WILDC.A.T.S
COVERT-ACTION-TEAMS

ZEALOT

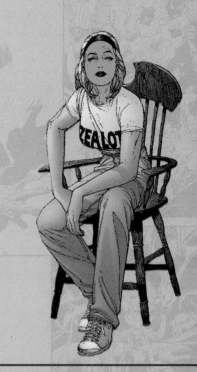

HOMECOMING

Table of Contents

Cover and Pinup Credits

Colors by Joe Chiodo and WildStorm FX
Lettering by Richard Starkings and Comicraft
Cover art by Travis Charest and Richard Friend

WILDC.A.T.S: HOMECOMING Published by WildStorm Productions. WILDC.A.T.S is ® WildStorm Productions, an imprint of DC Comics. Cover, design pages, and compilation © 1999 WildStorm Productions. All Rights Reserved. Originally published in single magazine form as WILDC.A.T.S #21-27. Copyright © 1995, 1996 WildStorm Productions. Editorial offices: 7910 Ivanhoe St., #438, La Jolla, CA 92037. Any similarities to persons living or dead is purely coincidental. PRINTED IN CANADA.

DC Comics, a division of Warner Bros.– A Time Warner Entertainment Company

WILDC.A.T.S #21

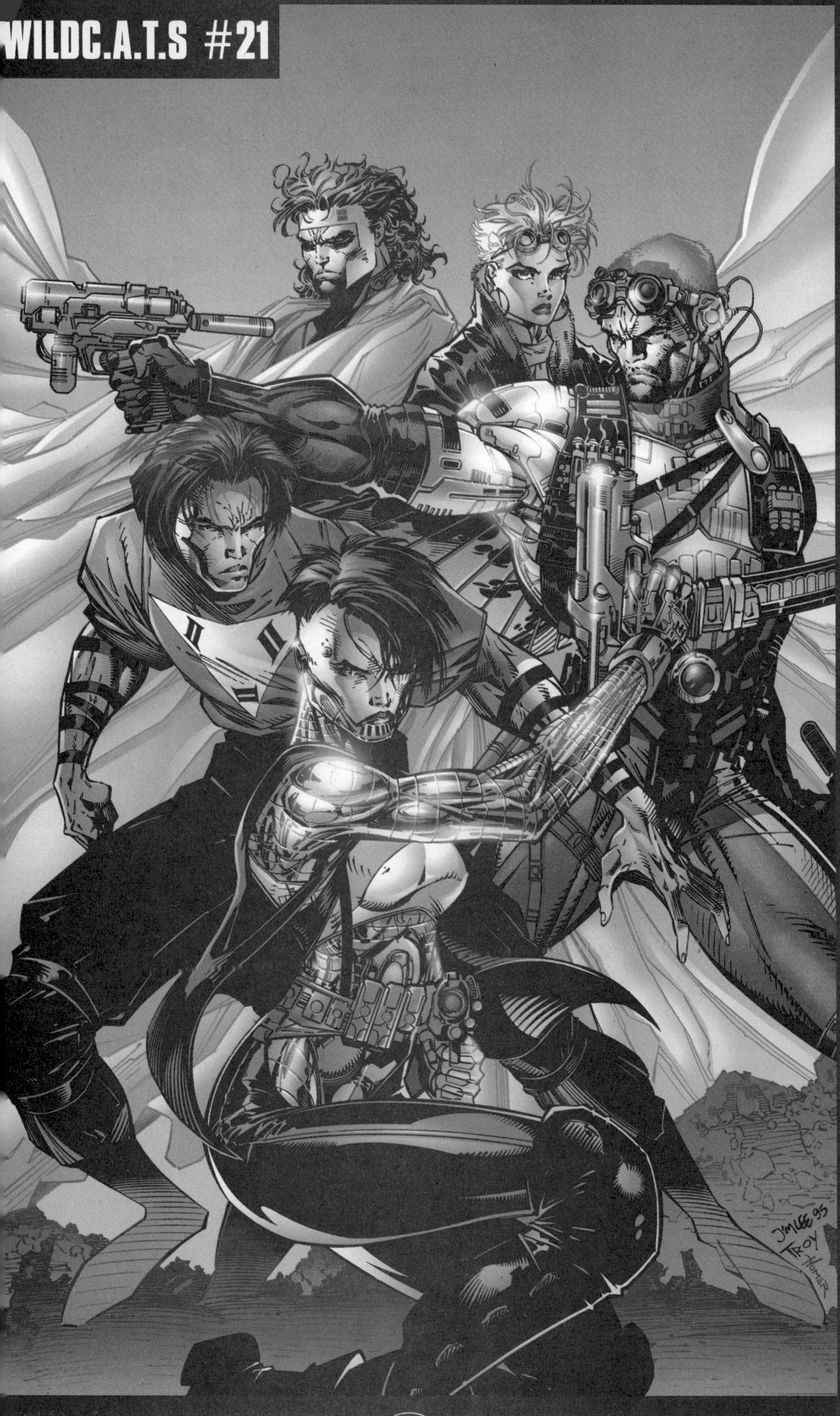

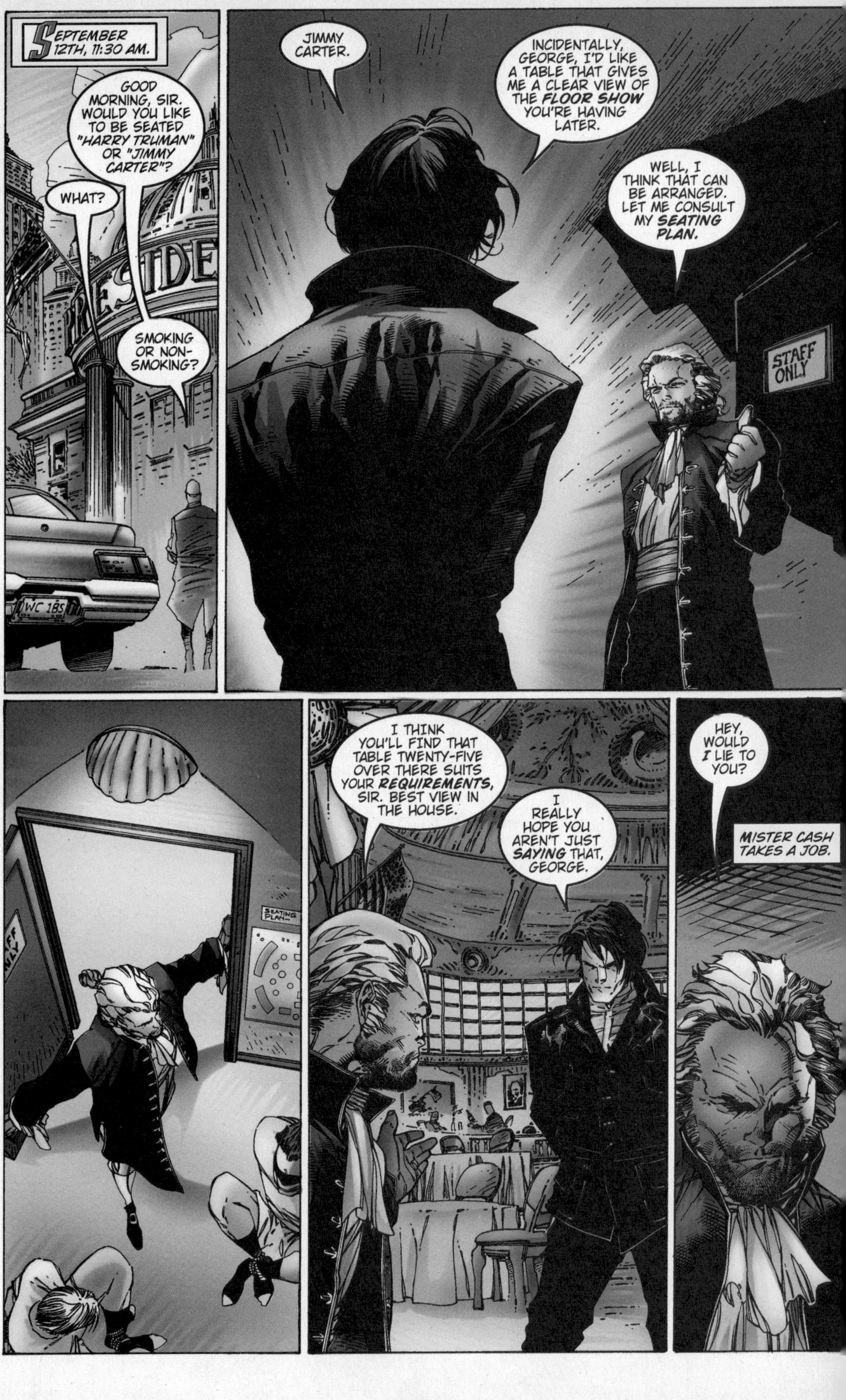
SEPTEMBER 12TH, 11:30 AM.
GOOD MORNING, SIR. WOULD YOU LIKE TO BE SEATED "HARRY TRUMAN" OR "JIMMY CARTER"?
WHAT?
SMOKING OR NON-SMOKING?
PRESIDE
WC 1BS
JIMMY CARTER.
INCIDENTALLY, GEORGE, I'D LIKE A TABLE THAT GIVES ME A CLEAR VIEW OF THE FLOOR SHOW YOU'RE HAVING LATER.
WELL, I THINK THAT CAN BE ARRANGED. LET ME CONSULT MY SEATING PLAN.
STAFF ONLY
SEATING PLAN
I THINK YOU'LL FIND THAT TABLE TWENTY-FIVE OVER THERE SUITS YOUR REQUIREMENTS, SIR. BEST VIEW IN THE HOUSE.
I REALLY HOPE YOU AREN'T JUST SAYING THAT, GEORGE.
HEY, WOULD I LIE TO YOU?
MISTER CASH TAKES A JOB.

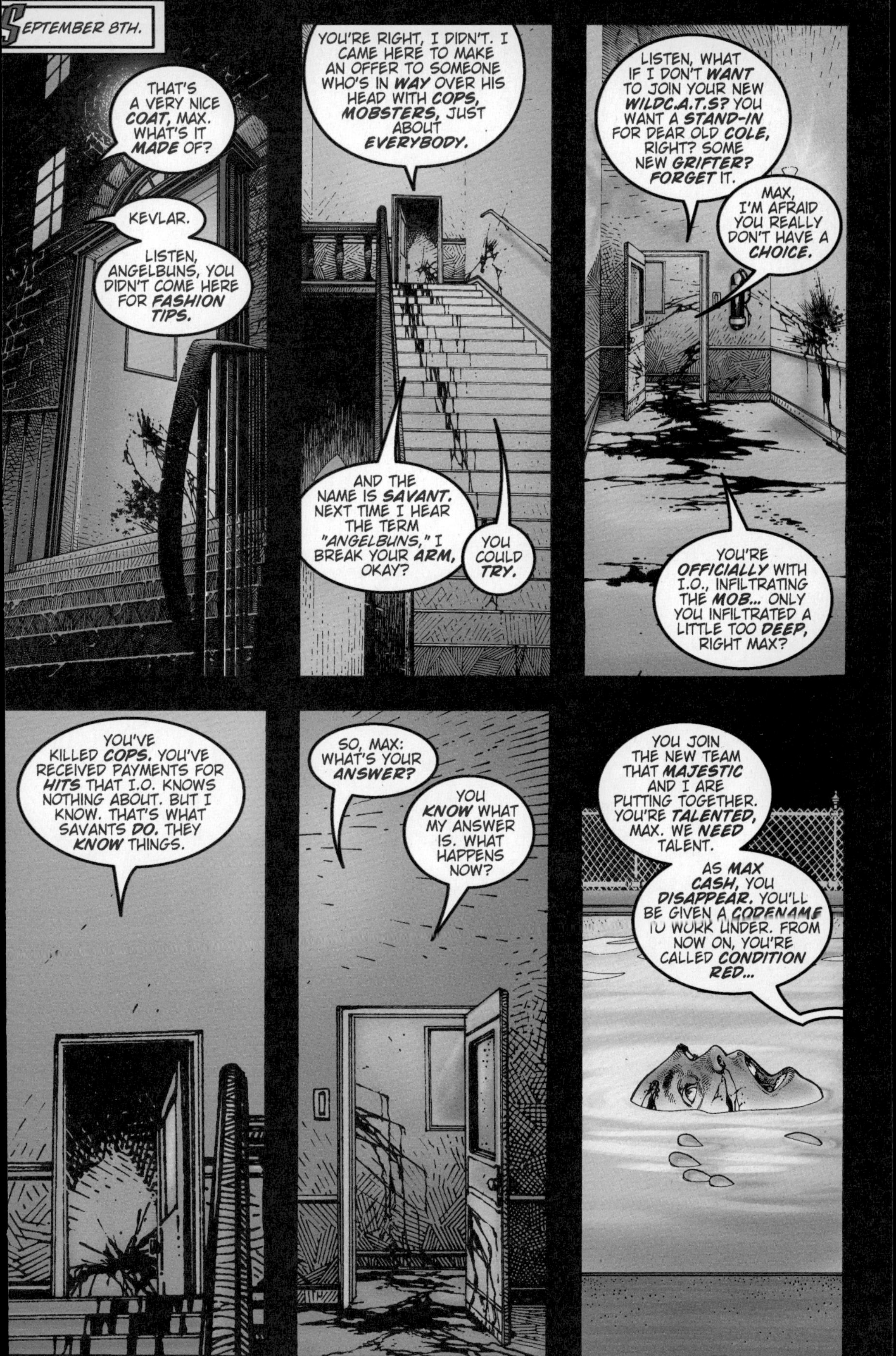
SEPTEMBER 8TH.
THAT'S A VERY NICE COAT, MAX. WHAT'S IT MADE OF?
KEVLAR.
LISTEN, ANGELBUNS, YOU DIDN'T COME HERE FOR FASHION TIPS.
YOU'RE RIGHT, I DIDN'T. I CAME HERE TO MAKE AN OFFER TO SOMEONE WHO'S IN WAY OVER HIS HEAD WITH COPS, MOBSTERS, JUST ABOUT EVERYBODY.
AND THE NAME IS SAVANT. NEXT TIME I HEAR THE TERM "ANGELBUNS," I BREAK YOUR ARM, OKAY?
YOU COULD TRY.
LISTEN, WHAT IF I DON'T WANT TO JOIN YOUR NEW WILDC.A.T.S? YOU WANT A STAND-IN FOR DEAR OLD COLE, RIGHT? SOME NEW GRIFTER? FORGET IT.
MAX, I'M AFRAID YOU REALLY DON'T HAVE A CHOICE.
YOU'RE OFFICIALLY WITH I.O., INFILTRATING THE MOB... ONLY YOU INFILTRATED A LITTLE TOO DEEP, RIGHT MAX?
YOU'VE KILLED COPS. YOU'VE RECEIVED PAYMENTS FOR HITS THAT I.O. KNOWS NOTHING ABOUT. BUT I KNOW. THAT'S WHAT SAVANTS DO. THEY KNOW THINGS.
SO, MAX: WHAT'S YOUR ANSWER?
YOU KNOW WHAT MY ANSWER IS. WHAT HAPPENS NOW?
YOU JOIN THE NEW TEAM THAT MAJESTIC AND I ARE PUTTING TOGETHER. YOU'RE TALENTED, MAX. WE NEED TALENT.
AS MAX CASH, YOU DISAPPEAR. YOU'LL BE GIVEN A CODENAME TO WORK UNDER. FROM NOW ON, YOU'RE CALLED CONDITION RED...

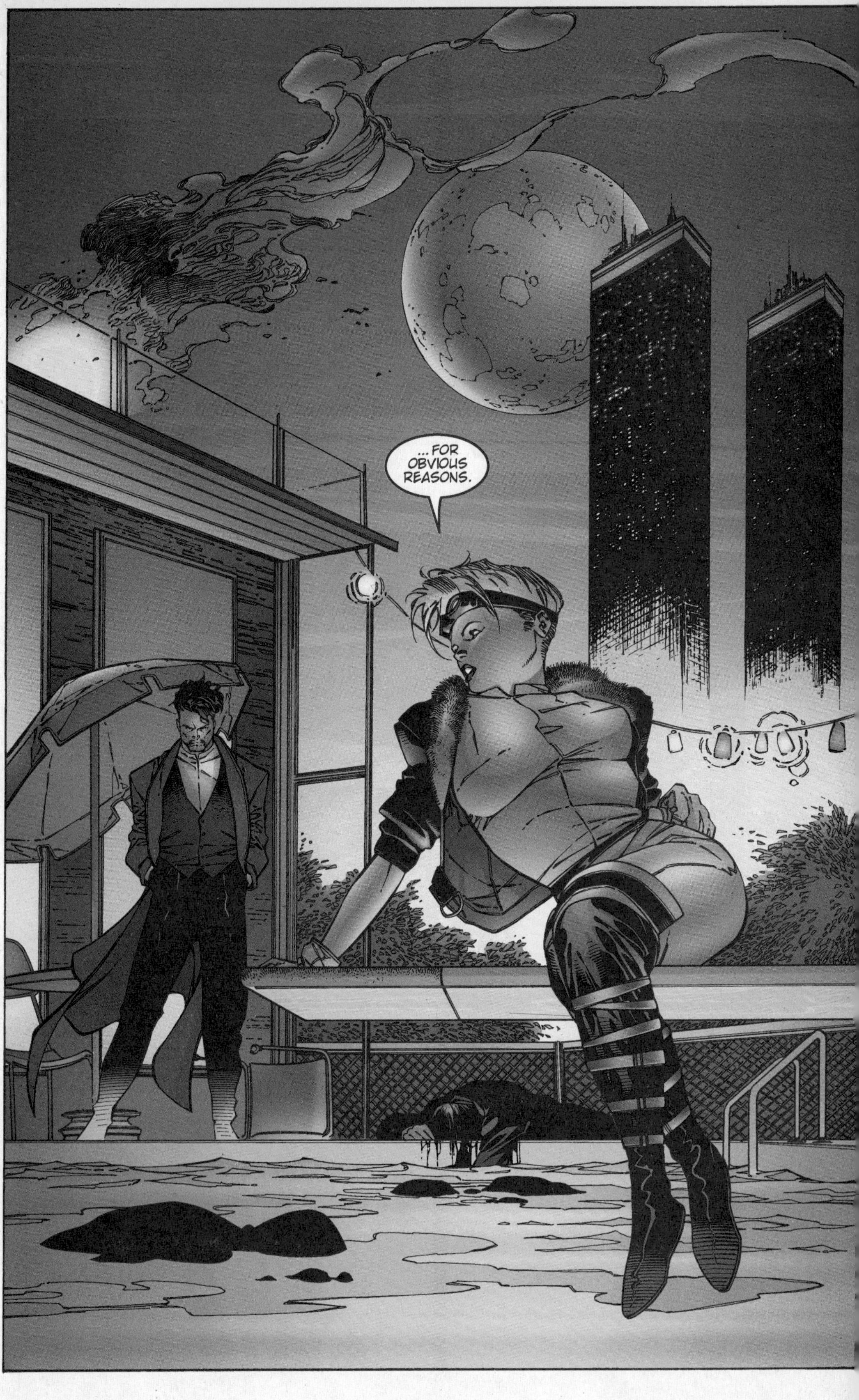
...FOR OBVIOUS REASONS.

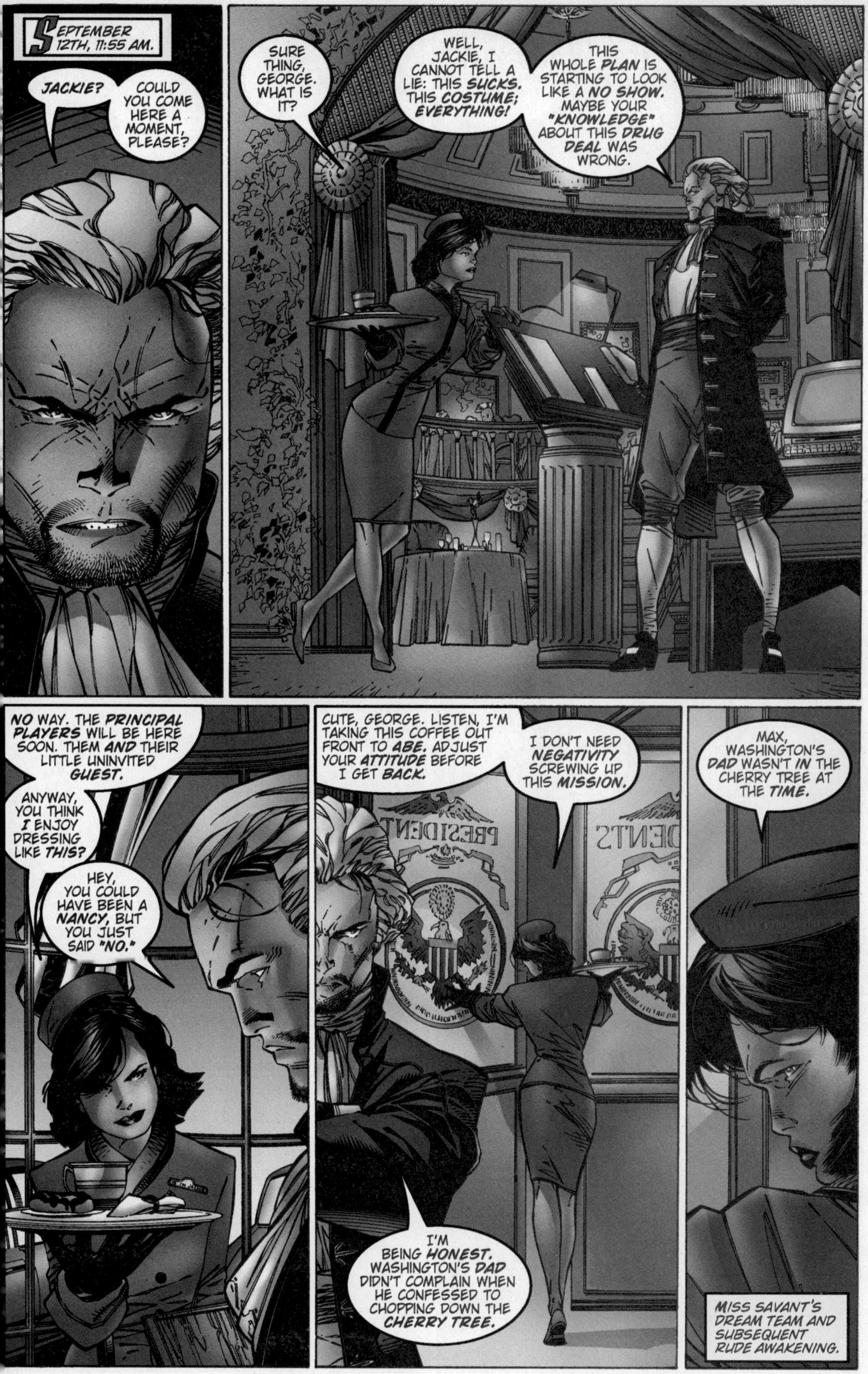
SEPTEMBER 12TH, 11:55 AM.
JACKIE?
COULD YOU COME HERE A MOMENT, PLEASE?
SURE THING, GEORGE. WHAT IS IT?
WELL, JACKIE, I CANNOT TELL A LIE: THIS SUCKS. THIS COSTUME; EVERYTHING!
THIS WHOLE PLAN IS STARTING TO LOOK LIKE A NO SHOW. MAYBE YOUR "KNOWLEDGE" ABOUT THIS DRUG DEAL WAS WRONG.
NO WAY. THE PRINCIPAL PLAYERS WILL BE HERE SOON. THEM AND THEIR LITTLE UNINVITED GUEST.
ANYWAY, YOU THINK I ENJOY DRESSING LIKE THIS?
HEY, YOU COULD HAVE BEEN A NANCY, BUT YOU JUST SAID "NO."
CUTE, GEORGE. LISTEN, I'M TAKING THIS COFFEE OUT FRONT TO ABE. ADJUST YOUR ATTITUDE BEFORE I GET BACK.
I DON'T NEED NEGATIVITY SCREWING UP THIS MISSION.
I'M BEING HONEST. WASHINGTON'S DAD DIDN'T COMPLAIN WHEN HE CONFESSED TO CHOPPING DOWN THE CHERRY TREE.
MAX, WASHINGTON'S DAD WASN'T IN THE CHERRY TREE AT THE TIME.
MISS SAVANT'S DREAM TEAM AND SUBSEQUENT RUDE AWAKENING.

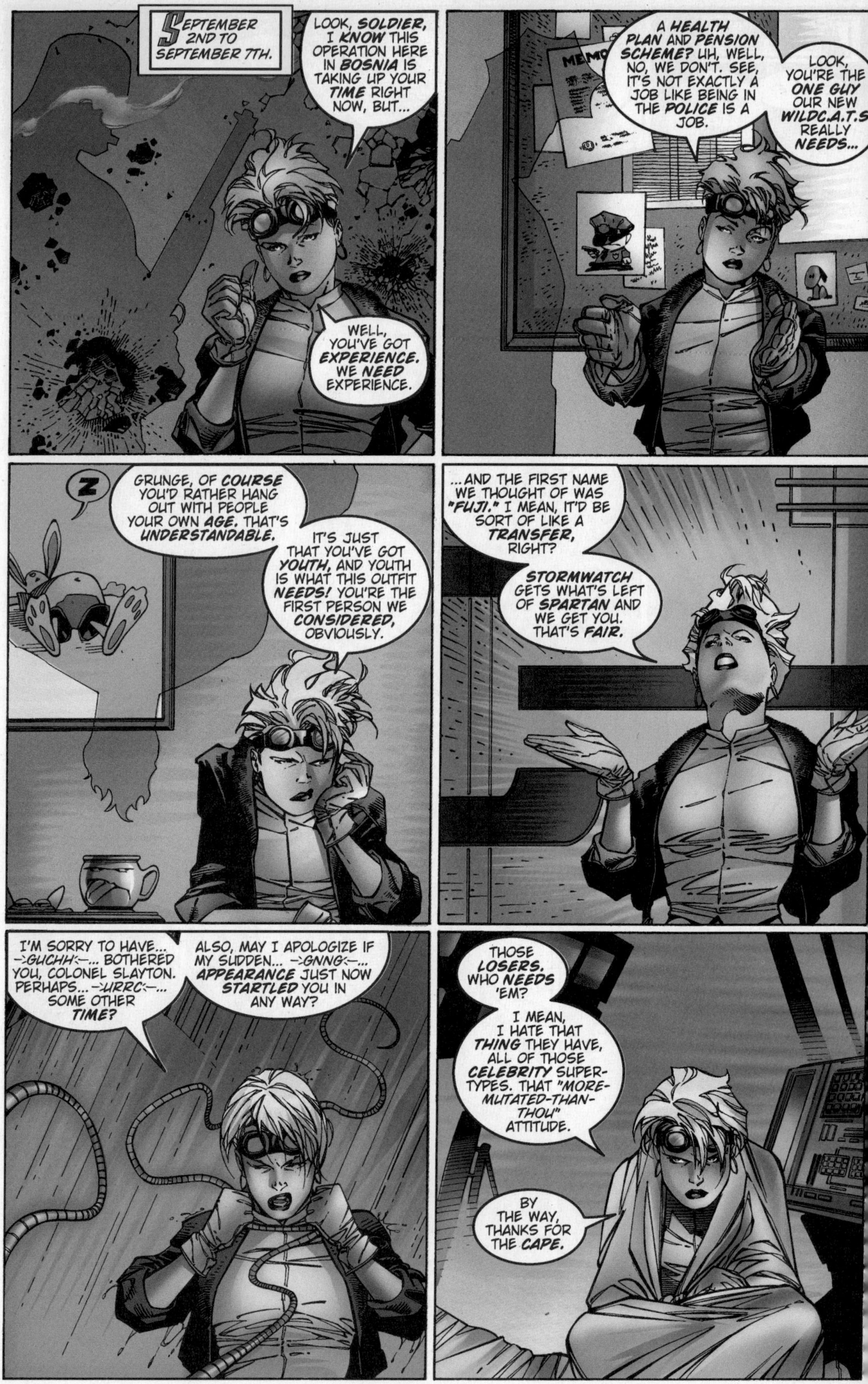
SEPTEMBER 2ND TO SEPTEMBER 7TH.
LOOK, SOLDIER, I KNOW THIS OPERATION HERE IN BOSNIA IS TAKING UP YOUR TIME RIGHT NOW, BUT...
WELL, YOU'VE GOT EXPERIENCE. WE NEED EXPERIENCE.
A HEALTH PLAN AND PENSION SCHEME? UH, WELL, NO, WE DON'T. SEE, IT'S NOT EXACTLY A JOB LIKE BEING IN THE POLICE IS A JOB.
LOOK, YOU'RE THE ONE GUY OUR NEW WILDC.A.T.S REALLY NEEDS...
Z
GRUNGE, OF COURSE YOU'D RATHER HANG OUT WITH PEOPLE YOUR OWN AGE. THAT'S UNDERSTANDABLE.
IT'S JUST THAT YOU'VE GOT YOUTH, AND YOUTH IS WHAT THIS OUTFIT NEEDS! YOU'RE THE FIRST PERSON WE CONSIDERED, OBVIOUSLY.
...AND THE FIRST NAME WE THOUGHT OF WAS "FUJI." I MEAN, IT'D BE SORT OF LIKE A TRANSFER, RIGHT?
STORMWATCH GETS WHAT'S LEFT OF SPARTAN AND WE GET YOU. THAT'S FAIR.
I'M SORRY TO HAVE... —GUCHH—... BOTHERED YOU, COLONEL SLAYTON. PERHAPS... —URRC—... SOME OTHER TIME?
ALSO, MAY I APOLOGIZE IF MY SUDDEN... —GNNG—... APPEARANCE JUST NOW STARTLED YOU IN ANY WAY?
THOSE LOSERS. WHO NEEDS 'EM?
I MEAN, I HATE THAT THING THEY HAVE, ALL OF THOSE CELEBRITY SUPER-TYPES. THAT "MORE-MUTATED-THAN-THOU" ATTITUDE.
BY THE WAY, THANKS FOR THE CAPE.

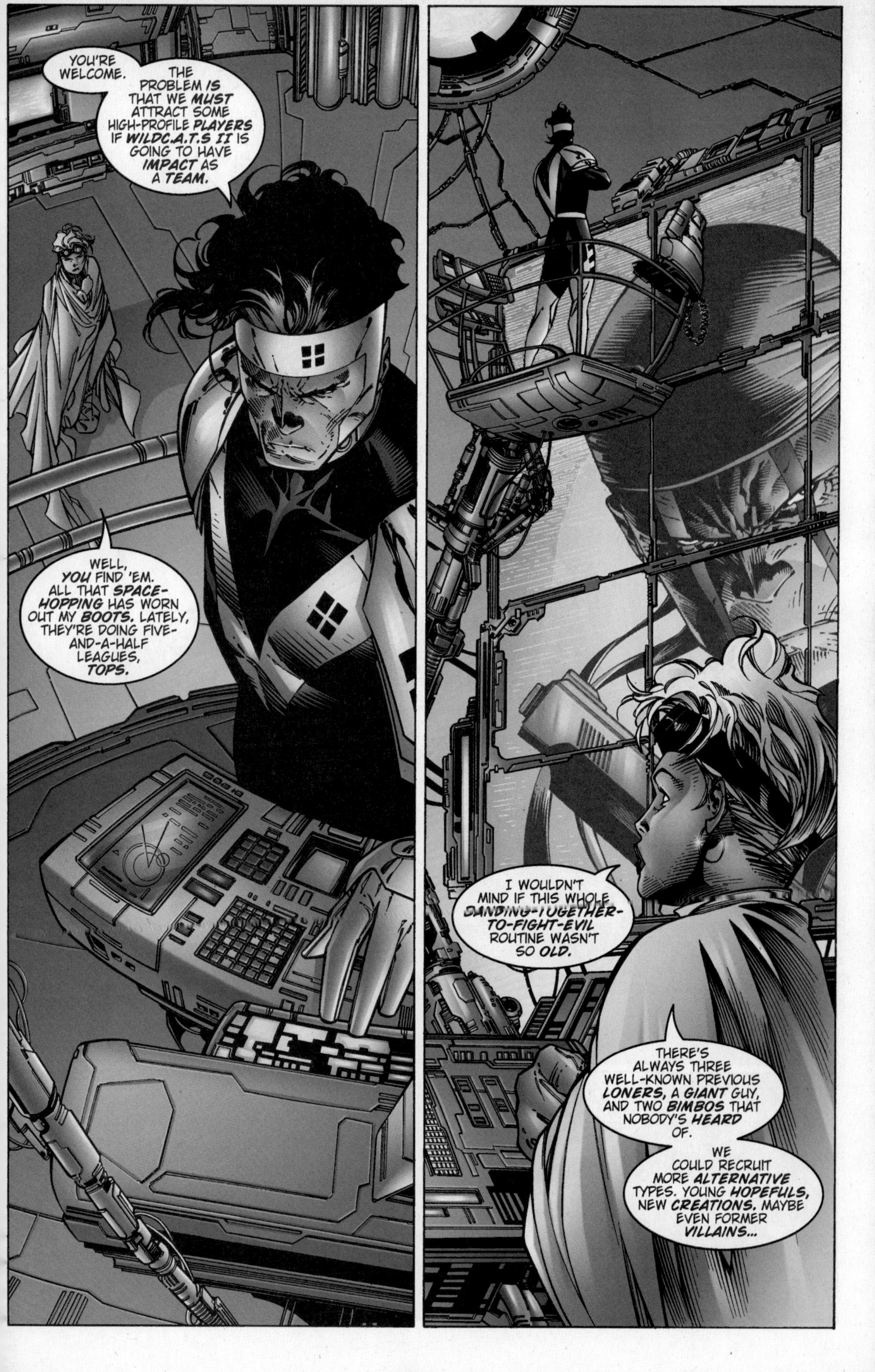
YOU'RE WELCOME.
THE PROBLEM *IS* THAT WE *MUST* ATTRACT SOME HIGH-PROFILE *PLAYERS* IF *WILDC.A.T.S II* IS GOING TO HAVE *IMPACT* AS A *TEAM.*
WELL, *YOU* FIND 'EM. ALL THAT *SPACE-HOPPING* HAS WORN OUT MY *BOOTS.* LATELY, THEY'RE DOING FIVE-AND-A-HALF LEAGUES, *TOPS.*
I WOULDN'T MIND IF THIS WHOLE *BANDING-TOGETHER-TO-FIGHT-EVIL* ROUTINE WASN'T SO *OLD.*
THERE'S ALWAYS THREE WELL-KNOWN PREVIOUS *LONERS,* A *GIANT* GUY, AND TWO *BIMBOS* THAT NOBODY'S *HEARD* OF.
WE COULD RECRUIT MORE *ALTERNATIVE* TYPES. YOUNG *HOPEFULS,* NEW *CREATIONS.* MAYBE EVEN FORMER *VILLAINS...*

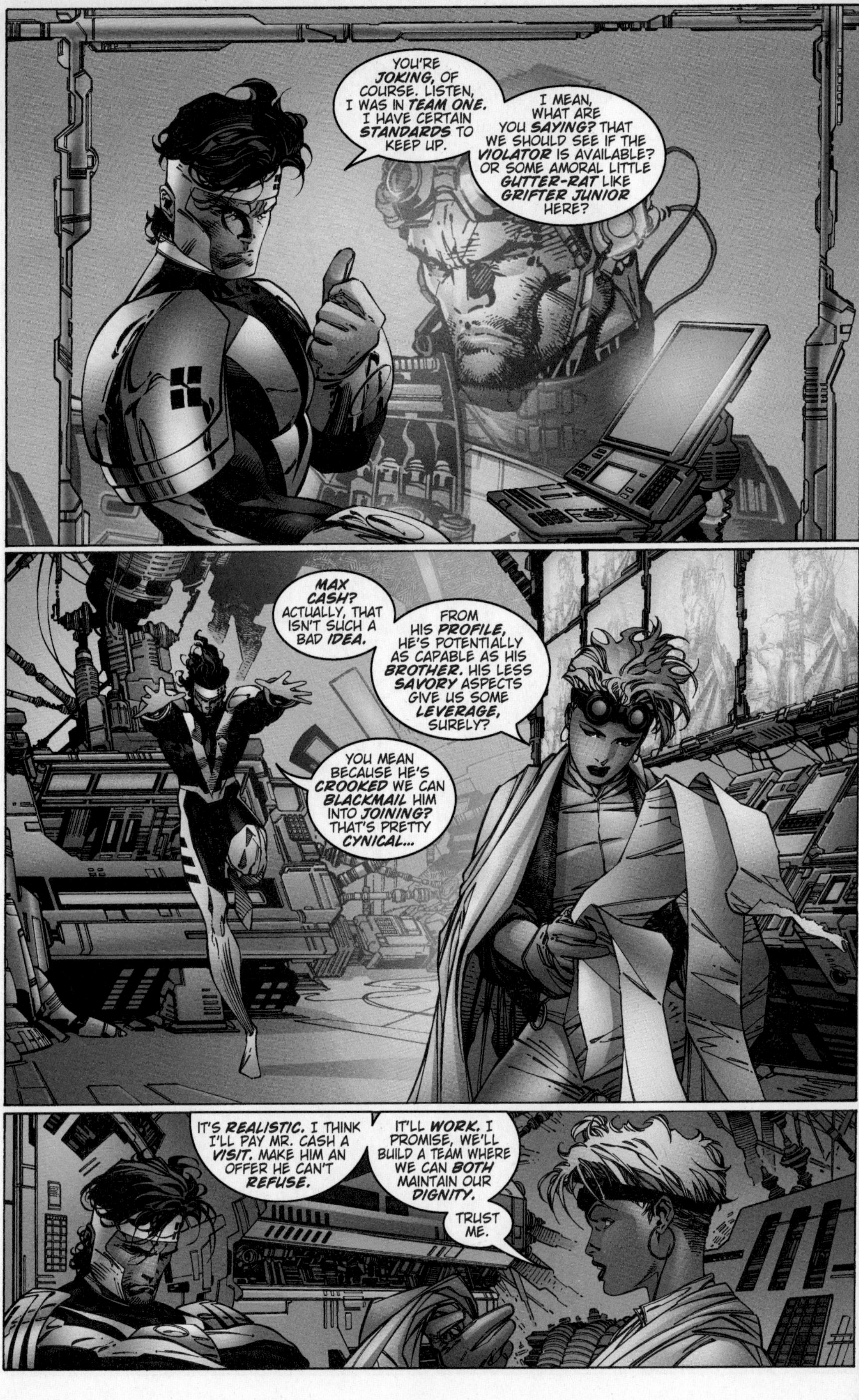
YOU'RE JOKING, OF COURSE. LISTEN, I WAS IN TEAM ONE. I HAVE CERTAIN STANDARDS TO KEEP UP.
I MEAN, WHAT ARE YOU SAYING? THAT WE SHOULD SEE IF THE VIOLATOR IS AVAILABLE? OR SOME AMORAL LITTLE GUTTER-RAT LIKE GRIFTER JUNIOR HERE?
MAX CASH? ACTUALLY, THAT ISN'T SUCH A BAD IDEA.
FROM HIS PROFILE, HE'S POTENTIALLY AS CAPABLE AS HIS BROTHER. HIS LESS SAVORY ASPECTS GIVE US SOME LEVERAGE, SURELY?
YOU MEAN BECAUSE HE'S CROOKED WE CAN BLACKMAIL HIM INTO JOINING? THAT'S PRETTY CYNICAL...
IT'S REALISTIC. I THINK I'LL PAY MR. CASH A VISIT. MAKE HIM AN OFFER HE CAN'T REFUSE.
IT'LL WORK. I PROMISE, WE'LL BUILD A TEAM WHERE WE CAN BOTH MAINTAIN OUR DIGNITY.
TRUST ME.

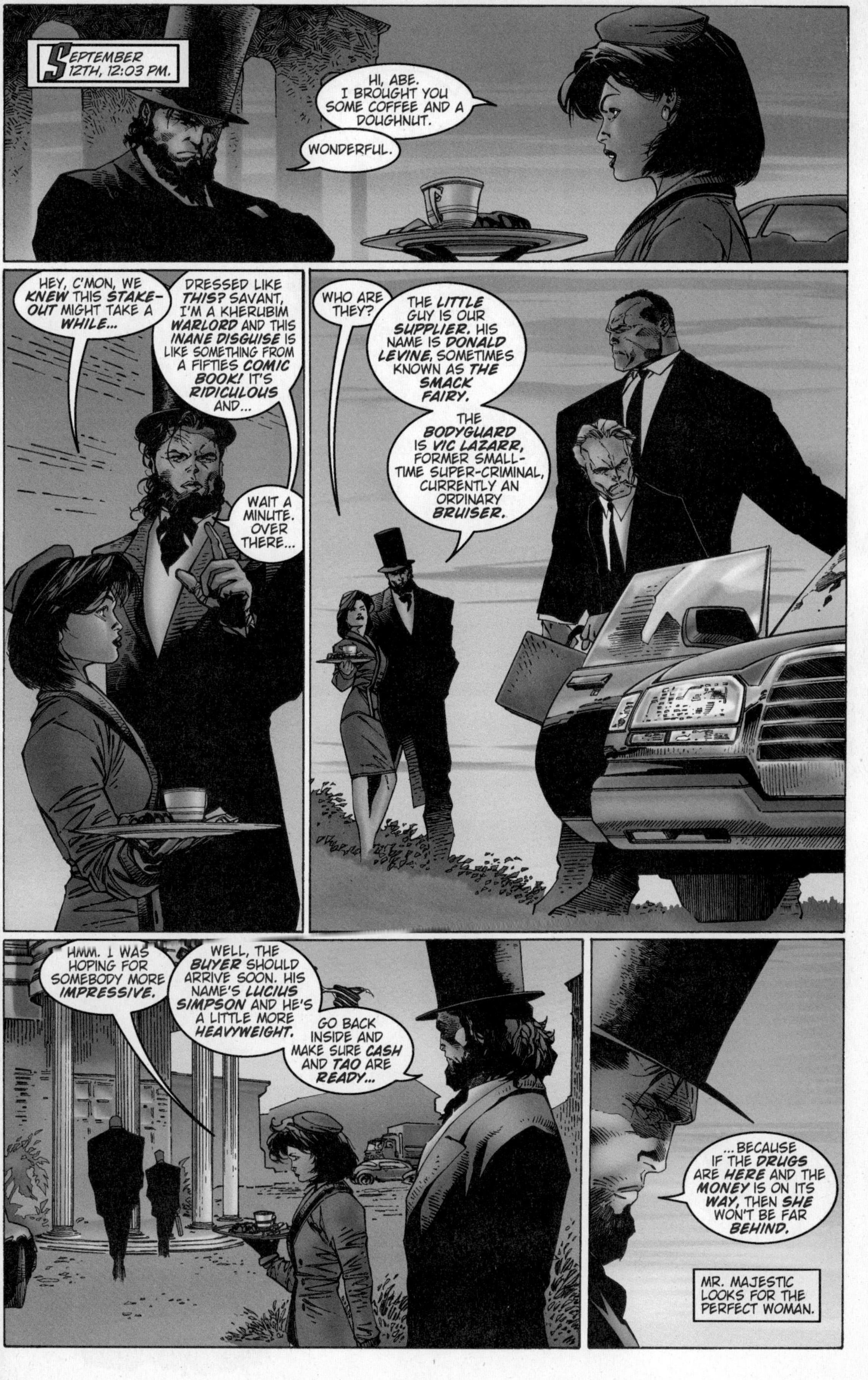
SEPTEMBER 12TH, 12:03 PM.
HI, ABE. I BROUGHT YOU SOME COFFEE AND A DOUGHNUT.
WONDERFUL.
HEY, C'MON, WE KNEW THIS STAKE-OUT MIGHT TAKE A WHILE...
DRESSED LIKE THIS? SAVANT, I'M A KHERUBIM WARLORD AND THIS INANE DISGUISE IS LIKE SOMETHING FROM A FIFTIES COMIC BOOK! IT'S RIDICULOUS AND...
WAIT A MINUTE. OVER THERE...
WHO ARE THEY?
THE LITTLE GUY IS OUR SUPPLIER. HIS NAME IS DONALD LEVINE, SOMETIMES KNOWN AS THE SMACK FAIRY.
THE BODYGUARD IS VIC LAZARR, FORMER SMALL-TIME SUPER-CRIMINAL, CURRENTLY AN ORDINARY BRUISER.
HMM. I WAS HOPING FOR SOMEBODY MORE IMPRESSIVE.
WELL, THE BUYER SHOULD ARRIVE SOON. HIS NAME'S LUCIUS SIMPSON AND HE'S A LITTLE MORE HEAVYWEIGHT.
GO BACK INSIDE AND MAKE SURE CASH AND TAO ARE READY...
...BECAUSE IF THE DRUGS ARE HERE AND THE MONEY IS ON ITS WAY, THEN SHE WON'T BE FAR BEHIND.
MR. MAJESTIC LOOKS FOR THE PERFECT WOMAN.

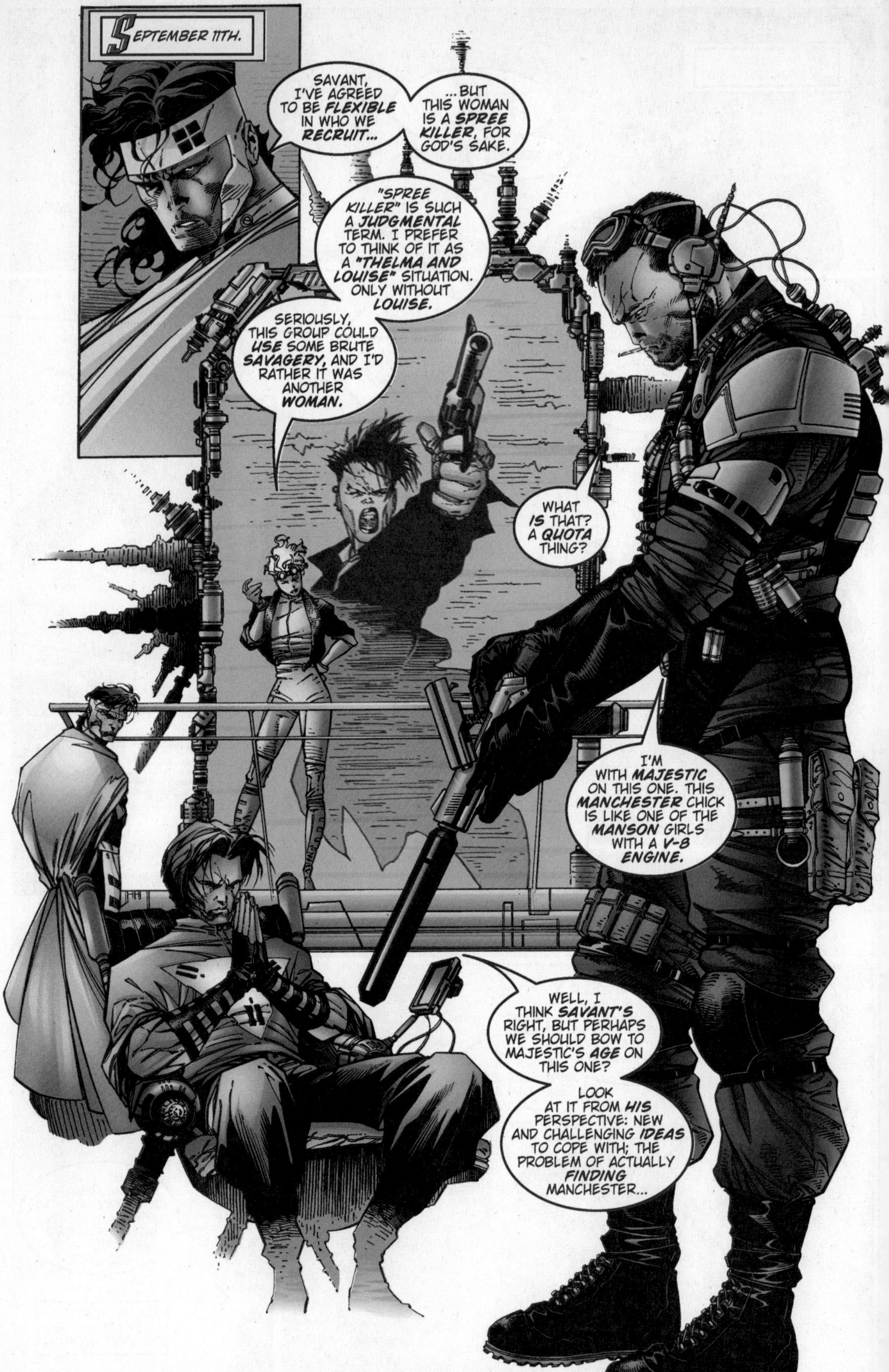
SEPTEMBER 11TH.
SAVANT, I'VE AGREED TO BE FLEXIBLE IN WHO WE RECRUIT...
...BUT THIS WOMAN IS A SPREE KILLER, FOR GOD'S SAKE.
"SPREE KILLER" IS SUCH A JUDGMENTAL TERM. I PREFER TO THINK OF IT AS A "THELMA AND LOUISE" SITUATION. ONLY WITHOUT LOUISE.
SERIOUSLY, THIS GROUP COULD USE SOME BRUTE SAVAGERY, AND I'D RATHER IT WAS ANOTHER WOMAN.
WHAT IS THAT? A QUOTA THING?
I'M WITH MAJESTIC ON THIS ONE. THIS MANCHESTER CHICK IS LIKE ONE OF THE MANSON GIRLS WITH A V-8 ENGINE.
WELL, I THINK SAVANT'S RIGHT, BUT PERHAPS WE SHOULD BOW TO MAJESTIC'S AGE ON THIS ONE?
LOOK AT IT FROM HIS PERSPECTIVE: NEW AND CHALLENGING IDEAS TO COPE WITH; THE PROBLEM OF ACTUALLY FINDING MANCHESTER...

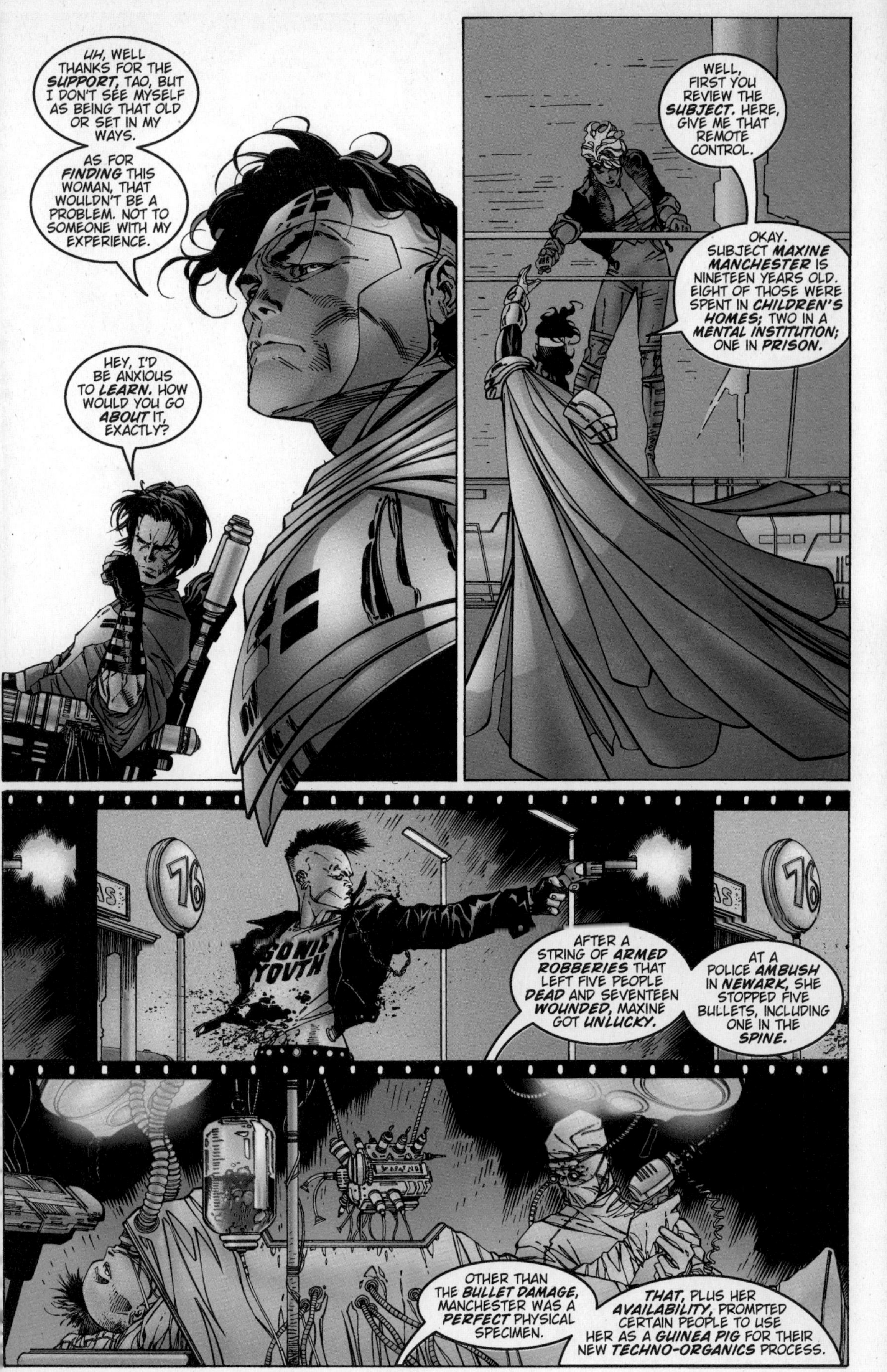
UH, WELL THANKS FOR THE SUPPORT, TAO, BUT I DON'T SEE MYSELF AS BEING THAT OLD OR SET IN MY WAYS.
AS FOR FINDING THIS WOMAN, THAT WOULDN'T BE A PROBLEM. NOT TO SOMEONE WITH MY EXPERIENCE.
HEY, I'D BE ANXIOUS TO LEARN. HOW WOULD YOU GO ABOUT IT, EXACTLY?
WELL, FIRST YOU REVIEW THE SUBJECT. HERE, GIVE ME THAT REMOTE CONTROL.
OKAY. SUBJECT MAXINE MANCHESTER IS NINETEEN YEARS OLD. EIGHT OF THOSE WERE SPENT IN CHILDREN'S HOMES; TWO IN A MENTAL INSTITUTION; ONE IN PRISON.
76
SONIC YOUTH
AFTER A STRING OF ARMED ROBBERIES THAT LEFT FIVE PEOPLE DEAD AND SEVENTEEN WOUNDED, MAXINE GOT UNLUCKY.
AT A POLICE AMBUSH IN NEWARK, SHE STOPPED FIVE BULLETS, INCLUDING ONE IN THE SPINE.
OTHER THAN THE BULLET DAMAGE, MANCHESTER WAS A PERFECT PHYSICAL SPECIMEN.
THAT, PLUS HER AVAILABILITY, PROMPTED CERTAIN PEOPLE TO USE HER AS A GUINEA PIG FOR THEIR NEW TECHNO-ORGANICS PROCESS.

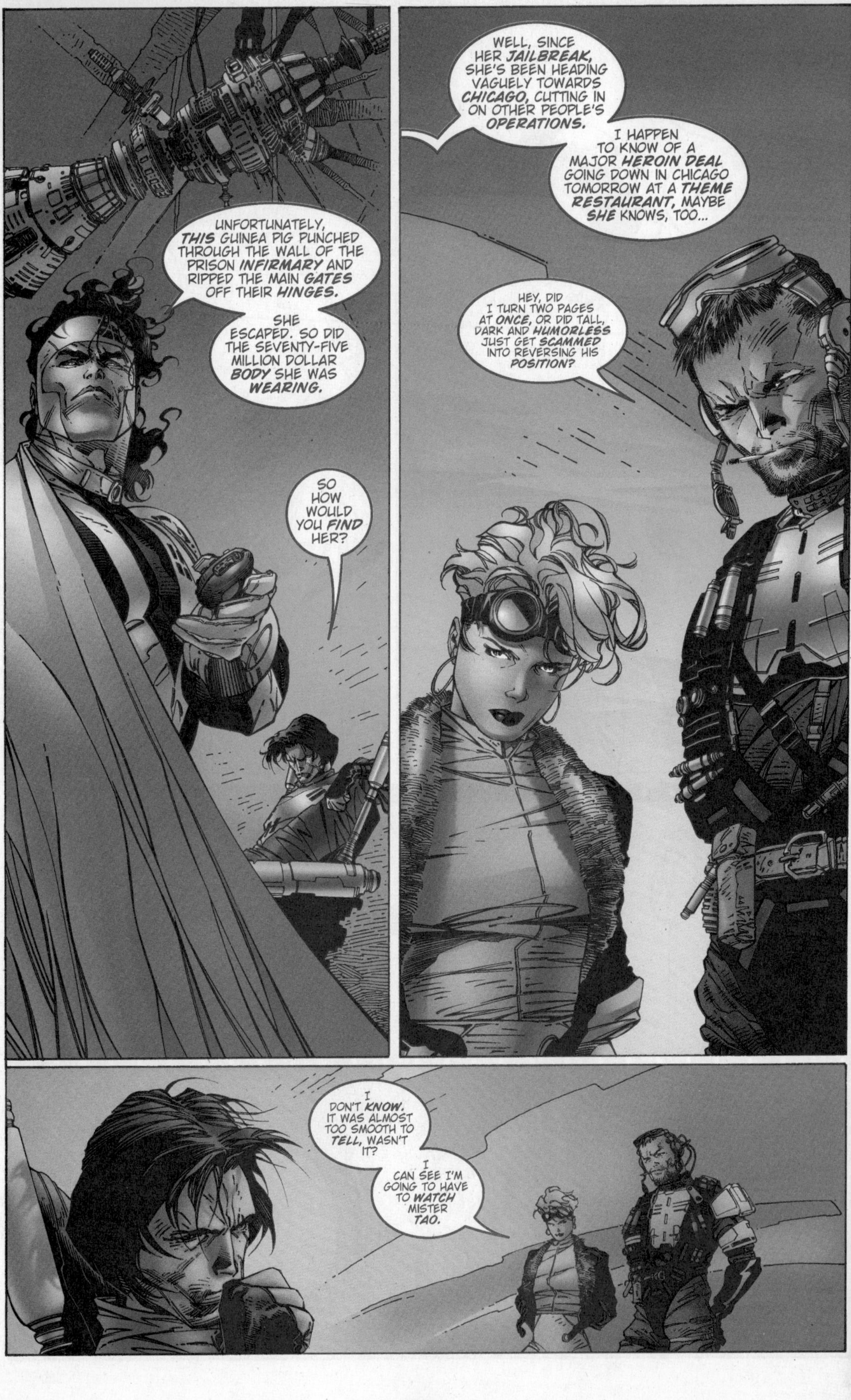
UNFORTUNATELY, THIS GUINEA PIG PUNCHED THROUGH THE WALL OF THE PRISON INFIRMARY AND RIPPED THE MAIN GATES OFF THEIR HINGES.
SHE ESCAPED. SO DID THE SEVENTY-FIVE MILLION DOLLAR BODY SHE WAS WEARING.
SO HOW WOULD YOU FIND HER?
WELL, SINCE HER JAILBREAK, SHE'S BEEN HEADING VAGUELY TOWARDS CHICAGO, CUTTING IN ON OTHER PEOPLE'S OPERATIONS.
I HAPPEN TO KNOW OF A MAJOR HEROIN DEAL GOING DOWN IN CHICAGO TOMORROW AT A THEME RESTAURANT, MAYBE SHE KNOWS, TOO...
HEY, DID I TURN TWO PAGES AT ONCE, OR DID TALL, DARK AND HUMORLESS JUST GET SCAMMED INTO REVERSING HIS POSITION?
I DON'T KNOW. IT WAS ALMOST TOO SMOOTH TO TELL, WASN'T IT?
I CAN SEE I'M GOING TO HAVE TO WATCH MISTER TAO.

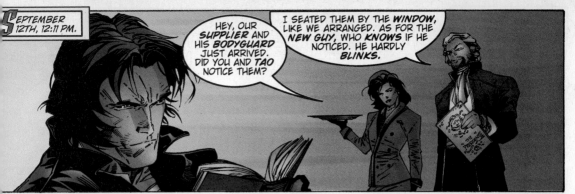

SEPTEMBER 12TH, 12:11 PM.
HEY, OUR SUPPLIER AND HIS BODYGUARD JUST ARRIVED. DID YOU AND TAO NOTICE THEM?
I SEATED THEM BY THE WINDOW, LIKE WE ARRANGED. AS FOR THE NEW GUY, WHO KNOWS IF HE NOTICED. HE HARDLY BLINKS.
THE PRESIDENTS
LEVINE LOOKS NERVOUS.
CAN YOU BLAME THE GUY? ACCORDING TO HONEST ABE, HE'S GOT TEN POUNDS OF CHINA WHITE IN THAT SUITCASE, SO...
WAIT A MINUTE. I'M GETTING A TRANSMISSION.
HELLO, GEORGE? THIS IS ABE. SIMPSON HAS JUST ARRIVED. HIS BODYGUARDS AREN'T CYBORGS LIKE WE EXPECTED.
I DON'T KNOW WHAT THEY ARE. THEY'RE ALL BIG GUYS, AND THEY'VE ALL GOT BAND-AIDS ON THEIR HEADS.
AW, NO. I HEARD ABOUT THESE THINGS. THEY'RE SOMETHING NEW, CALLED ZOMBOTS. DEAD MEN WITH MICRO-ELECTRONIC IMPLANTS.
THEY'RE CHEAP, VOICE-CONTROLLED, AND DISPOSABLE, FOR MOBSTERS WHO CAN'T AFFORD CYBORG HEAVIES.
I'D BETTER WARN TAO.
I MEAN, HE DOESN'T SEEM TO HAVE ANY POWERS OR WEAPONS.
MAYBE HE'LL GIVE THEM A MEANINGFUL LOOK, OR SOMETHING.
THE NEW GUY.

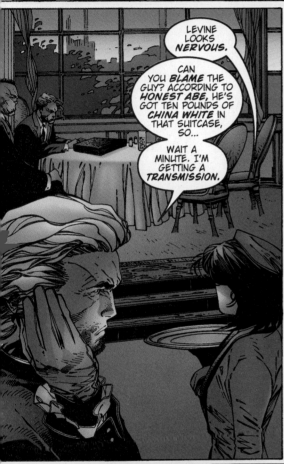

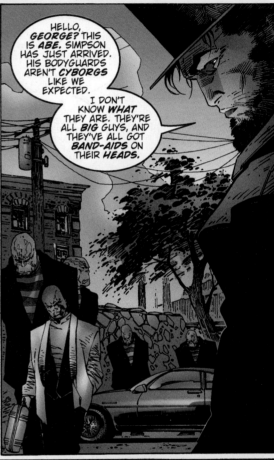

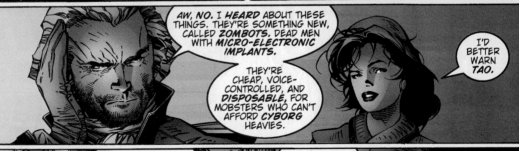

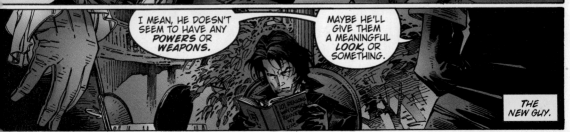

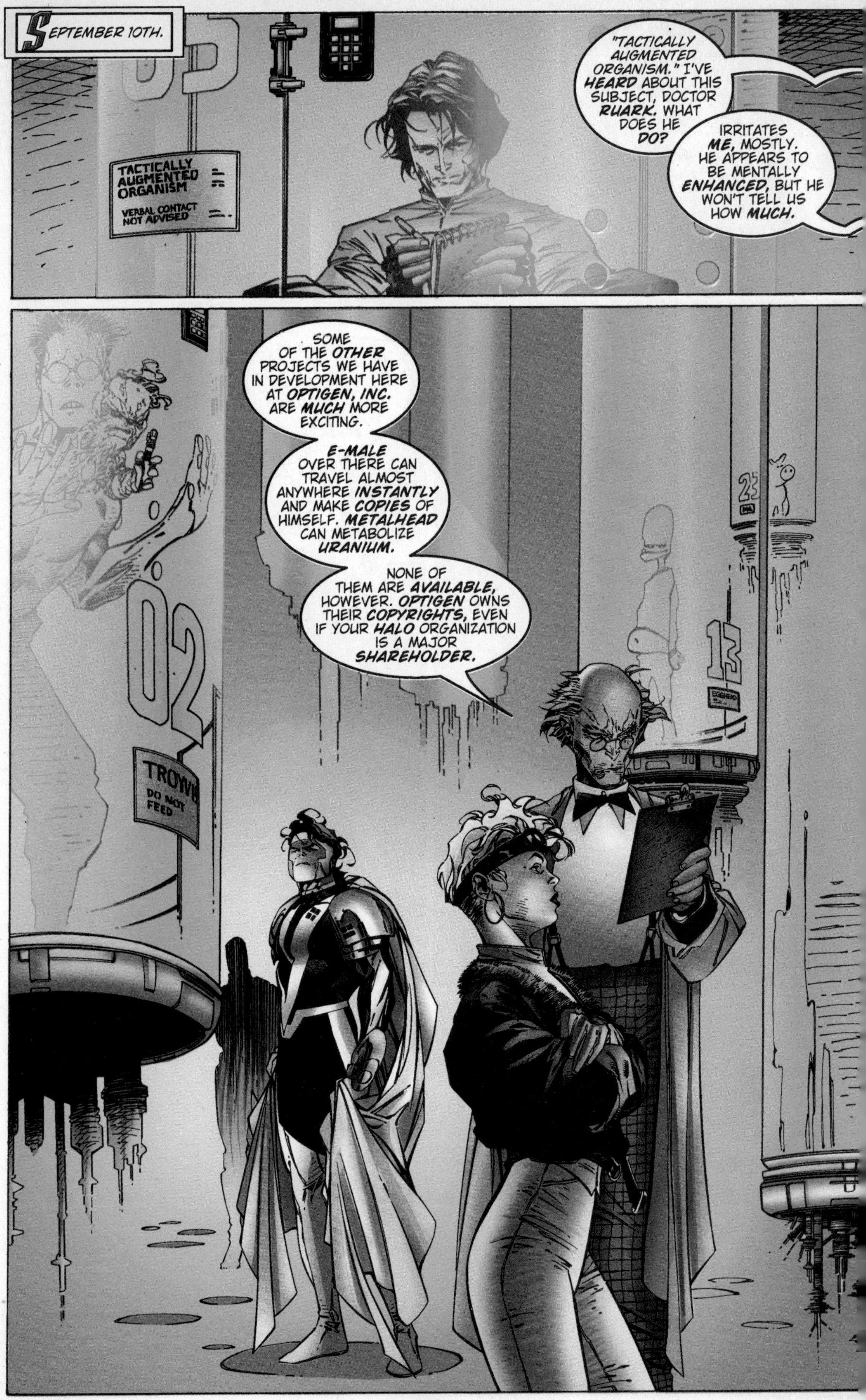

SEPTEMBER 10TH.
TACTICALLY AUGMENTED ORGANISM
VERBAL CONTACT NOT ADVISED
"TACTICALLY AUGMENTED ORGANISM." I'VE HEARD ABOUT THIS SUBJECT, DOCTOR RUARK. WHAT DOES HE DO?
IRRITATES ME, MOSTLY. HE APPEARS TO BE MENTALLY ENHANCED, BUT HE WON'T TELL US HOW MUCH.
SOME OF THE OTHER PROJECTS WE HAVE IN DEVELOPMENT HERE AT OPTIGEN, INC. ARE MUCH MORE EXCITING.
E-MALE OVER THERE CAN TRAVEL ALMOST ANYWHERE INSTANTLY AND MAKE COPIES OF HIMSELF. METALHEAD CAN METABOLIZE URANIUM.
NONE OF THEM ARE AVAILABLE, HOWEVER. OPTIGEN OWNS THEIR COPYRIGHTS, EVEN IF YOUR HALO ORGANIZATION IS A MAJOR SHAREHOLDER.
02
TROYV
DO NOT FEED
13

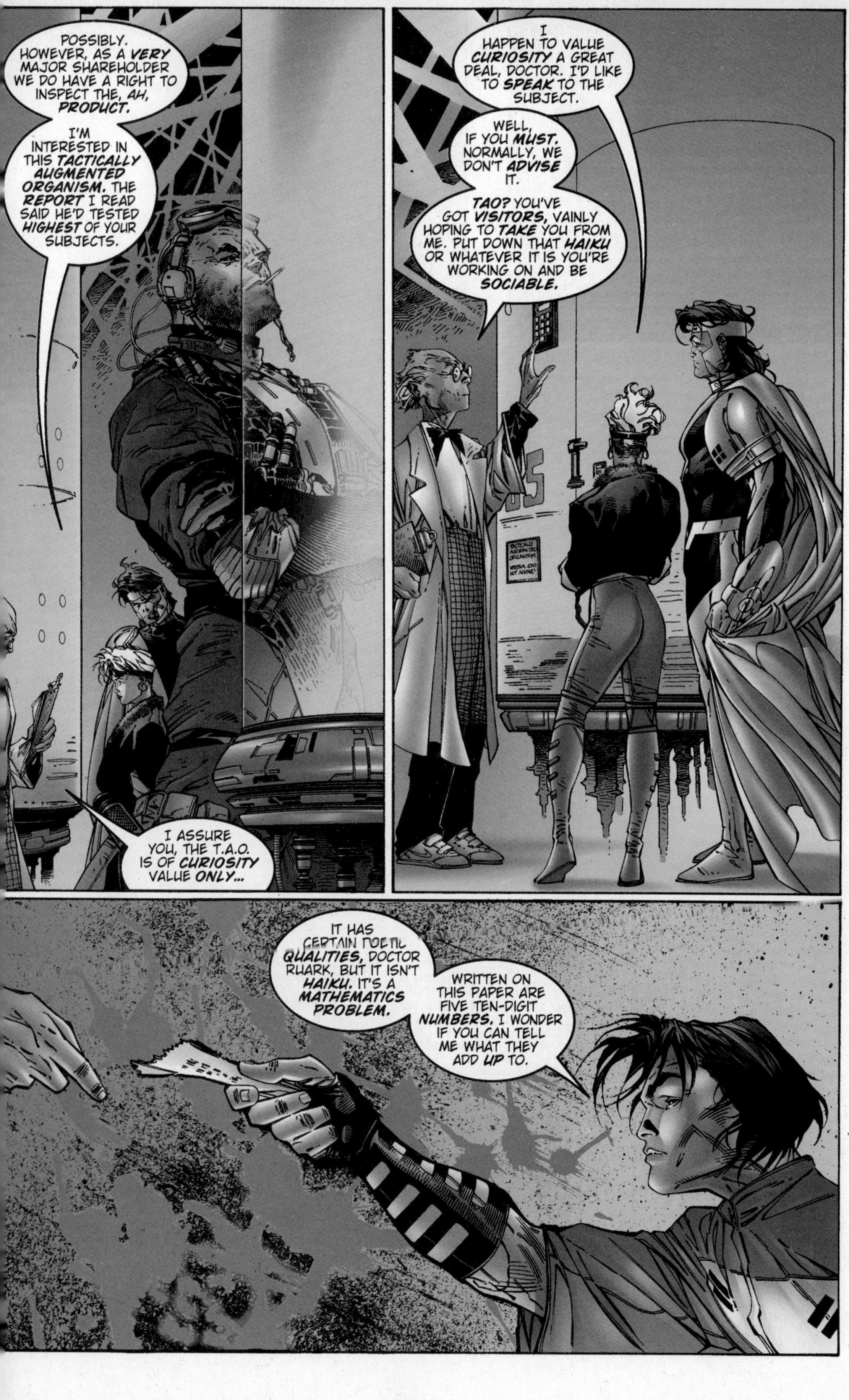
POSSIBLY. HOWEVER, AS A VERY MAJOR SHAREHOLDER WE DO HAVE A RIGHT TO INSPECT THE, AH, PRODUCT.
I'M INTERESTED IN THIS TACTICALLY AUGMENTED ORGANISM. THE REPORT I READ SAID HE'D TESTED HIGHEST OF YOUR SUBJECTS.
I ASSURE YOU, THE T.A.O. IS OF CURIOSITY VALUE ONLY...
I HAPPEN TO VALUE CURIOSITY A GREAT DEAL, DOCTOR. I'D LIKE TO SPEAK TO THE SUBJECT.
WELL, IF YOU MUST. NORMALLY, WE DON'T ADVISE IT.
TAO? YOU'VE GOT VISITORS, VAINLY HOPING TO TAKE YOU FROM ME. PUT DOWN THAT HAIKU OR WHATEVER IT IS YOU'RE WORKING ON AND BE SOCIABLE.
IT HAS CERTAIN POETIC QUALITIES, DOCTOR RUARK, BUT IT ISN'T HAIKU. IT'S A MATHEMATICS PROBLEM.
WRITTEN ON THIS PAPER ARE FIVE TEN-DIGIT NUMBERS. I WONDER IF YOU CAN TELL ME WHAT THEY ADD UP TO.

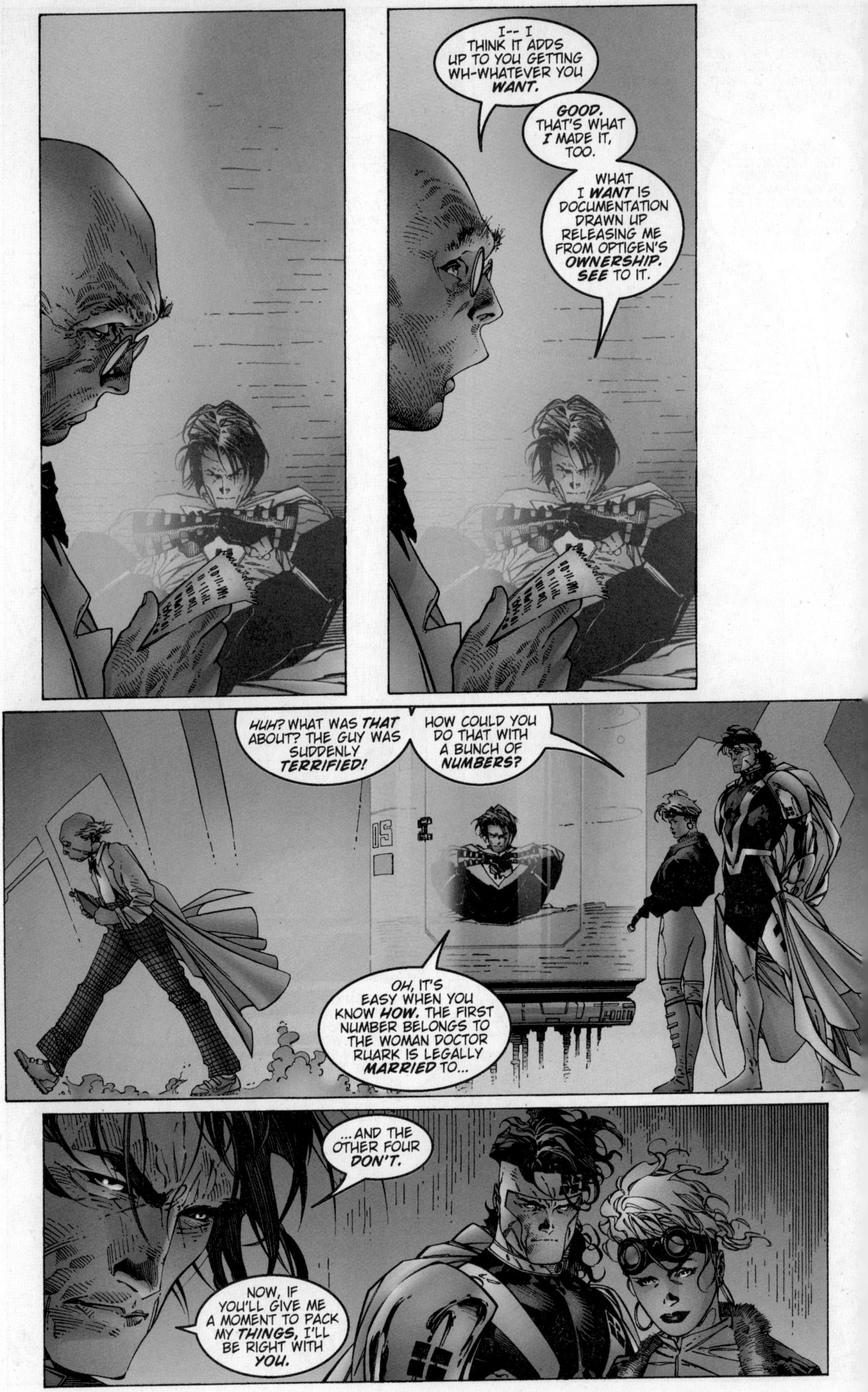
I-- I THINK IT ADDS UP TO YOU GETTING WH-WHATEVER YOU WANT.
GOOD. THAT'S WHAT I MADE IT, TOO.
WHAT I WANT IS DOCUMENTATION DRAWN UP RELEASING ME FROM OPTIGEN'S OWNERSHIP. SEE TO IT.
HUH? WHAT WAS THAT ABOUT? THE GUY WAS SUDDENLY TERRIFIED!
HOW COULD YOU DO THAT WITH A BUNCH OF NUMBERS?
15
OH, IT'S EASY WHEN YOU KNOW HOW. THE FIRST NUMBER BELONGS TO THE WOMAN DOCTOR RUARK IS LEGALLY MARRIED TO...
...AND THE OTHER FOUR DON'T.
NOW, IF YOU'LL GIVE ME A MOMENT TO PACK MY THINGS, I'LL BE RIGHT WITH YOU.

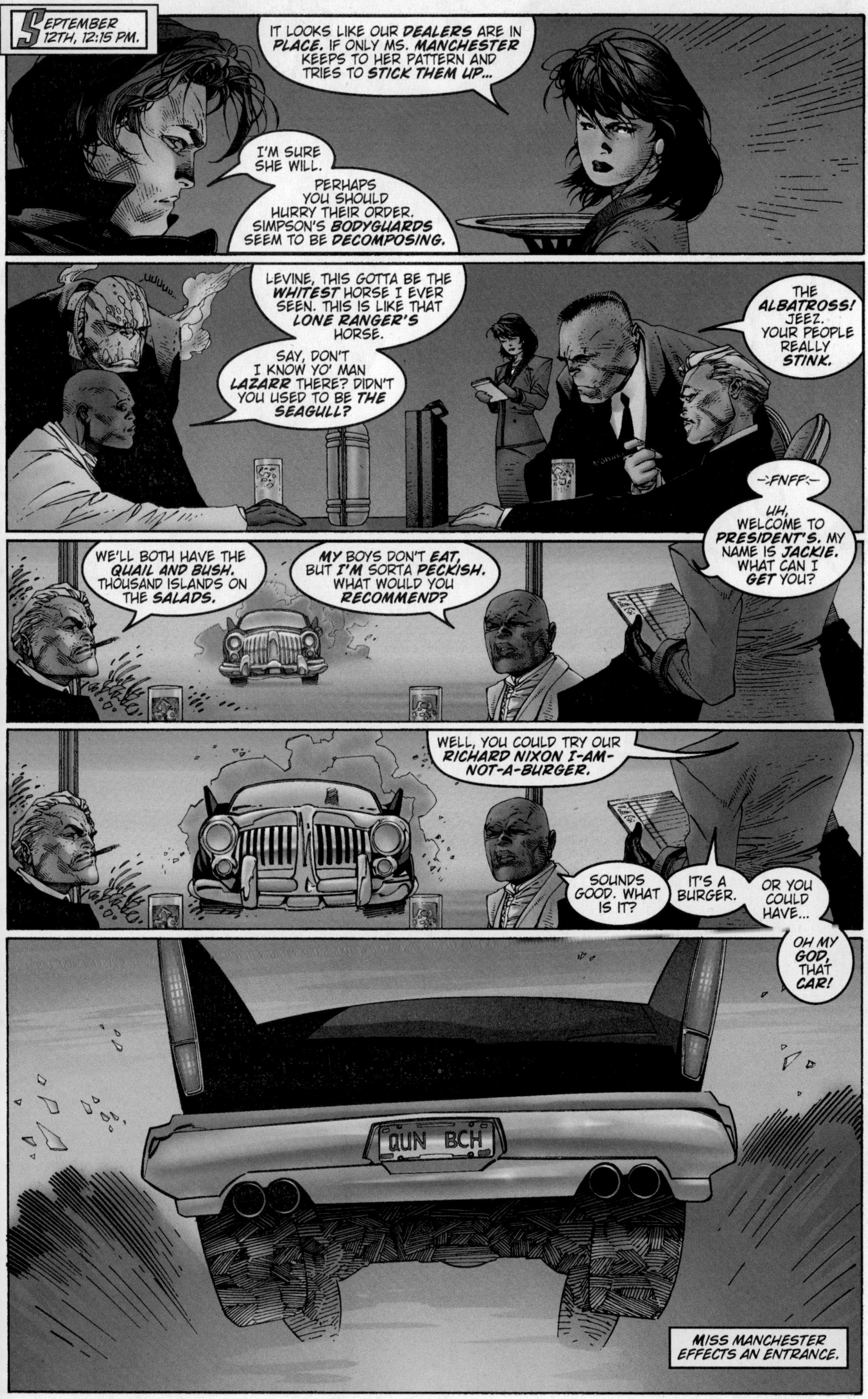
SEPTEMBER 12TH, 12:15 PM.
IT LOOKS LIKE OUR DEALERS ARE IN PLACE. IF ONLY MS. MANCHESTER KEEPS TO HER PATTERN AND TRIES TO STICK THEM UP...
I'M SURE SHE WILL.
PERHAPS YOU SHOULD HURRY THEIR ORDER. SIMPSON'S BODYGUARDS SEEM TO BE DECOMPOSING.
LEVINE, THIS GOTTA BE THE WHITEST HORSE I EVER SEEN. THIS IS LIKE THAT LONE RANGER'S HORSE.
SAY, DON'T I KNOW YO' MAN LAZARR THERE? DIDN'T YOU USED TO BE THE SEAGULL?
THE ALBATROSS! JEEZ. YOUR PEOPLE REALLY STINK.
-FNFF-
UH, WELCOME TO PRESIDENT'S. MY NAME IS JACKIE. WHAT CAN I GET YOU?
WE'LL BOTH HAVE THE QUAIL AND BUSH. THOUSAND ISLANDS ON THE SALADS.
MY BOYS DON'T EAT, BUT I'M SORTA PECKISH. WHAT WOULD YOU RECOMMEND?
WELL, YOU COULD TRY OUR RICHARD NIXON I-AM-NOT-A-BURGER.
SOUNDS GOOD. WHAT IS IT?
IT'S A BURGER.
OR YOU COULD HAVE...
OH MY GOD, THAT CAR!
QUN BCH
MISS MANCHESTER EFFECTS AN ENTRANCE.

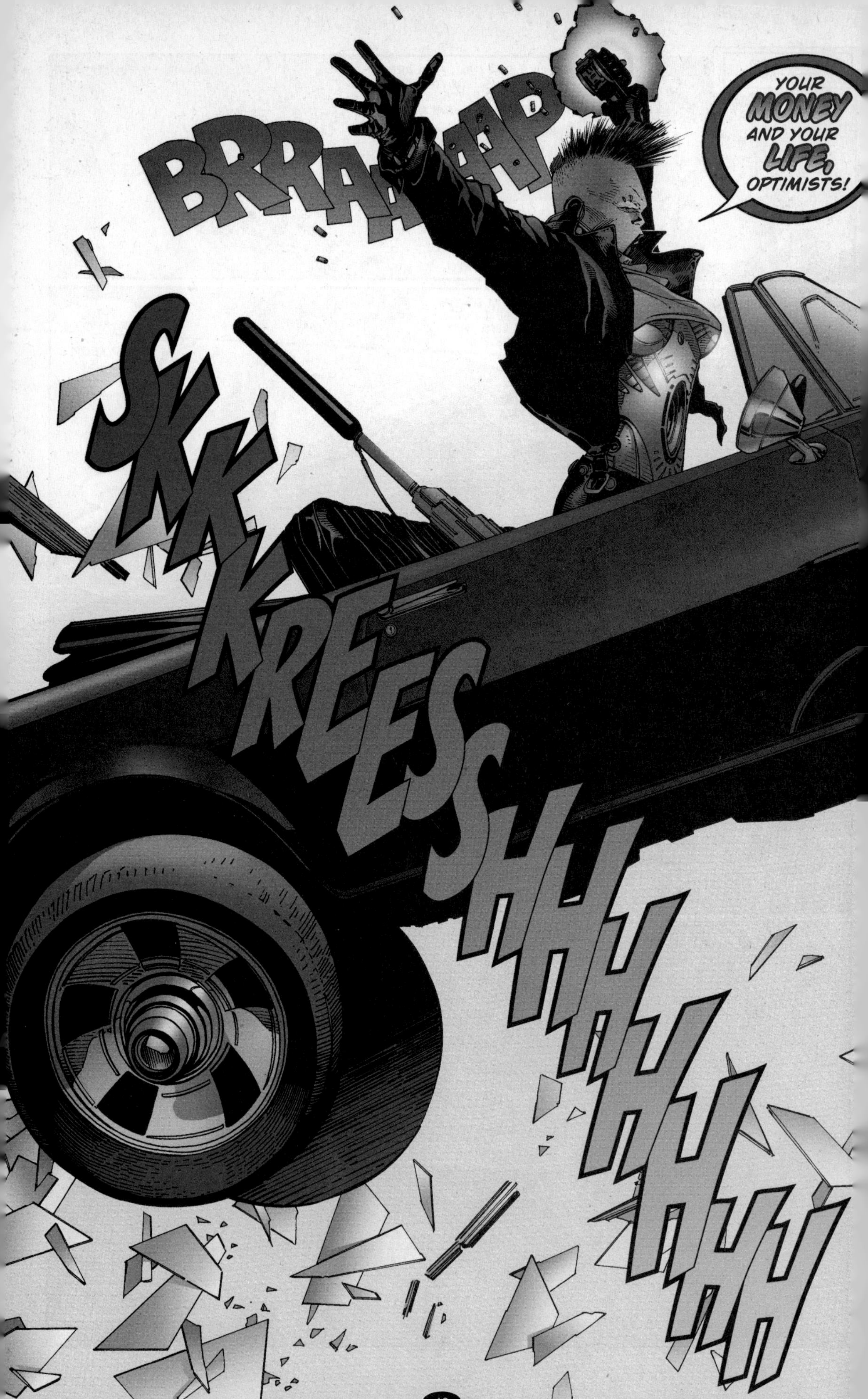
BRRAAAAAP
YOUR MONEY AND YOUR LIFE, OPTIMISTS!
SKKKREESSHHHHHHHH

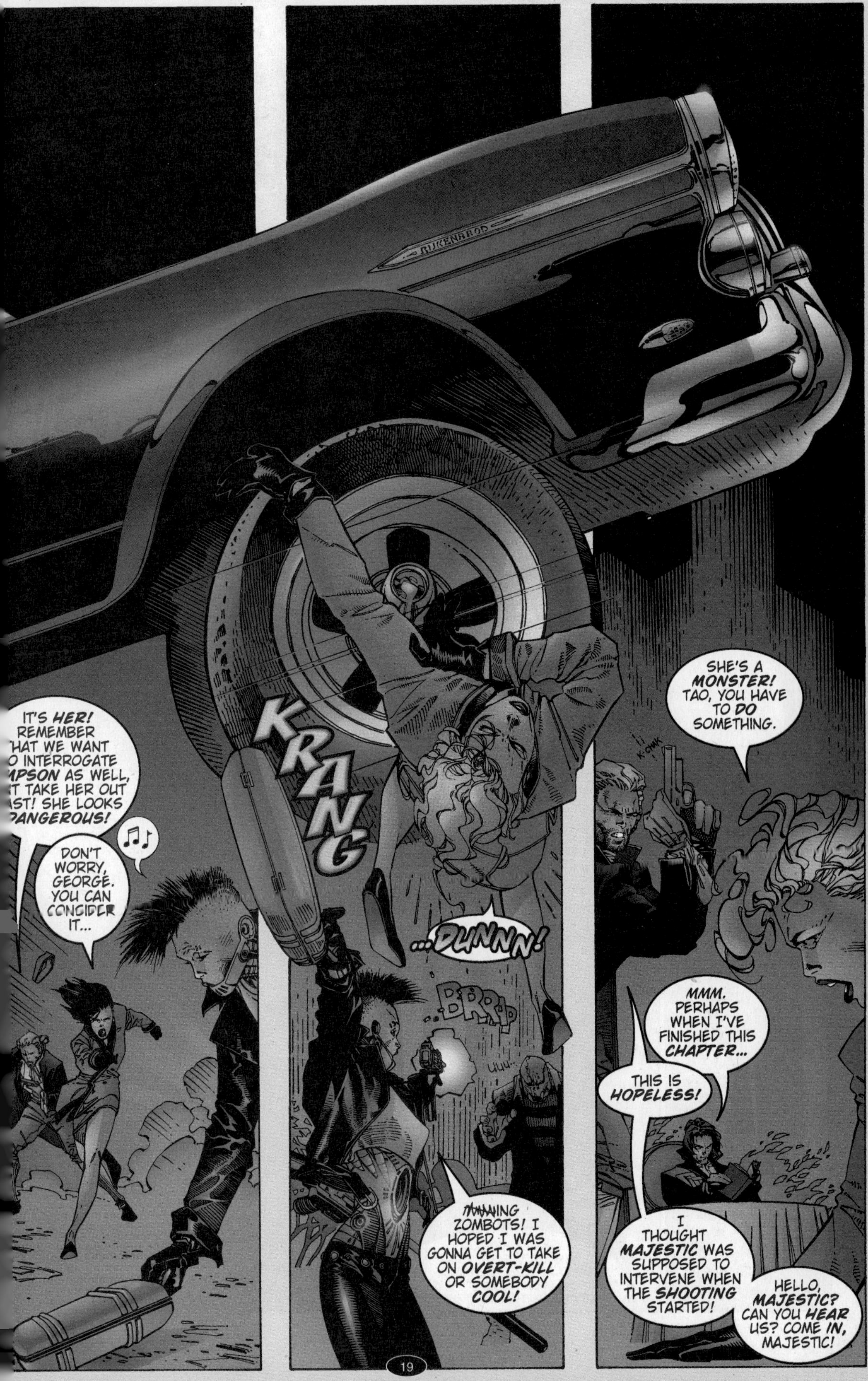
IT'S HER! REMEMBER THAT WE WANT O INTERROGATE MPSON AS WELL, T TAKE HER OUT AST! SHE LOOKS DANGEROUS!
DON'T WORRY, GEORGE. YOU CAN CONCIDER IT...
KRANG
...DUNNN!
BRRRAP
ING ZOMBOTS! I HOPED I WAS GONNA GET TO TAKE ON OVERT-KILL OR SOMEBODY COOL!
K-CHAK
SHE'S A MONSTER! TAO, YOU HAVE TO DO SOMETHING.
MMM. PERHAPS WHEN I'VE FINISHED THIS CHAPTER...
THIS IS HOPELESS!
I THOUGHT MAJESTIC WAS SUPPOSED TO INTERVENE WHEN THE SHOOTING STARTED!
HELLO, MAJESTIC? CAN YOU HEAR US? COME IN, MAJESTIC!

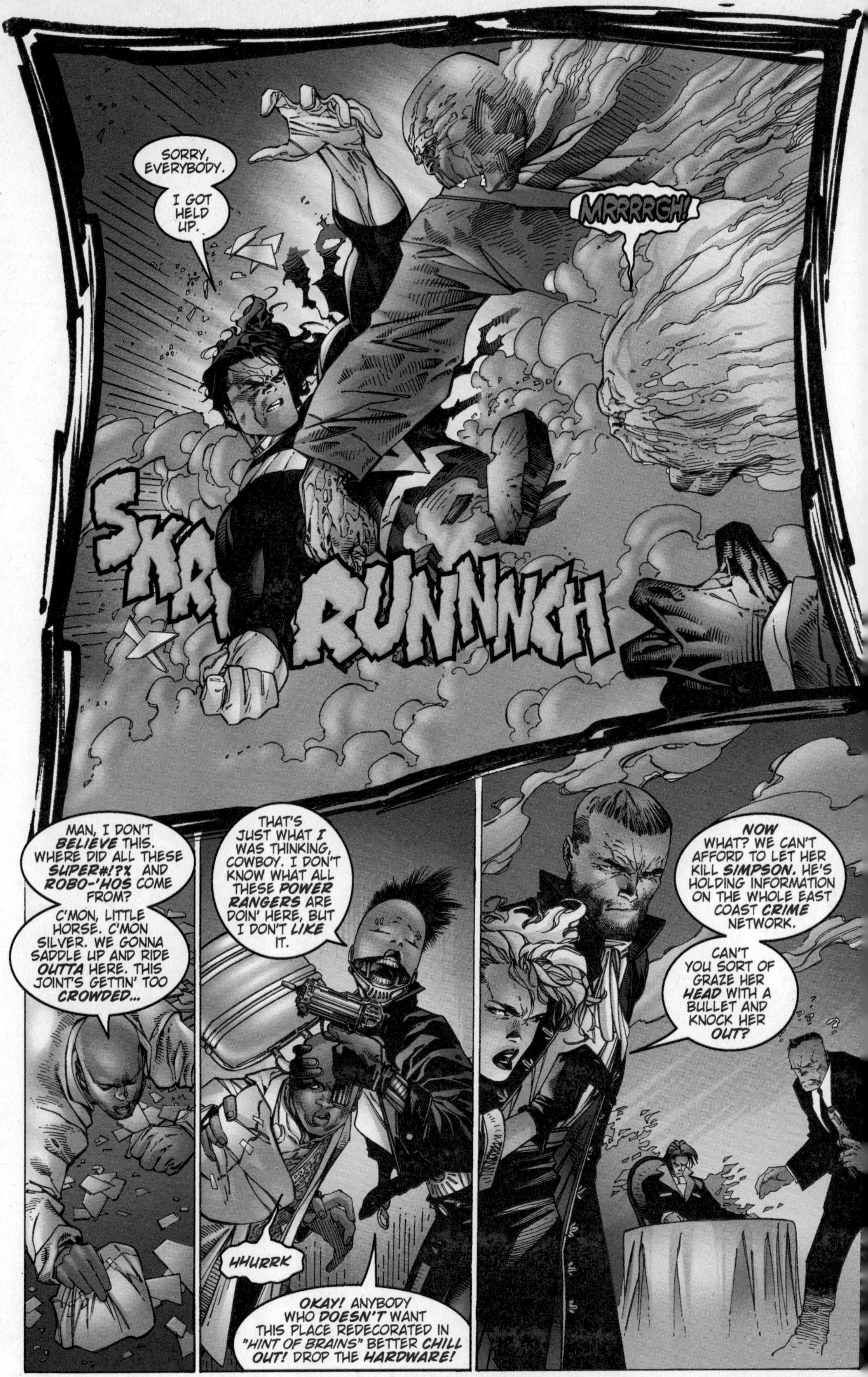

SORRY, EVERYBODY.
I GOT HELD UP.
MRRRRGH!
SKRRUNNNCH
MAN, I DON'T BELIEVE THIS. WHERE DID ALL THESE SUPER#!?% AND ROBO-'HOS COME FROM?
C'MON, LITTLE HORSE. C'MON SILVER. WE GONNA SADDLE UP AND RIDE OUTTA HERE. THIS JOINT'S GETTIN' TOO CROWDED...
THAT'S JUST WHAT I WAS THINKING, COWBOY. I DON'T KNOW WHAT ALL THESE POWER RANGERS ARE DOIN' HERE, BUT I DON'T LIKE IT.
HHURRK
OKAY! ANYBODY WHO DOESN'T WANT THIS PLACE REDECORATED IN "HINT OF BRAINS" BETTER CHILL OUT! DROP THE HARDWARE!
NOW WHAT? WE CAN'T AFFORD TO LET HER KILL SIMPSON. HE'S HOLDING INFORMATION ON THE WHOLE EAST COAST CRIME NETWORK.
CAN'T YOU SORT OF GRAZE HER HEAD WITH A BULLET AND KNOCK HER OUT?

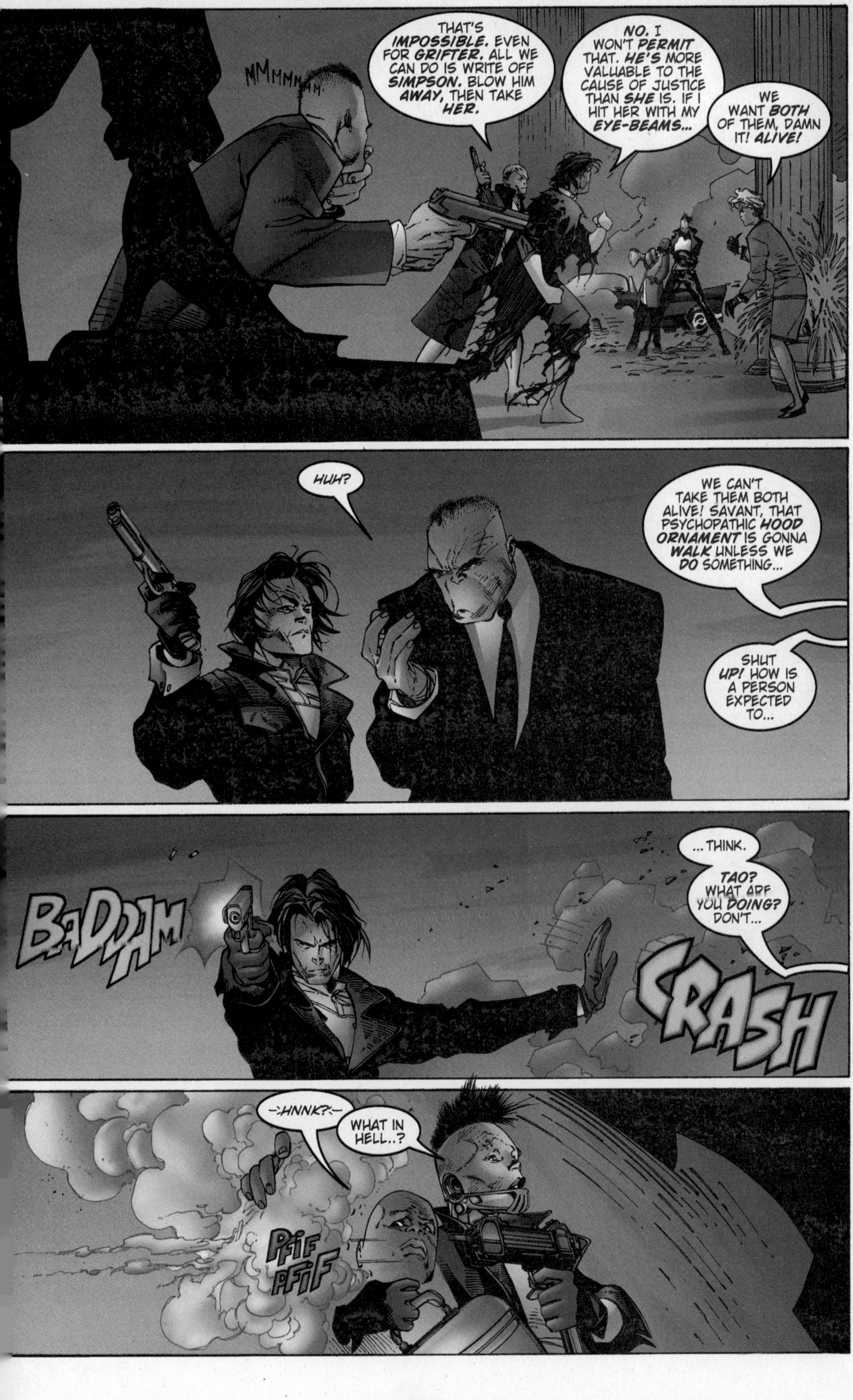
MMMMMMM
THAT'S IMPOSSIBLE. EVEN FOR GRIFTER. ALL WE CAN DO IS WRITE OFF SIMPSON. BLOW HIM AWAY, THEN TAKE HER.
NO. I WON'T PERMIT THAT. HE'S MORE VALUABLE TO THE CAUSE OF JUSTICE THAN SHE IS. IF I HIT HER WITH MY EYE-BEAMS...
WE WANT BOTH OF THEM, DAMN IT! ALIVE!
HUH?
WE CAN'T TAKE THEM BOTH ALIVE! SAVANT, THAT PSYCHOPATHIC HOOD ORNAMENT IS GONNA WALK UNLESS WE DO SOMETHING...
SHUT UP! HOW IS A PERSON EXPECTED TO...
BADDAM
...THINK.
TAO? WHAT ARE YOU DOING? DON'T...
CRASH
-HNNK?-
WHAT IN HELL..?
PFIF PFIF

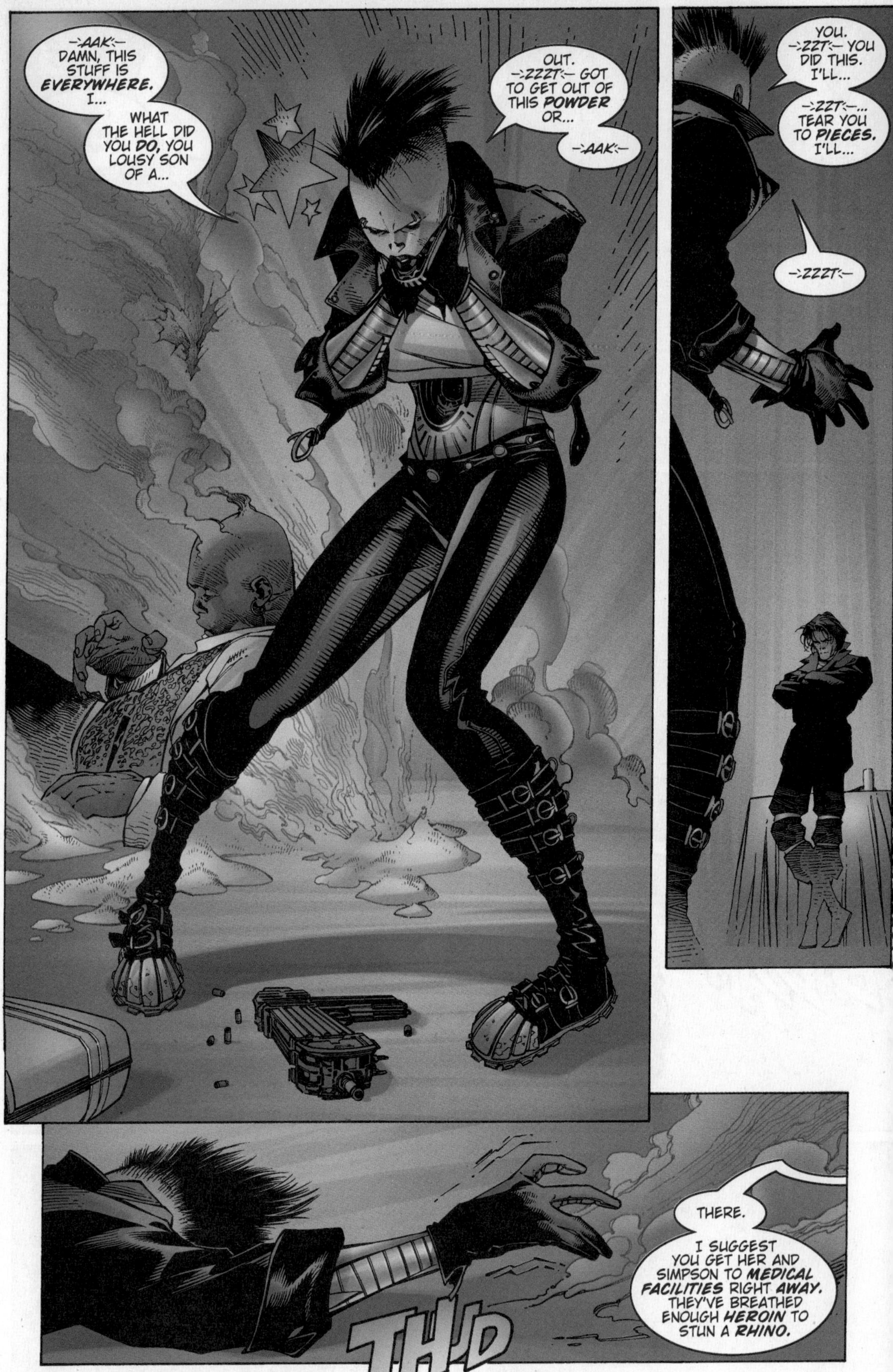

—AAK— DAMN, THIS STUFF IS EVERYWHERE. I...
WHAT THE HELL DID YOU DO, YOU LOUSY SON OF A...
OUT. —ZZZT— GOT TO GET OUT OF THIS POWDER OR...
—AAK—
YOU. —ZZT— YOU DID THIS. I'LL...
—ZZT—... TEAR YOU TO PIECES. I'LL...
—ZZZT—
THUD
THERE.
I SUGGEST YOU GET HER AND SIMPSON TO MEDICAL FACILITIES RIGHT AWAY. THEY'VE BREATHED ENOUGH HEROIN TO STUN A RHINO.

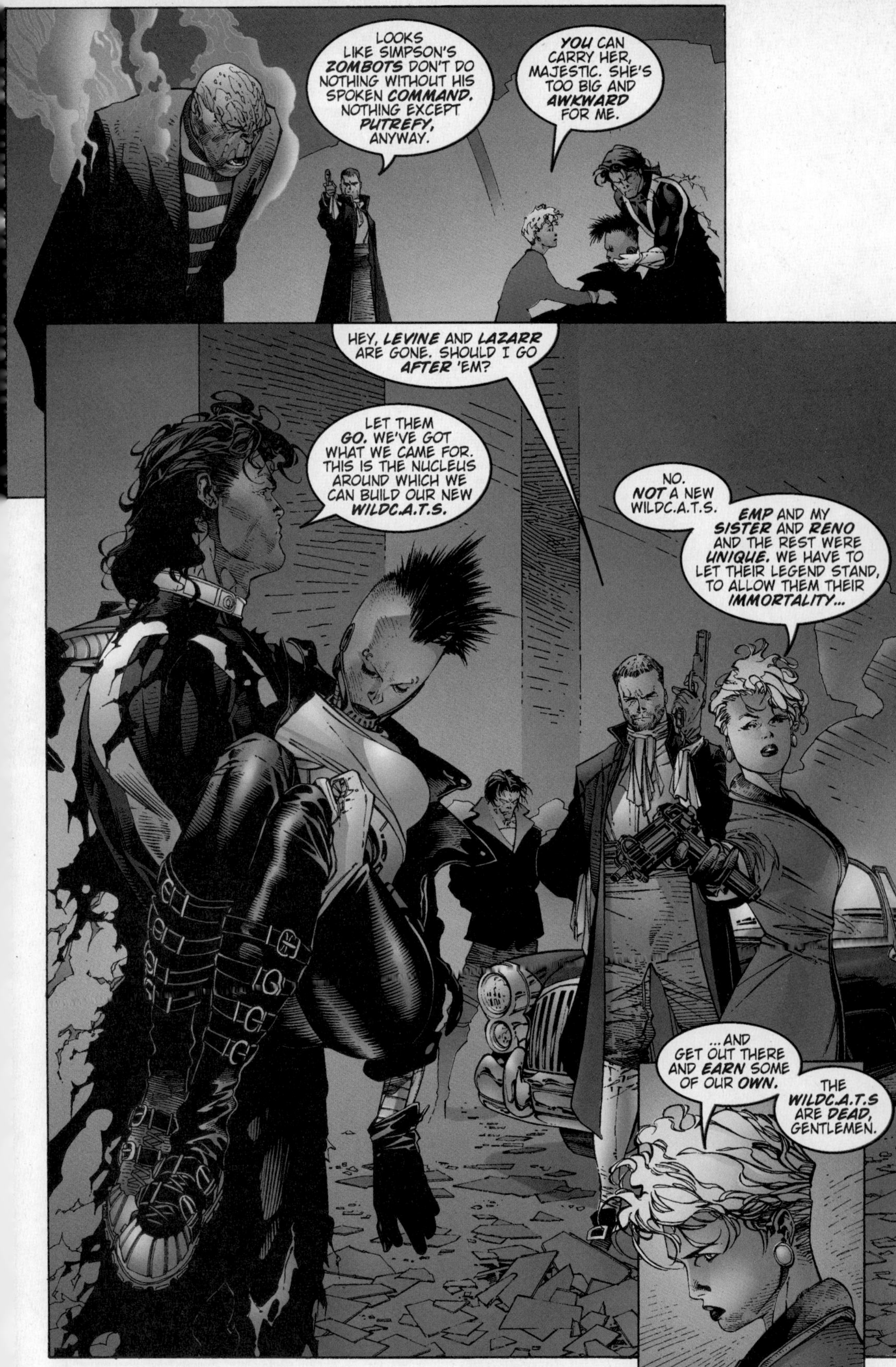
LOOKS LIKE SIMPSON'S ZOMBOTS DON'T DO NOTHING WITHOUT HIS SPOKEN COMMAND. NOTHING EXCEPT PUTREFY, ANYWAY.
YOU CAN CARRY HER, MAJESTIC. SHE'S TOO BIG AND AWKWARD FOR ME.
HEY, LEVINE AND LAZARR ARE GONE. SHOULD I GO AFTER 'EM?
LET THEM GO. WE'VE GOT WHAT WE CAME FOR. THIS IS THE NUCLEUS AROUND WHICH WE CAN BUILD OUR NEW WILDC.A.T.S.
NO. NOT A NEW WILDC.A.T.S.
EMP AND MY SISTER AND RENO AND THE REST WERE UNIQUE. WE HAVE TO LET THEIR LEGEND STAND, TO ALLOW THEM THEIR IMMORTALITY...
...AND GET OUT THERE AND EARN SOME OF OUR OWN.
THE WILDC.A.T.S ARE DEAD, GENTLEMEN.

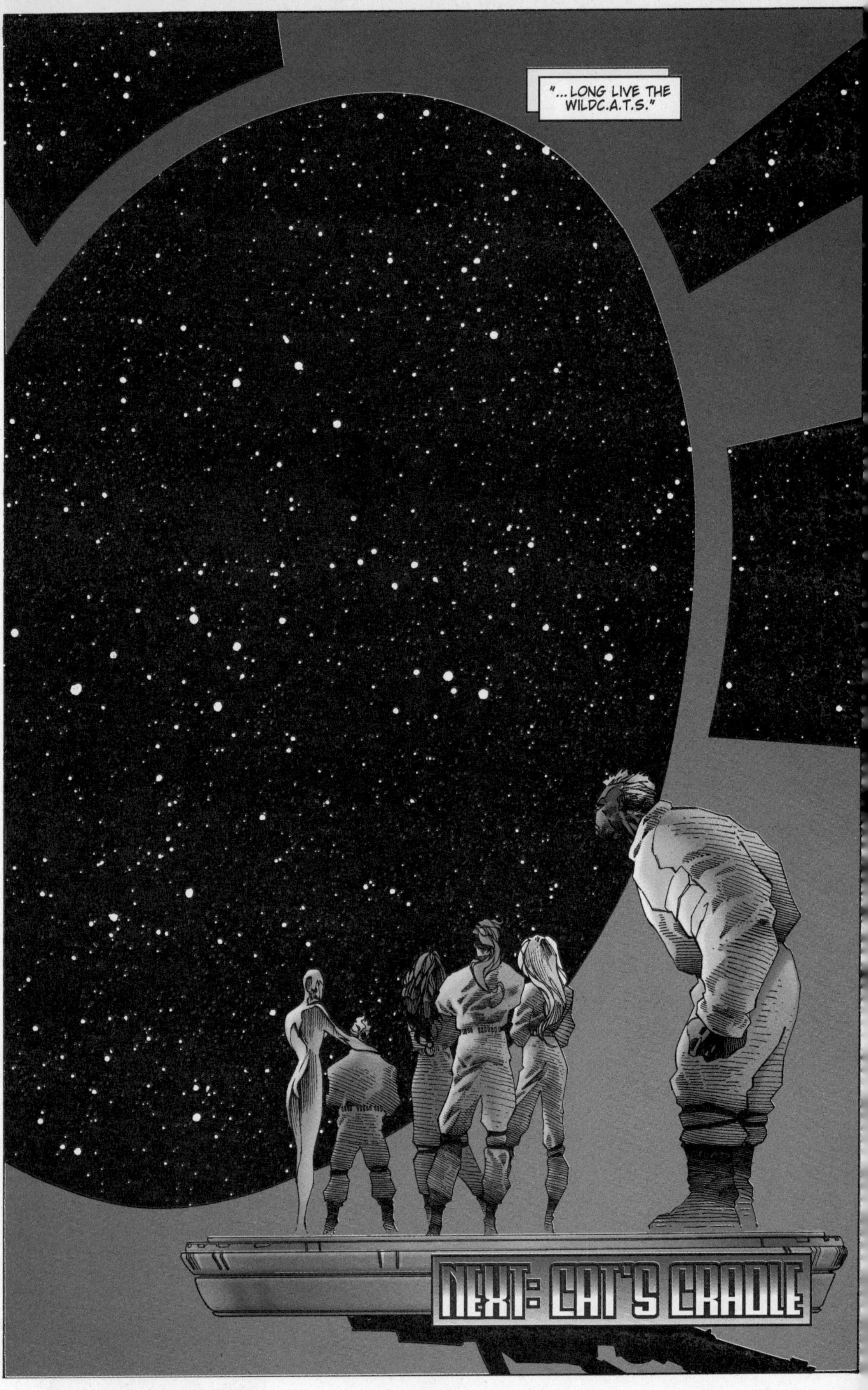
"...LONG LIVE THE WILDC.A.T.S."
NEXT: CAT'S CRADLE

WILDC.A.T.S #22

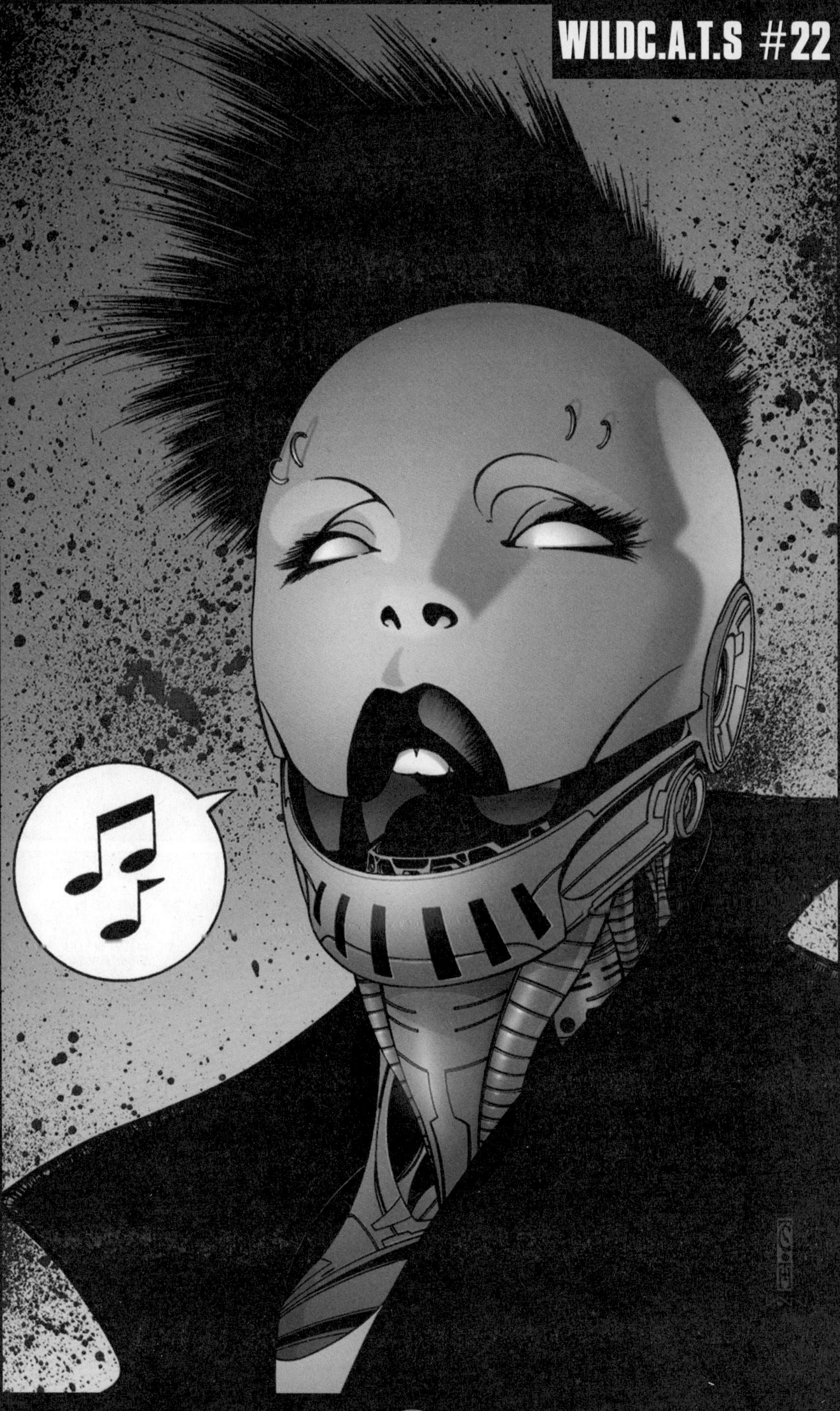

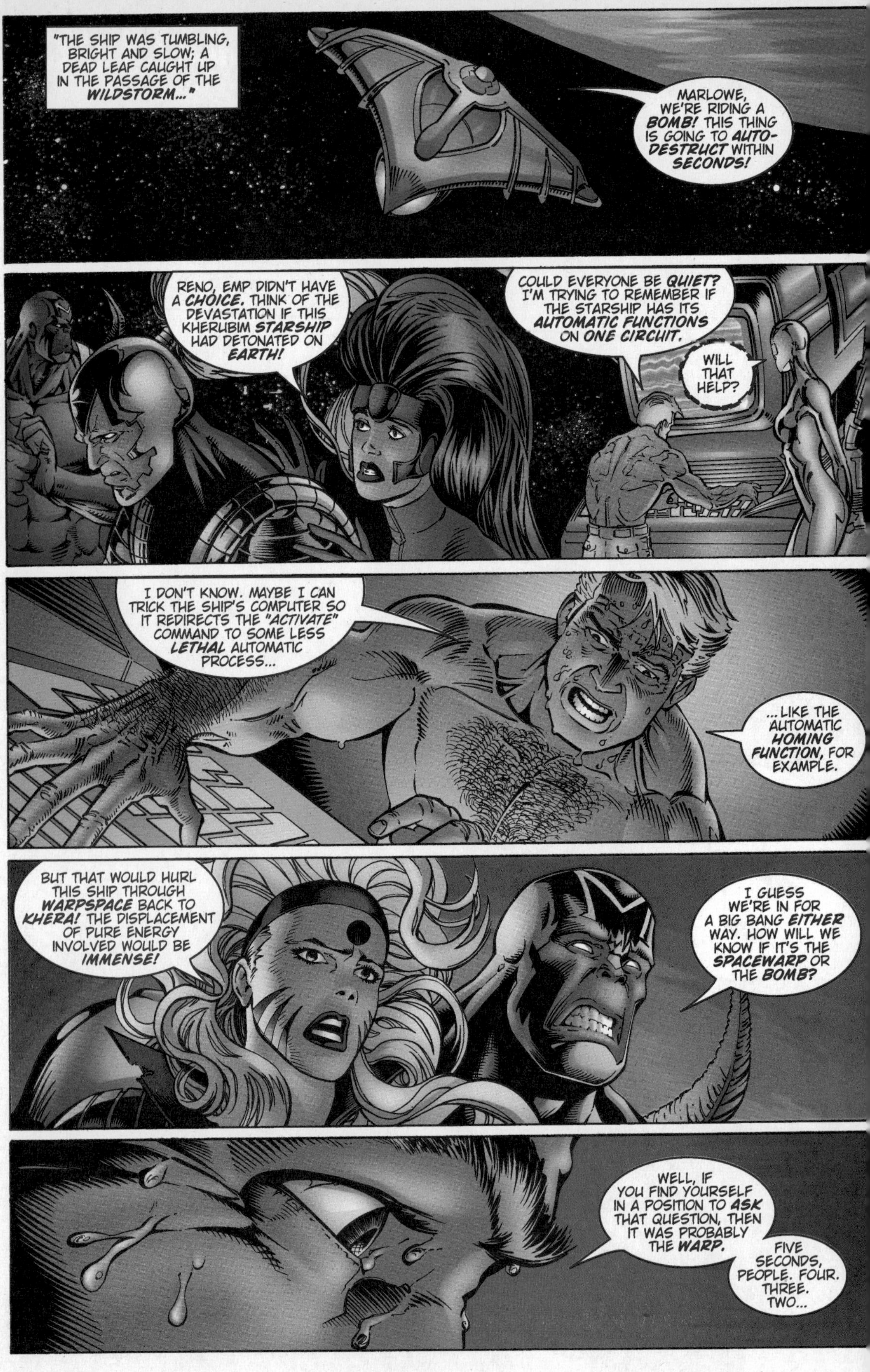
"THE SHIP WAS TUMBLING, BRIGHT AND SLOW; A DEAD LEAF CAUGHT UP IN THE PASSAGE OF THE WILDSTORM..."
MARLOWE, WE'RE RIDING A BOMB! THIS THING IS GOING TO AUTO-DESTRUCT WITHIN SECONDS!
RENO, EMP DIDN'T HAVE A CHOICE. THINK OF THE DEVASTATION IF THIS KHERUBIM STARSHIP HAD DETONATED ON EARTH!
COULD EVERYONE BE QUIET? I'M TRYING TO REMEMBER IF THE STARSHIP HAS ITS AUTOMATIC FUNCTIONS ON ONE CIRCUIT.
WILL THAT HELP?
I DON'T KNOW. MAYBE I CAN TRICK THE SHIP'S COMPUTER SO IT REDIRECTS THE "ACTIVATE" COMMAND TO SOME LESS LETHAL AUTOMATIC PROCESS...
...LIKE THE AUTOMATIC HOMING FUNCTION, FOR EXAMPLE.
BUT THAT WOULD HURL THIS SHIP THROUGH WARPSPACE BACK TO KHERA! THE DISPLACEMENT OF PURE ENERGY INVOLVED WOULD BE IMMENSE!
I GUESS WE'RE IN FOR A BIG BANG EITHER WAY. HOW WILL WE KNOW IF IT'S THE SPACEWARP OR THE BOMB?
WELL, IF YOU FIND YOURSELF IN A POSITION TO ASK THAT QUESTION, THEN IT WAS PROBABLY THE WARP.
FIVE SECONDS, PEOPLE. FOUR. THREE. TWO...

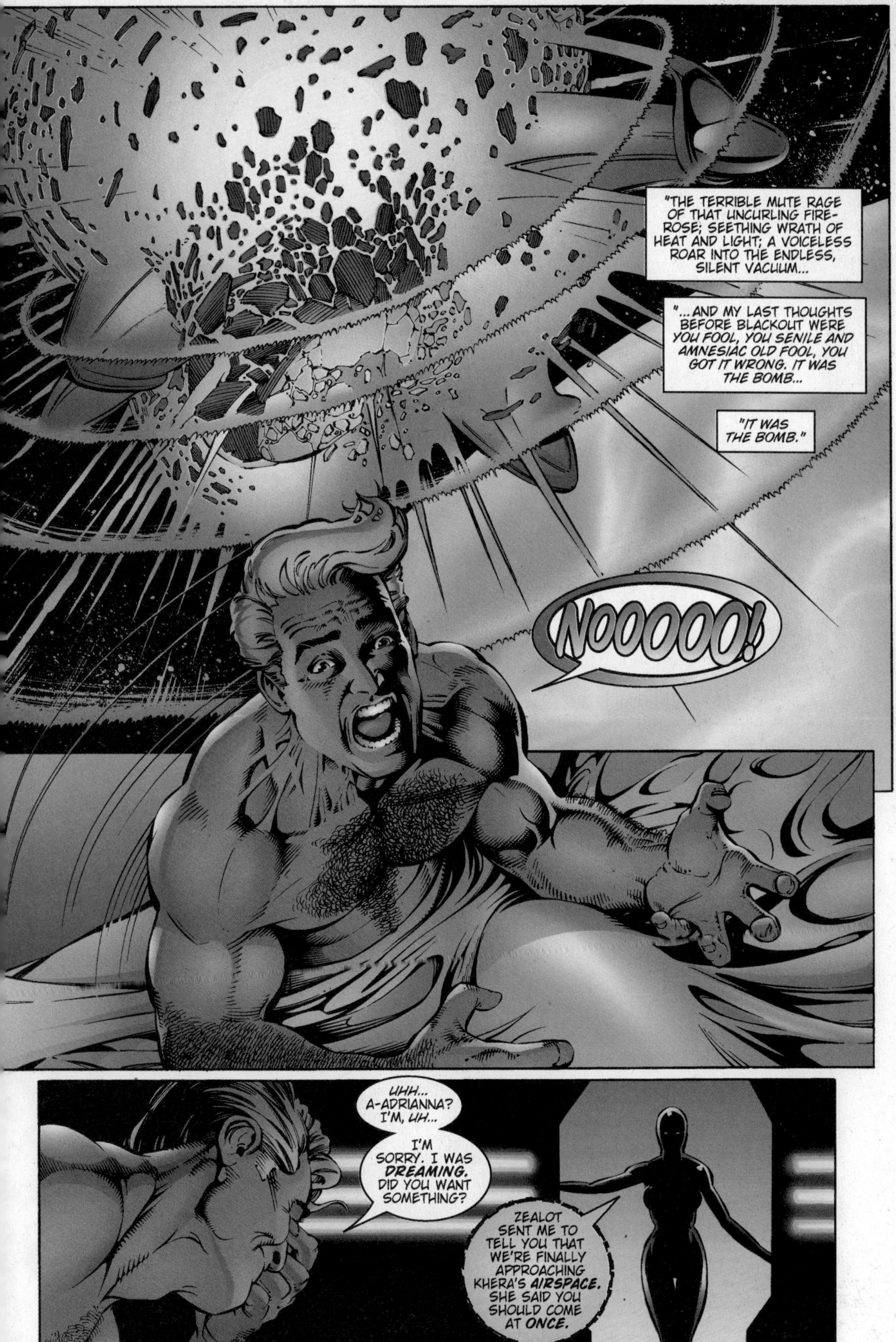
"THE TERRIBLE MUTE RAGE OF THAT UNCURLING FIRE-ROSE; SEETHING WRATH OF HEAT AND LIGHT; A VOICELESS ROAR INTO THE ENDLESS, SILENT VACUUM...
"...AND MY LAST THOUGHTS BEFORE BLACKOUT WERE *YOU FOOL, YOU SENILE AND AMNESIAC OLD FOOL, YOU GOT IT WRONG. IT WAS THE BOMB...*
"IT WAS THE BOMB."
NOOOOO!
UHH... A-ADRIANNA? I'M, *UH*...
I'M SORRY. I WAS ***DREAMING.*** DID YOU WANT SOMETHING?
ZEALOT SENT ME TO TELL YOU THAT WE'RE FINALLY APPROACHING KHERA'S ***AIRSPACE.*** SHE SAID YOU SHOULD COME AT ***ONCE.***

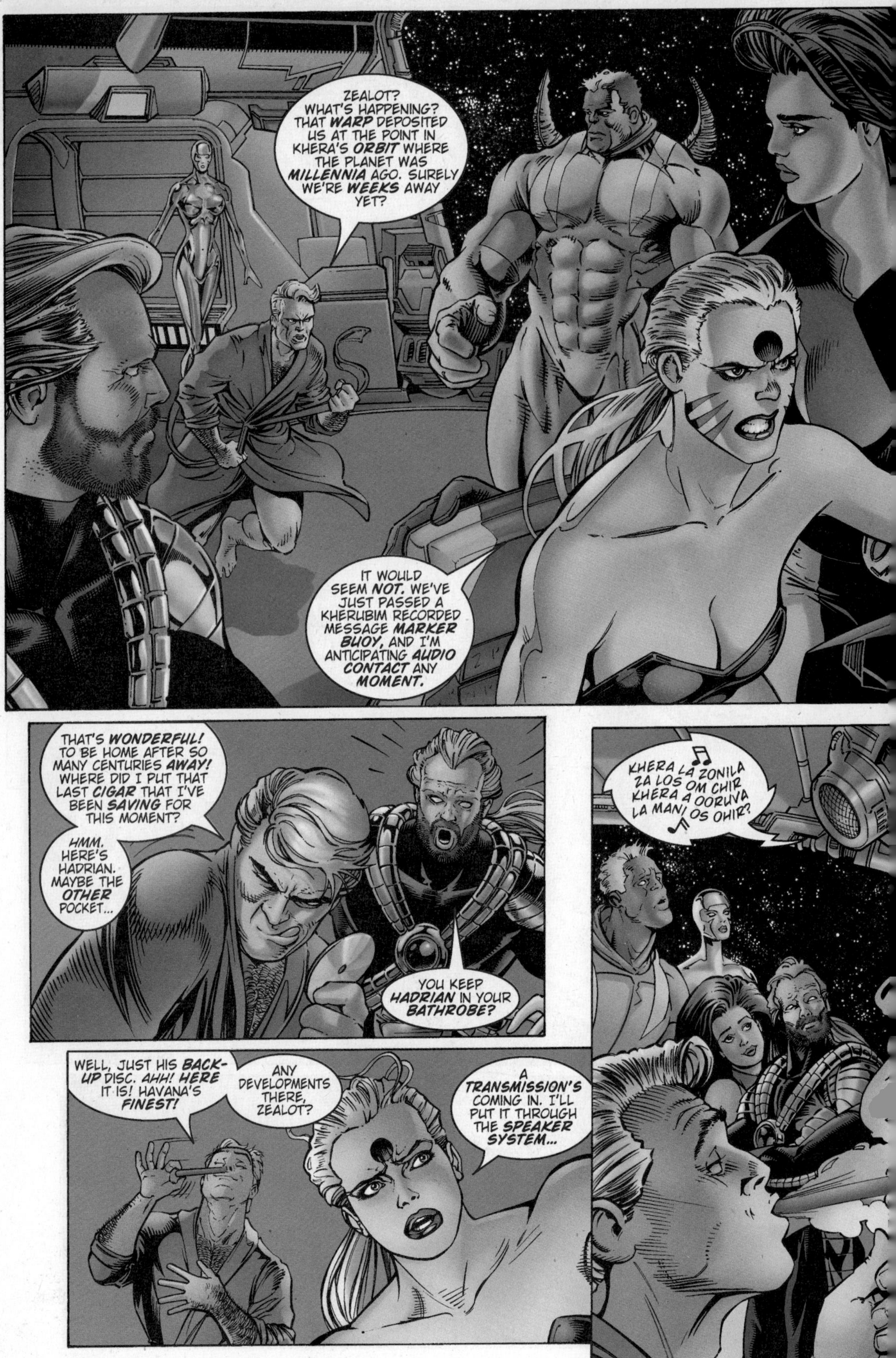
ZEALOT? WHAT'S HAPPENING? THAT WARP DEPOSITED US AT THE POINT IN KHERA'S ORBIT WHERE THE PLANET WAS MILLENNIA AGO. SURELY WE'RE WEEKS AWAY YET?
IT WOULD SEEM NOT. WE'VE JUST PASSED A KHERUBIM RECORDED MESSAGE MARKER BUOY, AND I'M ANTICIPATING AUDIO CONTACT ANY MOMENT.
THAT'S WONDERFUL! TO BE HOME AFTER SO MANY CENTURIES AWAY! WHERE DID I PUT THAT LAST CIGAR THAT I'VE BEEN SAVING FOR THIS MOMENT?
HMM. HERE'S HADRIAN. MAYBE THE OTHER POCKET...
YOU KEEP HADRIAN IN YOUR BATHROBE?
WELL, JUST HIS BACK-UP DISC. AHH! HERE IT IS! HAVANA'S FINEST!
ANY DEVELOPMENTS THERE, ZEALOT?
A TRANSMISSION'S COMING IN. I'LL PUT IT THROUGH THE SPEAKER SYSTEM...
KHERA LA ZONILA ZA LOS OM CHIR KHERA A OORUVA LA MAN! OS OHIR?

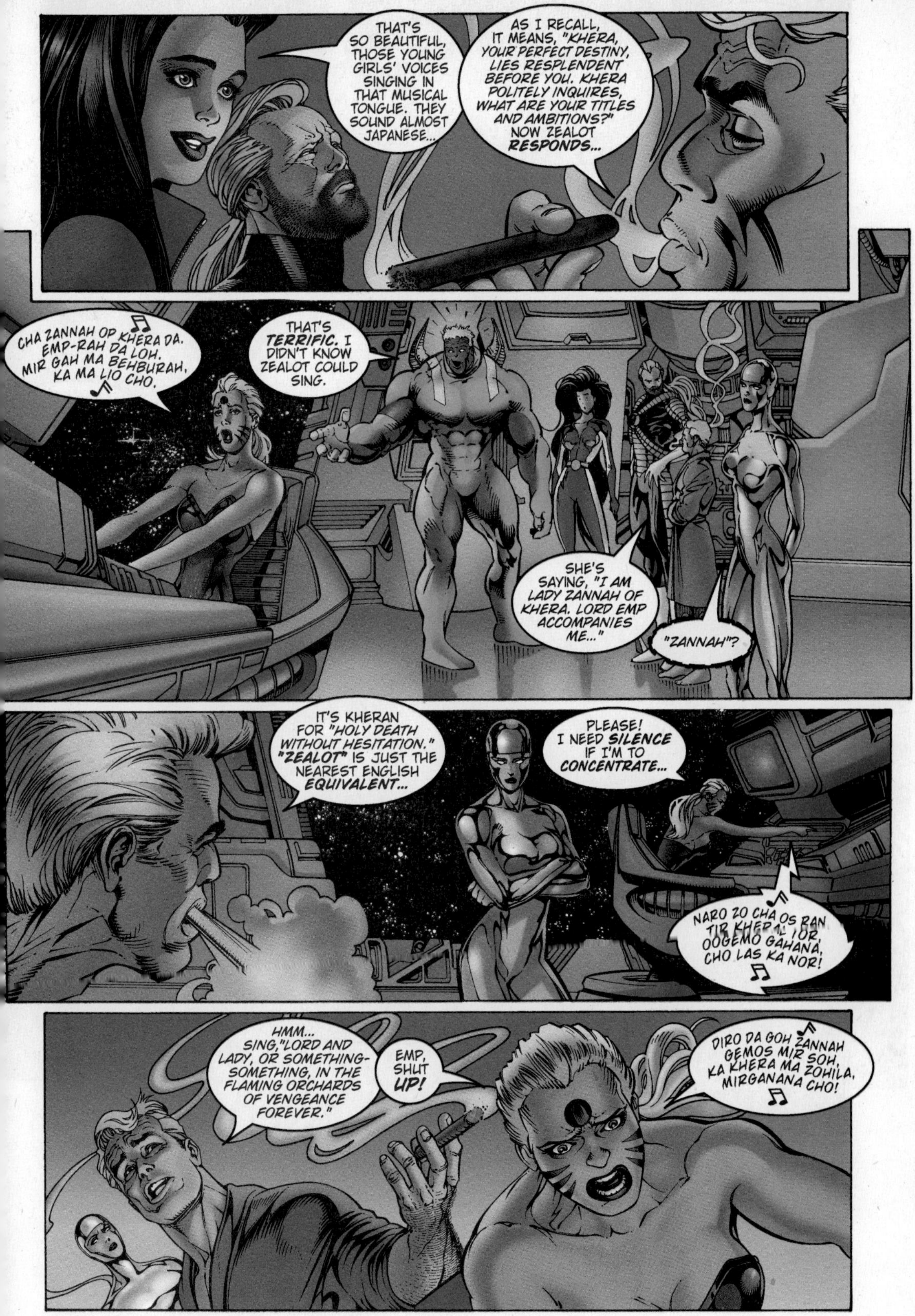
THAT'S SO BEAUTIFUL, THOSE YOUNG GIRLS' VOICES SINGING IN THAT MUSICAL TONGUE. THEY SOUND ALMOST JAPANESE...
AS I RECALL, IT MEANS, "KHERA, YOUR PERFECT DESTINY, LIES RESPLENDENT BEFORE YOU. KHERA POLITELY INQUIRES, WHAT ARE YOUR TITLES AND AMBITIONS?" NOW ZEALOT RESPONDS...
CHA ZANNAH OP KHERA DA. EMP-RAH DA LOH. MIR GAH MA BEHBURAH, KA MA LIO CHO.
THAT'S TERRIFIC. I DIDN'T KNOW ZEALOT COULD SING.
SHE'S SAYING, "I AM LADY ZANNAH OF KHERA. LORD EMP ACCOMPANIES ME..."
"ZANNAH"?
IT'S KHERAN FOR "HOLY DEATH WITHOUT HESITATION." "ZEALOT" IS JUST THE NEAREST ENGLISH EQUIVALENT...
PLEASE! I NEED SILENCE IF I'M TO CONCENTRATE...
NARO ZO CHA OS RAN TIR KHER IOR OOGEMO GAHANA, CHO LAS KA NOR!
HMM... SING, "LORD AND LADY, OR SOMETHING-SOMETHING, IN THE FLAMING ORCHARDS OF VENGEANCE FOREVER."
EMP, SHUT UP!
DIRO DA GOH ZANNAH GEMOS MIR SOH, KA KHERA MA ZOHILA, MIRGANANA CHO!

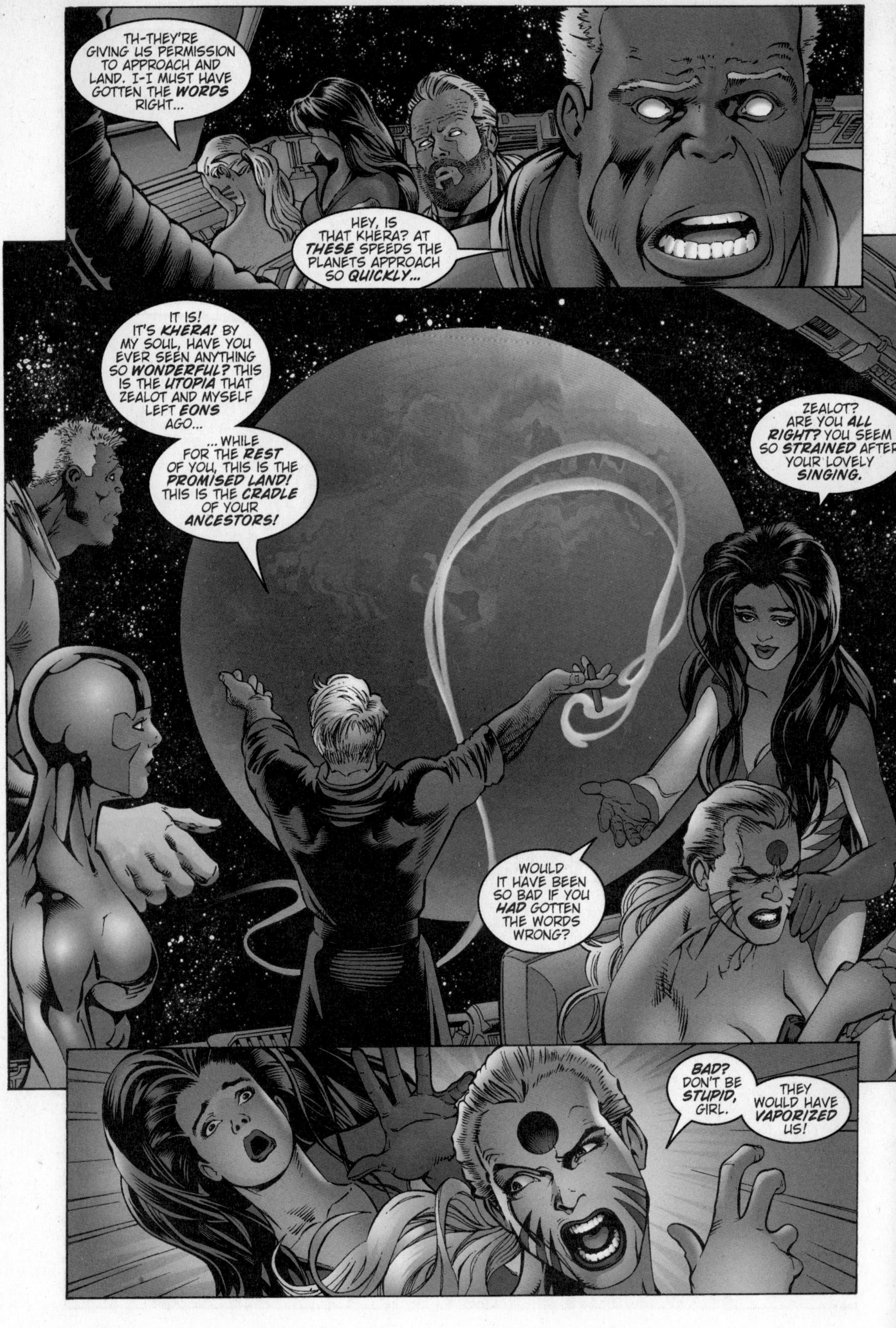
TH-THEY'RE GIVING US PERMISSION TO APPROACH AND LAND. I-I MUST HAVE GOTTEN THE WORDS RIGHT...
HEY, IS THAT KHERA? AT THESE SPEEDS THE PLANETS APPROACH SO QUICKLY...
IT IS! IT'S KHERA! BY MY SOUL, HAVE YOU EVER SEEN ANYTHING SO WONDERFUL? THIS IS THE UTOPIA THAT ZEALOT AND MYSELF LEFT EONS AGO...
...WHILE FOR THE REST OF YOU, THIS IS THE PROMISED LAND! THIS IS THE CRADLE OF YOUR ANCESTORS!
ZEALOT? ARE YOU ALL RIGHT? YOU SEEM SO STRAINED AFTER YOUR LOVELY SINGING.
WOULD IT HAVE BEEN SO BAD IF YOU HAD GOTTEN THE WORDS WRONG?
BAD? DON'T BE STUPID, GIRL.
THEY WOULD HAVE VAPORIZED US!

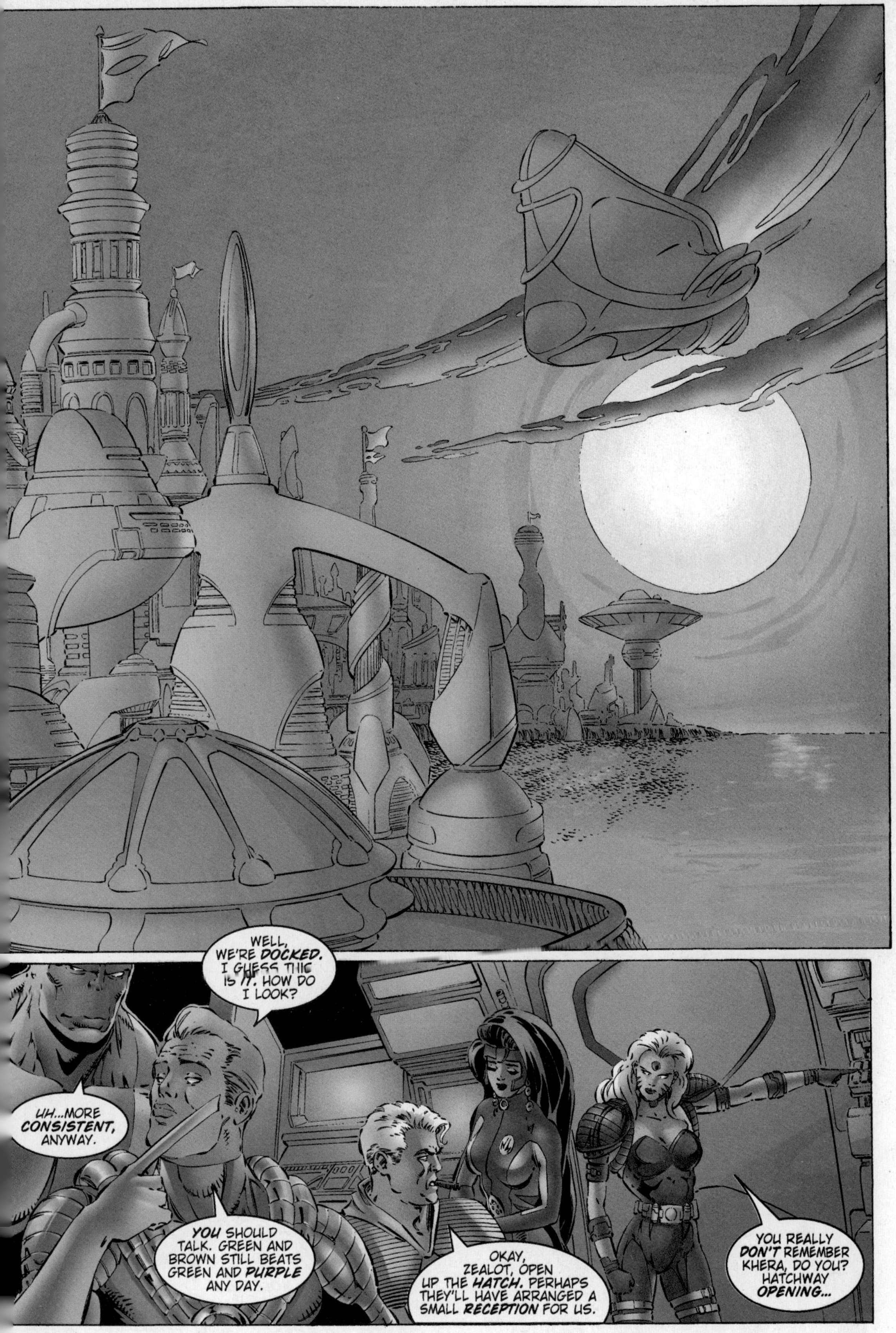
WELL, WE'RE **DOCKED.** I GUESS THIS IS *IT.* HOW DO I LOOK?
UH...MORE **CONSISTENT,** ANYWAY.
YOU SHOULD TALK. GREEN AND BROWN STILL BEATS GREEN AND ***PURPLE*** ANY DAY.
OKAY, ZEALOT, OPEN UP THE ***HATCH.*** PERHAPS THEY'LL HAVE ARRANGED A SMALL ***RECEPTION*** FOR US.
YOU REALLY ***DON'T*** REMEMBER KHERA, DO YOU? HATCHWAY ***OPENING...***

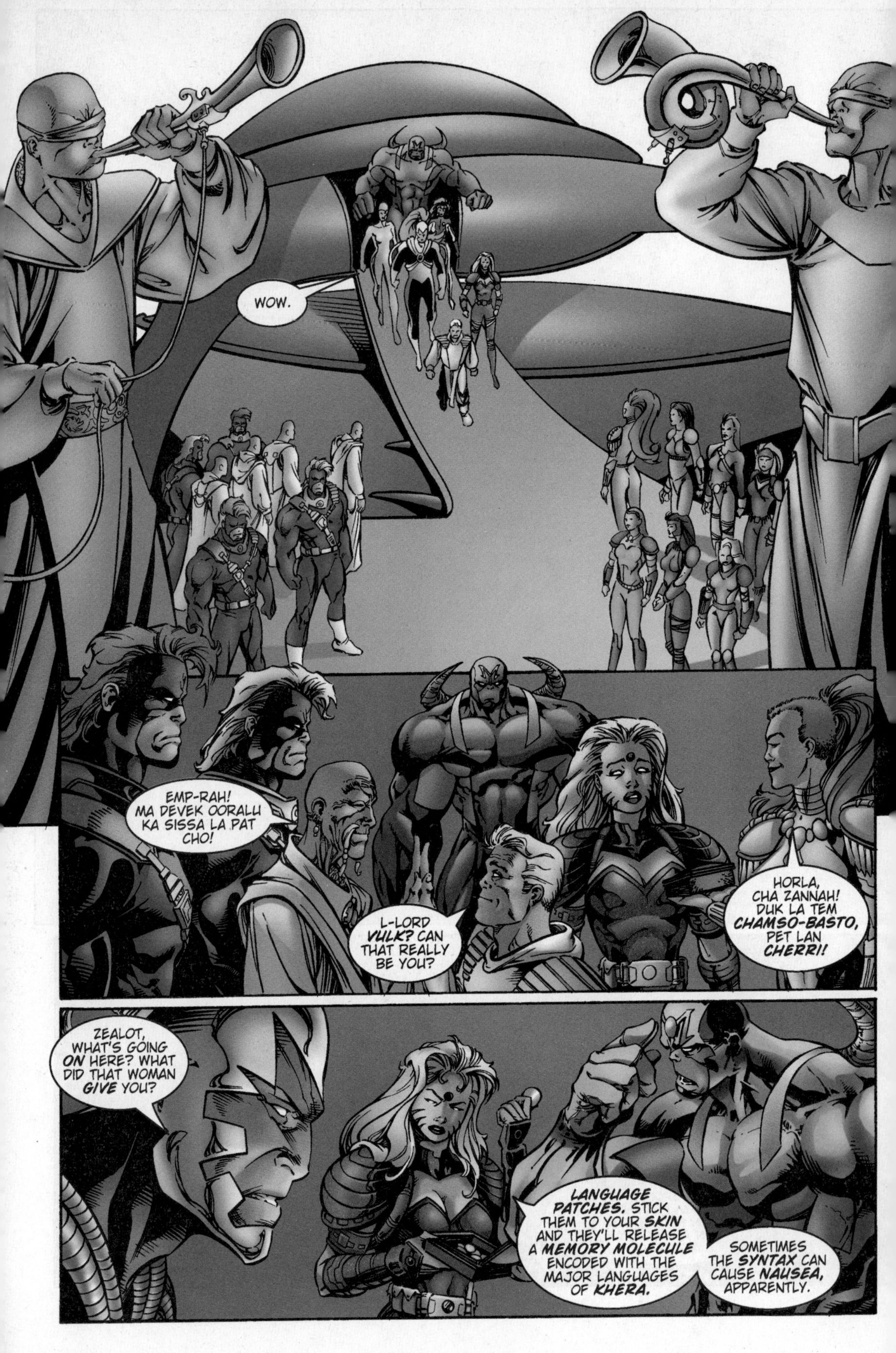
WOW.
EMP-RAH! MA DEVEK OORALU KA SISSA LA PAT CHO!
L-LORD VULK? CAN THAT REALLY BE YOU?
HORLA, CHA ZANNAH! DUK LA TEM CHAMSO-BASTO, PET LAN CHERRI!
ZEALOT, WHAT'S GOING ON HERE? WHAT DID THAT WOMAN GIVE YOU?
LANGUAGE PATCHES. STICK THEM TO YOUR SKIN AND THEY'LL RELEASE A MEMORY MOLECULE ENCODED WITH THE MAJOR LANGUAGES OF KHERA.
SOMETIMES THE SYNTAX CAN CAUSE NAUSEA, APPARENTLY.

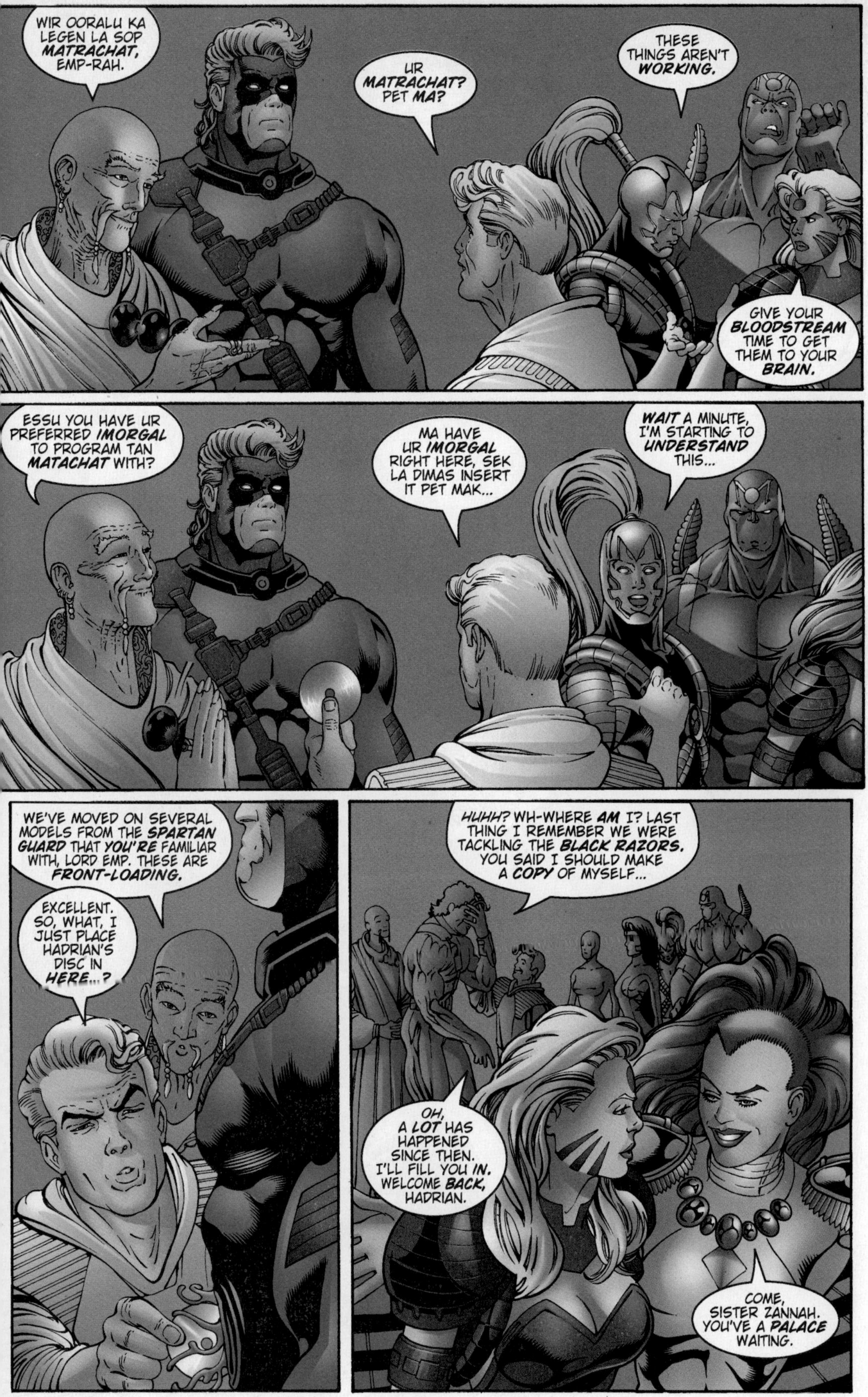
WIR OORALU KA LEGEN LA SOP MATRACHAT, EMP-RAH.
UR MATRACHAT? PET MA?
THESE THINGS AREN'T WORKING.
GIVE YOUR BLOODSTREAM TIME TO GET THEM TO YOUR BRAIN.
ESSU YOU HAVE UR PREFERRED IMORGAL TO PROGRAM TAN MATACHAT WITH?
MA HAVE UR IMORGAL RIGHT HERE, SEK LA DIMAS INSERT IT PET MAK...
WAIT A MINUTE, I'M STARTING TO UNDERSTAND THIS...
WE'VE MOVED ON SEVERAL MODELS FROM THE SPARTAN GUARD THAT YOU'RE FAMILIAR WITH, LORD EMP. THESE ARE FRONT-LOADING.
EXCELLENT. SO, WHAT, I JUST PLACE HADRIAN'S DISC IN HERE...?
HUHH? WH-WHERE AM I? LAST THING I REMEMBER WE WERE TACKLING THE BLACK RAZORS. YOU SAID I SHOULD MAKE A COPY OF MYSELF...
OH, A LOT HAS HAPPENED SINCE THEN. I'LL FILL YOU IN. WELCOME BACK, HADRIAN.
COME, SISTER ZANNAH. YOU'VE A PALACE WAITING.

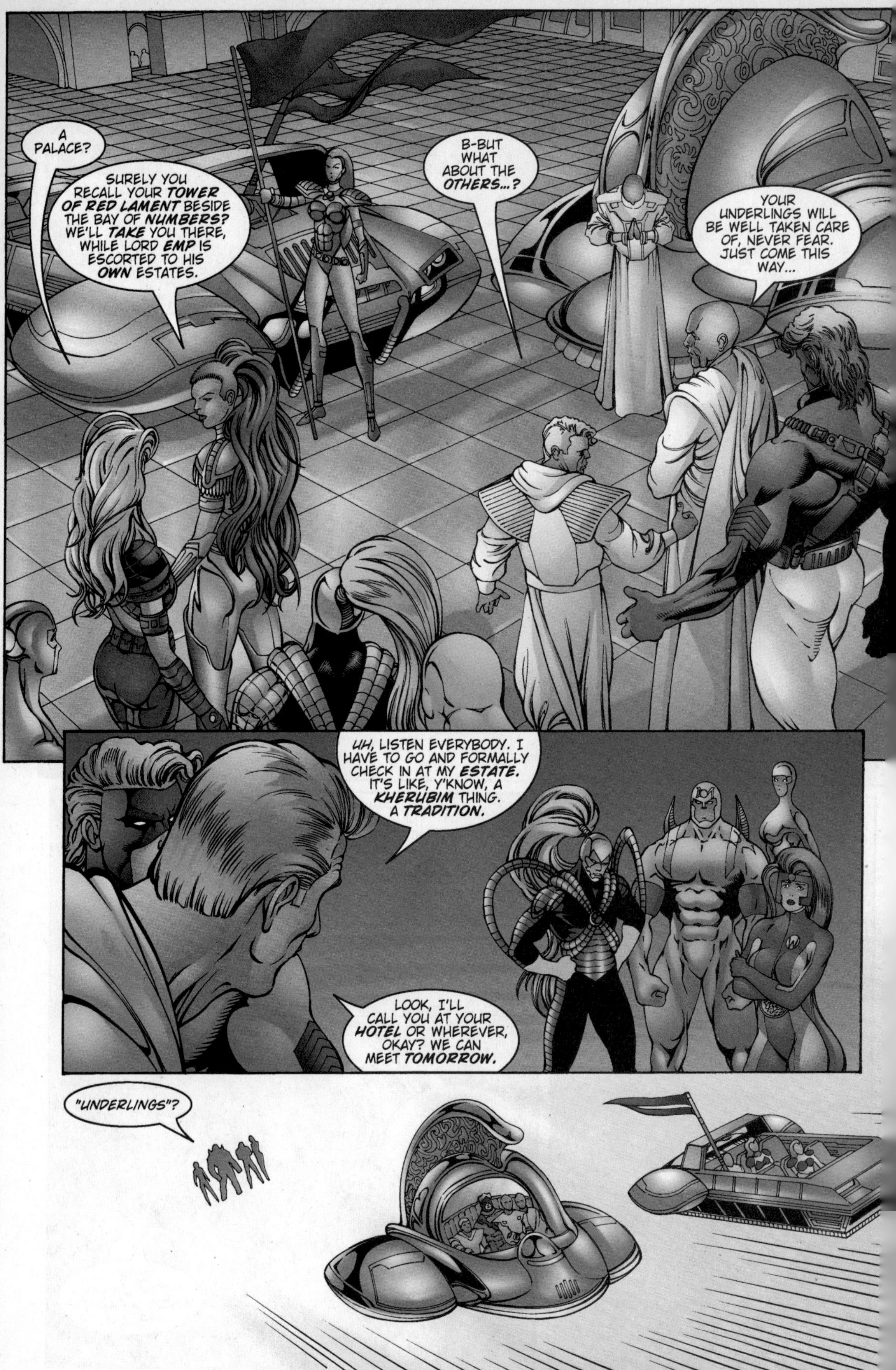
A PALACE?
SURELY YOU RECALL YOUR TOWER OF RED LAMENT BESIDE THE BAY OF NUMBERS? WE'LL TAKE YOU THERE, WHILE LORD EMP IS ESCORTED TO HIS OWN ESTATES.
B-BUT WHAT ABOUT THE OTHERS...?
YOUR UNDERLINGS WILL BE WELL TAKEN CARE OF, NEVER FEAR. JUST COME THIS WAY...
UH, LISTEN EVERYBODY. I HAVE TO GO AND FORMALLY CHECK IN AT MY ESTATE. IT'S LIKE, Y'KNOW, A KHERUBIM THING. A TRADITION.
LOOK, I'LL CALL YOU AT YOUR HOTEL OR WHEREVER, OKAY? WE CAN MEET TOMORROW.
"UNDERLINGS"?

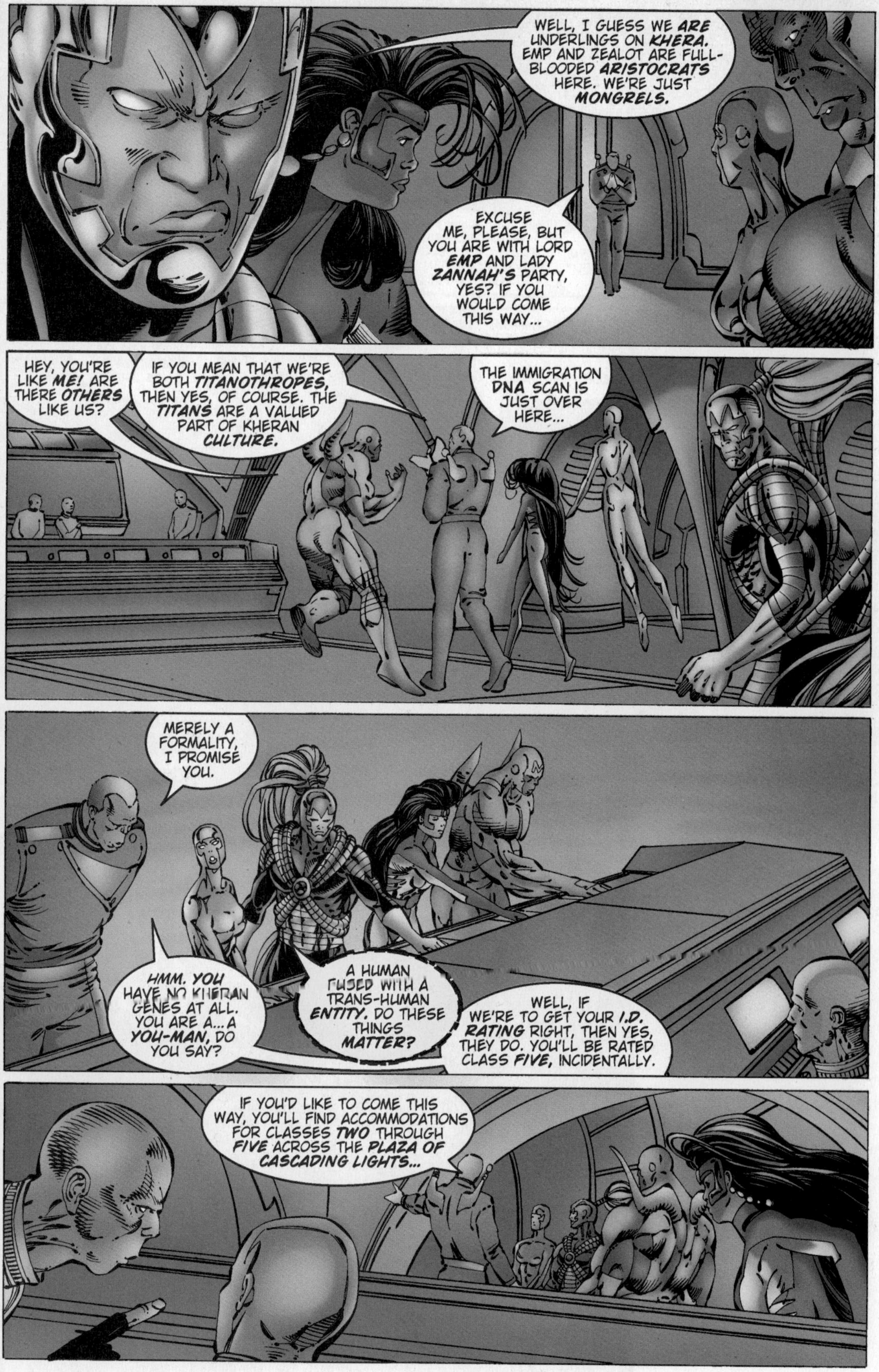
WELL, I GUESS WE ARE UNDERLINGS ON KHERA. EMP AND ZEALOT ARE FULL-BLOODED ARISTOCRATS HERE. WE'RE JUST MONGRELS.
EXCUSE ME, PLEASE, BUT YOU ARE WITH LORD EMP AND LADY ZANNAH'S PARTY, YES? IF YOU WOULD COME THIS WAY...
HEY, YOU'RE LIKE ME! ARE THERE OTHERS LIKE US?
IF YOU MEAN THAT WE'RE BOTH TITANOTHROPES, THEN YES, OF COURSE. THE TITANS ARE A VALUED PART OF KHERAN CULTURE.
THE IMMIGRATION DNA SCAN IS JUST OVER HERE...
MERELY A FORMALITY, I PROMISE YOU.
HMM. YOU HAVE NO KHERAN GENES AT ALL. YOU ARE A... A YOU-MAN, DO YOU SAY?
A HUMAN FUSED WITH A TRANS-HUMAN ENTITY. DO THESE THINGS MATTER?
WELL, IF WE'RE TO GET YOUR I.D. RATING RIGHT, THEN YES, THEY DO. YOU'LL BE RATED CLASS FIVE, INCIDENTALLY.
IF YOU'D LIKE TO COME THIS WAY, YOU'LL FIND ACCOMMODATIONS FOR CLASSES TWO THROUGH FIVE ACROSS THE PLAZA OF CASCADING LIGHTS...

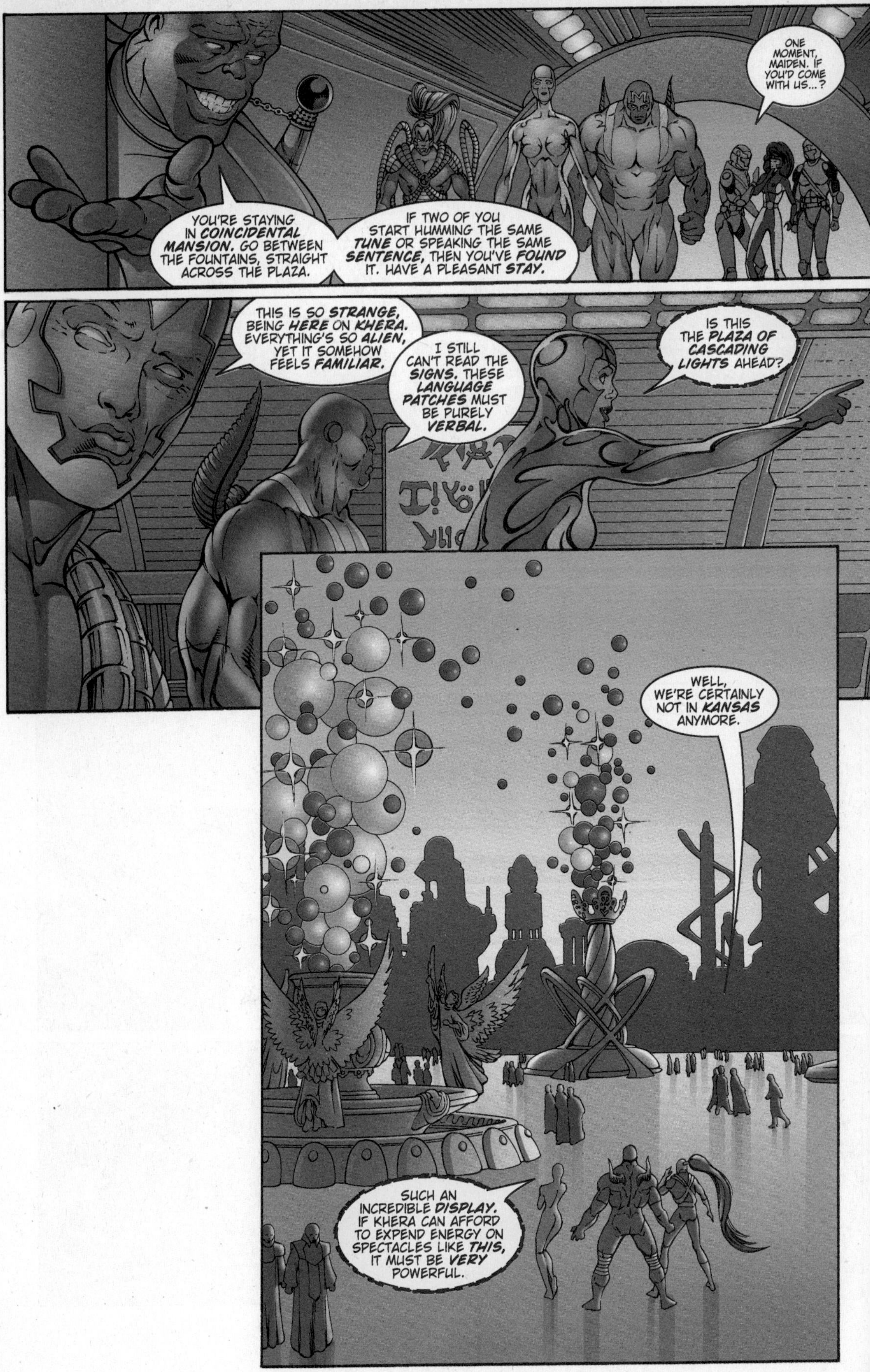
YOU'RE STAYING IN COINCIDENTAL MANSION. GO BETWEEN THE FOUNTAINS, STRAIGHT ACROSS THE PLAZA.
IF TWO OF YOU START HUMMING THE SAME TUNE OR SPEAKING THE SAME SENTENCE, THEN YOU'VE FOUND IT. HAVE A PLEASANT STAY.
ONE MOMENT, MAIDEN. IF YOU'D COME WITH US...?
THIS IS SO STRANGE, BEING HERE ON KHERA. EVERYTHING'S SO ALIEN, YET IT SOMEHOW FEELS FAMILIAR.
I STILL CAN'T READ THE SIGNS. THESE LANGUAGE PATCHES MUST BE PURELY VERBAL.
IS THIS THE PLAZA OF CASCADING LIGHTS AHEAD?
WELL, WE'RE CERTAINLY NOT IN KANSAS ANYMORE.
SUCH AN INCREDIBLE DISPLAY. IF KHERA CAN AFFORD TO EXPEND ENERGY ON SPECTACLES LIKE THIS, IT MUST BE VERY POWERFUL.

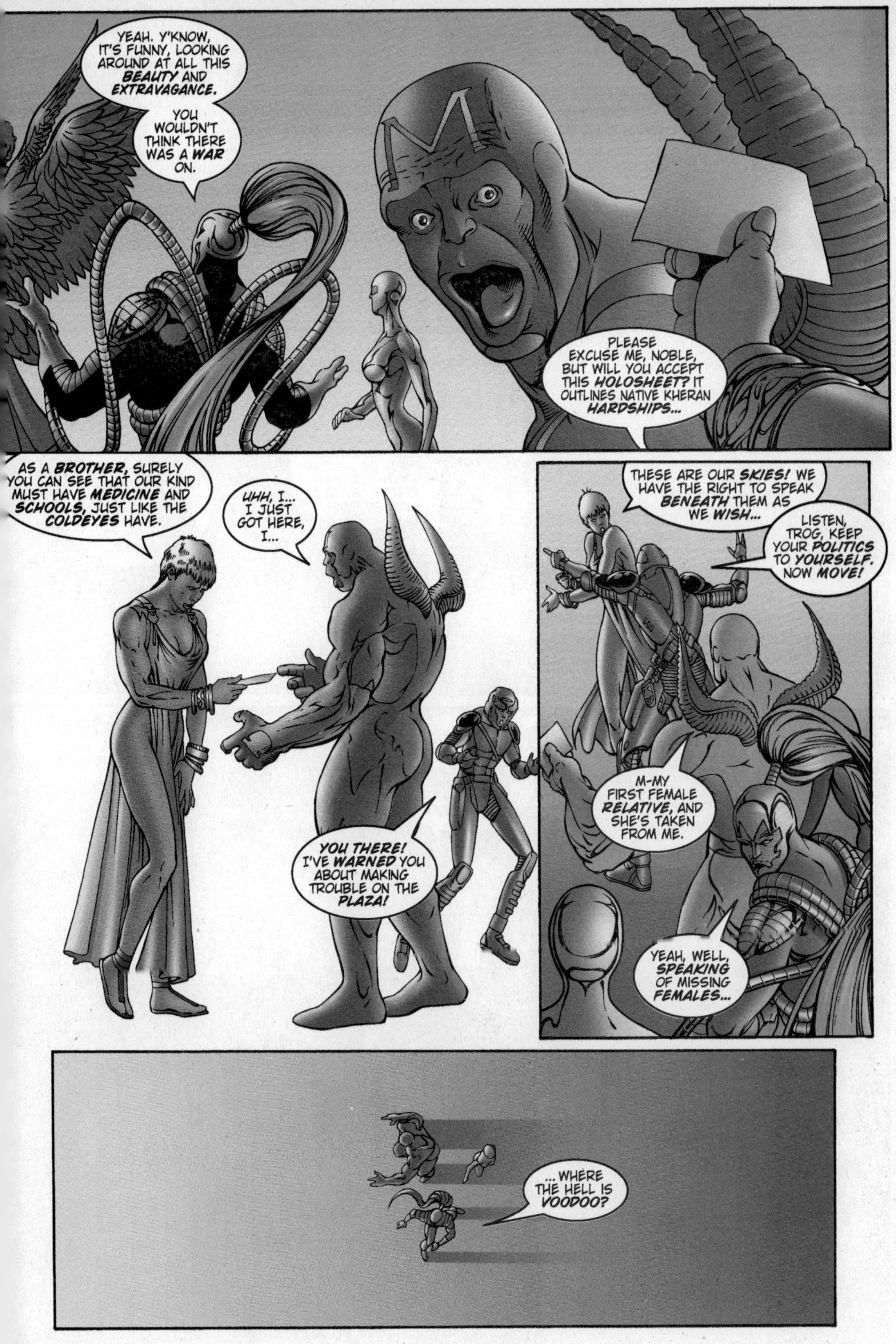
YEAH. Y'KNOW, IT'S FUNNY, LOOKING AROUND AT ALL THIS BEAUTY AND EXTRAVAGANCE.
YOU WOULDN'T THINK THERE WAS A WAR ON.
PLEASE EXCUSE ME, NOBLE, BUT WILL YOU ACCEPT THIS HOLOSHEET? IT OUTLINES NATIVE KHERAN HARDSHIPS...
AS A BROTHER, SURELY YOU CAN SEE THAT OUR KIND MUST HAVE MEDICINE AND SCHOOLS, JUST LIKE THE COLDEYES HAVE.
UHH, I... I JUST GOT HERE, I...
YOU THERE! I'VE WARNED YOU ABOUT MAKING TROUBLE ON THE PLAZA!
THESE ARE OUR SKIES! WE HAVE THE RIGHT TO SPEAK BENEATH THEM AS WE WISH...
LISTEN, TROG, KEEP YOUR POLITICS TO YOURSELF. NOW MOVE!
M-MY FIRST FEMALE RELATIVE, AND SHE'S TAKEN FROM ME.
YEAH, WELL, SPEAKING OF MISSING FEMALES...
...WHERE THE HELL IS VOODOO?

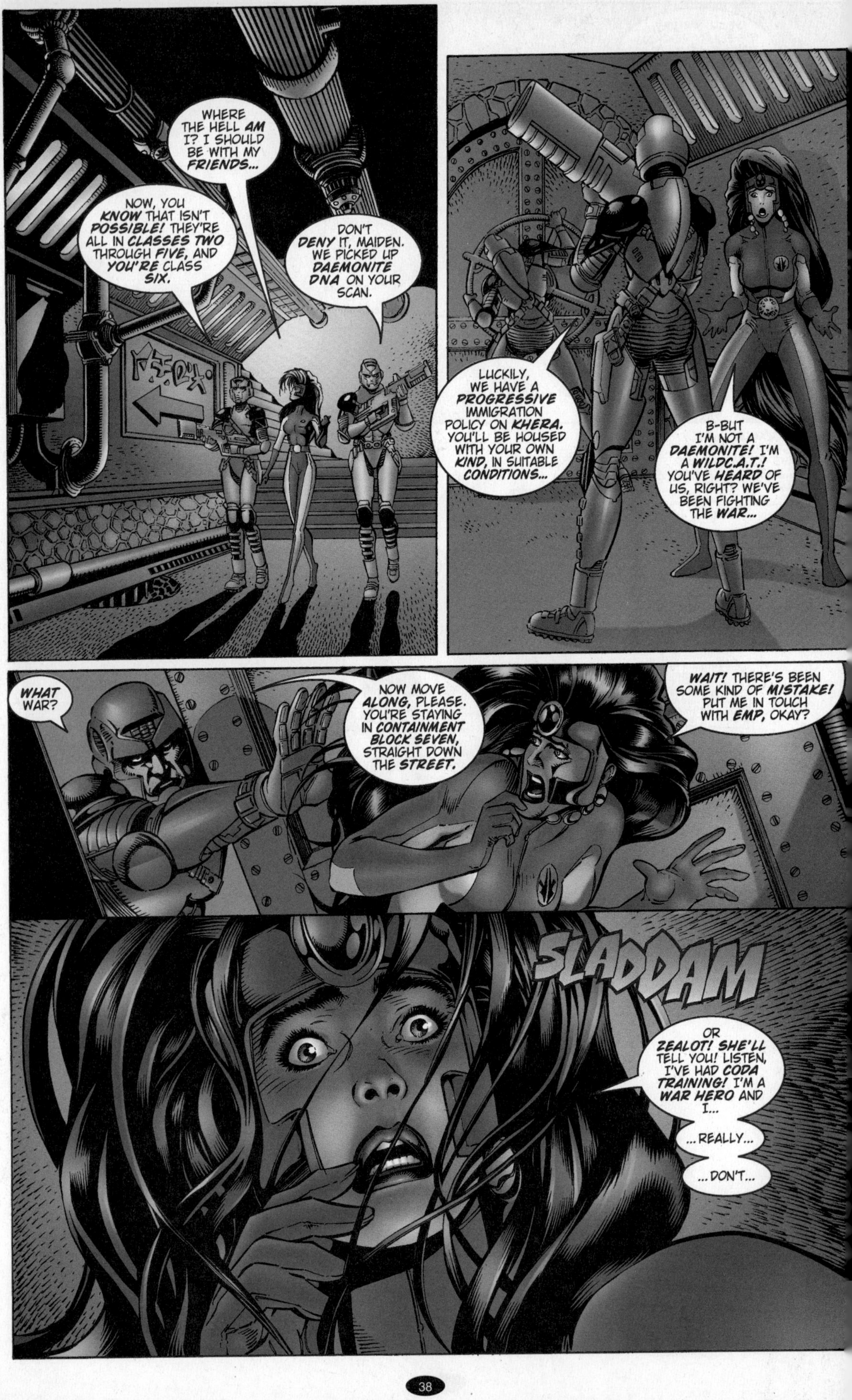
WHERE THE HELL AM I? I SHOULD BE WITH MY FRIENDS...
NOW, YOU KNOW THAT ISN'T POSSIBLE! THEY'RE ALL IN CLASSES TWO THROUGH FIVE, AND YOU'RE CLASS SIX.
DON'T DENY IT, MAIDEN. WE PICKED UP DAEMONITE DNA ON YOUR SCAN.
LUCKILY, WE HAVE A PROGRESSIVE IMMIGRATION POLICY ON KHERA. YOU'LL BE HOUSED WITH YOUR OWN KIND, IN SUITABLE CONDITIONS...
B-BUT I'M NOT A DAEMONITE! I'M A WILDC.A.T.! YOU'VE HEARD OF US, RIGHT? WE'VE BEEN FIGHTING THE WAR...
WHAT WAR?
NOW MOVE ALONG, PLEASE. YOU'RE STAYING IN CONTAINMENT BLOCK SEVEN, STRAIGHT DOWN THE STREET.
WAIT! THERE'S BEEN SOME KIND OF MISTAKE! PUT ME IN TOUCH WITH EMP, OKAY?
SLADDAM
OR ZEALOT! SHE'LL TELL YOU! LISTEN, I'VE HAD CODA TRAINING! I'M A WAR HERO AND I...
...REALLY...
...DON'T...

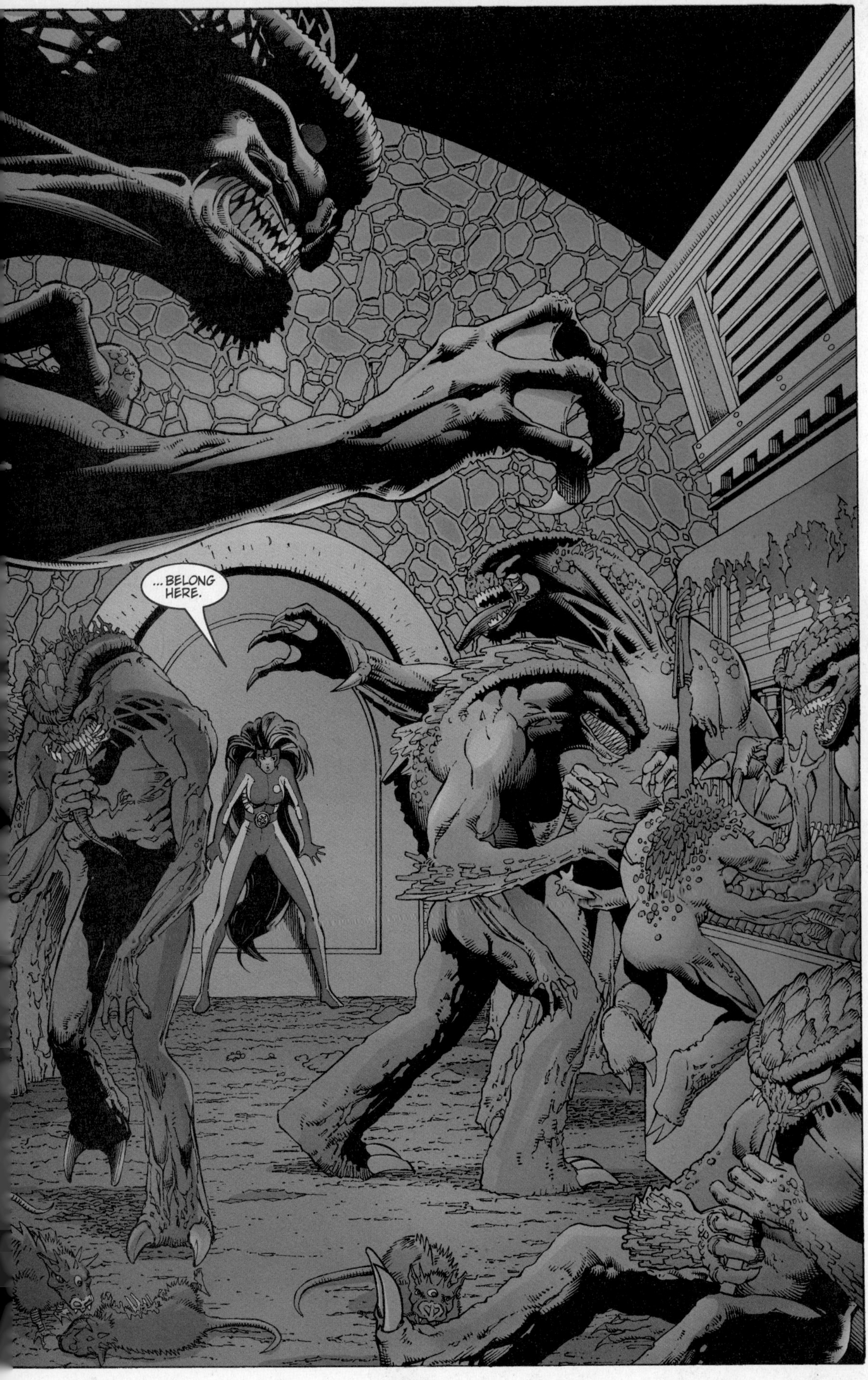
...BELONG HERE.

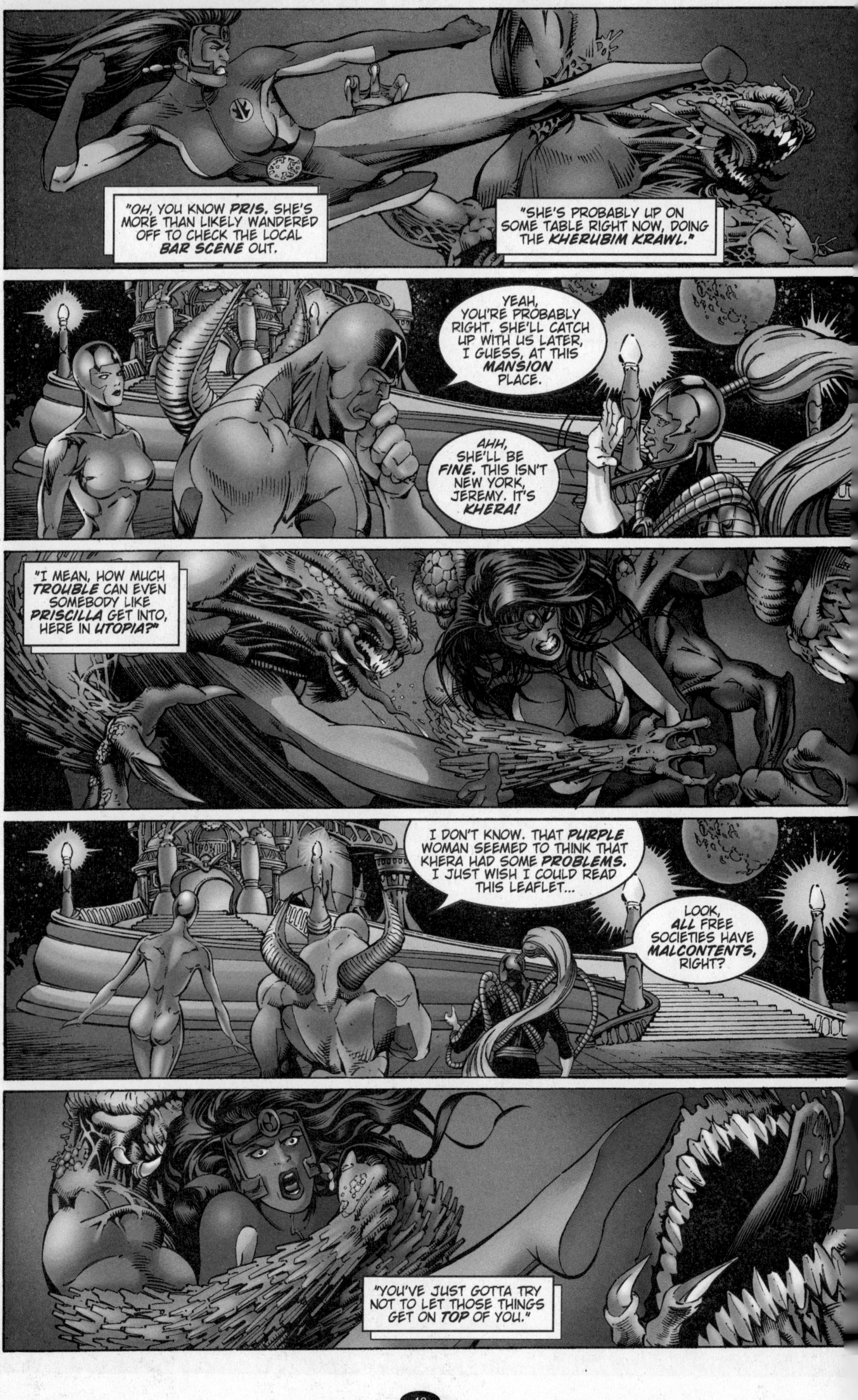
"OH, YOU KNOW PRIS. SHE'S MORE THAN LIKELY WANDERED OFF TO CHECK THE LOCAL BAR SCENE OUT.
"SHE'S PROBABLY UP ON SOME TABLE RIGHT NOW, DOING THE KHERUBIM KRAWL."
YEAH, YOU'RE PROBABLY RIGHT. SHE'LL CATCH UP WITH US LATER, I GUESS, AT THIS MANSION PLACE.
AHH, SHE'LL BE FINE. THIS ISN'T NEW YORK, JEREMY. IT'S KHERA!
"I MEAN, HOW MUCH TROUBLE CAN EVEN SOMEBODY LIKE PRISCILLA GET INTO, HERE IN UTOPIA?"
I DON'T KNOW. THAT PURPLE WOMAN SEEMED TO THINK THAT KHERA HAD SOME PROBLEMS. I JUST WISH I COULD READ THIS LEAFLET...
LOOK, ALL FREE SOCIETIES HAVE MALCONTENTS, RIGHT?
"YOU'VE JUST GOTTA TRY NOT TO LET THOSE THINGS GET ON TOP OF YOU."

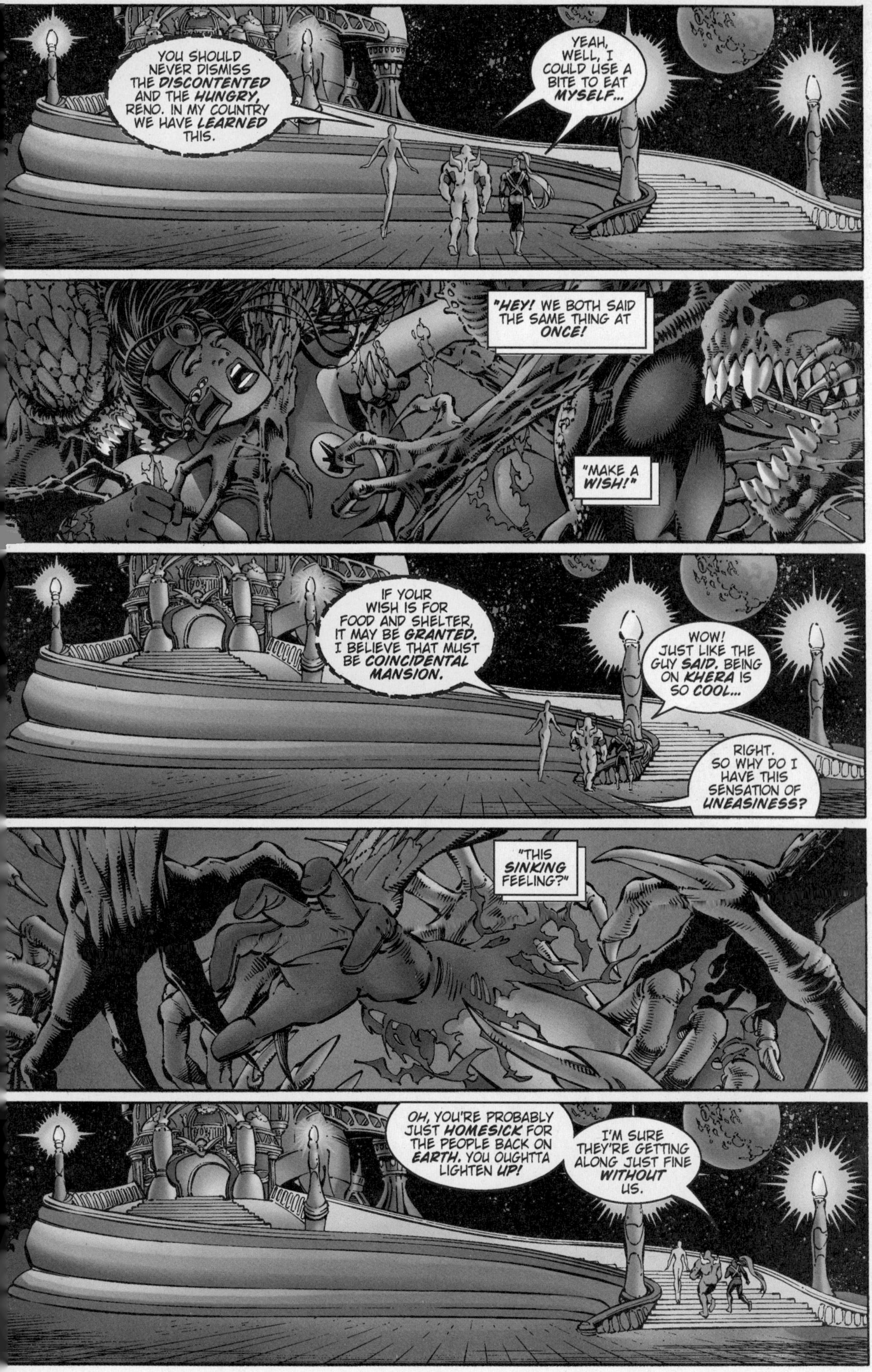

YOU SHOULD NEVER DISMISS THE DISCONTENTED AND THE HUNGRY, RENO. IN MY COUNTRY WE HAVE LEARNED THIS.
YEAH, WELL, I COULD USE A BITE TO EAT MYSELF...
"HEY! WE BOTH SAID THE SAME THING AT ONCE!
"MAKE A WISH!"
IF YOUR WISH IS FOR FOOD AND SHELTER, IT MAY BE GRANTED. I BELIEVE THAT MUST BE COINCIDENTAL MANSION.
WOW! JUST LIKE THE GUY SAID. BEING ON KHERA IS SO COOL...
RIGHT. SO WHY DO I HAVE THIS SENSATION OF UNEASINESS?
"THIS SINKING FEELING?"
OH, YOU'RE PROBABLY JUST HOMESICK FOR THE PEOPLE BACK ON EARTH. YOU OUGHTTA LIGHTEN UP!
I'M SURE THEY'RE GETTING ALONG JUST FINE WITHOUT US.

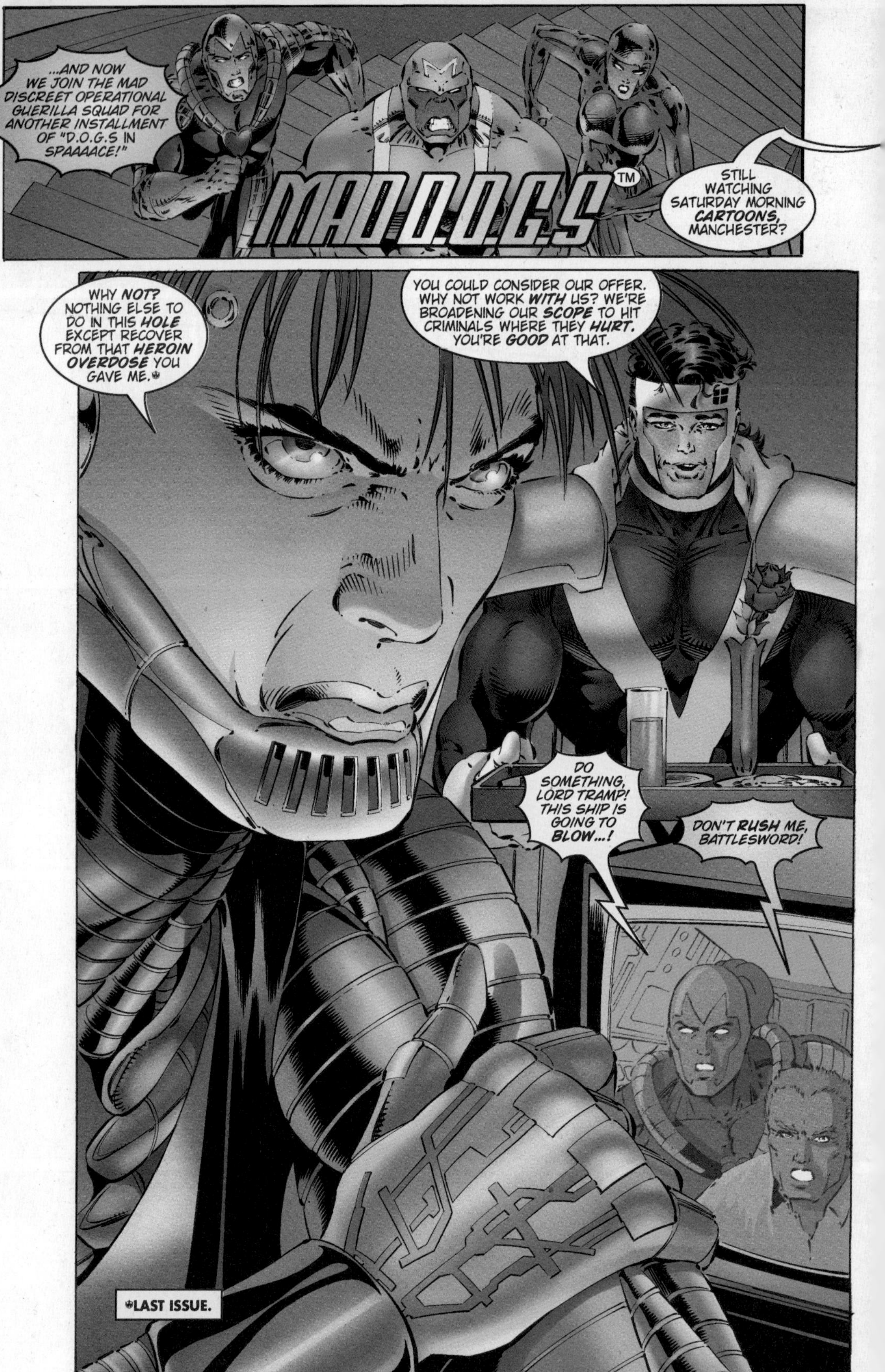
...AND NOW WE JOIN THE MAD DISCREET OPERATIONAL GUERILLA SQUAD FOR ANOTHER INSTALLMENT OF "D.O.G.S IN SPAAAAACE!"
MAD D.O.G.S™
STILL WATCHING SATURDAY MORNING CARTOONS, MANCHESTER?
WHY NOT? NOTHING ELSE TO DO IN THIS HOLE EXCEPT RECOVER FROM THAT HEROIN OVERDOSE YOU GAVE ME.*
YOU COULD CONSIDER OUR OFFER. WHY NOT WORK WITH US? WE'RE BROADENING OUR SCOPE TO HIT CRIMINALS WHERE THEY HURT. YOU'RE GOOD AT THAT.
DO SOMETHING, LORD TRAMP! THIS SHIP IS GOING TO BLOW...!
DON'T RUSH ME, BATTLESWORD!
*LAST ISSUE.

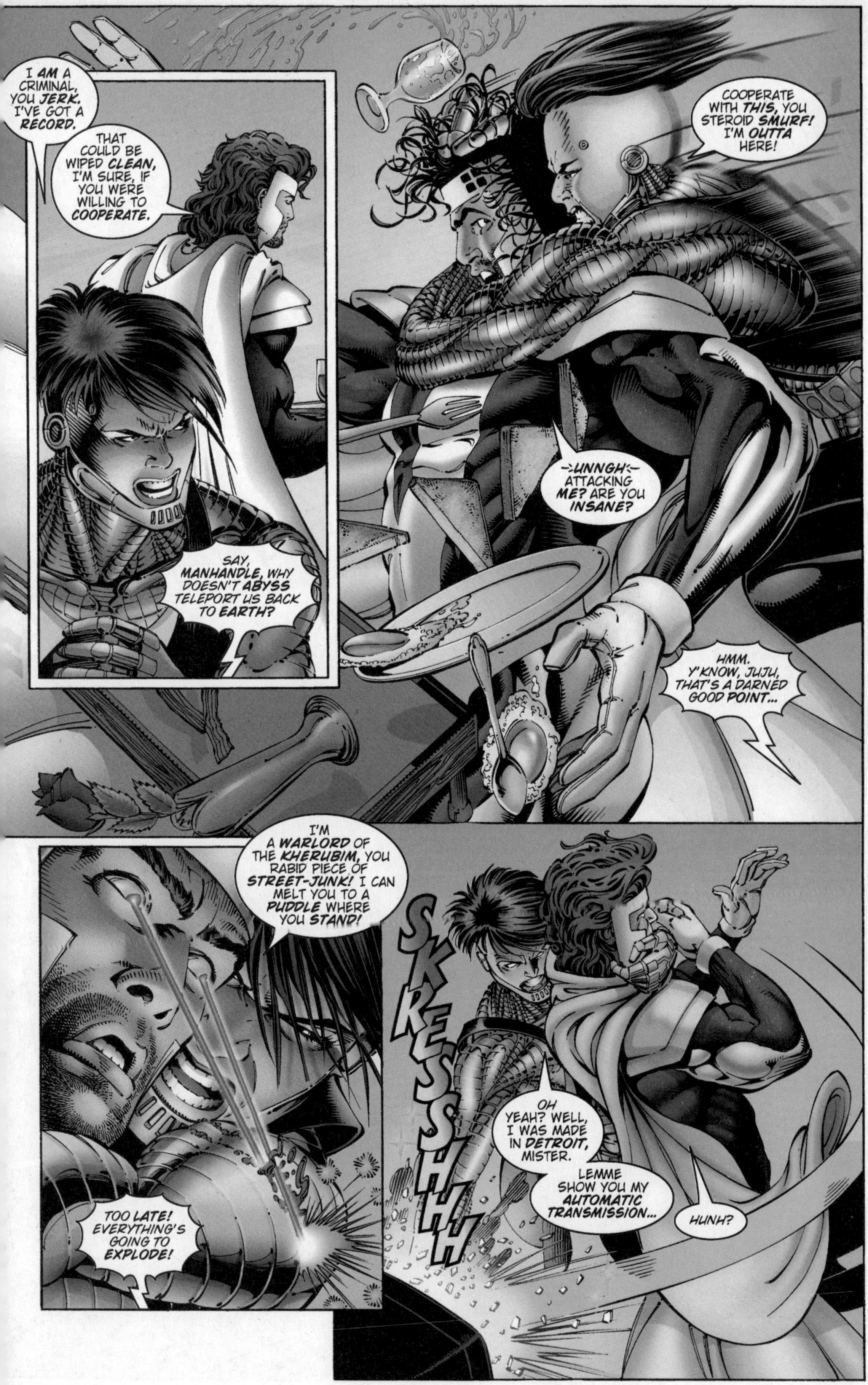
I AM A CRIMINAL, YOU JERK. I'VE GOT A RECORD.
THAT COULD BE WIPED CLEAN, I'M SURE, IF YOU WERE WILLING TO COOPERATE.
SAY, MANHANDLE, WHY DOESN'T ABYSS TELEPORT US BACK TO EARTH?
COOPERATE WITH THIS, YOU STEROID SMURF! I'M OUTTA HERE!
-UNNGH- ATTACKING ME? ARE YOU INSANE?
HMM. Y'KNOW, JUJU, THAT'S A DARNED GOOD POINT...
I'M A WARLORD OF THE KHERUBIM, YOU RABID PIECE OF STREET-JUNK! I CAN MELT YOU TO A PUDDLE WHERE YOU STAND!
TOO LATE! EVERYTHING'S GOING TO EXPLODE!
SKRESSHHH
OH YEAH? WELL, I WAS MADE IN DETROIT, MISTER.
LEMME SHOW YOU MY AUTOMATIC TRANSMISSION...
HUNH?

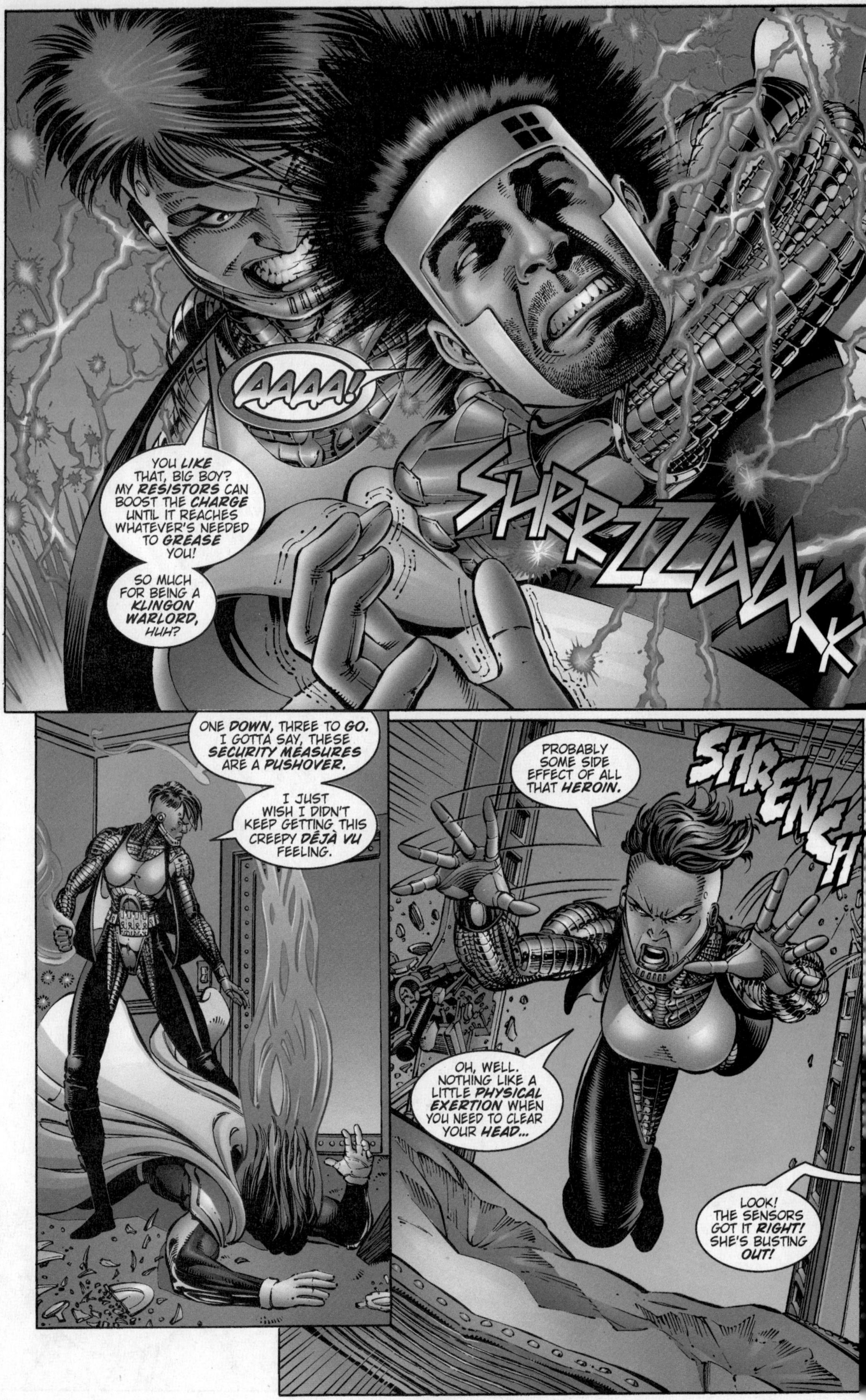
AAAA!
YOU LIKE THAT, BIG BOY? MY RESISTORS CAN BOOST THE CHARGE UNTIL IT REACHES WHATEVER'S NEEDED TO GREASE YOU!
SO MUCH FOR BEING A KLINGON WARLORD, HUH?
SHRRZZAAKK
ONE DOWN, THREE TO GO. I GOTTA SAY, THESE SECURITY MEASURES ARE A PUSHOVER.
I JUST WISH I DIDN'T KEEP GETTING THIS CREEPY DÉJÀ VU FEELING.
SHRENCH
PROBABLY SOME SIDE EFFECT OF ALL THAT HEROIN.
OH, WELL. NOTHING LIKE A LITTLE PHYSICAL EXERTION WHEN YOU NEED TO CLEAR YOUR HEAD...
LOOK! THE SENSORS GOT IT RIGHT! SHE'S BUSTING OUT!

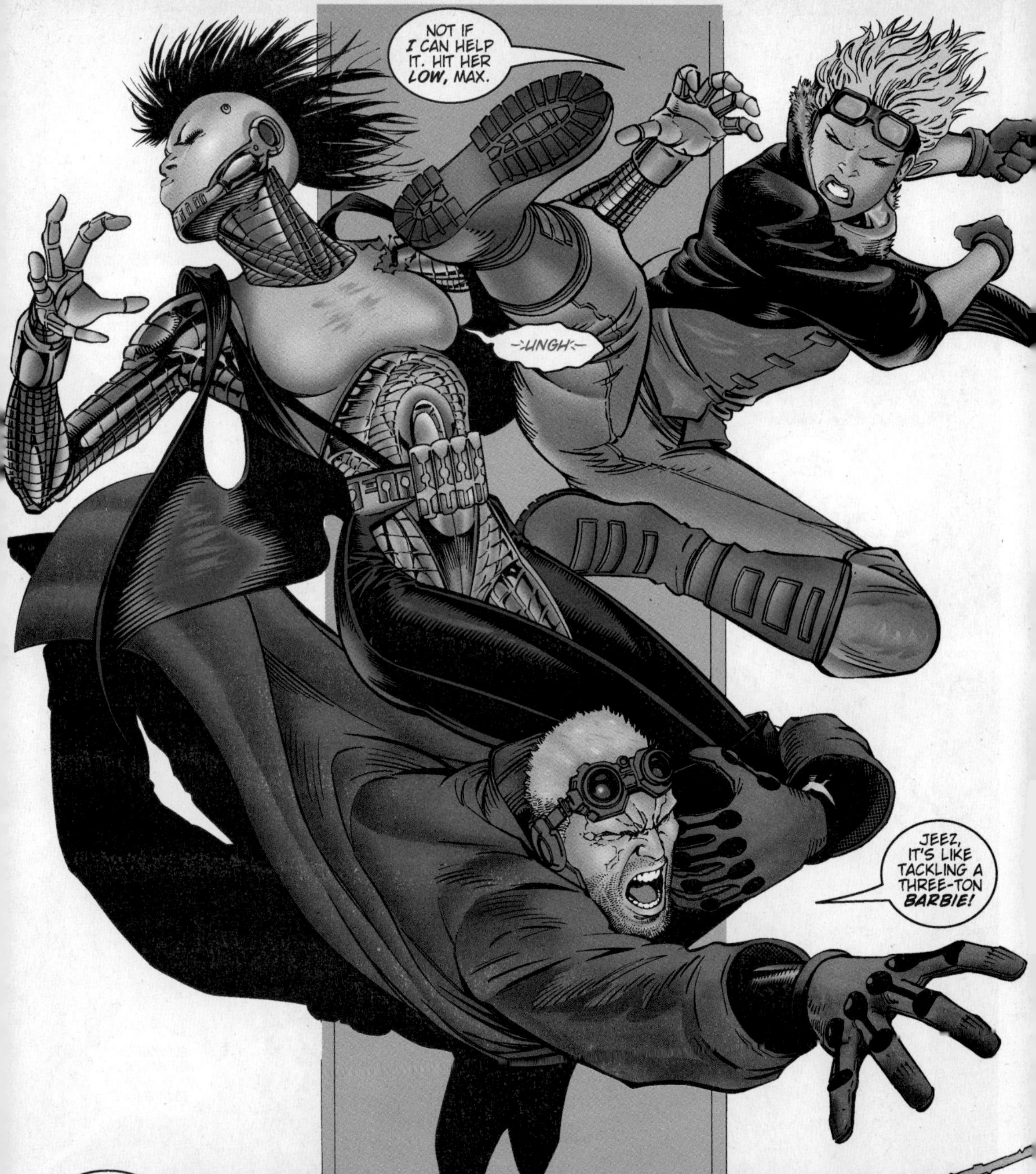
NOT IF I CAN HELP IT. HIT HER LOW, MAX.
-UNGH-
JEEZ, IT'S LIKE TACKLING A THREE-TON BARBIE!

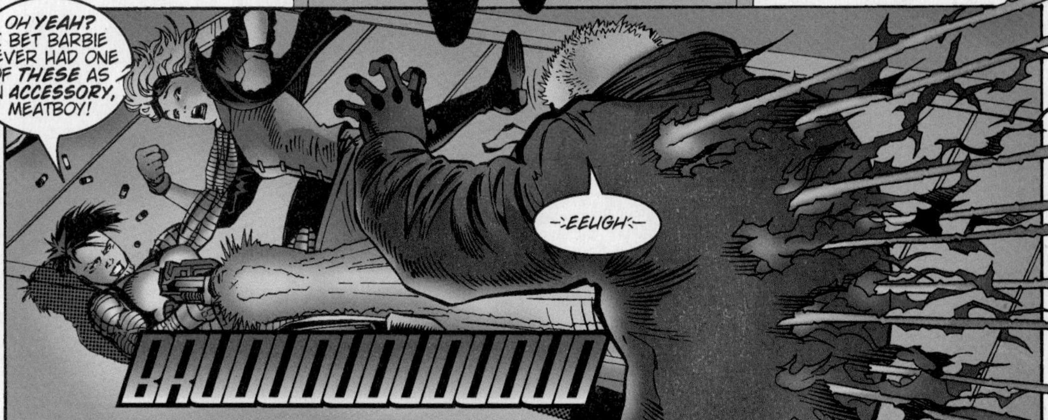
OH YEAH? I BET BARBIE NEVER HAD ONE OF THESE AS AN ACCESSORY, MEATBOY!
-EEUGH-
BRUUUUUUUUUUD

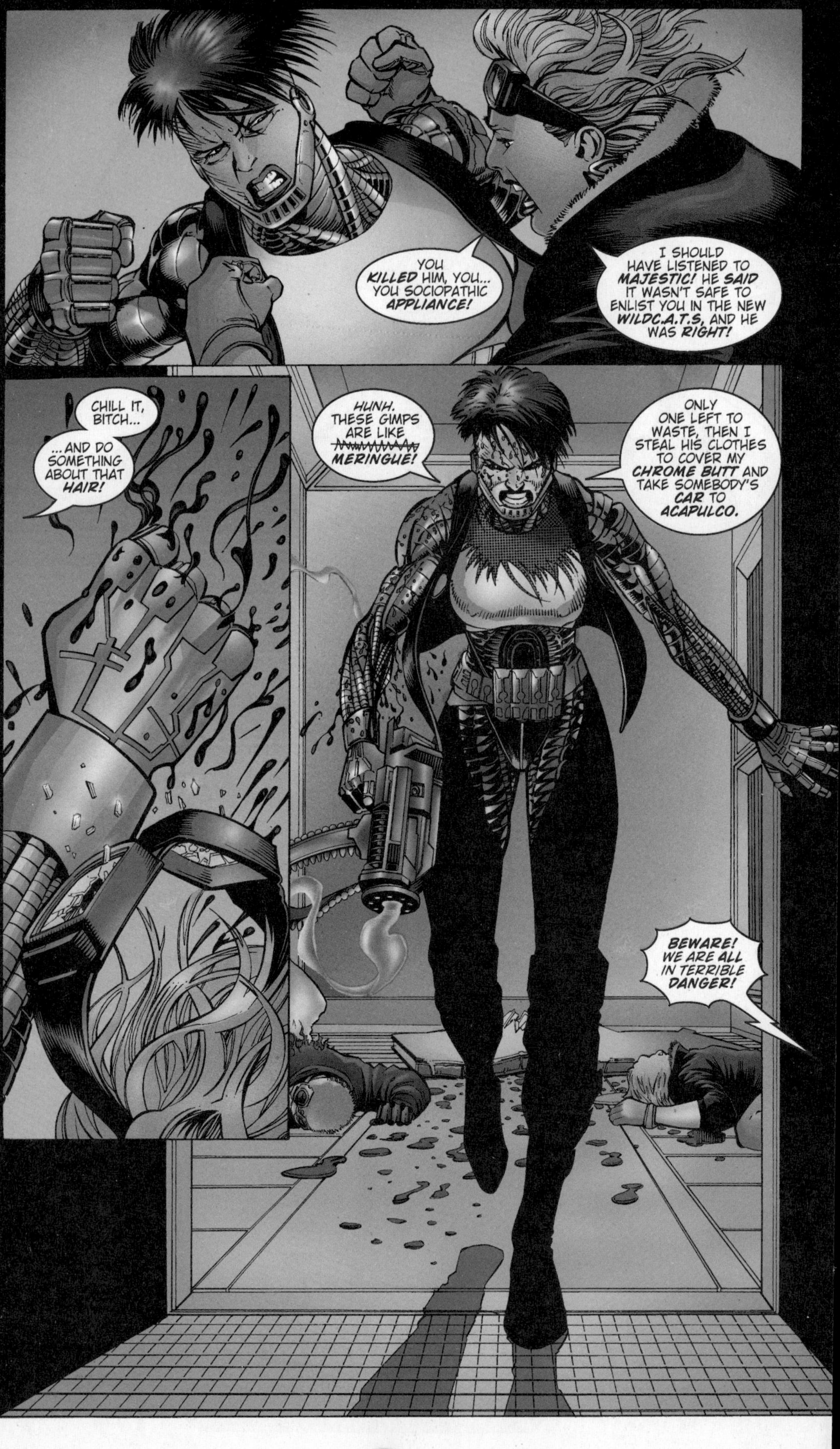
YOU KILLED HIM, YOU... YOU SOCIOPATHIC APPLIANCE!
I SHOULD HAVE LISTENED TO MAJESTIC! HE SAID IT WASN'T SAFE TO ENLIST YOU IN THE NEW WILDC.A.T.S, AND HE WAS RIGHT!
CHILL IT, BITCH...
...AND DO SOMETHING ABOUT THAT HAIR!
HUNH. THESE GIMPS ARE LIKE MERINGUE!
ONLY ONE LEFT TO WASTE, THEN I STEAL HIS CLOTHES TO COVER MY CHROME BUTT AND TAKE SOMEBODY'S CAR TO ACAPULCO.
BEWARE! WE ARE ALL IN TERRIBLE DANGER!

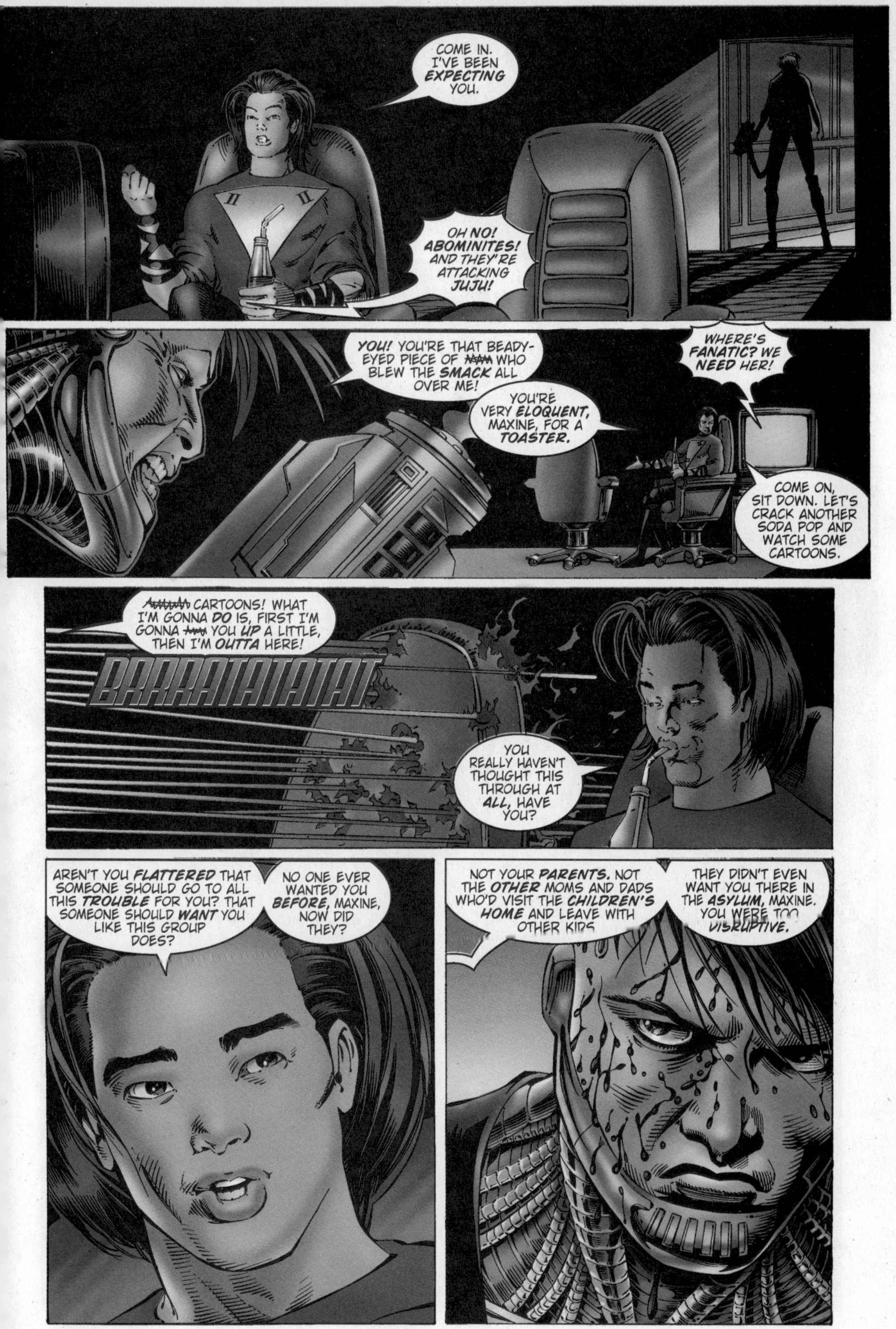
COME IN. I'VE BEEN EXPECTING YOU.
OH NO! ABOMINITES! AND THEY'RE ATTACKING JUJU!
YOU! YOU'RE THAT BEADY-EYED PIECE OF WHO BLEW THE SMACK ALL OVER ME!
YOU'RE VERY ELOQUENT, MAXINE, FOR A TOASTER.
WHERE'S FANATIC? WE NEED HER!
COME ON, SIT DOWN. LET'S CRACK ANOTHER SODA POP AND WATCH SOME CARTOONS.
CARTOONS! WHAT I'M GONNA DO IS, FIRST I'M GONNA YOU UP A LITTLE, THEN I'M OUTTA HERE!
BRRRATATATAT
YOU REALLY HAVEN'T THOUGHT THIS THROUGH AT ALL, HAVE YOU?
AREN'T YOU FLATTERED THAT SOMEONE SHOULD GO TO ALL THIS TROUBLE FOR YOU? THAT SOMEONE SHOULD WANT YOU LIKE THIS GROUP DOES?
NO ONE EVER WANTED YOU BEFORE, MAXINE, NOW DID THEY?
NOT YOUR PARENTS. NOT THE OTHER MOMS AND DADS WHO'D VISIT THE CHILDREN'S HOME AND LEAVE WITH OTHER KIDS
THEY DIDN'T EVEN WANT YOU THERE IN THE ASYLUM, MAXINE. YOU WERE TOO DISRUPTIVE.

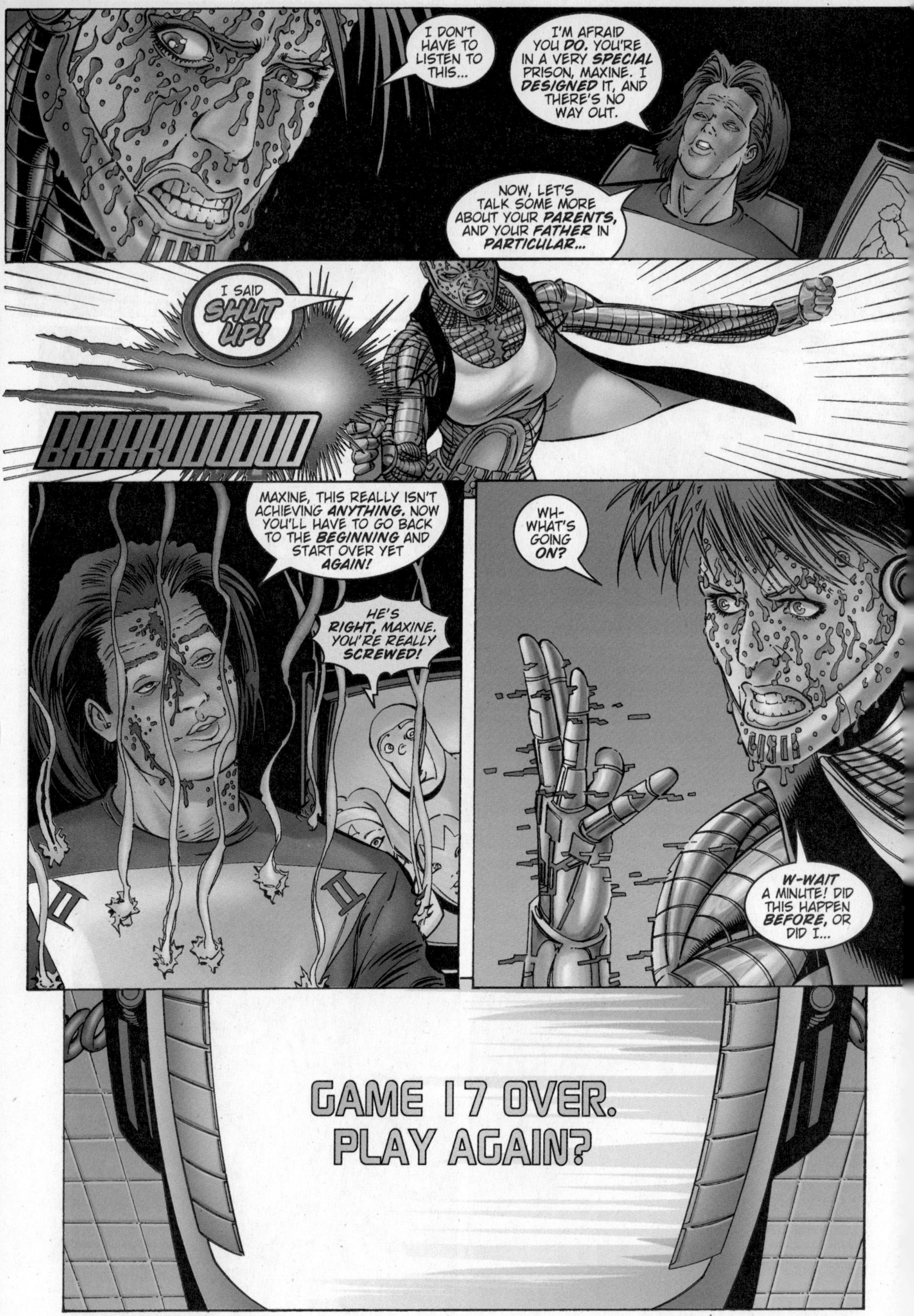
I DON'T HAVE TO LISTEN TO THIS...
I'M AFRAID YOU **DO.** YOU'RE IN A VERY **SPECIAL** PRISON, MAXINE. I **DESIGNED** IT, AND THERE'S NO WAY OUT.
NOW, LET'S TALK SOME MORE ABOUT YOUR **PARENTS,** AND YOUR **FATHER** IN **PARTICULAR...**
I SAID SHUT UP!
BRRRRUDUDUD
MAXINE, THIS REALLY ISN'T ACHIEVING **ANYTHING.** NOW YOU'LL HAVE TO GO BACK TO THE **BEGINNING** AND START OVER YET **AGAIN!**
HE'S **RIGHT,** MAXINE. YOU'RE REALLY **SCREWED!**
WH-WHAT'S GOING **ON?**
W-WAIT A MINUTE! DID THIS HAPPEN **BEFORE,** OR DID I...
GAME 17 OVER. PLAY AGAIN?

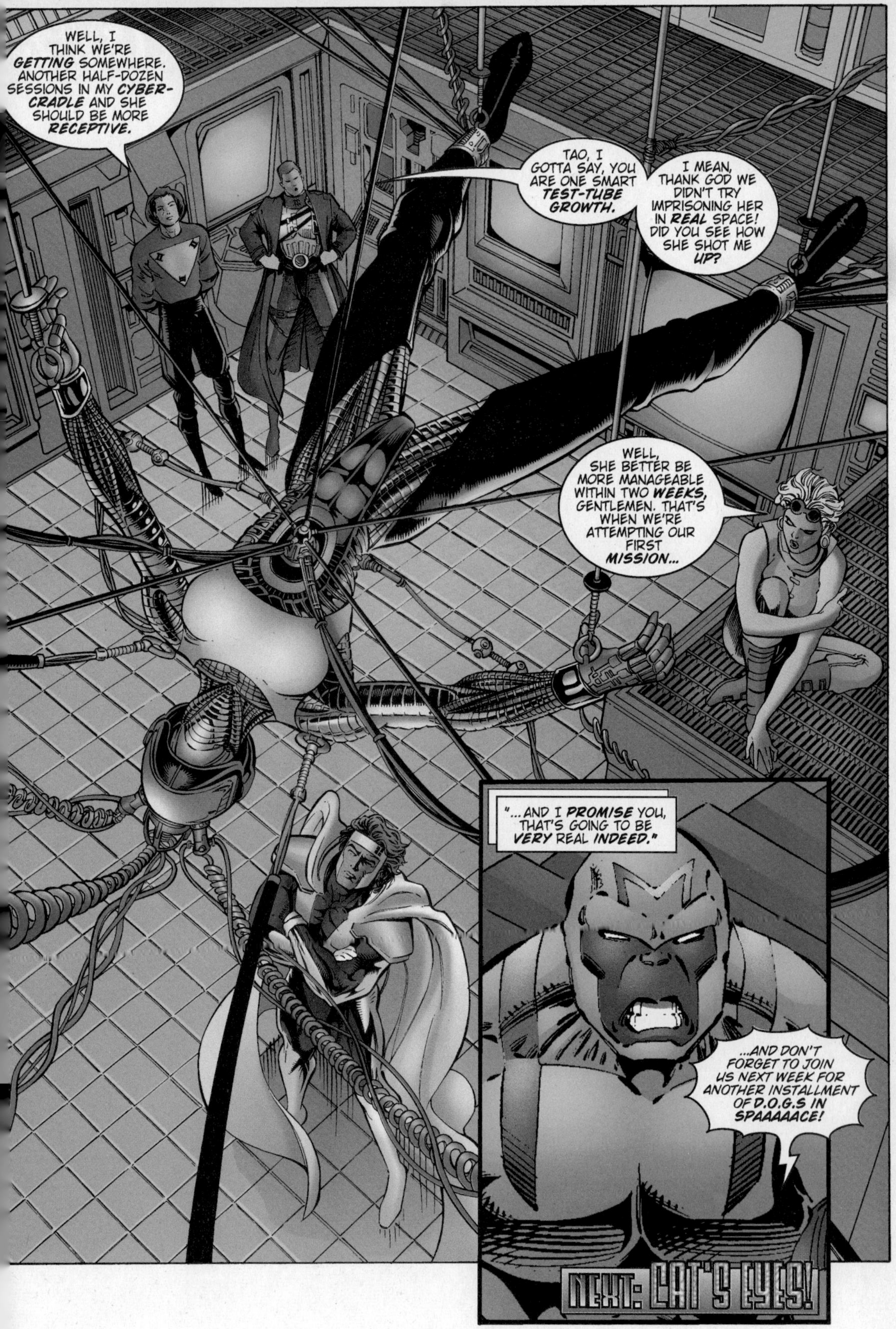
WELL, I THINK WE'RE GETTING SOMEWHERE. ANOTHER HALF-DOZEN SESSIONS IN MY CYBER-CRADLE AND SHE SHOULD BE MORE RECEPTIVE.
TAO, I GOTTA SAY, YOU ARE ONE SMART TEST-TUBE GROWTH.
I MEAN, THANK GOD WE DIDN'T TRY IMPRISONING HER IN REAL SPACE! DID YOU SEE HOW SHE SHOT ME UP?
WELL, SHE BETTER BE MORE MANAGEABLE WITHIN TWO WEEKS, GENTLEMEN. THAT'S WHEN WE'RE ATTEMPTING OUR FIRST MISSION...
"...AND I PROMISE YOU, THAT'S GOING TO BE VERY REAL INDEED."
...AND DON'T FORGET TO JOIN US NEXT WEEK FOR ANOTHER INSTALLMENT OF D.O.G.S IN SPAAAAACE!
NEXT: CAT'S EYES!

WILDC.A.T.S #23

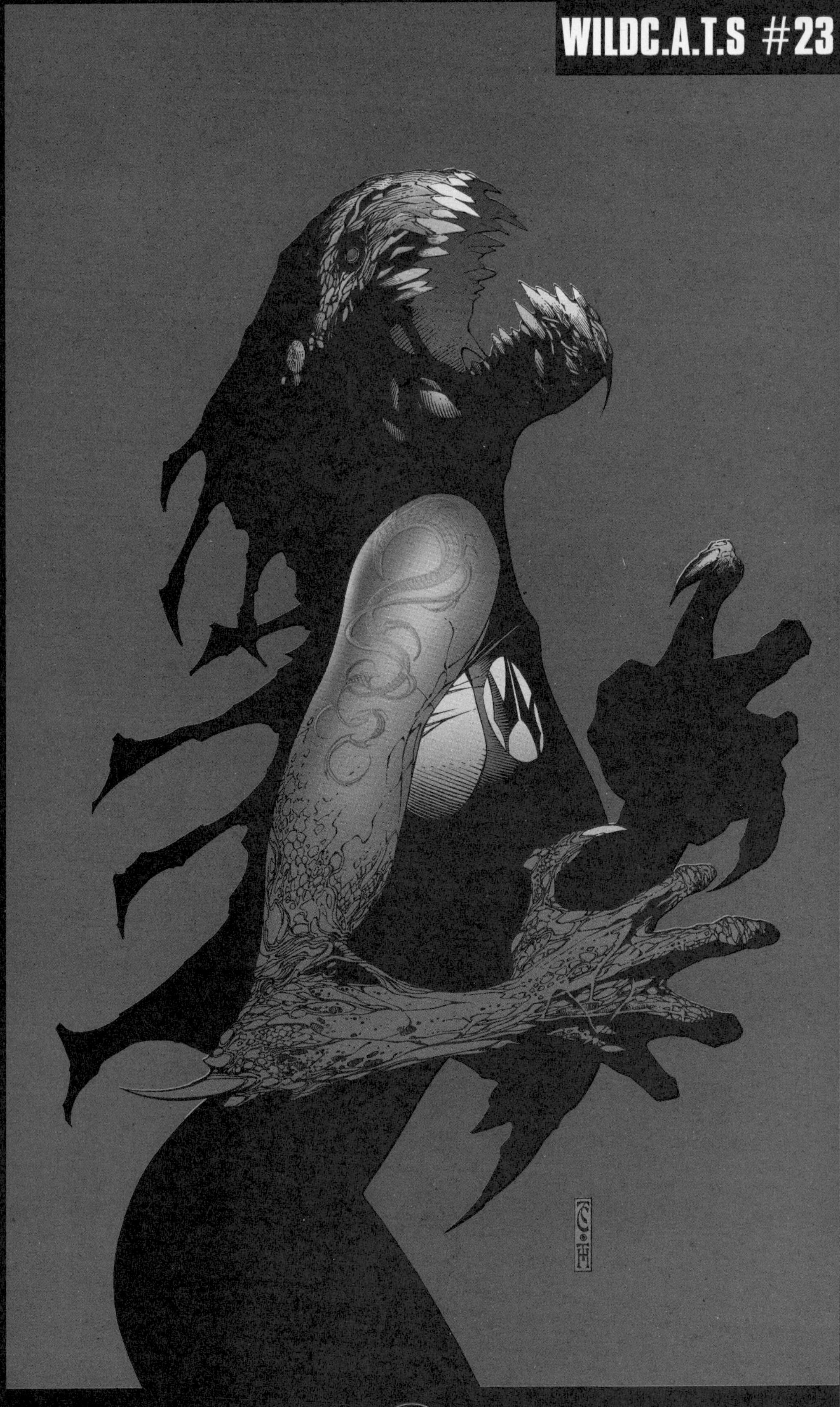

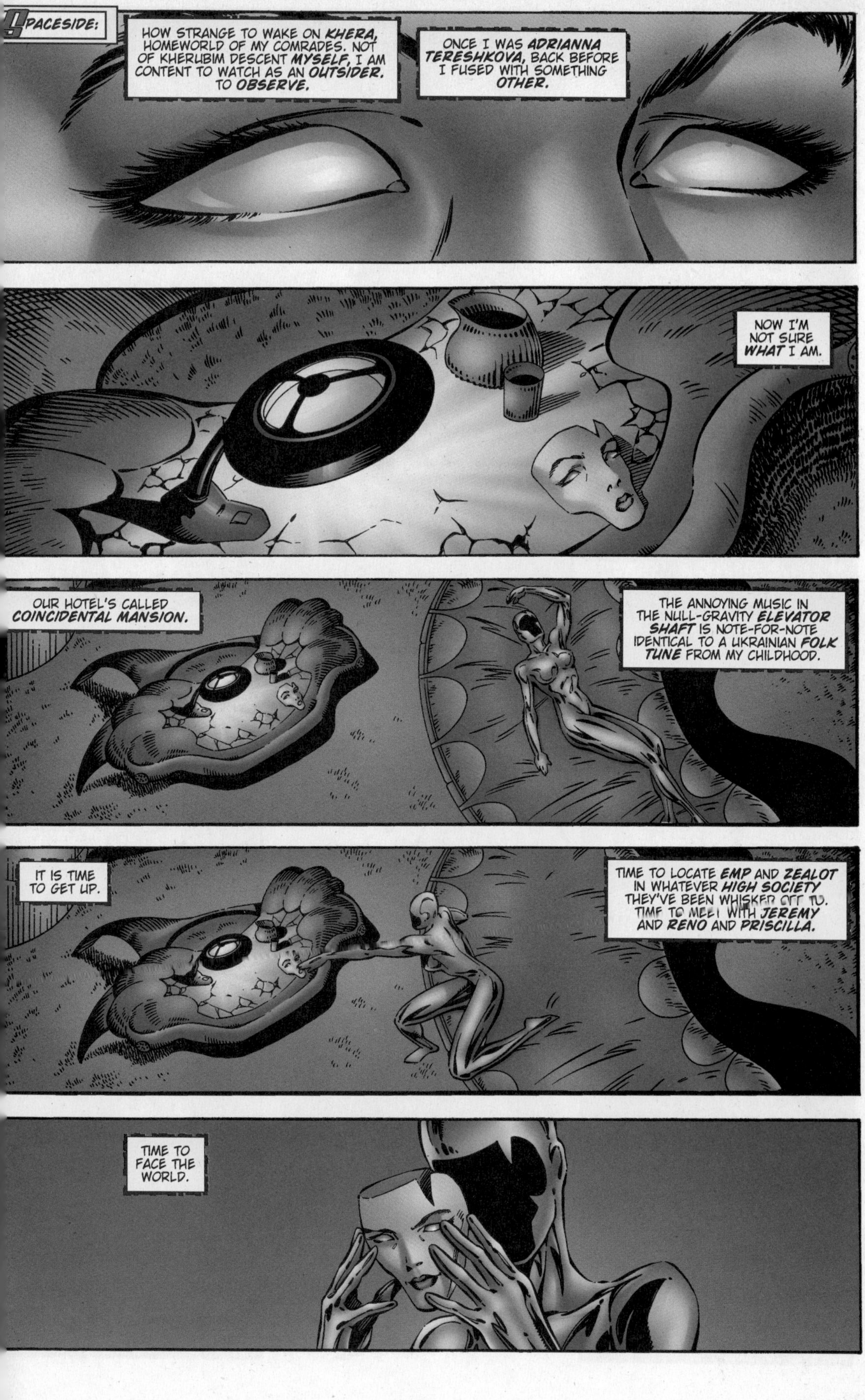
SPACESIDE:
HOW STRANGE TO WAKE ON KHERA, HOMEWORLD OF MY COMRADES. NOT OF KHERUBIM DESCENT MYSELF, I AM CONTENT TO WATCH AS AN OUTSIDER. TO OBSERVE.
ONCE I WAS ADRIANNA TERESHKOVA, BACK BEFORE I FUSED WITH SOMETHING OTHER.
NOW I'M NOT SURE WHAT I AM.
OUR HOTEL'S CALLED COINCIDENTAL MANSION.
THE ANNOYING MUSIC IN THE NULL-GRAVITY ELEVATOR SHAFT IS NOTE-FOR-NOTE IDENTICAL TO A UKRAINIAN FOLK TUNE FROM MY CHILDHOOD.
IT IS TIME TO GET UP.
TIME TO LOCATE EMP AND ZEALOT IN WHATEVER HIGH SOCIETY THEY'VE BEEN WHISKED OFF TO. TIME TO MEET WITH JEREMY AND RENO AND PRISCILLA.
TIME TO FACE THE WORLD.

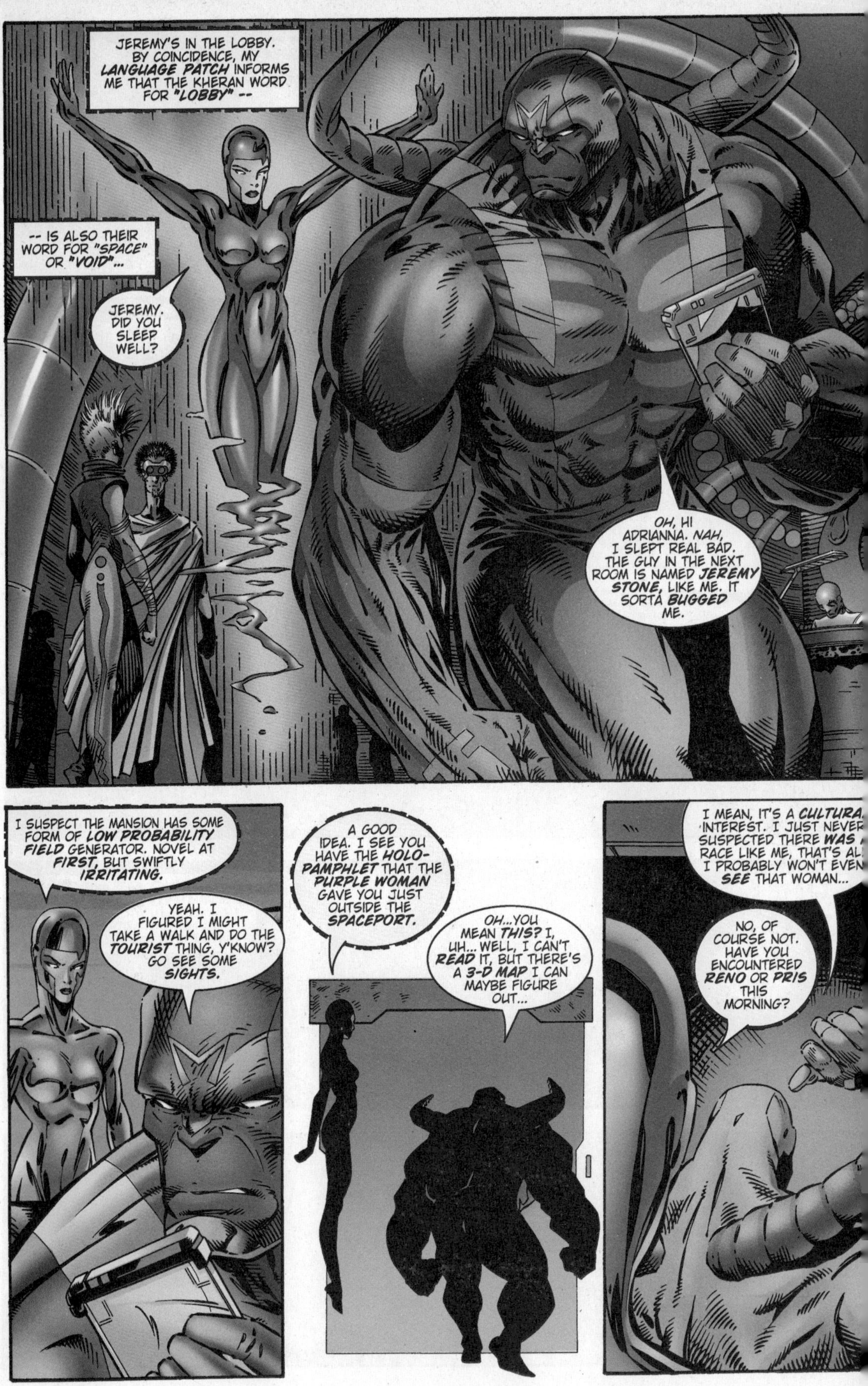
JEREMY'S IN THE LOBBY. BY COINCIDENCE, MY LANGUAGE PATCH INFORMS ME THAT THE KHERAN WORD FOR "LOBBY" --
-- IS ALSO THEIR WORD FOR "SPACE" OR "VOID"...
JEREMY. DID YOU SLEEP WELL?
OH, HI ADRIANNA. NAH, I SLEPT REAL BAD. THE GUY IN THE NEXT ROOM IS NAMED JEREMY STONE, LIKE ME. IT SORTA BUGGED ME.
I SUSPECT THE MANSION HAS SOME FORM OF LOW PROBABILITY FIELD GENERATOR. NOVEL AT FIRST, BUT SWIFTLY IRRITATING.
YEAH. I FIGURED I MIGHT TAKE A WALK AND DO THE TOURIST THING, Y'KNOW? GO SEE SOME SIGHTS.
A GOOD IDEA. I SEE YOU HAVE THE HOLO-PAMPHLET THAT THE PURPLE WOMAN GAVE YOU JUST OUTSIDE THE SPACEPORT.
OH...YOU MEAN THIS? I, UH... WELL, I CAN'T READ IT, BUT THERE'S A 3-D MAP I CAN MAYBE FIGURE OUT...
I MEAN, IT'S A CULTURA INTEREST. I JUST NEVER SUSPECTED THERE WAS RACE LIKE ME, THAT'S AL I PROBABLY WON'T EVEN SEE THAT WOMAN...
NO, OF COURSE NOT. HAVE YOU ENCOUNTERED RENO OR PRIS THIS MORNING?

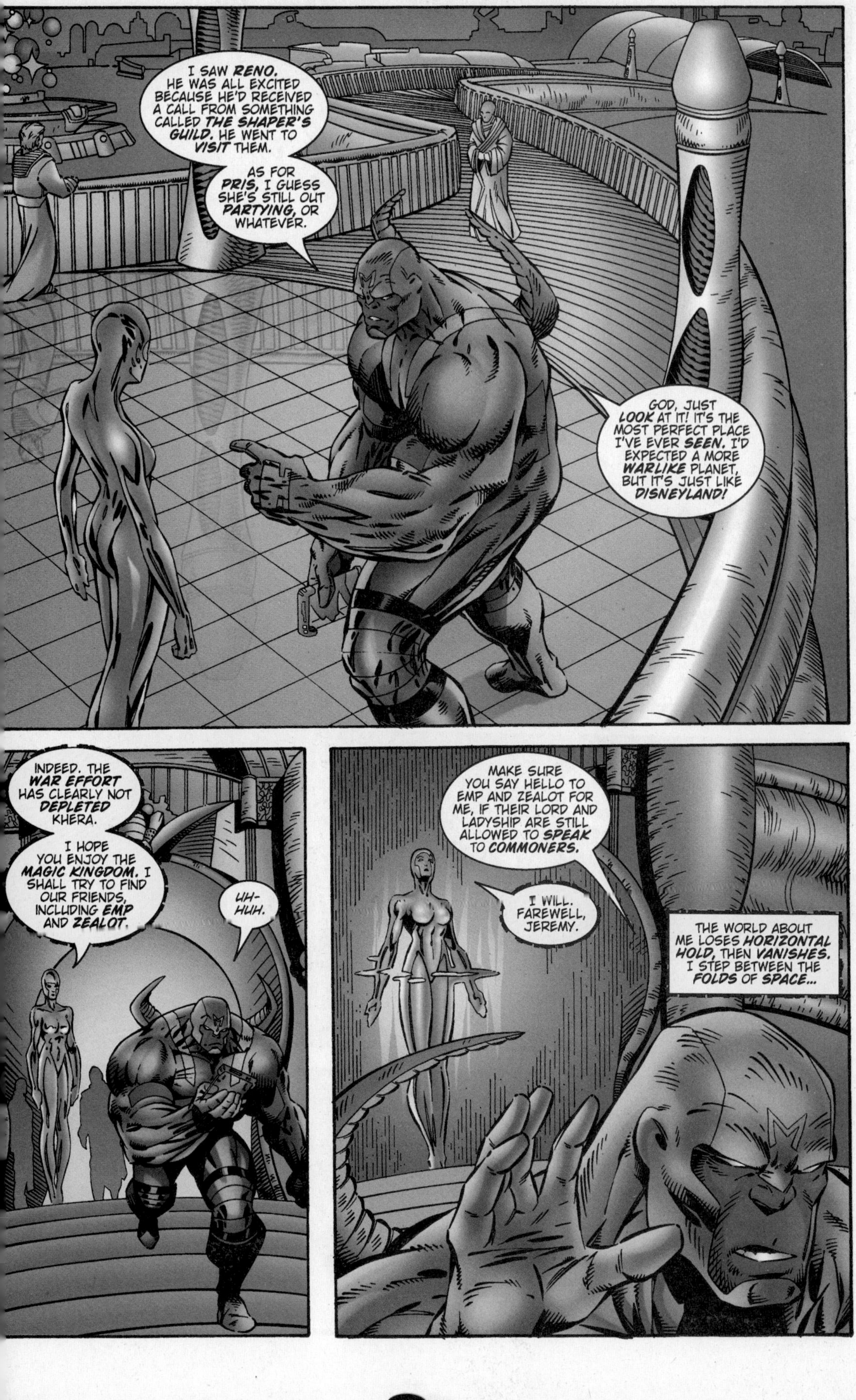
I SAW RENO. HE WAS ALL EXCITED BECAUSE HE'D RECEIVED A CALL FROM SOMETHING CALLED THE SHAPER'S GUILD. HE WENT TO VISIT THEM.
AS FOR PRIS, I GUESS SHE'S STILL OUT PARTYING, OR WHATEVER.
GOD, JUST LOOK AT IT! IT'S THE MOST PERFECT PLACE I'VE EVER SEEN. I'D EXPECTED A MORE WARLIKE PLANET, BUT IT'S JUST LIKE DISNEYLAND!
INDEED. THE WAR EFFORT HAS CLEARLY NOT DEPLETED KHERA.
I HOPE YOU ENJOY THE MAGIC KINGDOM. I SHALL TRY TO FIND OUR FRIENDS, INCLUDING EMP AND ZEALOT.
UH-HUH.
MAKE SURE YOU SAY HELLO TO EMP AND ZEALOT FOR ME, IF THEIR LORD AND LADYSHIP ARE STILL ALLOWED TO SPEAK TO COMMONERS.
I WILL. FAREWELL, JEREMY.
THE WORLD ABOUT ME LOSES HORIZONTAL HOLD, THEN VANISHES. I STEP BETWEEN THE FOLDS OF SPACE...

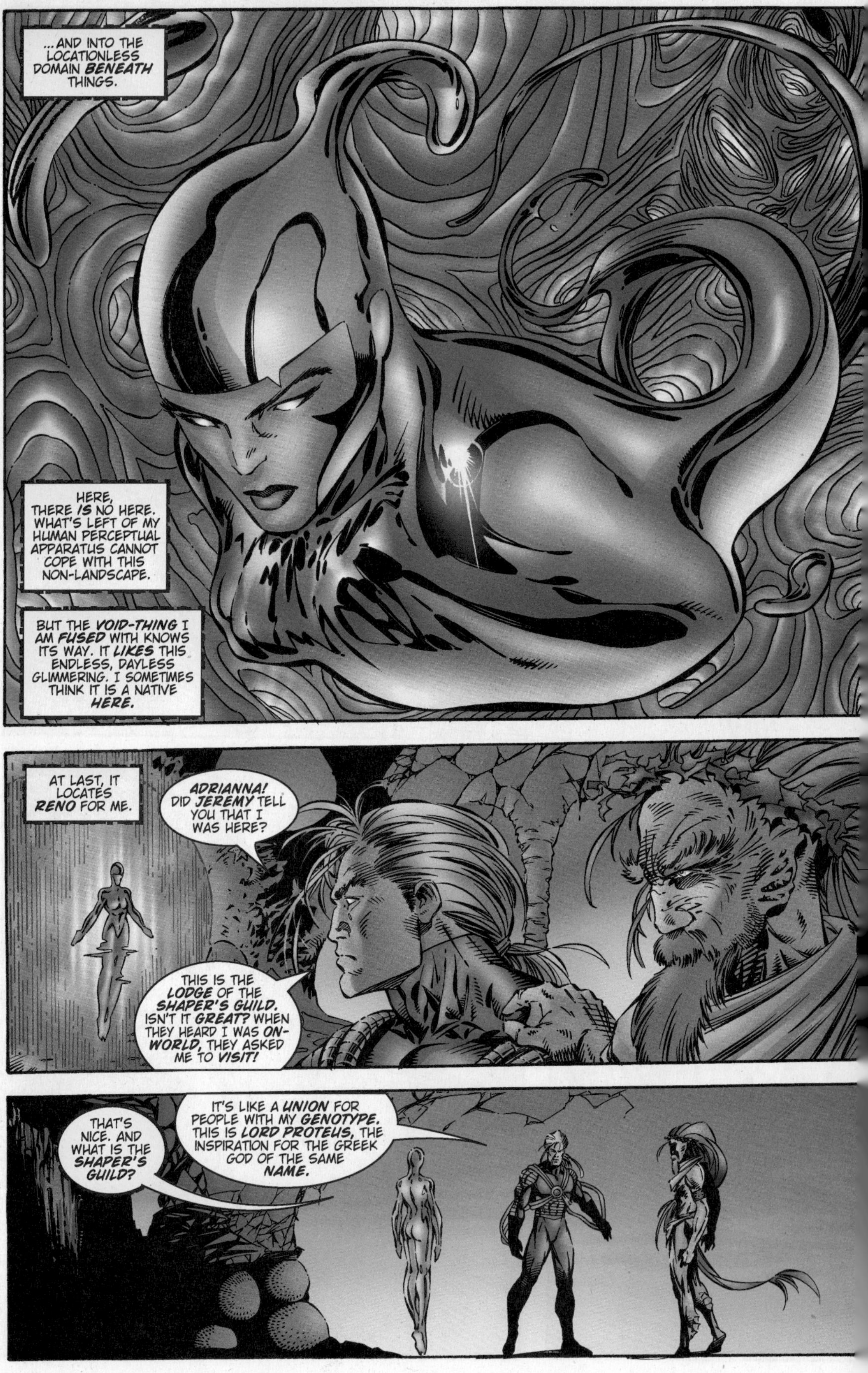
...AND INTO THE LOCATIONLESS DOMAIN BENEATH THINGS.
HERE, THERE IS NO HERE. WHAT'S LEFT OF MY HUMAN PERCEPTUAL APPARATUS CANNOT COPE WITH THIS NON-LANDSCAPE.
BUT THE VOID-THING I AM FUSED WITH KNOWS ITS WAY. IT LIKES THIS ENDLESS, DAYLESS GLIMMERING. I SOMETIMES THINK IT IS A NATIVE HERE.
AT LAST, IT LOCATES RENO FOR ME.
ADRIANNA! DID JEREMY TELL YOU THAT I WAS HERE?
THIS IS THE LODGE OF THE SHAPER'S GUILD. ISN'T IT GREAT? WHEN THEY HEARD I WAS ON-WORLD, THEY ASKED ME TO VISIT!
THAT'S NICE. AND WHAT IS THE SHAPER'S GUILD?
IT'S LIKE A UNION FOR PEOPLE WITH MY GENOTYPE. THIS IS LORD PROTEUS, THE INSPIRATION FOR THE GREEK GOD OF THE SAME NAME.

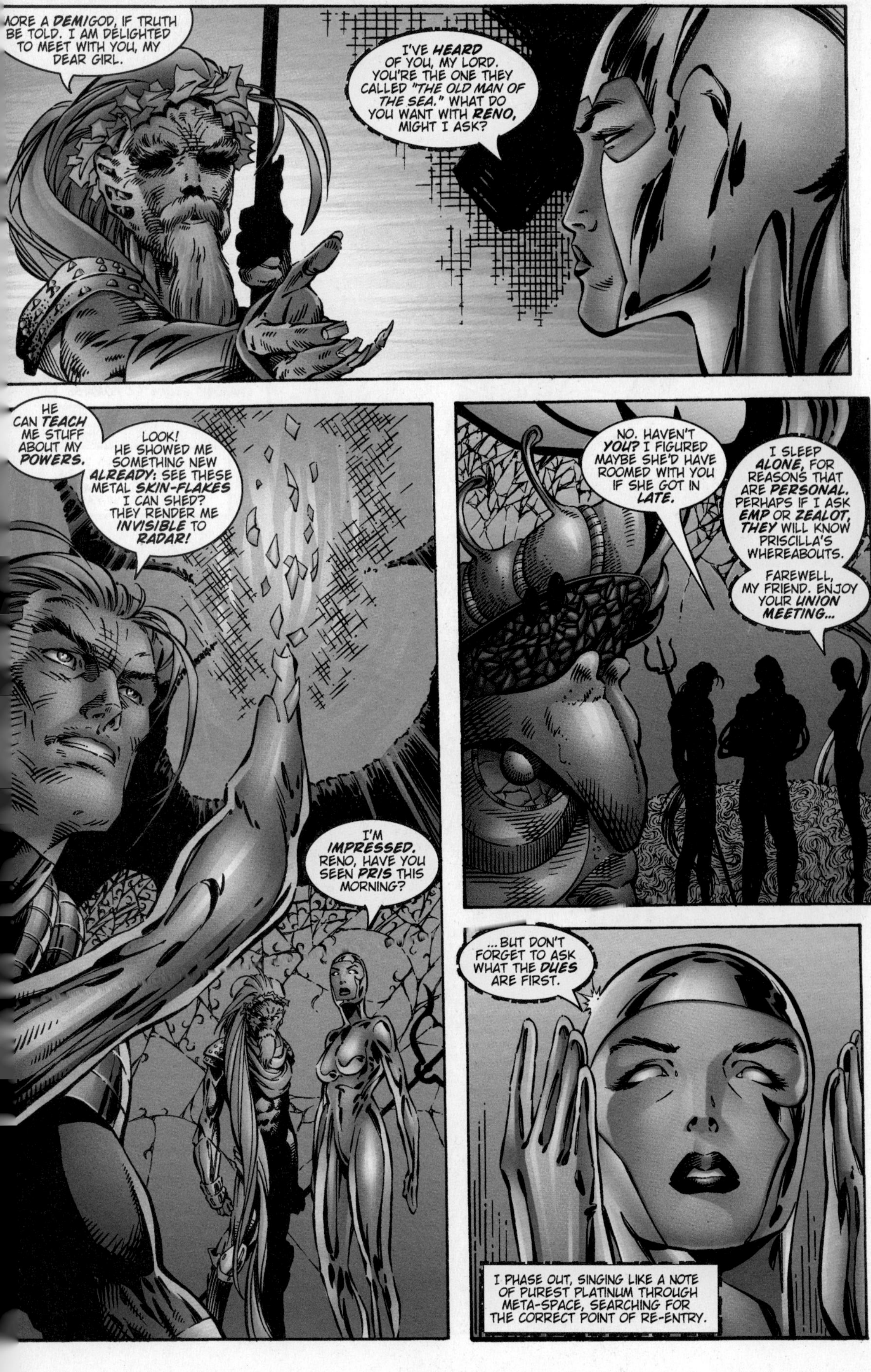
MORE A DEMIGOD, IF TRUTH BE TOLD. I AM DELIGHTED TO MEET WITH YOU, MY DEAR GIRL.
I'VE HEARD OF YOU, MY LORD. YOU'RE THE ONE THEY CALLED "THE OLD MAN OF THE SEA." WHAT DO YOU WANT WITH RENO, MIGHT I ASK?
HE CAN TEACH ME STUFF ABOUT MY POWERS.
LOOK! HE SHOWED ME SOMETHING NEW ALREADY: SEE THESE METAL SKIN-FLAKES I CAN SHED? THEY RENDER ME INVISIBLE TO RADAR!
I'M IMPRESSED. RENO, HAVE YOU SEEN PRIS THIS MORNING?
NO. HAVEN'T YOU? I FIGURED MAYBE SHE'D HAVE ROOMED WITH YOU IF SHE GOT IN LATE.
I SLEEP ALONE, FOR REASONS THAT ARE PERSONAL. PERHAPS IF I ASK EMP OR ZEALOT, THEY WILL KNOW PRISCILLA'S WHEREABOUTS.
FAREWELL, MY FRIEND. ENJOY YOUR UNION MEETING...
...BUT DON'T FORGET TO ASK WHAT THE DUES ARE FIRST.
I PHASE OUT, SINGING LIKE A NOTE OF PUREST PLATINUM THROUGH META-SPACE, SEARCHING FOR THE CORRECT POINT OF RE-ENTRY.

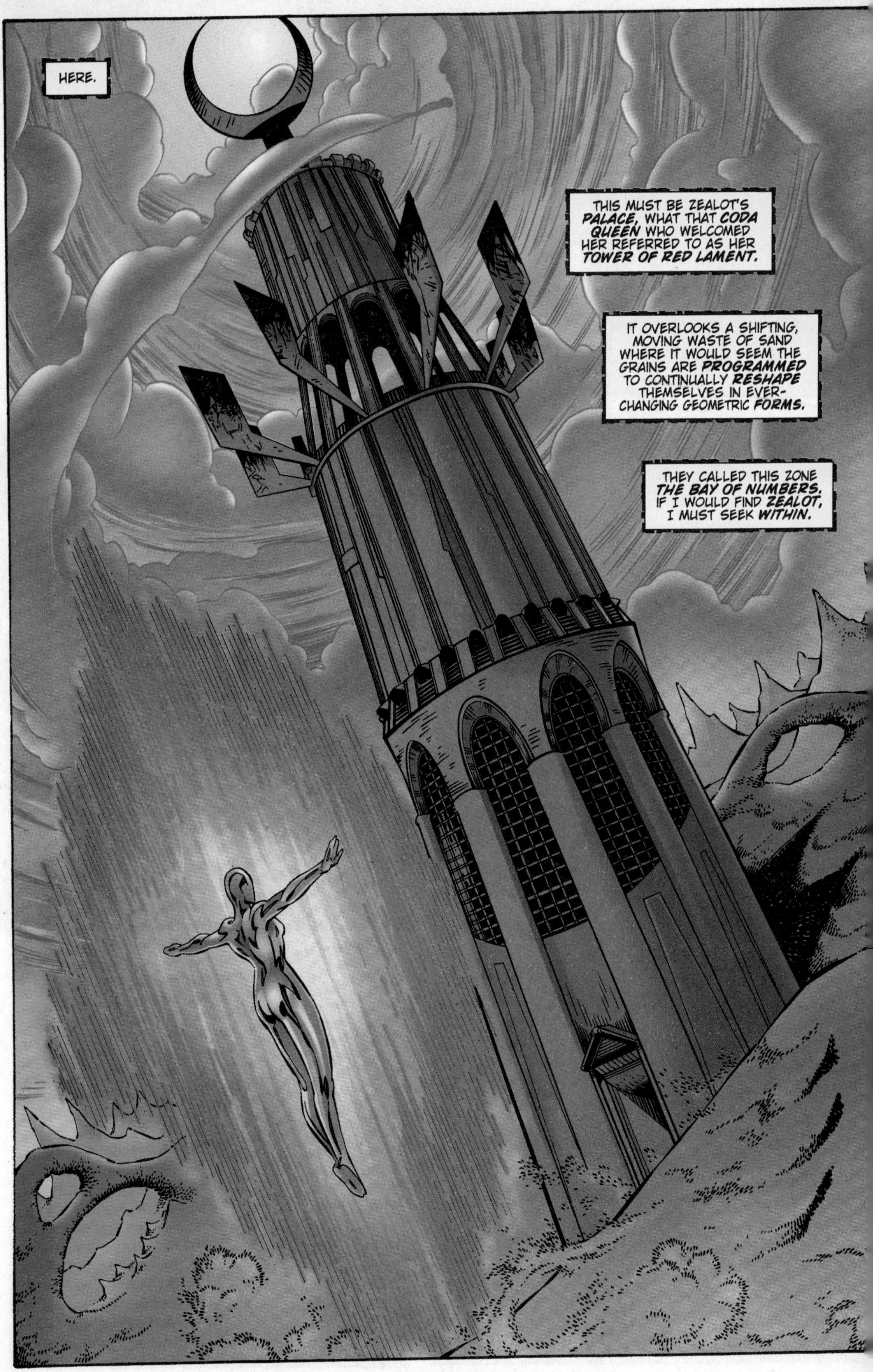
HERE.
THIS MUST BE ZEALOT'S PALACE, WHAT THAT CODA QUEEN WHO WELCOMED HER REFERRED TO AS HER TOWER OF RED LAMENT.
IT OVERLOOKS A SHIFTING, MOVING WASTE OF SAND WHERE IT WOULD SEEM THE GRAINS ARE PROGRAMMED TO CONTINUALLY RESHAPE THEMSELVES IN EVER-CHANGING GEOMETRIC FORMS.
THEY CALLED THIS ZONE THE BAY OF NUMBERS. IF I WOULD FIND ZEALOT, I MUST SEEK WITHIN.

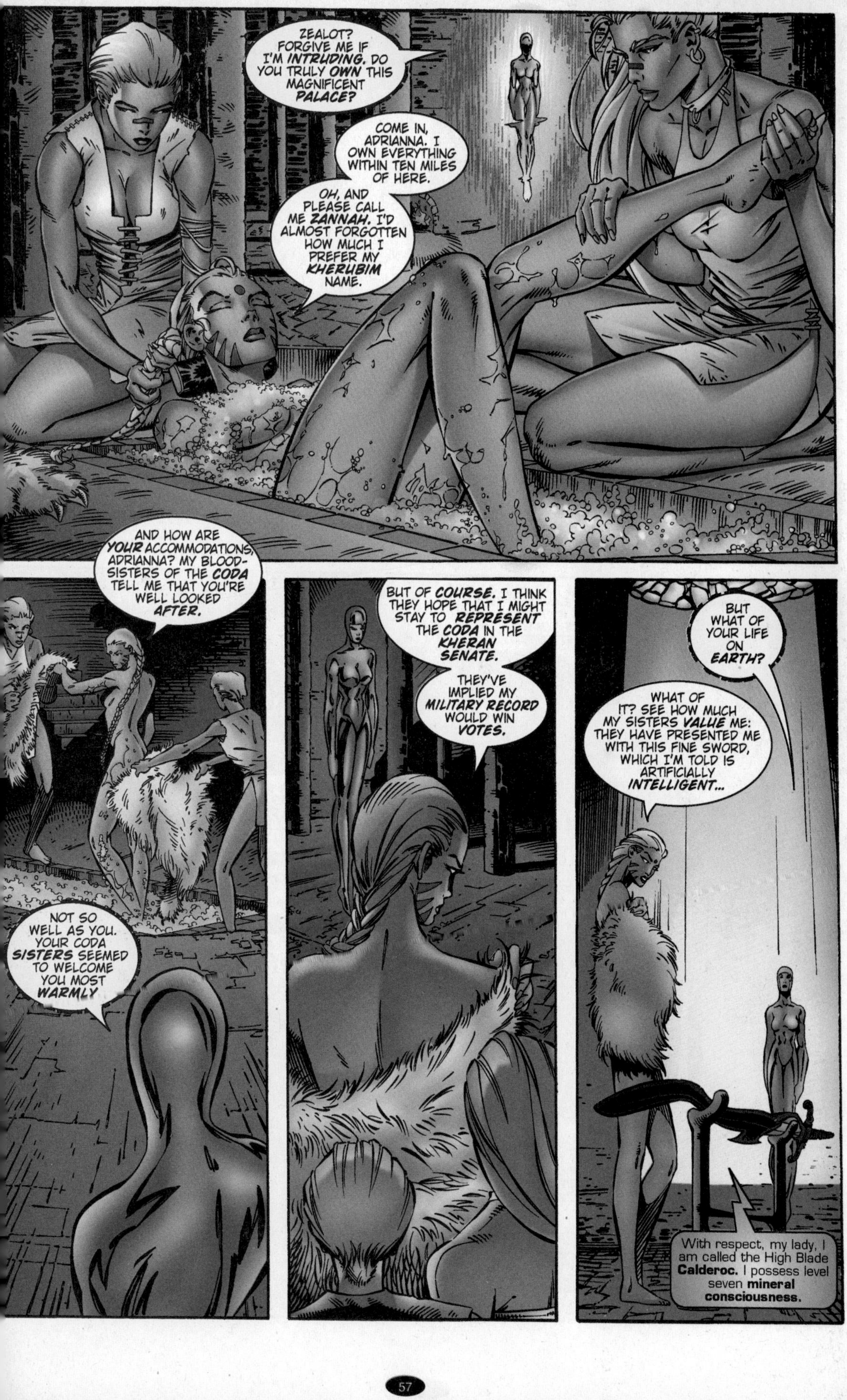
ZEALOT? FORGIVE ME IF I'M INTRUDING. DO YOU TRULY OWN THIS MAGNIFICENT PALACE?
COME IN, ADRIANNA. I OWN EVERYTHING WITHIN TEN MILES OF HERE.
OH, AND PLEASE CALL ME ZANNAH. I'D ALMOST FORGOTTEN HOW MUCH I PREFER MY KHERUBIM NAME.
AND HOW ARE YOUR ACCOMMODATIONS, ADRIANNA? MY BLOOD-SISTERS OF THE CODA TELL ME THAT YOU'RE WELL LOOKED AFTER.
NOT SO WELL AS YOU. YOUR CODA SISTERS SEEMED TO WELCOME YOU MOST WARMLY.
BUT OF COURSE. I THINK THEY HOPE THAT I MIGHT STAY TO REPRESENT THE CODA IN THE KHERAN SENATE.
THEY'VE IMPLIED MY MILITARY RECORD WOULD WIN VOTES.
BUT WHAT OF YOUR LIFE ON EARTH?
WHAT OF IT? SEE HOW MUCH MY SISTERS VALUE ME: THEY HAVE PRESENTED ME WITH THIS FINE SWORD, WHICH I'M TOLD IS ARTIFICIALLY INTELLIGENT...
With respect, my lady, I am called the High Blade Calderoc. I possess level seven mineral consciousness.

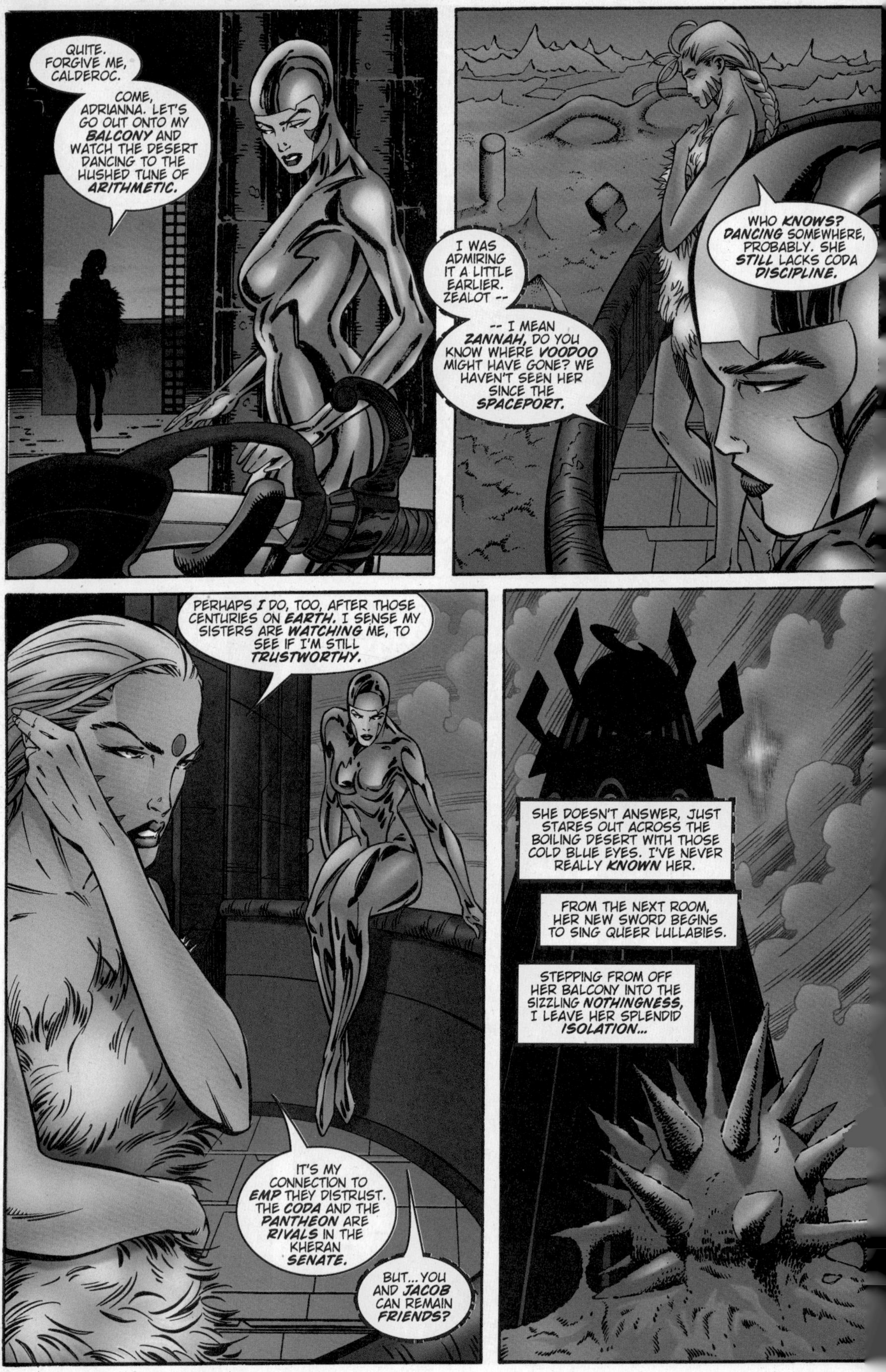
QUITE. FORGIVE ME, CALDEROC.
COME, ADRIANNA. LET'S GO OUT ONTO MY BALCONY AND WATCH THE DESERT DANCING TO THE HUSHED TUNE OF ARITHMETIC.
I WAS ADMIRING IT A LITTLE EARLIER. ZEALOT --
-- I MEAN ZANNAH, DO YOU KNOW WHERE VOODOO MIGHT HAVE GONE? WE HAVEN'T SEEN HER SINCE THE SPACEPORT.
WHO KNOWS? DANCING SOMEWHERE, PROBABLY. SHE STILL LACKS CODA DISCIPLINE.
PERHAPS I DO, TOO, AFTER THOSE CENTURIES ON EARTH. I SENSE MY SISTERS ARE WATCHING ME, TO SEE IF I'M STILL TRUSTWORTHY.
IT'S MY CONNECTION TO EMP THEY DISTRUST. THE CODA AND THE PANTHEON ARE RIVALS IN THE KHERAN SENATE.
BUT... YOU AND JACOB CAN REMAIN FRIENDS?
SHE DOESN'T ANSWER, JUST STARES OUT ACROSS THE BOILING DESERT WITH THOSE COLD BLUE EYES. I'VE NEVER REALLY KNOWN HER.
FROM THE NEXT ROOM, HER NEW SWORD BEGINS TO SING QUEER LULLABIES.
STEPPING FROM OFF HER BALCONY INTO THE SIZZLING NOTHINGNESS, I LEAVE HER SPLENDID ISOLATION...

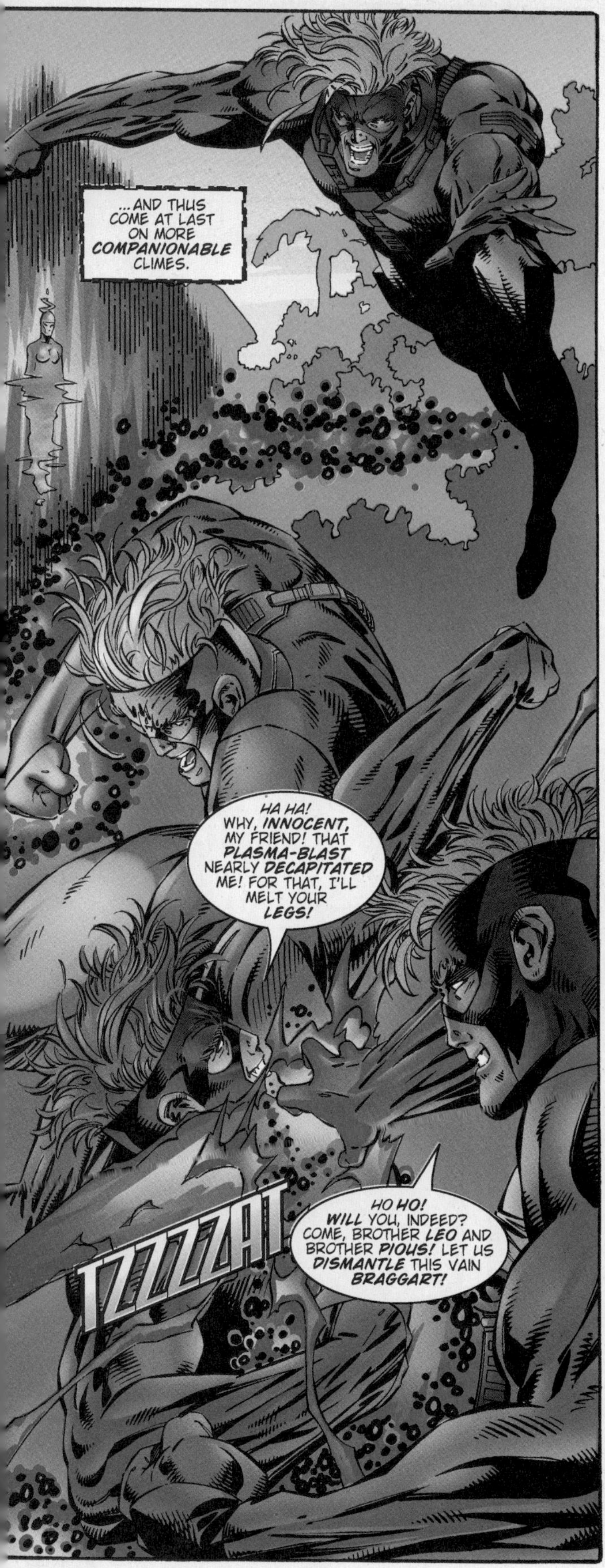
...AND THUS COME AT LAST ON MORE COMPANIONABLE CLIMES.
HA HA! WHY, INNOCENT, MY FRIEND! THAT PLASMA-BLAST NEARLY DECAPITATED ME! FOR THAT, I'LL MELT YOUR LEGS!
TZZZZZAT
HO HO! WILL YOU, INDEED? COME, BROTHER LEO AND BROTHER PIOUS! LET US DISMANTLE THIS VAIN BRAGGART!
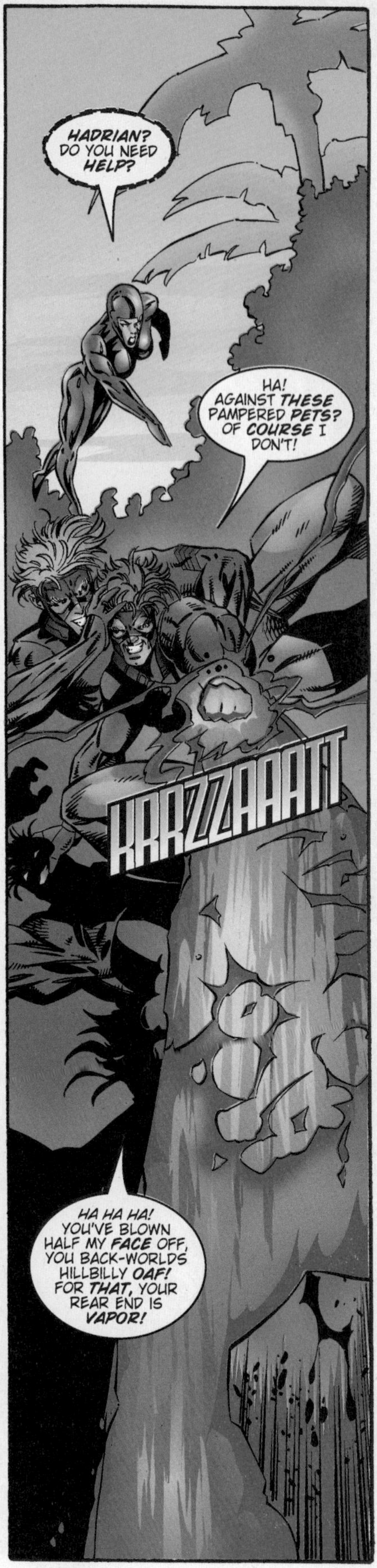
HADRIAN? DO YOU NEED HELP?
HA! AGAINST THESE PAMPERED PETS? OF COURSE I DON'T!
KRRZZZAAATT
HA HA HA! YOU'VE BLOWN HALF MY FACE OFF, YOU BACK-WORLDS HILLBILLY OAF! FOR THAT, YOUR REAR END IS VAPOR!

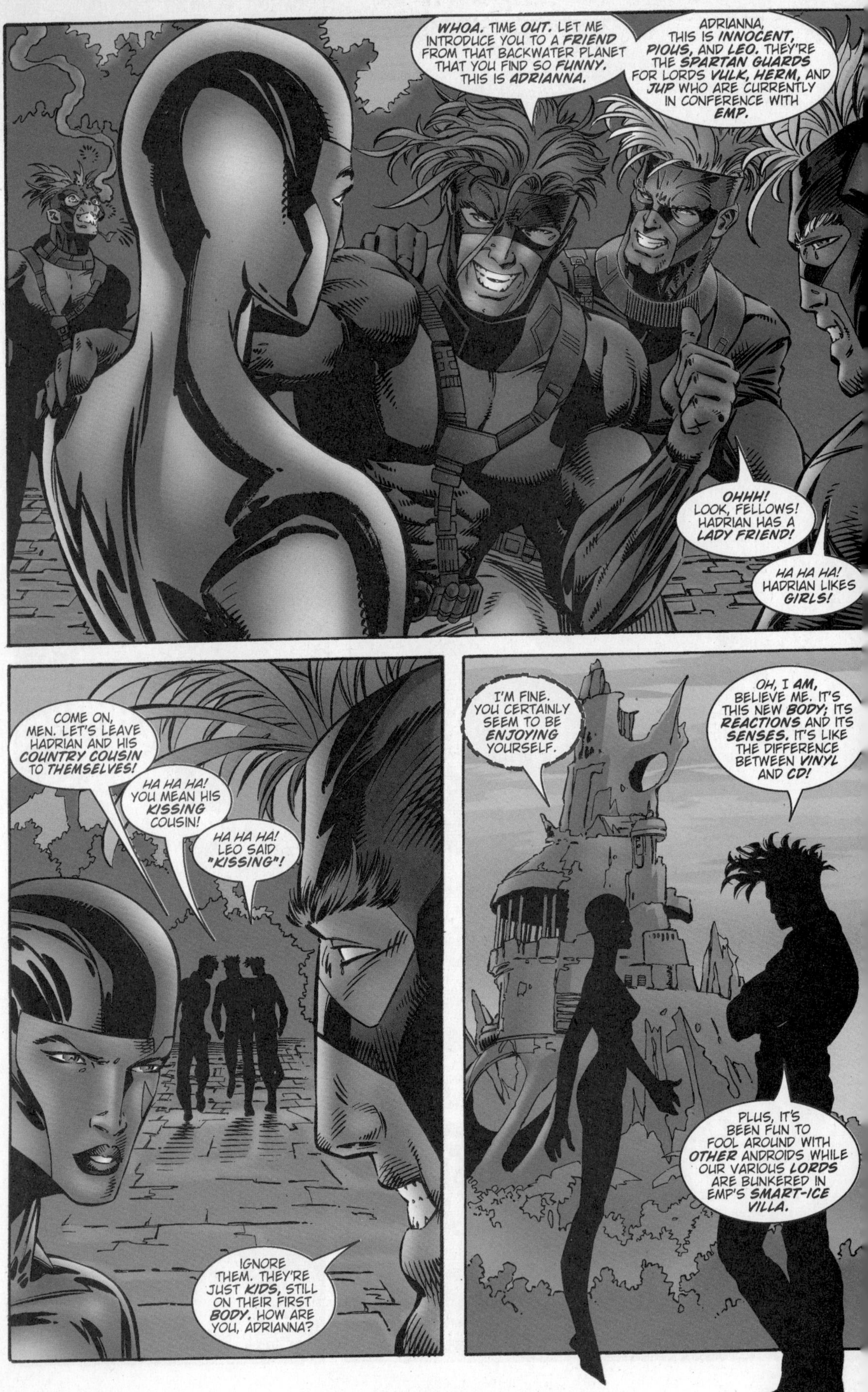
WHOA. TIME OUT. LET ME INTRODUCE YOU TO A FRIEND FROM THAT BACKWATER PLANET THAT YOU FIND SO FUNNY. THIS IS ADRIANNA.
ADRIANNA, THIS IS INNOCENT, PIOUS, AND LEO. THEY'RE THE SPARTAN GUARDS FOR LORDS VULK, HERM, AND JUP WHO ARE CURRENTLY IN CONFERENCE WITH EMP.
OHHH! LOOK, FELLOWS! HADRIAN HAS A LADY FRIEND!
HA HA HA! HADRIAN LIKES GIRLS!
COME ON, MEN. LET'S LEAVE HADRIAN AND HIS COUNTRY COUSIN TO THEMSELVES!
HA HA HA! YOU MEAN HIS KISSING COUSIN!
HA HA HA! LEO SAID "KISSING"!
IGNORE THEM. THEY'RE JUST KIDS, STILL ON THEIR FIRST BODY. HOW ARE YOU, ADRIANNA?
I'M FINE. YOU CERTAINLY SEEM TO BE ENJOYING YOURSELF.
OH, I AM, BELIEVE ME. IT'S THIS NEW BODY; ITS REACTIONS AND ITS SENSES. IT'S LIKE THE DIFFERENCE BETWEEN VINYL AND CD!
PLUS, IT'S BEEN FUN TO FOOL AROUND WITH OTHER ANDROIDS WHILE OUR VARIOUS LORDS ARE BUNKERED IN EMP'S SMART-ICE VILLA.

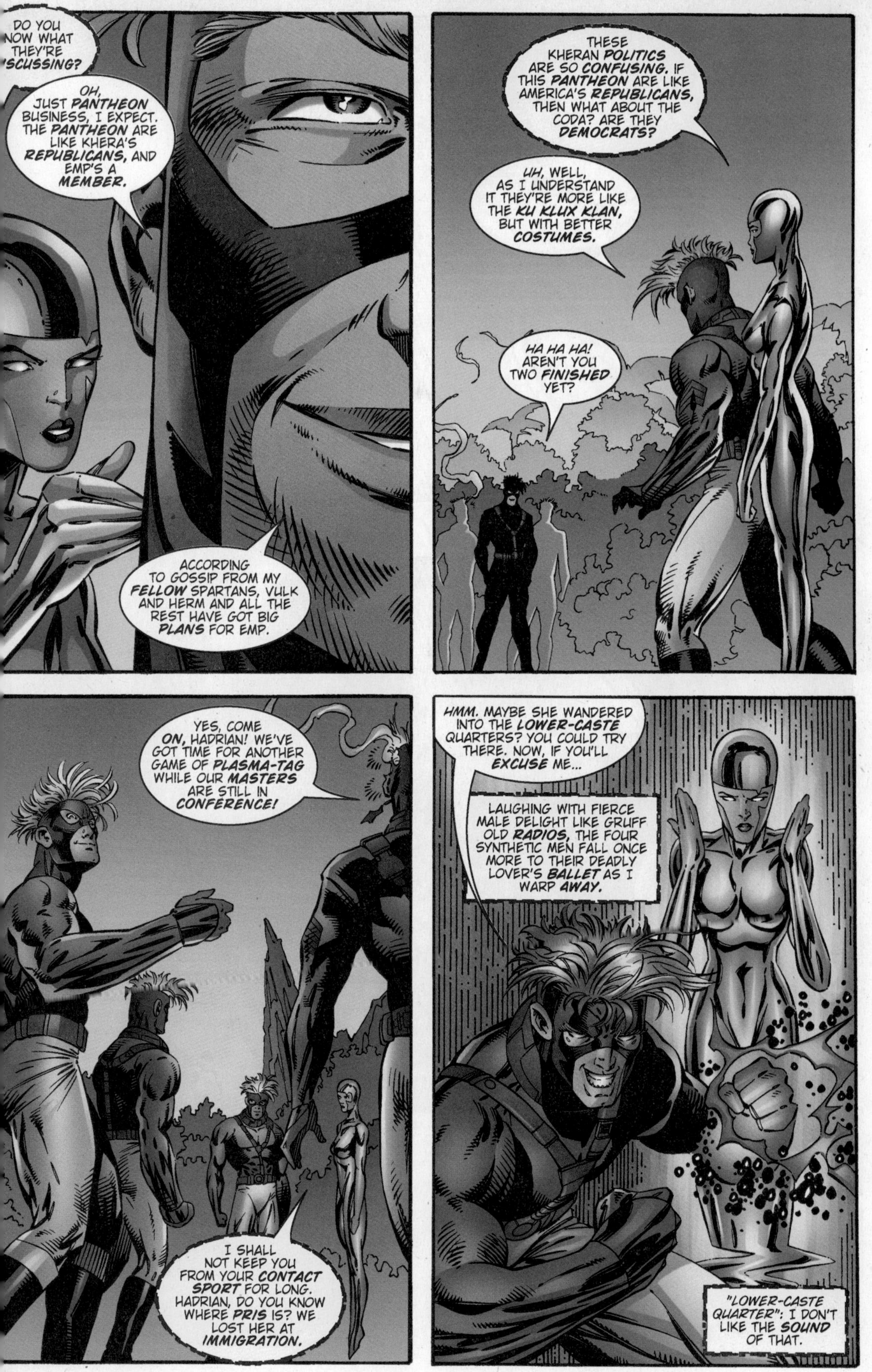
DO YOU NOW WHAT THEY'RE 'SCUSSING?
OH, JUST PANTHEON BUSINESS, I EXPECT. THE PANTHEON ARE LIKE KHERA'S REPUBLICANS, AND EMP'S A MEMBER.
ACCORDING TO GOSSIP FROM MY FELLOW SPARTANS, VULK AND HERM AND ALL THE REST HAVE GOT BIG PLANS FOR EMP.
THESE KHERAN POLITICS ARE SO CONFUSING. IF THIS PANTHEON ARE LIKE AMERICA'S REPUBLICANS, THEN WHAT ABOUT THE CODA? ARE THEY DEMOCRATS?
UH, WELL, AS I UNDERSTAND IT THEY'RE MORE LIKE THE KU KLUX KLAN, BUT WITH BETTER COSTUMES.
HA HA HA! AREN'T YOU TWO FINISHED YET?
YES, COME ON, HADRIAN! WE'VE GOT TIME FOR ANOTHER GAME OF PLASMA-TAG WHILE OUR MASTERS ARE STILL IN CONFERENCE!
I SHALL NOT KEEP YOU FROM YOUR CONTACT SPORT FOR LONG. HADRIAN, DO YOU KNOW WHERE PRIS IS? WE LOST HER AT IMMIGRATION.
HMM. MAYBE SHE WANDERED INTO THE LOWER-CASTE QUARTERS? YOU COULD TRY THERE. NOW, IF YOU'LL EXCUSE ME...
LAUGHING WITH FIERCE MALE DELIGHT LIKE GRUFF OLD RADIOS, THE FOUR SYNTHETIC MEN FALL ONCE MORE TO THEIR DEADLY LOVER'S BALLET AS I WARP AWAY.
"LOWER-CASTE QUARTER": I DON'T LIKE THE SOUND OF THAT.

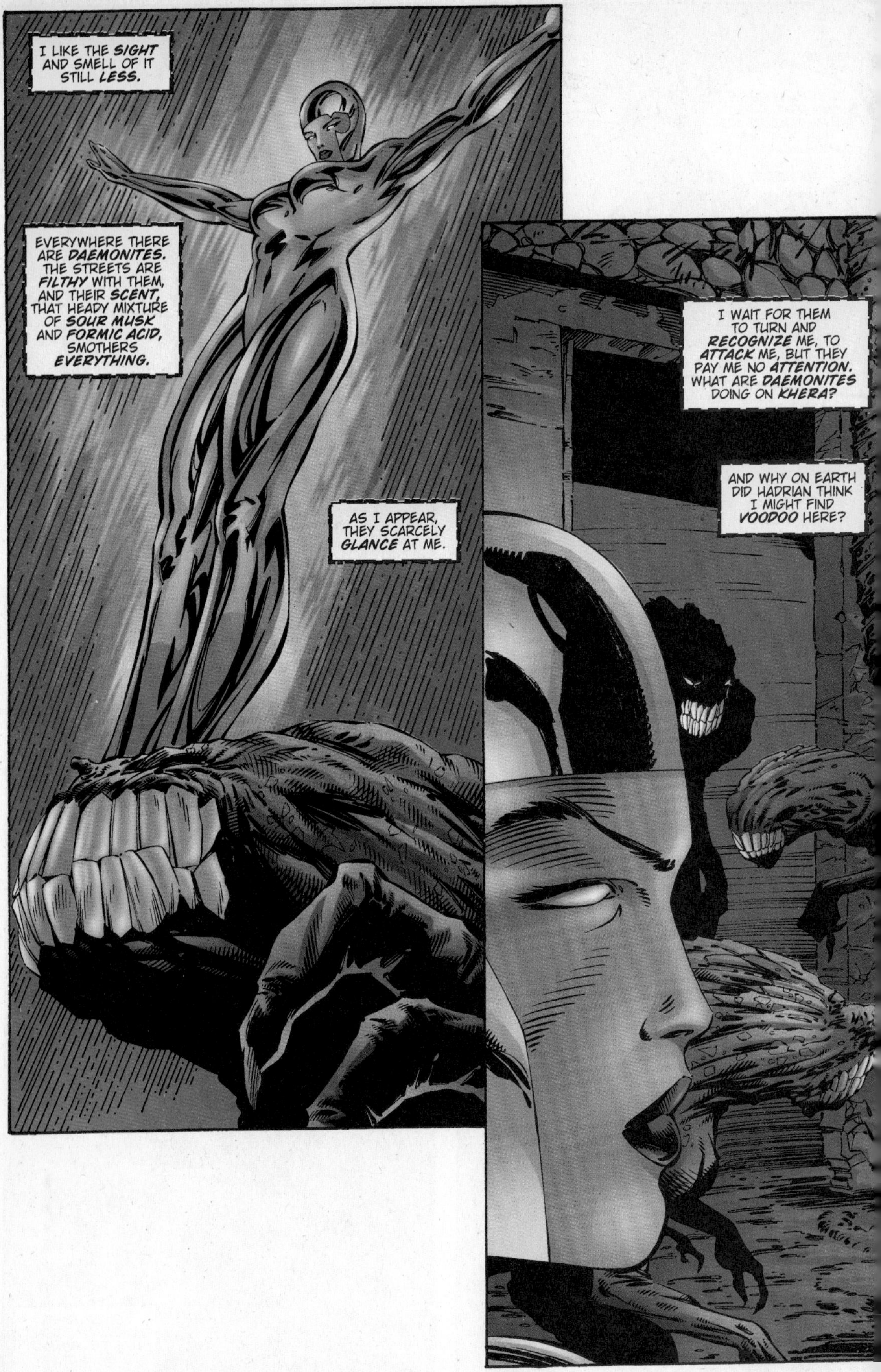
I LIKE THE SIGHT AND SMELL OF IT STILL LESS.
EVERYWHERE THERE ARE DAEMONITES. THE STREETS ARE FILTHY WITH THEM, AND THEIR SCENT, THAT HEADY MIXTURE OF SOUR MUSK AND FORMIC ACID, SMOTHERS EVERYTHING.
AS I APPEAR, THEY SCARCELY GLANCE AT ME.
I WAIT FOR THEM TO TURN AND RECOGNIZE ME, TO ATTACK ME, BUT THEY PAY ME NO ATTENTION. WHAT ARE DAEMONITES DOING ON KHERA?
AND WHY ON EARTH DID HADRIAN THINK I MIGHT FIND VOODOO HERE?

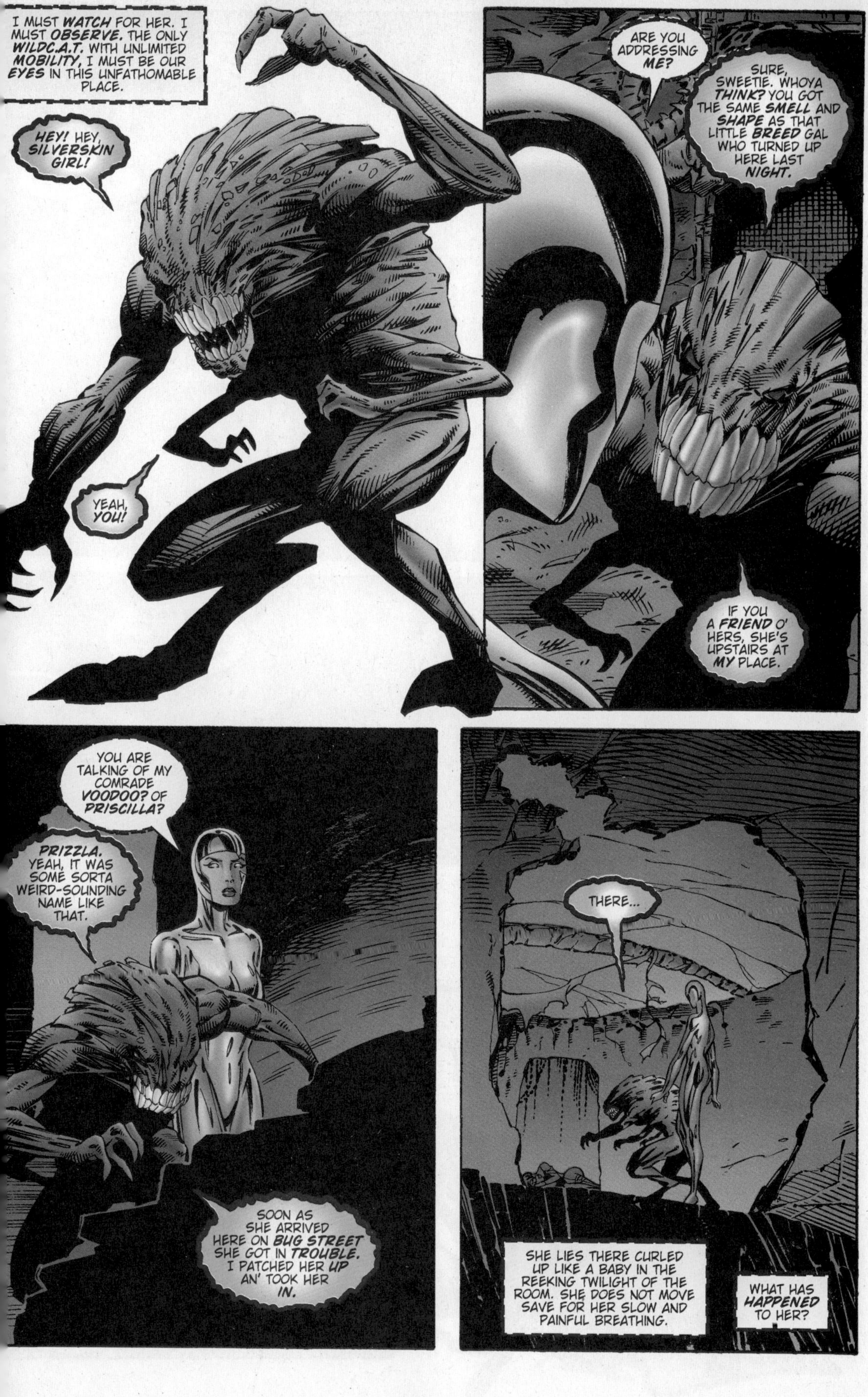
I MUST **WATCH** FOR HER. I MUST **OBSERVE.** THE ONLY **WILDC.A.T.** WITH UNLIMITED **MOBILITY,** I MUST BE OUR **EYES** IN THIS UNFATHOMABLE PLACE.
HEY! HEY, **SILVERSKIN GIRL!**
YEAH, **YOU!**
ARE YOU ADDRESSING **ME?**
SURE, SWEETIE. WHOYA **THINK?** YOU GOT THE SAME **SMELL** AND **SHAPE** AS THAT LITTLE **BREED** GAL WHO TURNED UP HERE LAST **NIGHT.**
IF YOU A **FRIEND** O' HERS, SHE'S UPSTAIRS AT **MY** PLACE.
YOU ARE TALKING OF MY COMRADE **VOODOO?** OF **PRISCILLA?**
PRIZZLA. YEAH, IT WAS SOME SORTA WEIRD-SOUNDING NAME LIKE THAT.
SOON AS SHE ARRIVED HERE ON **BUG STREET** SHE GOT IN **TROUBLE.** I PATCHED HER **UP** AN' TOOK HER **IN.**
THERE...
SHE LIES THERE CURLED UP LIKE A BABY IN THE REEKING TWILIGHT OF THE ROOM. SHE DOES NOT MOVE SAVE FOR HER SLOW AND PAINFUL BREATHING.
WHAT HAS **HAPPENED** TO HER?

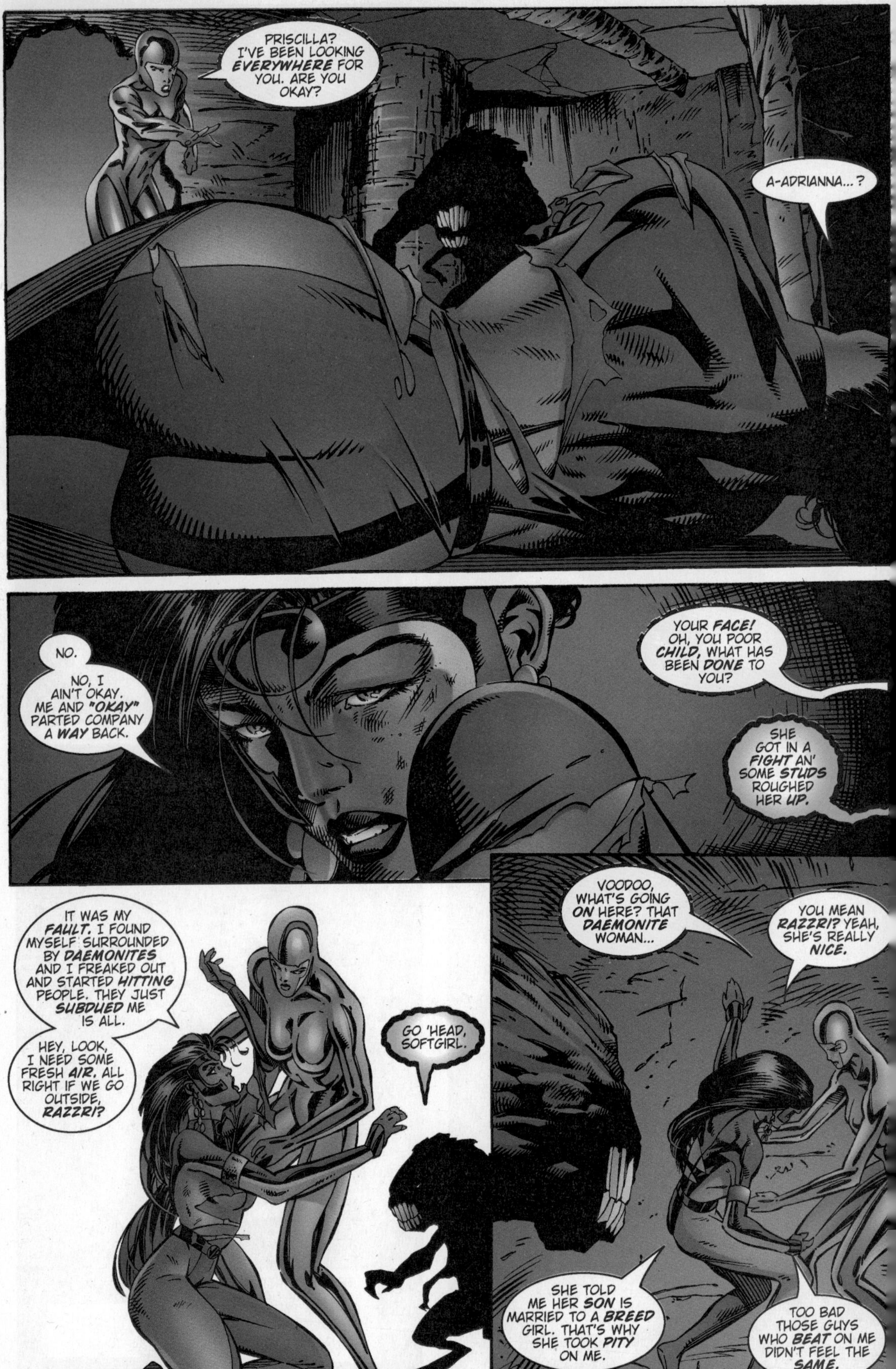
PRISCILLA? I'VE BEEN LOOKING EVERYWHERE FOR YOU. ARE YOU OKAY?
A-ADRIANNA...?
NO.
NO, I AIN'T OKAY. ME AND "OKAY" PARTED COMPANY A WAY BACK.
YOUR FACE! OH, YOU POOR CHILD, WHAT HAS BEEN DONE TO YOU?
SHE GOT IN A FIGHT AN' SOME STUDS ROUGHED HER UP.
IT WAS MY FAULT. I FOUND MYSELF SURROUNDED BY DAEMONITES AND I FREAKED OUT AND STARTED HITTING PEOPLE. THEY JUST SUBDUED ME IS ALL.
HEY, LOOK, I NEED SOME FRESH AIR. ALL RIGHT IF WE GO OUTSIDE, RAZZRI?
GO 'HEAD, SOFTGIRL.
VOODOO, WHAT'S GOING ON HERE? THAT DAEMONITE WOMAN...
YOU MEAN RAZZRI? YEAH, SHE'S REALLY NICE.
SHE TOLD ME HER SON IS MARRIED TO A BREED GIRL. THAT'S WHY SHE TOOK PITY ON ME.
TOO BAD THOSE GUYS WHO BEAT ON ME DIDN'T FEEL THE SAME.

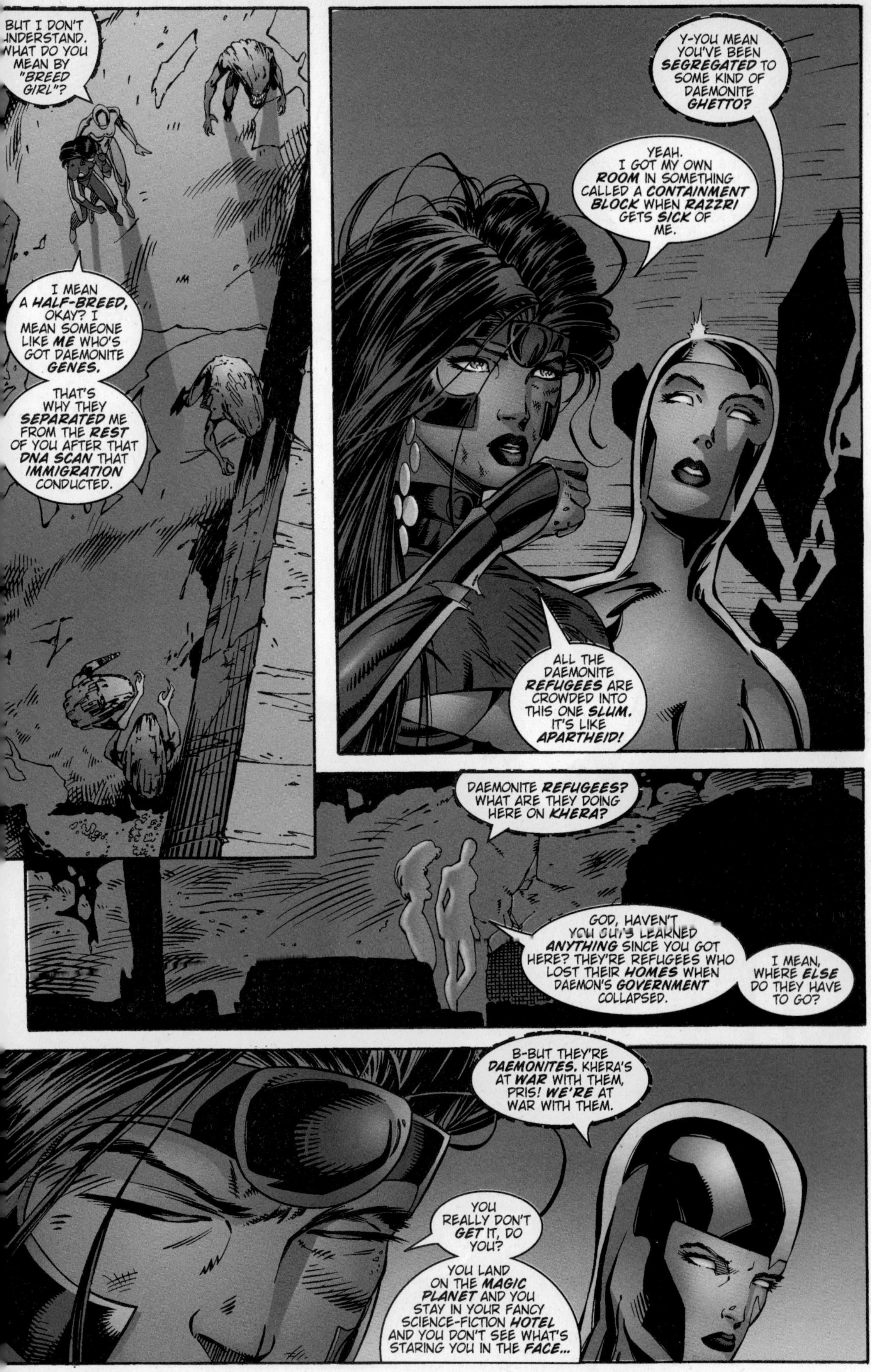
BUT I DON'T UNDERSTAND. WHAT DO YOU MEAN BY "BREED GIRL"?
I MEAN A HALF-BREED, OKAY? I MEAN SOMEONE LIKE ME WHO'S GOT DAEMONITE GENES.
THAT'S WHY THEY SEPARATED ME FROM THE REST OF YOU AFTER THAT DNA SCAN THAT IMMIGRATION CONDUCTED.
Y-YOU MEAN YOU'VE BEEN SEGREGATED TO SOME KIND OF DAEMONITE GHETTO?
YEAH. I GOT MY OWN ROOM IN SOMETHING CALLED A CONTAINMENT BLOCK WHEN RAZZRI GETS SICK OF ME.
ALL THE DAEMONITE REFUGEES ARE CROWDED INTO THIS ONE SLUM. IT'S LIKE APARTHEID!
DAEMONITE REFUGEES? WHAT ARE THEY DOING HERE ON KHERA?
GOD, HAVEN'T YOU GUYS LEARNED ANYTHING SINCE YOU GOT HERE? THEY'RE REFUGEES WHO LOST THEIR HOMES WHEN DAEMON'S GOVERNMENT COLLAPSED.
I MEAN, WHERE ELSE DO THEY HAVE TO GO?
B-BUT THEY'RE DAEMONITES. KHERA'S AT WAR WITH THEM, PRIS! WE'RE AT WAR WITH THEM.
YOU REALLY DON'T GET IT, DO YOU?
YOU LAND ON THE MAGIC PLANET AND YOU STAY IN YOUR FANCY SCIENCE-FICTION HOTEL AND YOU DON'T SEE WHAT'S STARING YOU IN THE FACE...

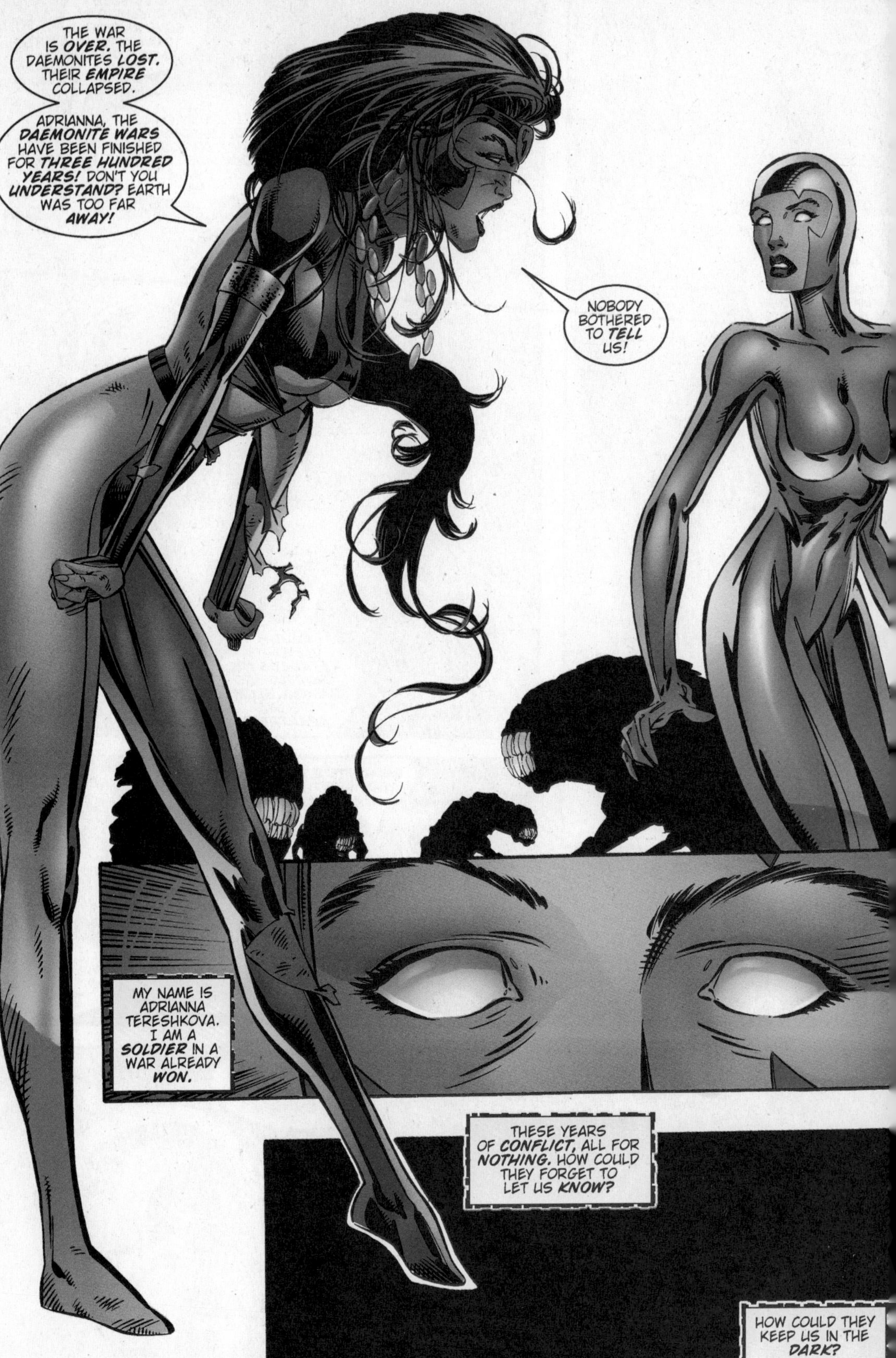
THE WAR IS OVER. THE DAEMONITES LOST. THEIR EMPIRE COLLAPSED.
ADRIANNA, THE DAEMONITE WARS HAVE BEEN FINISHED FOR THREE HUNDRED YEARS! DON'T YOU UNDERSTAND? EARTH WAS TOO FAR AWAY!
NOBODY BOTHERED TO TELL US!
MY NAME IS ADRIANNA TERESHKOVA. I AM A SOLDIER IN A WAR ALREADY WON.
THESE YEARS OF CONFLICT, ALL FOR NOTHING. HOW COULD THEY FORGET TO LET US KNOW?
HOW COULD THEY KEEP US IN THE DARK?

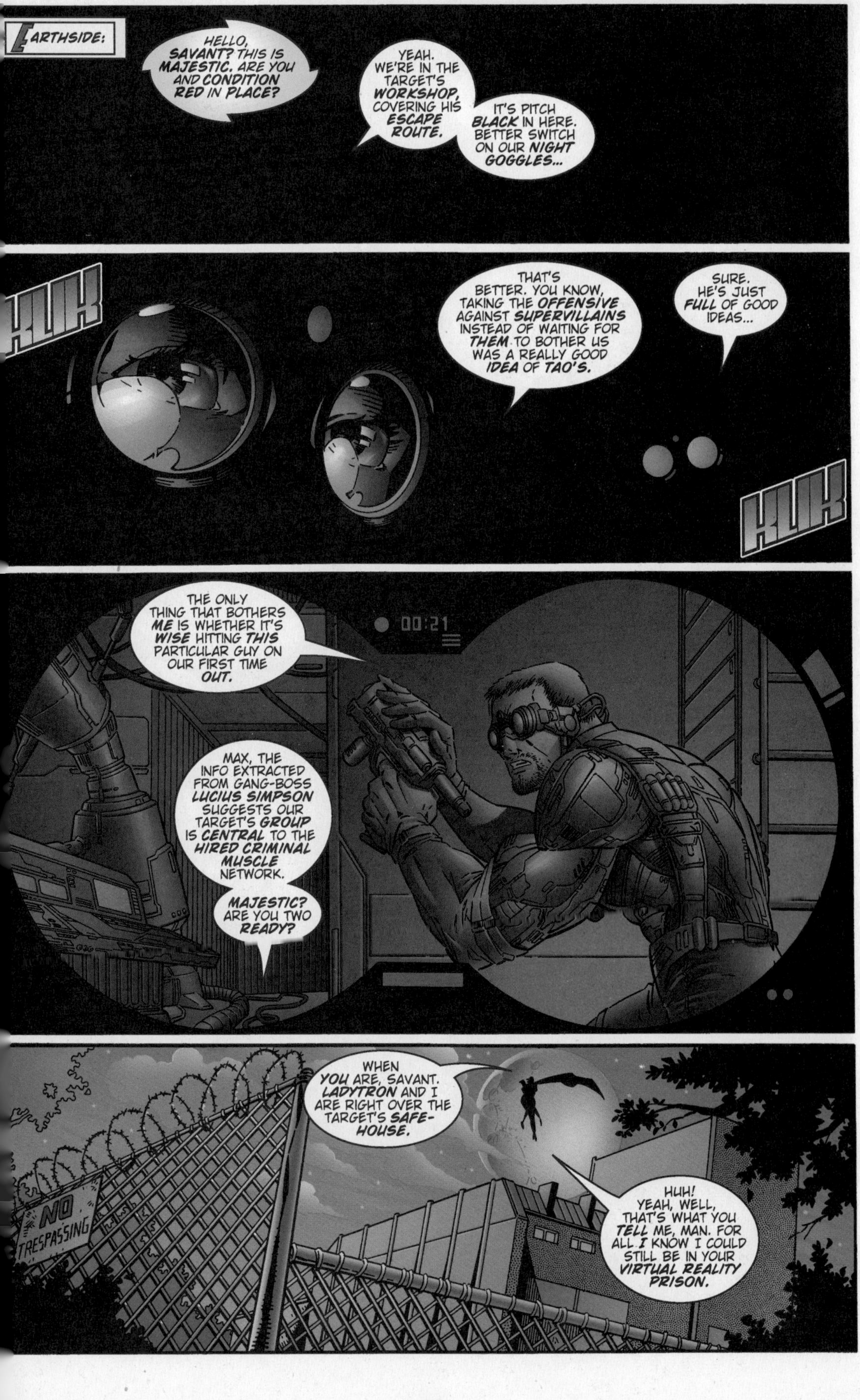
EARTHSIDE:
HELLO, SAVANT? THIS IS MAJESTIC. ARE YOU AND CONDITION RED IN PLACE?
YEAH. WE'RE IN THE TARGET'S WORKSHOP, COVERING HIS ESCAPE ROUTE.
IT'S PITCH BLACK IN HERE. BETTER SWITCH ON OUR NIGHT GOGGLES...
KLIK
THAT'S BETTER. YOU KNOW, TAKING THE OFFENSIVE AGAINST SUPERVILLAINS INSTEAD OF WAITING FOR THEM TO BOTHER US WAS A REALLY GOOD IDEA OF TAO'S.
SURE. HE'S JUST FULL OF GOOD IDEAS...
KLIK
THE ONLY THING THAT BOTHERS ME IS WHETHER IT'S WISE HITTING THIS PARTICULAR GUY ON OUR FIRST TIME OUT.
00:21
MAX, THE INFO EXTRACTED FROM GANG-BOSS LUCIUS SIMPSON SUGGESTS OUR TARGET'S GROUP IS CENTRAL TO THE HIRED CRIMINAL MUSCLE NETWORK.
MAJESTIC? ARE YOU TWO READY?
NO TRESPASSING
WHEN YOU ARE, SAVANT. LADYTRON AND I ARE RIGHT OVER THE TARGET'S SAFE-HOUSE.
HUH! YEAH, WELL, THAT'S WHAT YOU TELL ME, MAN. FOR ALL I KNOW I COULD STILL BE IN YOUR VIRTUAL REALITY PRISON.

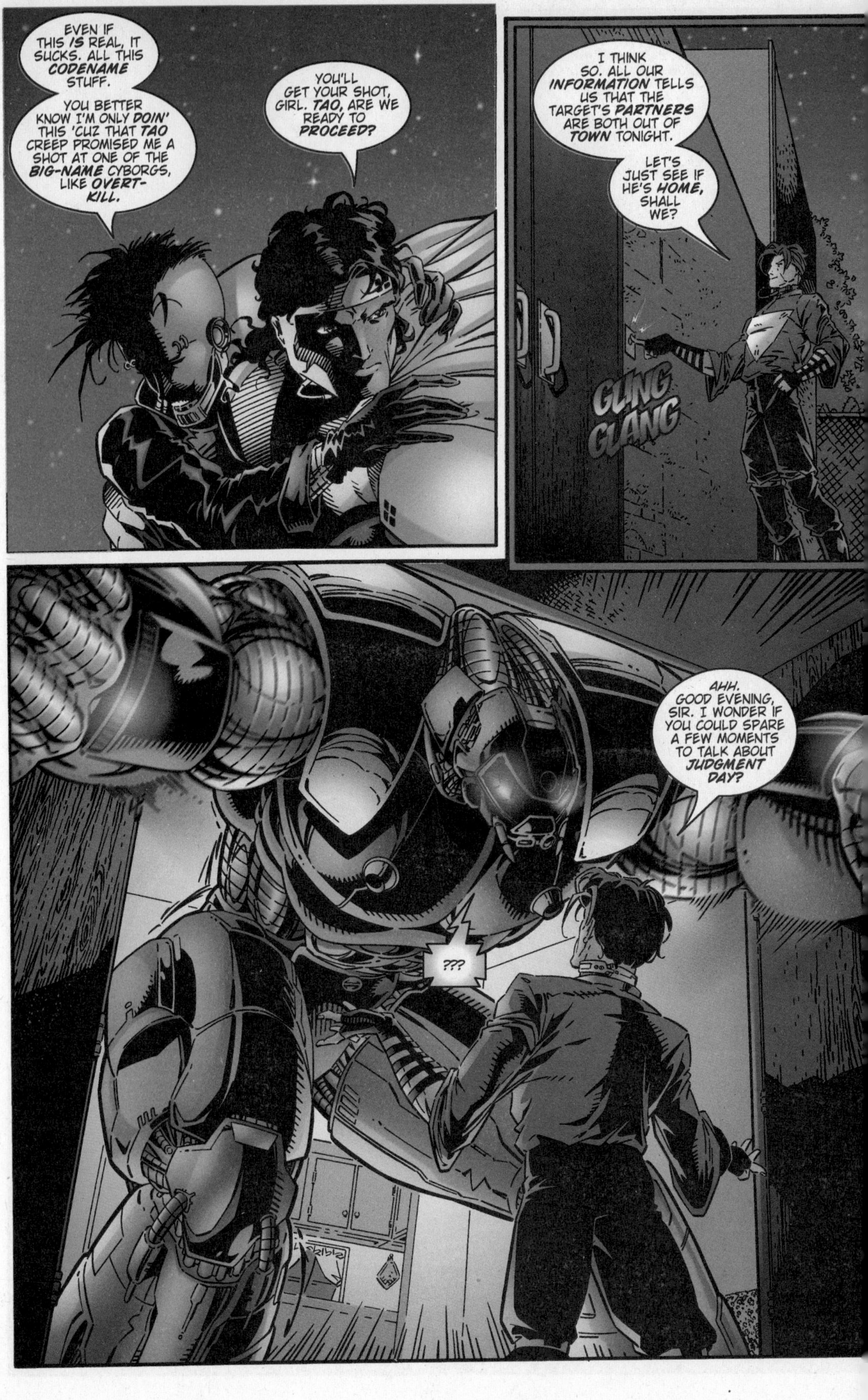
EVEN IF THIS IS REAL, IT SUCKS. ALL THIS CODENAME STUFF.
YOU BETTER KNOW I'M ONLY DOIN' THIS 'CUZ THAT TAO CREEP PROMISED ME A SHOT AT ONE OF THE BIG-NAME CYBORGS, LIKE OVERT-KILL.
YOU'LL GET YOUR SHOT, GIRL. TAO, ARE WE READY TO PROCEED?
I THINK SO. ALL OUR INFORMATION TELLS US THAT THE TARGET'S PARTNERS ARE BOTH OUT OF TOWN TONIGHT.
LET'S JUST SEE IF HE'S HOME, SHALL WE?
CLING CLANG
AHH. GOOD EVENING, SIR. I WONDER IF YOU COULD SPARE A FEW MOMENTS TO TALK ABOUT JUDGMENT DAY?
???

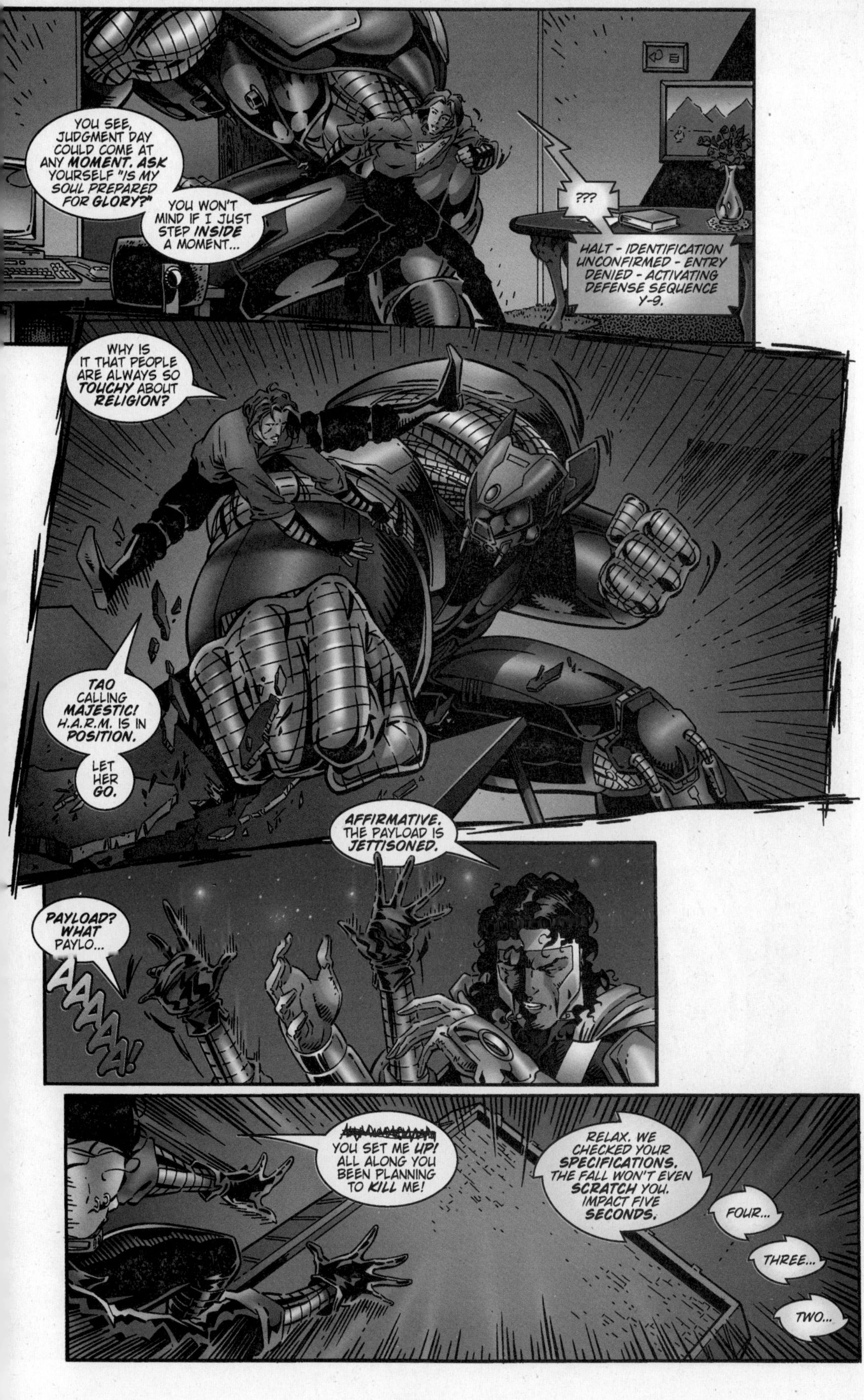

YOU SEE, JUDGMENT DAY COULD COME AT ANY MOMENT. ASK YOURSELF "IS MY SOUL PREPARED FOR GLORY?"
YOU WON'T MIND IF I JUST STEP INSIDE A MOMENT...
???
HALT - IDENTIFICATION UNCONFIRMED - ENTRY DENIED - ACTIVATING DEFENSE SEQUENCE Y-9.
WHY IS IT THAT PEOPLE ARE ALWAYS SO TOUCHY ABOUT RELIGION?
TAO CALLING MAJESTIC! H.A.R.M. IS IN POSITION.
LET HER GO.
AFFIRMATIVE. THE PAYLOAD IS JETTISONED.
PAYLOAD? WHAT PAYLO...
AAAAAA!
YOU SET ME UP! ALL ALONG YOU BEEN PLANNING TO KILL ME!
RELAX. WE CHECKED YOUR SPECIFICATIONS. THE FALL WON'T EVEN SCRATCH YOU. IMPACT FIVE SECONDS.
FOUR...
THREE...
TWO...

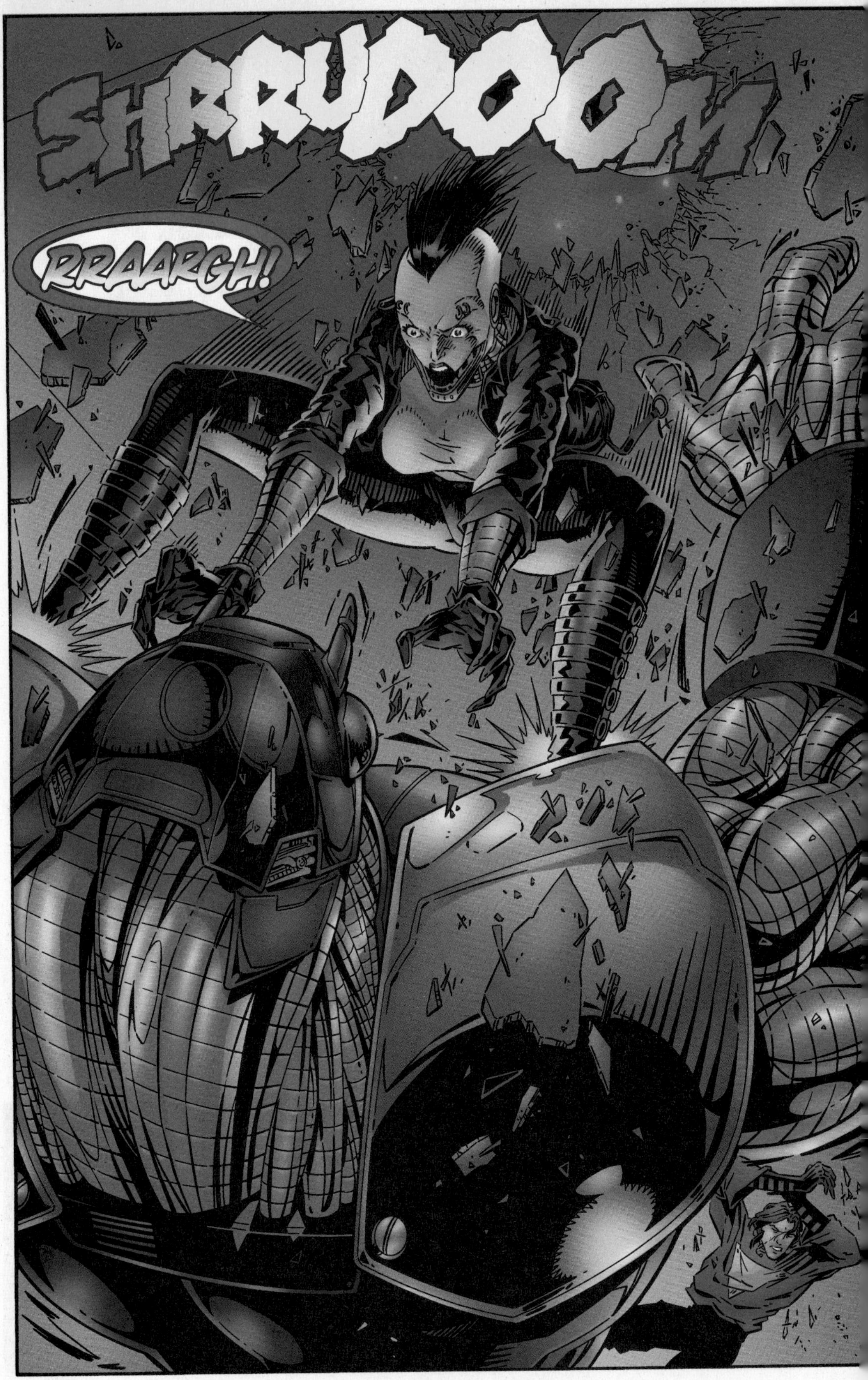
SHRRUDOOM!
RRAARGH!

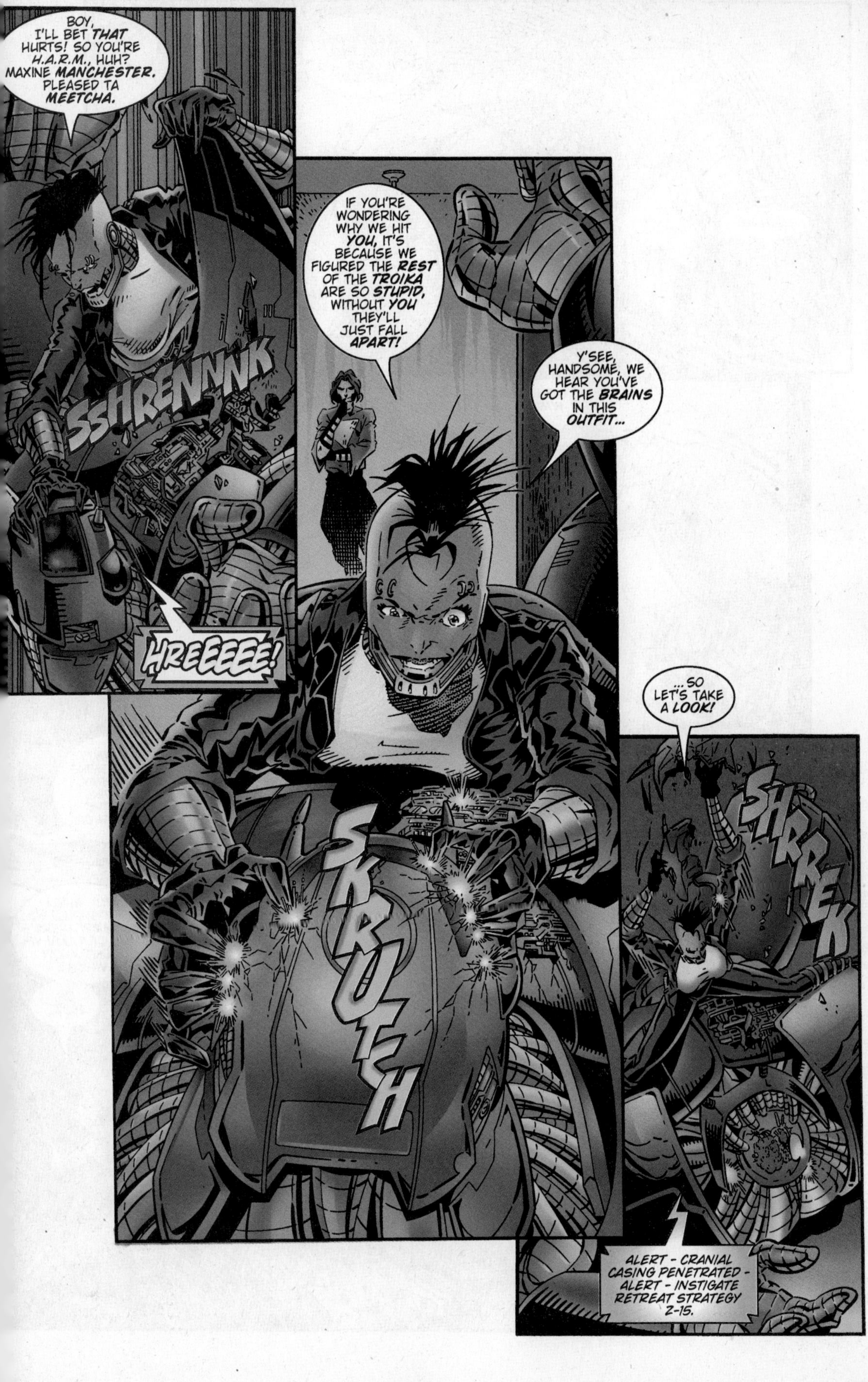
BOY, I'LL BET THAT HURTS! SO YOU'RE H.A.R.M., HUH? MAXINE MANCHESTER. PLEASED TA MEETCHA.
SSHRENNNK
HREEEEE!
IF YOU'RE WONDERING WHY WE HIT YOU, IT'S BECAUSE WE FIGURED THE REST OF THE TROIKA ARE SO STUPID, WITHOUT YOU THEY'LL JUST FALL APART!
Y'SEE, HANDSOME, WE HEAR YOU'VE GOT THE BRAINS IN THIS OUTFIT...
SKRUTCH
...SO LET'S TAKE A LOOK!
SHRREK
ALERT - CRANIAL CASING PENETRATED - ALERT - INSTIGATE RETREAT STRATEGY 2-15.

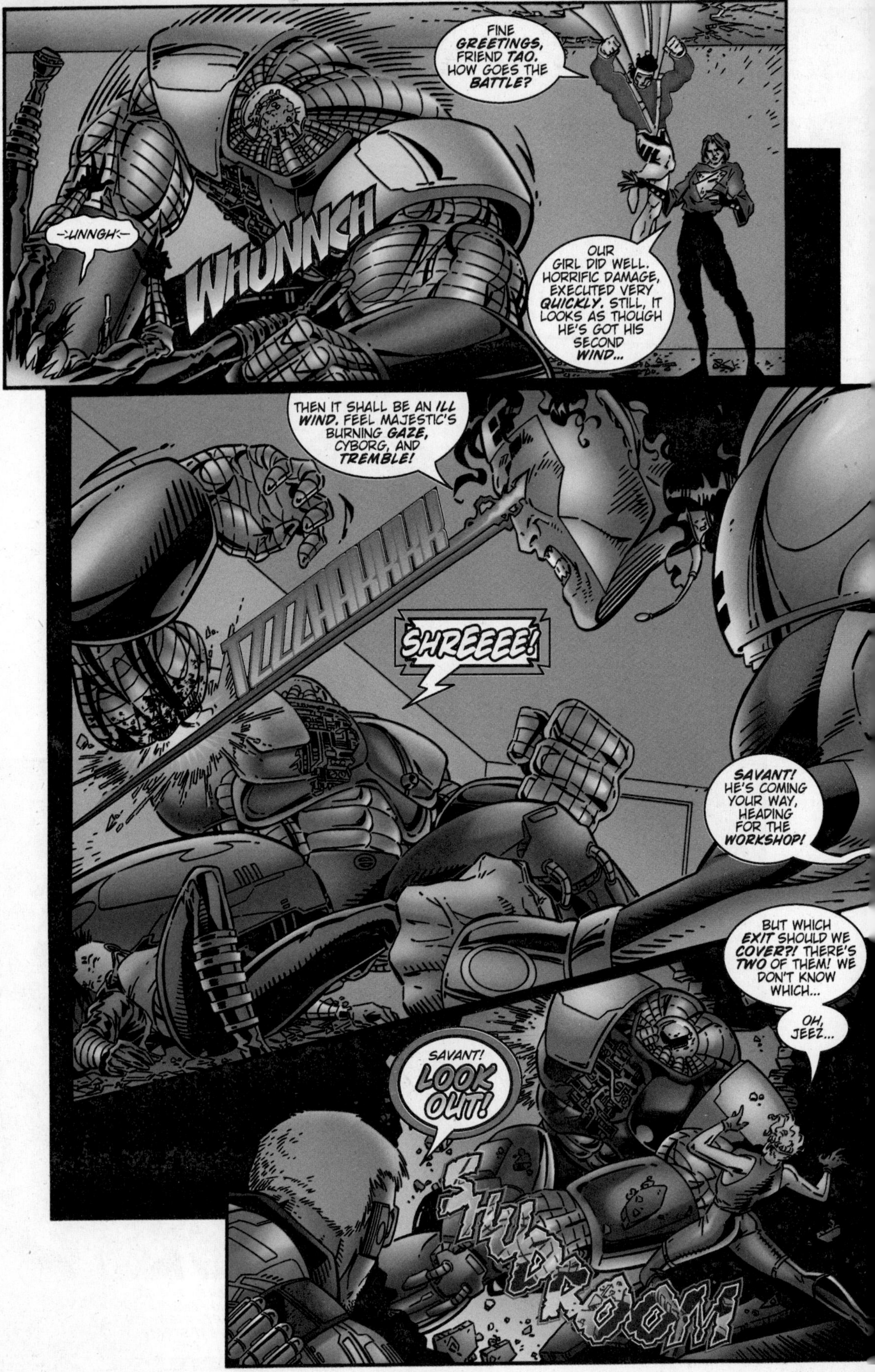
FINE GREETINGS, FRIEND TAO. HOW GOES THE BATTLE?
-UNNGH-
WHUNNCH
OUR GIRL DID WELL. HORRIFIC DAMAGE, EXECUTED VERY QUICKLY. STILL, IT LOOKS AS THOUGH HE'S GOT HIS SECOND WIND...
THEN IT SHALL BE AN ILL WIND. FEEL MAJESTIC'S BURNING GAZE, CYBORG, AND TREMBLE!
SHREEEE!
SAVANT! HE'S COMING YOUR WAY, HEADING FOR THE WORKSHOP!
BUT WHICH EXIT SHOULD WE COVER?! THERE'S TWO OF THEM! WE DON'T KNOW WHICH...
OH, JEEZ...
SAVANT! LOOK OUT!

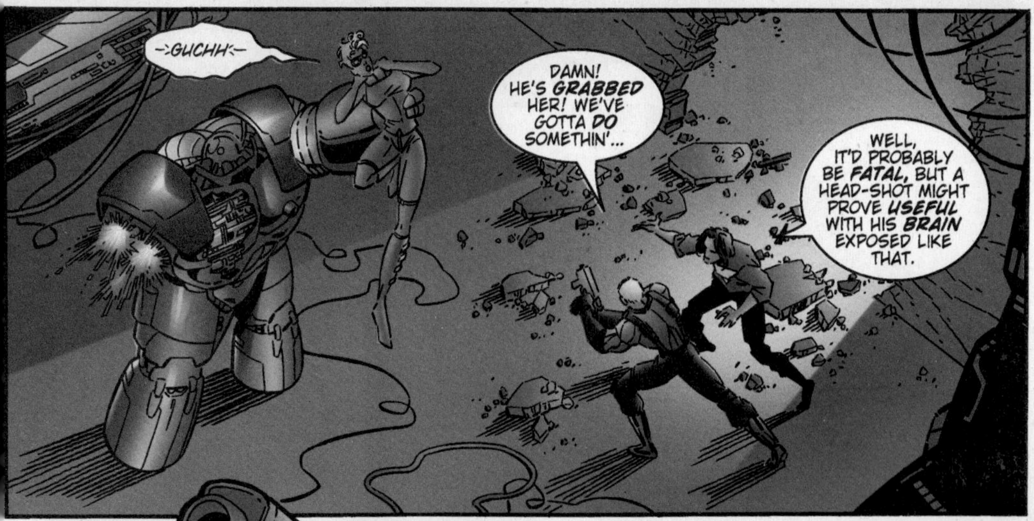
-GUCHH-
DAMN! HE'S GRABBED HER! WE'VE GOTTA DO SOMETHIN'...
WELL, IT'D PROBABLY BE FATAL, BUT A HEAD-SHOT MIGHT PROVE USEFUL WITH HIS BRAIN EXPOSED LIKE THAT.
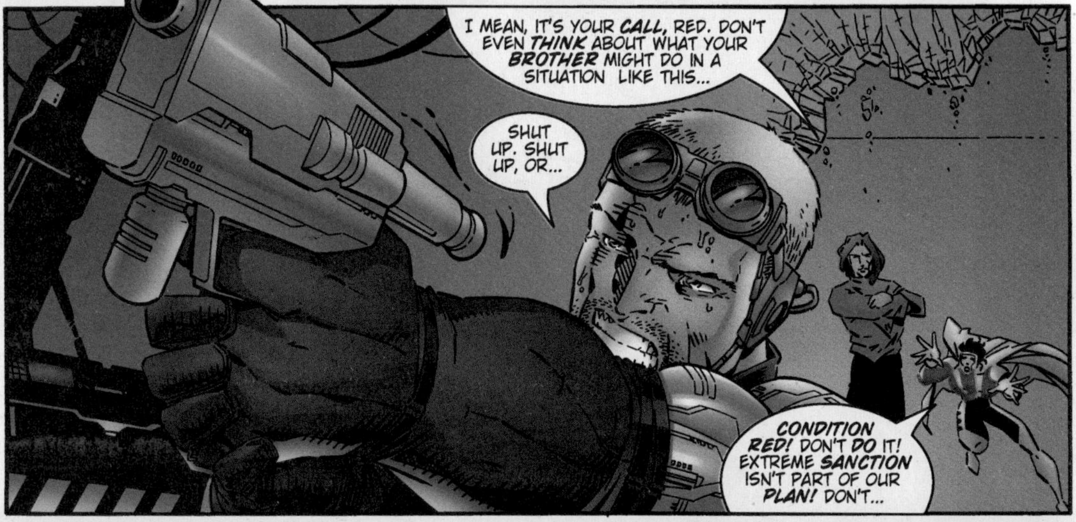
I MEAN, IT'S YOUR CALL, RED. DON'T EVEN THINK ABOUT WHAT YOUR BROTHER MIGHT DO IN A SITUATION LIKE THIS...
SHUT UP. SHUT UP, OR...
CONDITION RED! DON'T DO IT! EXTREME SANCTION ISN'T PART OF OUR PLAN! DON'T...
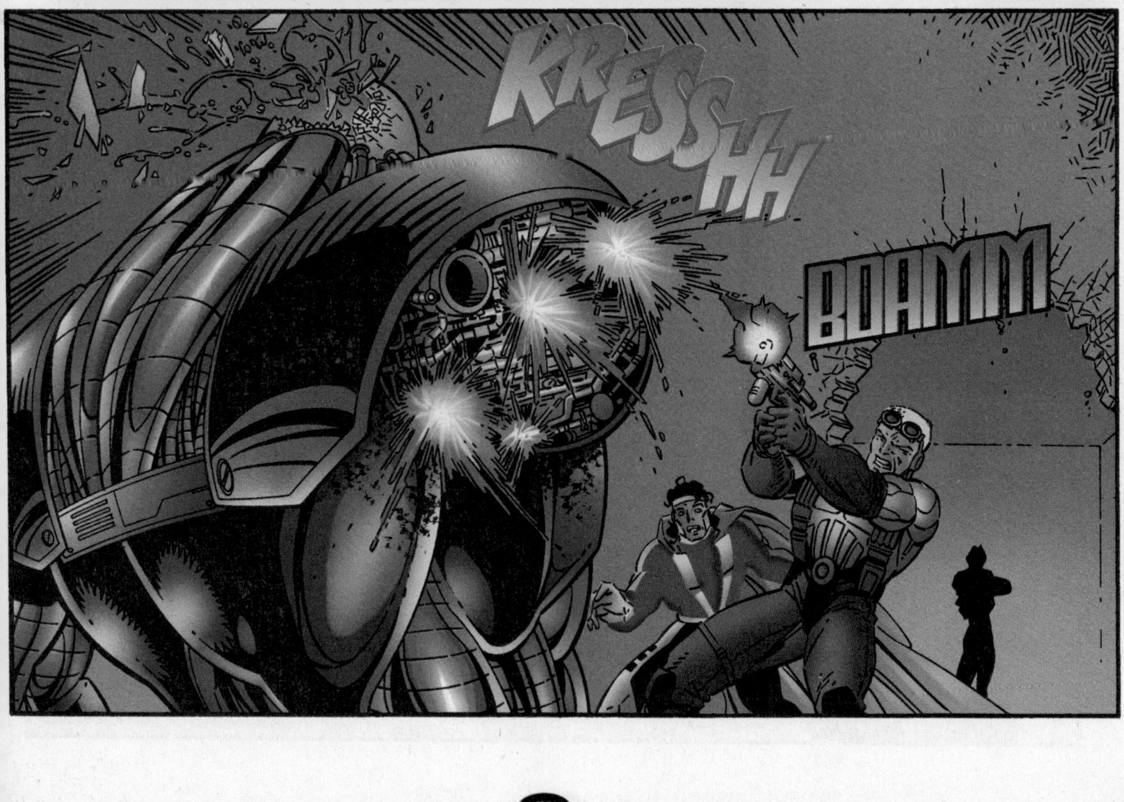
KRESSHH
BOAMM

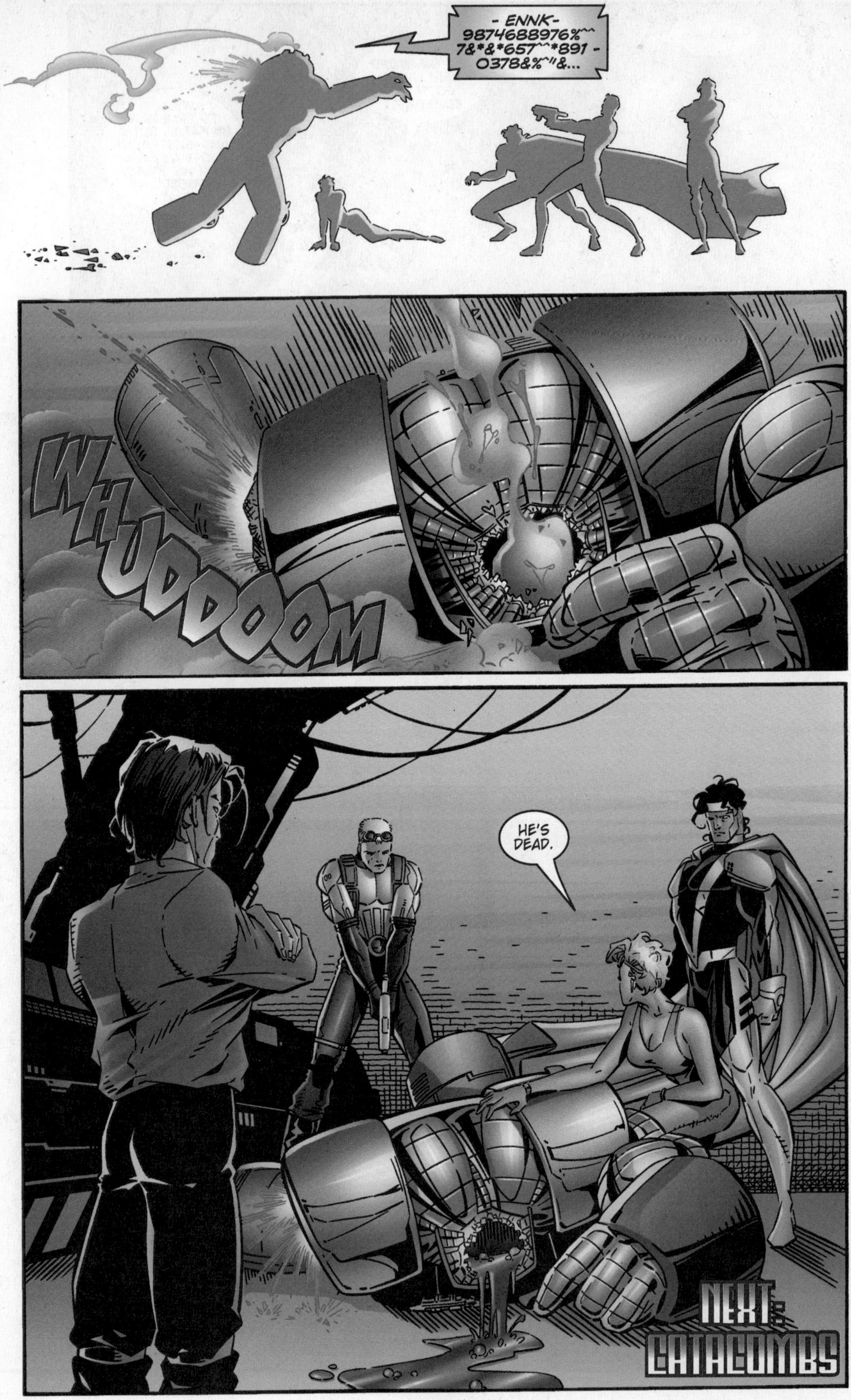
- ENNK- 9874688976%^^ 7&*&*657^^*891 - 0378&%^"&...
WHUDDOOM
HE'S DEAD.
NEXT CATACOMBS

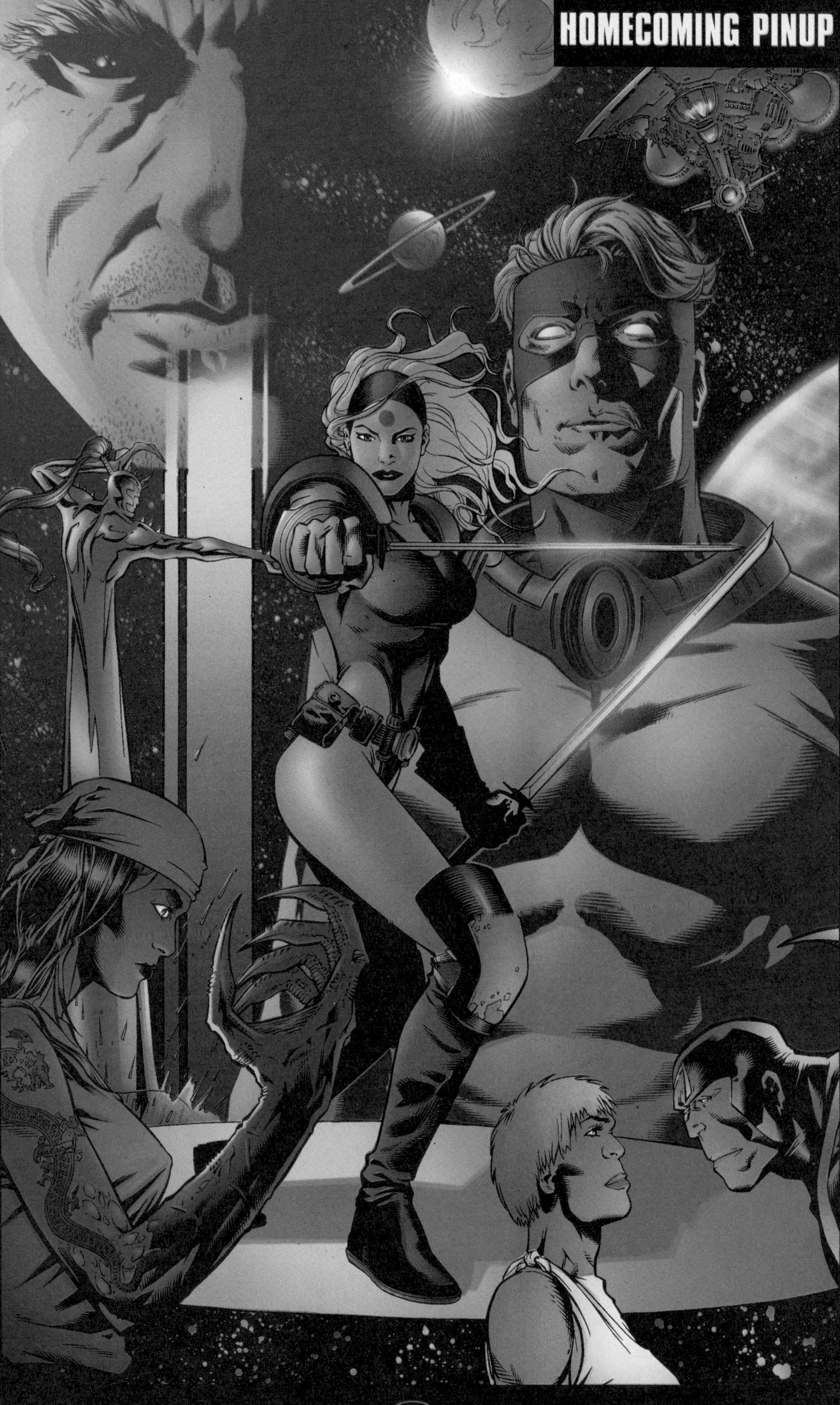
HOMECOMING PINUP

WILDC.A.T.S #24

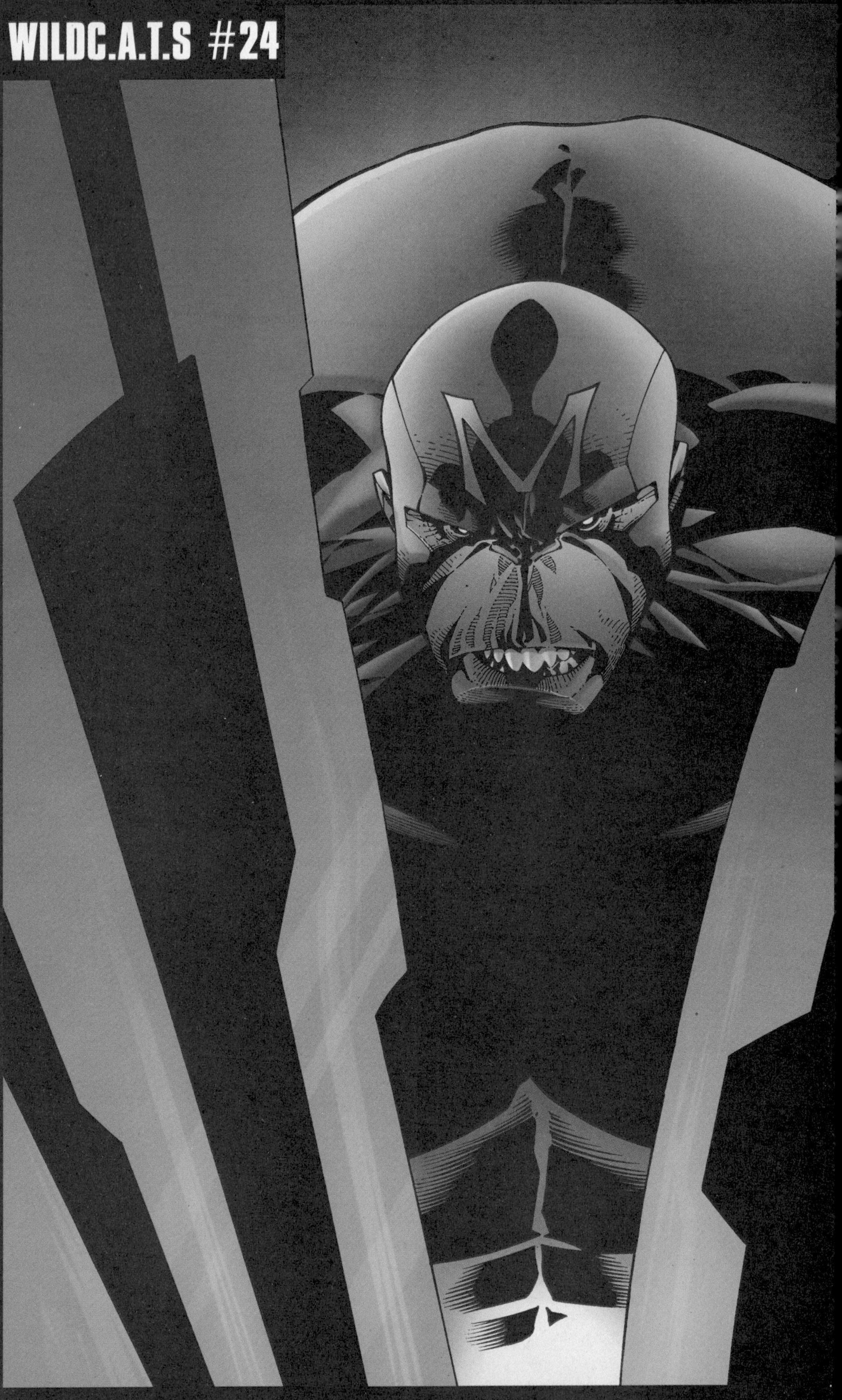

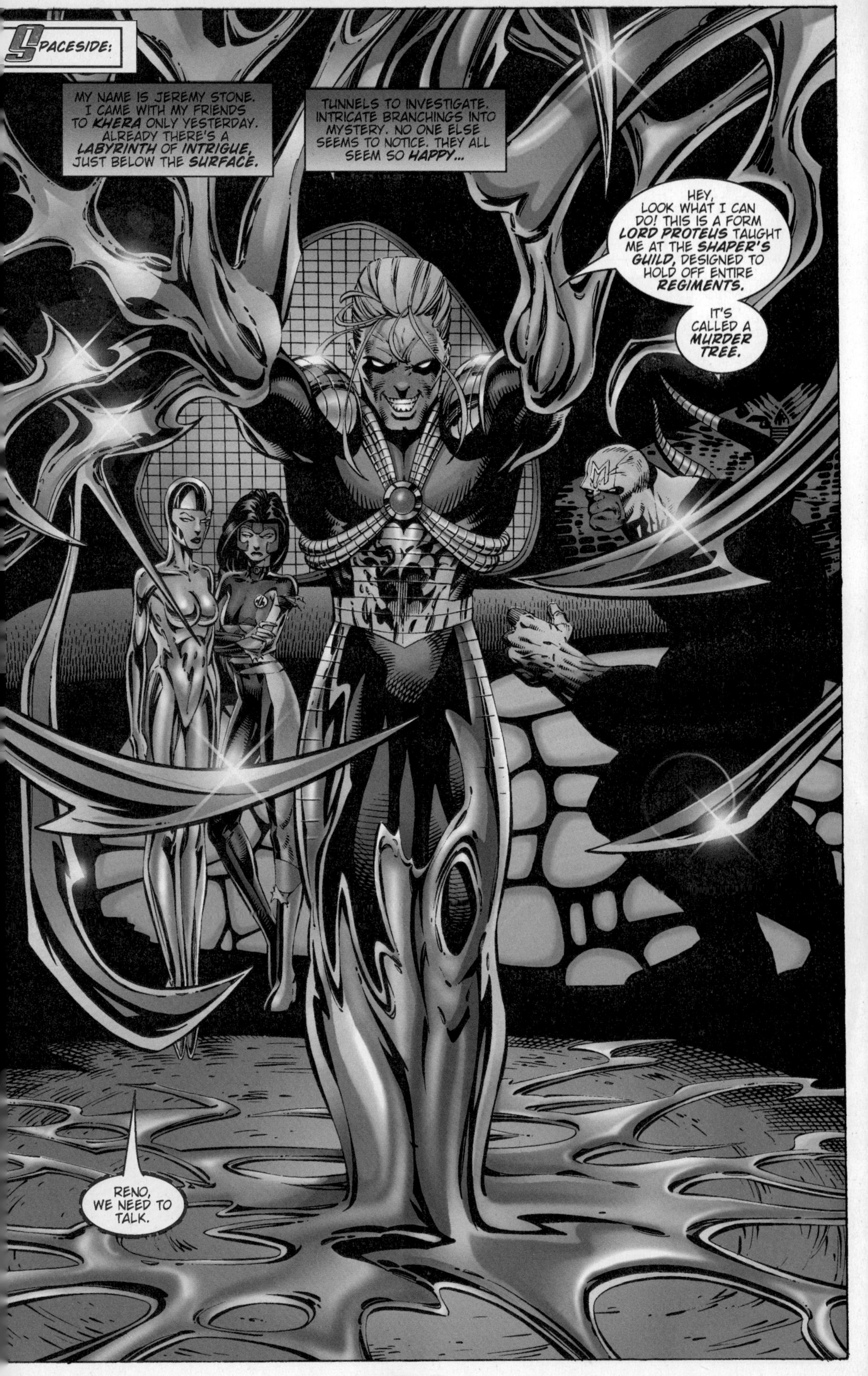
SPACESIDE:
MY NAME IS JEREMY STONE. I CAME WITH MY FRIENDS TO KHERA ONLY YESTERDAY. ALREADY THERE'S A LABYRINTH OF INTRIGUE, JUST BELOW THE SURFACE.
TUNNELS TO INVESTIGATE. INTRICATE BRANCHINGS INTO MYSTERY. NO ONE ELSE SEEMS TO NOTICE. THEY ALL SEEM SO HAPPY...
HEY, LOOK WHAT I CAN DO! THIS IS A FORM LORD PROTEUS TAUGHT ME AT THE SHAPER'S GUILD, DESIGNED TO HOLD OFF ENTIRE REGIMENTS.
IT'S CALLED A MURDER TREE.
RENO, WE NEED TO TALK.

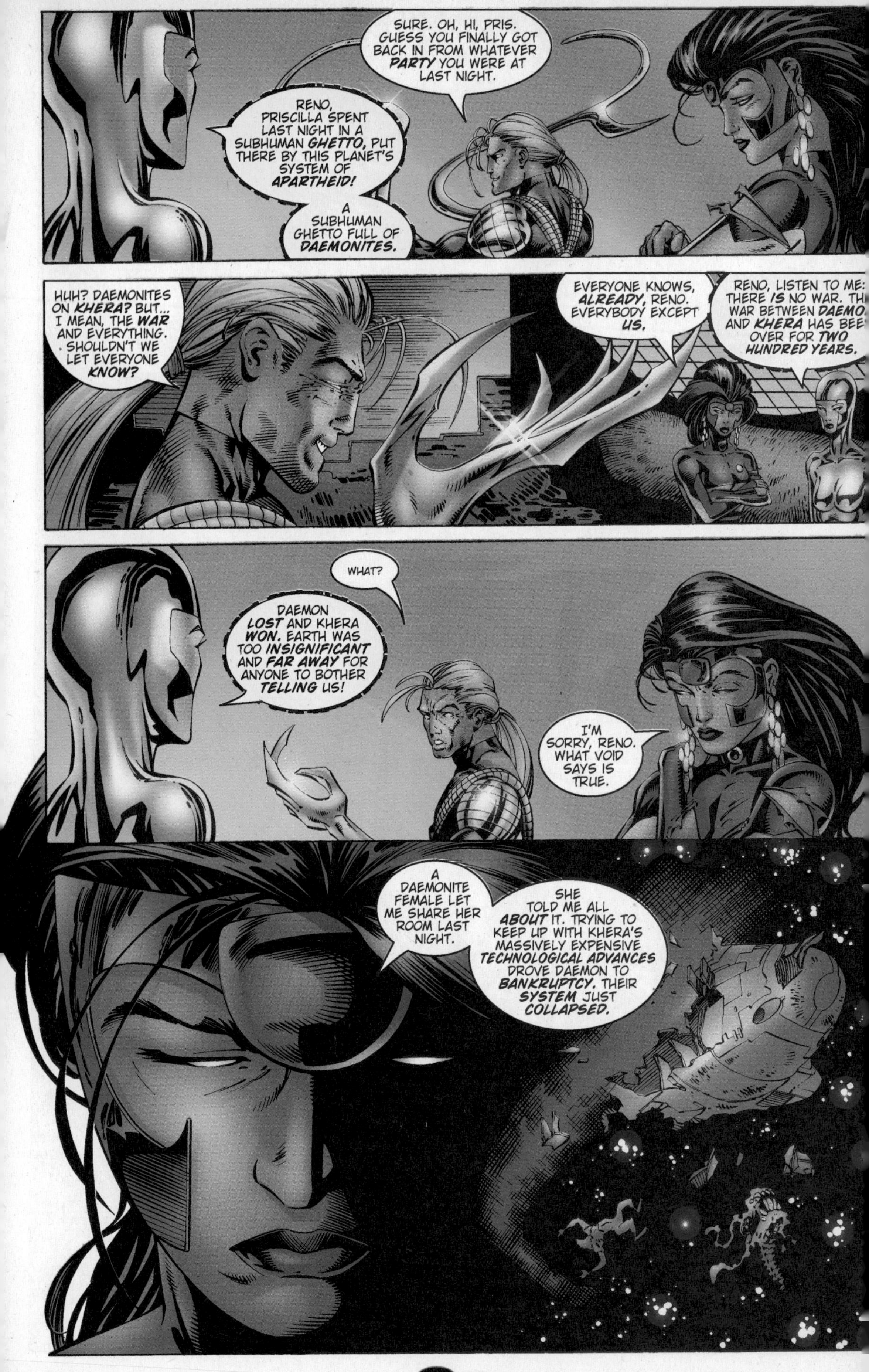
SURE. OH, HI, PRIS. GUESS YOU FINALLY GOT BACK IN FROM WHATEVER PARTY YOU WERE AT LAST NIGHT.
RENO, PRISCILLA SPENT LAST NIGHT IN A SUBHUMAN GHETTO, PUT THERE BY THIS PLANET'S SYSTEM OF APARTHEID!
A SUBHUMAN GHETTO FULL OF DAEMONITES.
HUH? DAEMONITES ON KHERA? BUT... I MEAN, THE WAR AND EVERYTHING. SHOULDN'T WE LET EVERYONE KNOW?
EVERYONE KNOWS, ALREADY, RENO. EVERYBODY EXCEPT US.
RENO, LISTEN TO ME: THERE IS NO WAR. TH WAR BETWEEN DAEMO AND KHERA HAS BEE OVER FOR TWO HUNDRED YEARS.
WHAT?
DAEMON LOST AND KHERA WON. EARTH WAS TOO INSIGNIFICANT AND FAR AWAY FOR ANYONE TO BOTHER TELLING US!
I'M SORRY, RENO. WHAT VOID SAYS IS TRUE.
A DAEMONITE FEMALE LET ME SHARE HER ROOM LAST NIGHT.
SHE TOLD ME ALL ABOUT IT. TRYING TO KEEP UP WITH KHERA'S MASSIVELY EXPENSIVE TECHNOLOGICAL ADVANCES DROVE DAEMON TO BANKRUPTCY. THEIR SYSTEM JUST COLLAPSED.

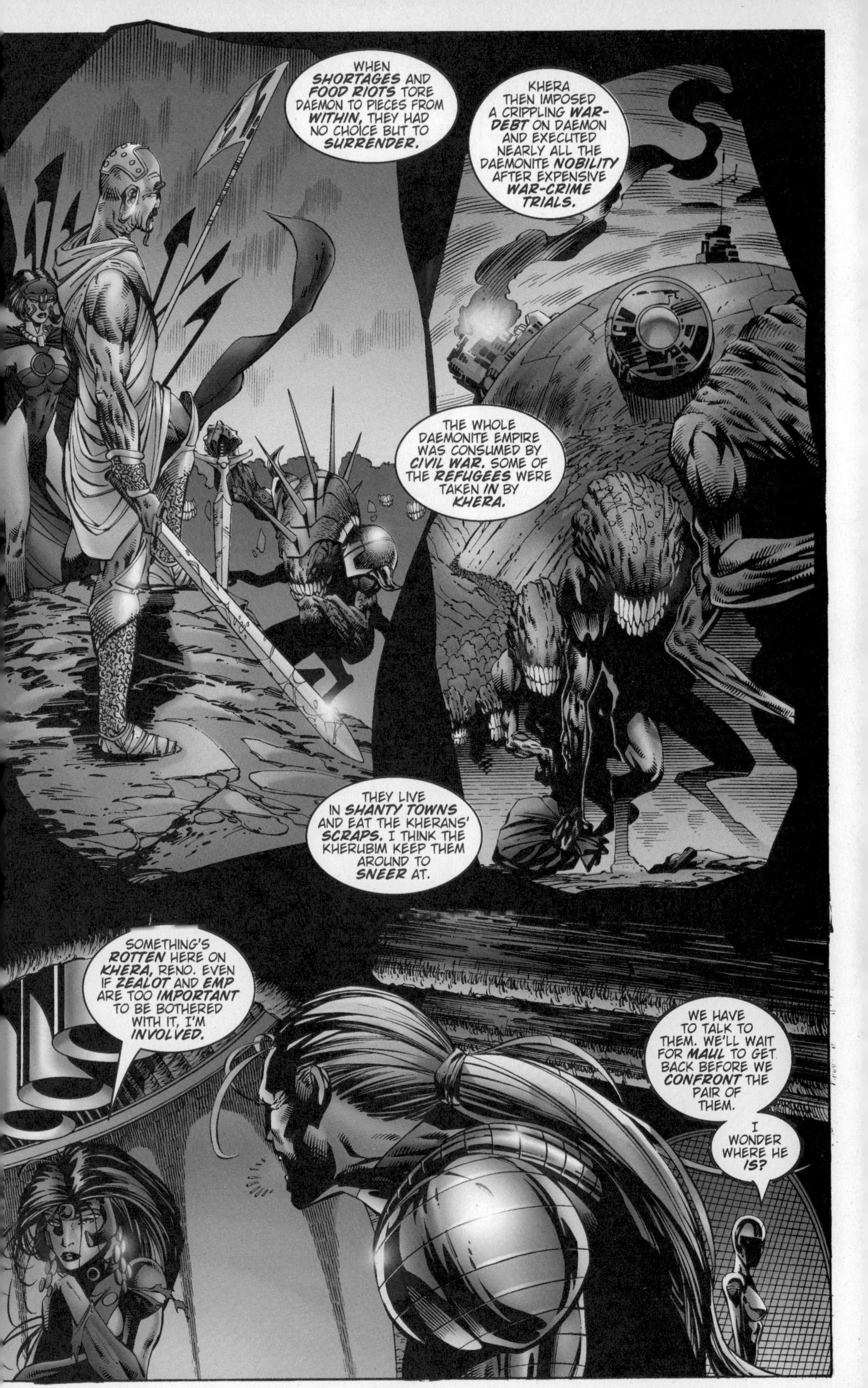

WHEN SHORTAGES AND FOOD RIOTS TORE DAEMON TO PIECES FROM WITHIN, THEY HAD NO CHOICE BUT TO SURRENDER.
KHERA THEN IMPOSED A CRIPPLING WAR-DEBT ON DAEMON AND EXECUTED NEARLY ALL THE DAEMONITE NOBILITY AFTER EXPENSIVE WAR-CRIME TRIALS.
THE WHOLE DAEMONITE EMPIRE WAS CONSUMED BY CIVIL WAR. SOME OF THE REFUGEES WERE TAKEN IN BY KHERA.
THEY LIVE IN SHANTY TOWNS AND EAT THE KHERANS' SCRAPS. I THINK THE KHERUBIM KEEP THEM AROUND TO SNEER AT.
SOMETHING'S ROTTEN HERE ON KHERA, RENO. EVEN IF ZEALOT AND EMP ARE TOO IMPORTANT TO BE BOTHERED WITH IT, I'M INVOLVED.
WE HAVE TO TALK TO THEM. WE'LL WAIT FOR MAUL TO GET BACK BEFORE WE CONFRONT THE PAIR OF THEM.
I WONDER WHERE HE IS?

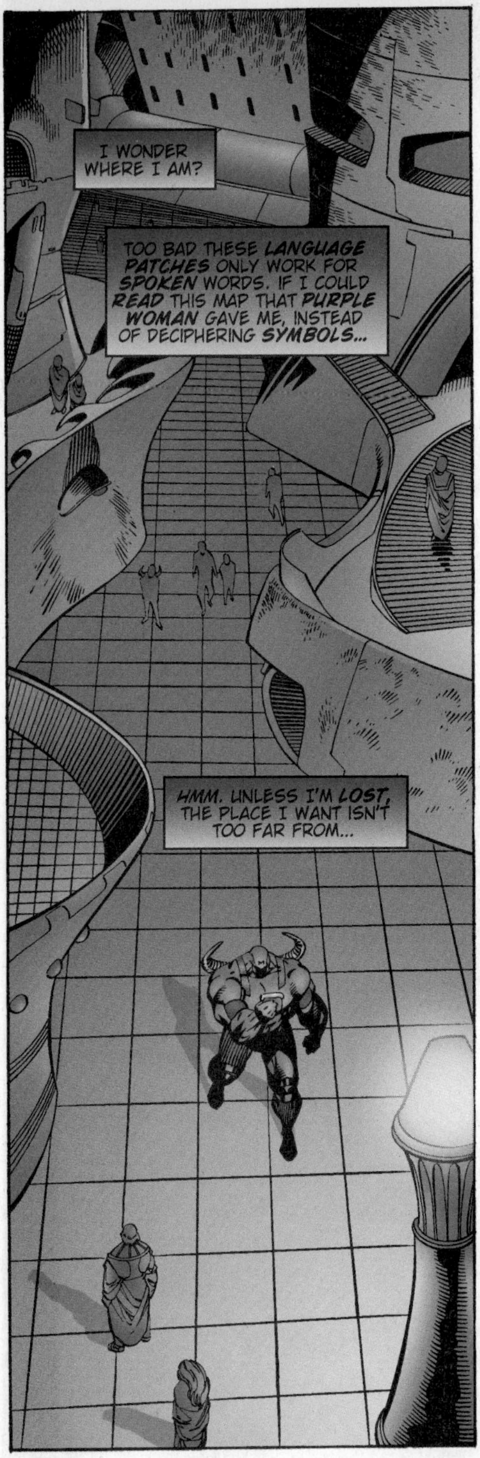
I WONDER WHERE I AM?
TOO BAD THESE LANGUAGE PATCHES ONLY WORK FOR SPOKEN WORDS. IF I COULD READ THIS MAP THAT PURPLE WOMAN GAVE ME, INSTEAD OF DECIPHERING SYMBOLS...
HMM. UNLESS I'M LOST, THE PLACE I WANT ISN'T TOO FAR FROM...
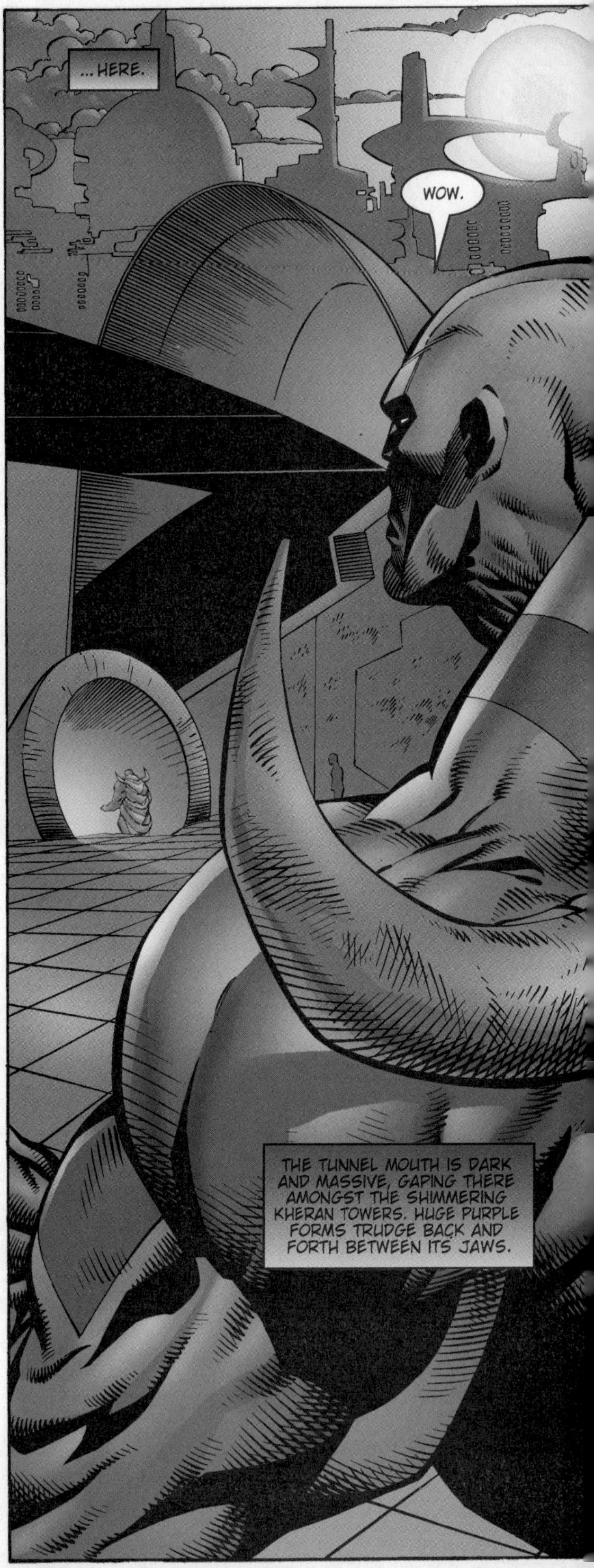
...HERE.
WOW.
THE TUNNEL MOUTH IS DARK AND MASSIVE, GAPING THERE AMONGST THE SHIMMERING KHERAN TOWERS. HUGE PURPLE FORMS TRUDGE BACK AND FORTH BETWEEN ITS JAWS.

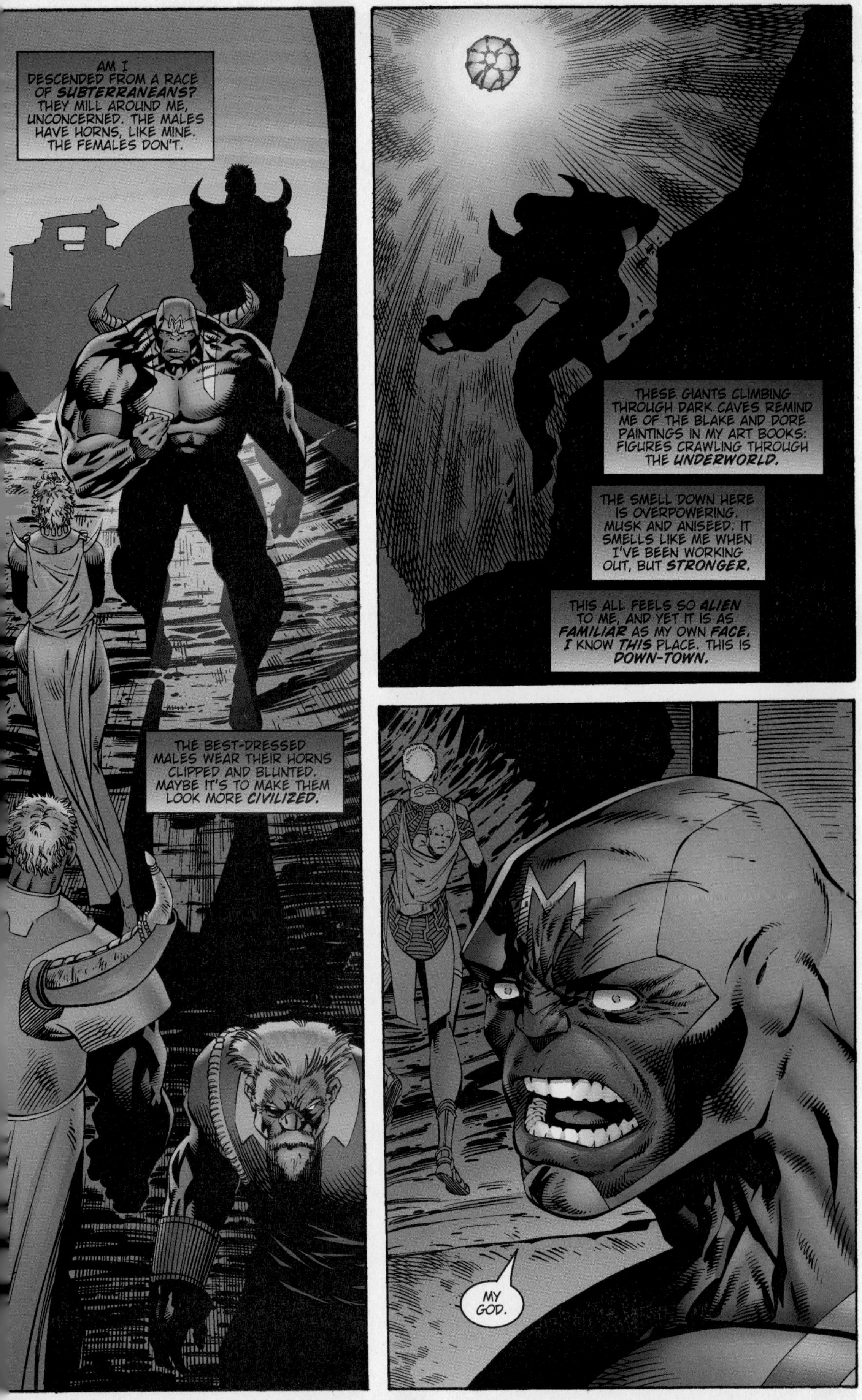
AM I DESCENDED FROM A RACE OF SUBTERRANEANS? THEY MILL AROUND ME, UNCONCERNED. THE MALES HAVE HORNS, LIKE MINE. THE FEMALES DON'T.
THE BEST-DRESSED MALES WEAR THEIR HORNS CLIPPED AND BLUNTED. MAYBE IT'S TO MAKE THEM LOOK MORE CIVILIZED.
THESE GIANTS CLIMBING THROUGH DARK CAVES REMIND ME OF THE BLAKE AND DORE PAINTINGS IN MY ART BOOKS: FIGURES CRAWLING THROUGH THE UNDERWORLD.
THE SMELL DOWN HERE IS OVERPOWERING. MUSK AND ANISEED. IT SMELLS LIKE ME WHEN I'VE BEEN WORKING OUT, BUT STRONGER.
THIS ALL FEELS SO ALIEN TO ME, AND YET IT IS AS FAMILIAR AS MY OWN FACE. I KNOW THIS PLACE. THIS IS DOWN-TOWN.
MY GOD.

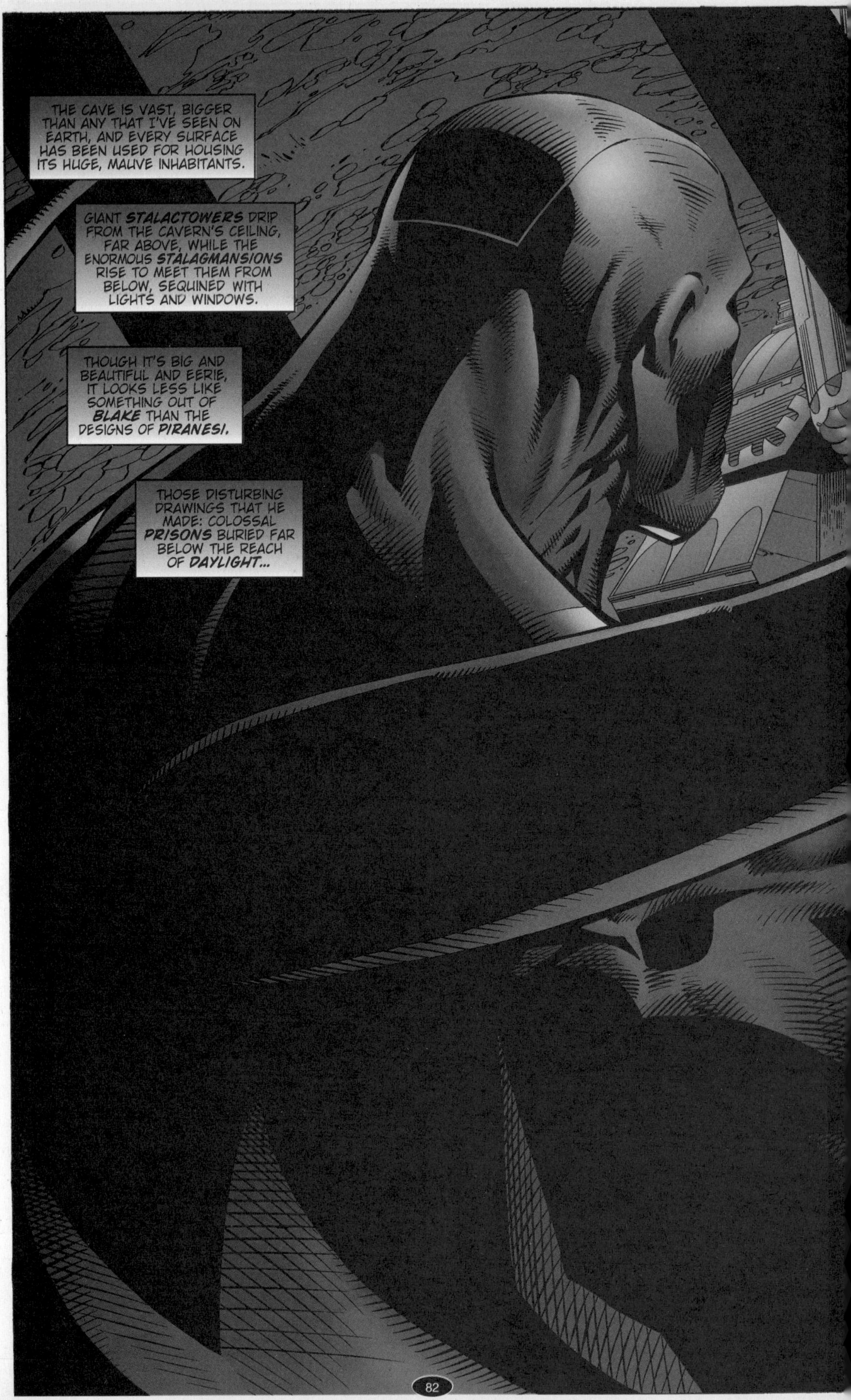
THE CAVE IS VAST, BIGGER THAN ANY THAT I'VE SEEN ON EARTH, AND EVERY SURFACE HAS BEEN USED FOR HOUSING ITS HUGE, MAUVE INHABITANTS.
GIANT STALACTOWERS DRIP FROM THE CAVERN'S CEILING, FAR ABOVE, WHILE THE ENORMOUS STALAGMANSIONS RISE TO MEET THEM FROM BELOW, SEQUINED WITH LIGHTS AND WINDOWS.
THOUGH IT'S BIG AND BEAUTIFUL AND EERIE, IT LOOKS LESS LIKE SOMETHING OUT OF BLAKE THAN THE DESIGNS OF PIRANESI.
THOSE DISTURBING DRAWINGS THAT HE MADE: COLOSSAL PRISONS BURIED FAR BELOW THE REACH OF DAYLIGHT...

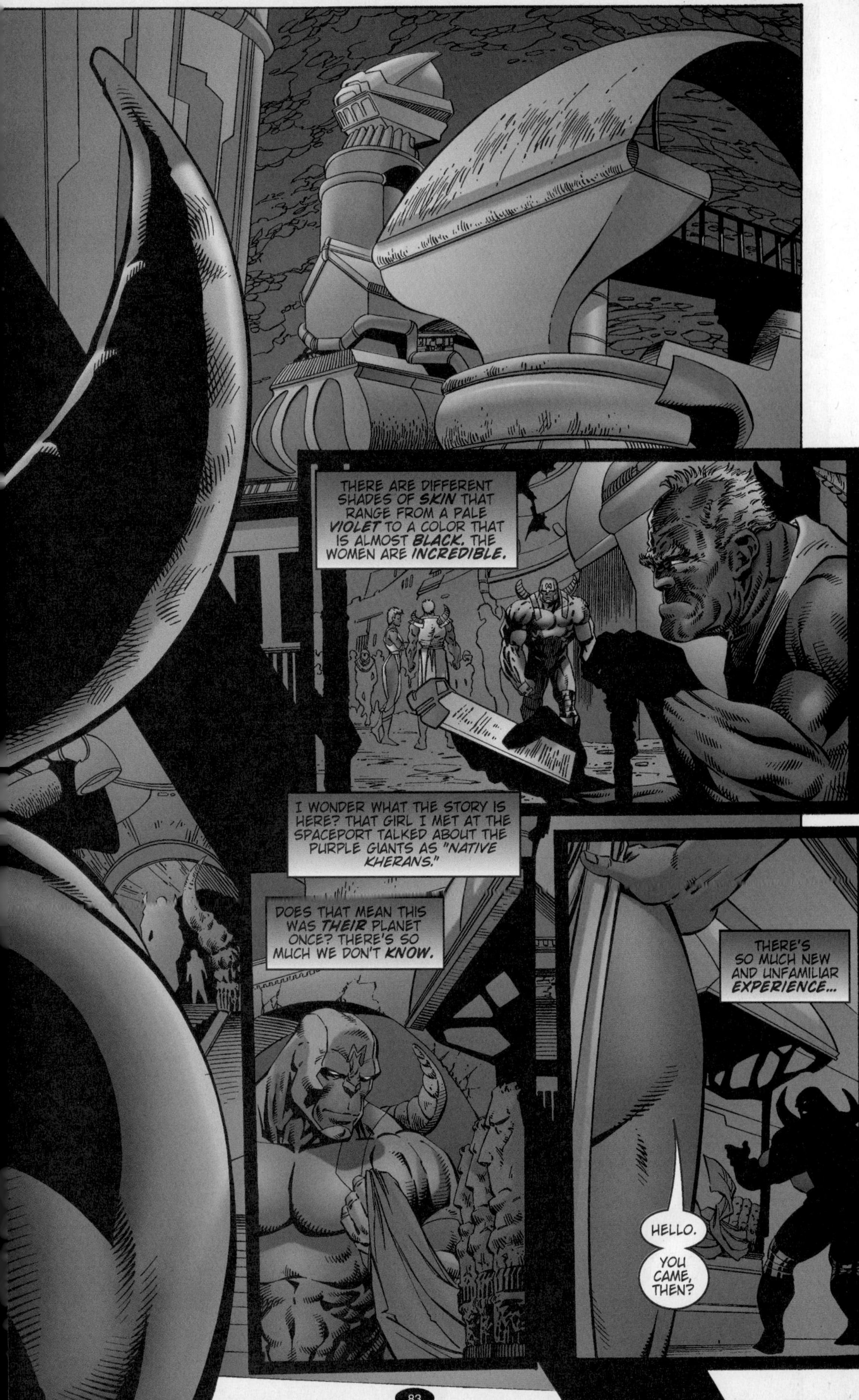
THERE ARE DIFFERENT SHADES OF SKIN THAT RANGE FROM A PALE VIOLET TO A COLOR THAT IS ALMOST BLACK. THE WOMEN ARE INCREDIBLE.
I WONDER WHAT THE STORY IS HERE? THAT GIRL I MET AT THE SPACEPORT TALKED ABOUT THE PURPLE GIANTS AS "NATIVE KHERANS."
DOES THAT MEAN THIS WAS THEIR PLANET ONCE? THERE'S SO MUCH WE DON'T KNOW.
THERE'S SO MUCH NEW AND UNFAMILIAR EXPERIENCE...
HELLO.
YOU CAME, THEN?

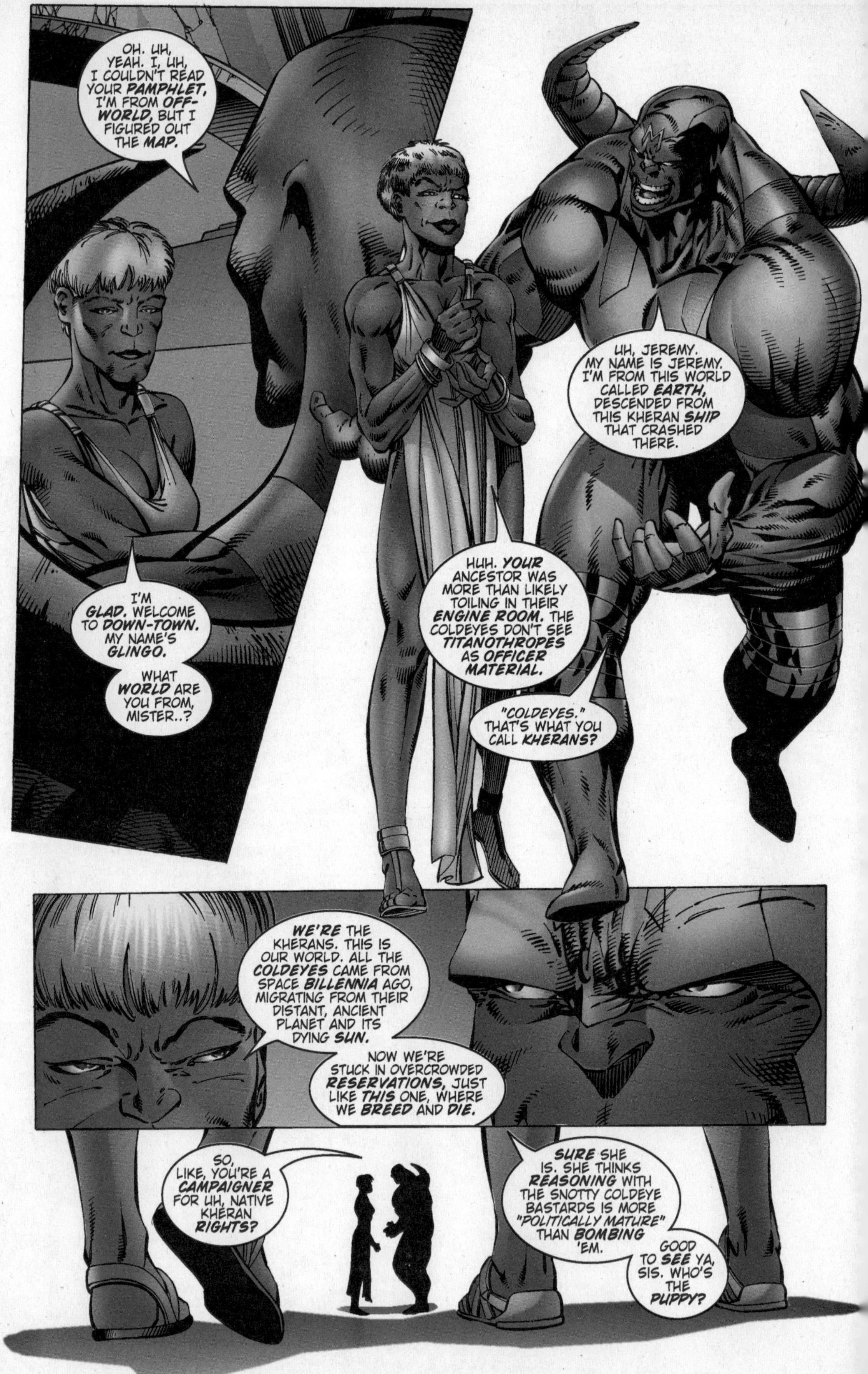

OH. UH, YEAH. I, UH, I COULDN'T READ YOUR PAMPHLET, I'M FROM OFF-WORLD, BUT I FIGURED OUT THE MAP.
I'M GLAD. WELCOME TO DOWN-TOWN. MY NAME'S GLINGO.
WHAT WORLD ARE YOU FROM, MISTER..?
UH, JEREMY. MY NAME IS JEREMY. I'M FROM THIS WORLD CALLED EARTH, DESCENDED FROM THIS KHERAN SHIP THAT CRASHED THERE.
HUH. YOUR ANCESTOR WAS MORE THAN LIKELY TOILING IN THEIR ENGINE ROOM. THE COLDEYES DON'T SEE TITANOTHROPES AS OFFICER MATERIAL.
"COLDEYES." THAT'S WHAT YOU CALL KHERANS?
WE'RE THE KHERANS. THIS IS OUR WORLD. ALL THE COLDEYES CAME FROM SPACE BILLENNIA AGO, MIGRATING FROM THEIR DISTANT, ANCIENT PLANET AND ITS DYING SUN.
NOW WE'RE STUCK IN OVERCROWDED RESERVATIONS, JUST LIKE THIS ONE, WHERE WE BREED AND DIE.
SO, LIKE, YOU'RE A CAMPAIGNER FOR UH, NATIVE KHERAN RIGHTS?
SURE SHE IS. SHE THINKS REASONING WITH THE SNOTTY COLDEYE BASTARDS IS MORE "POLITICALLY MATURE" THAN BOMBING 'EM.
GOOD TO SEE YA, SIS. WHO'S THE PUPPY?

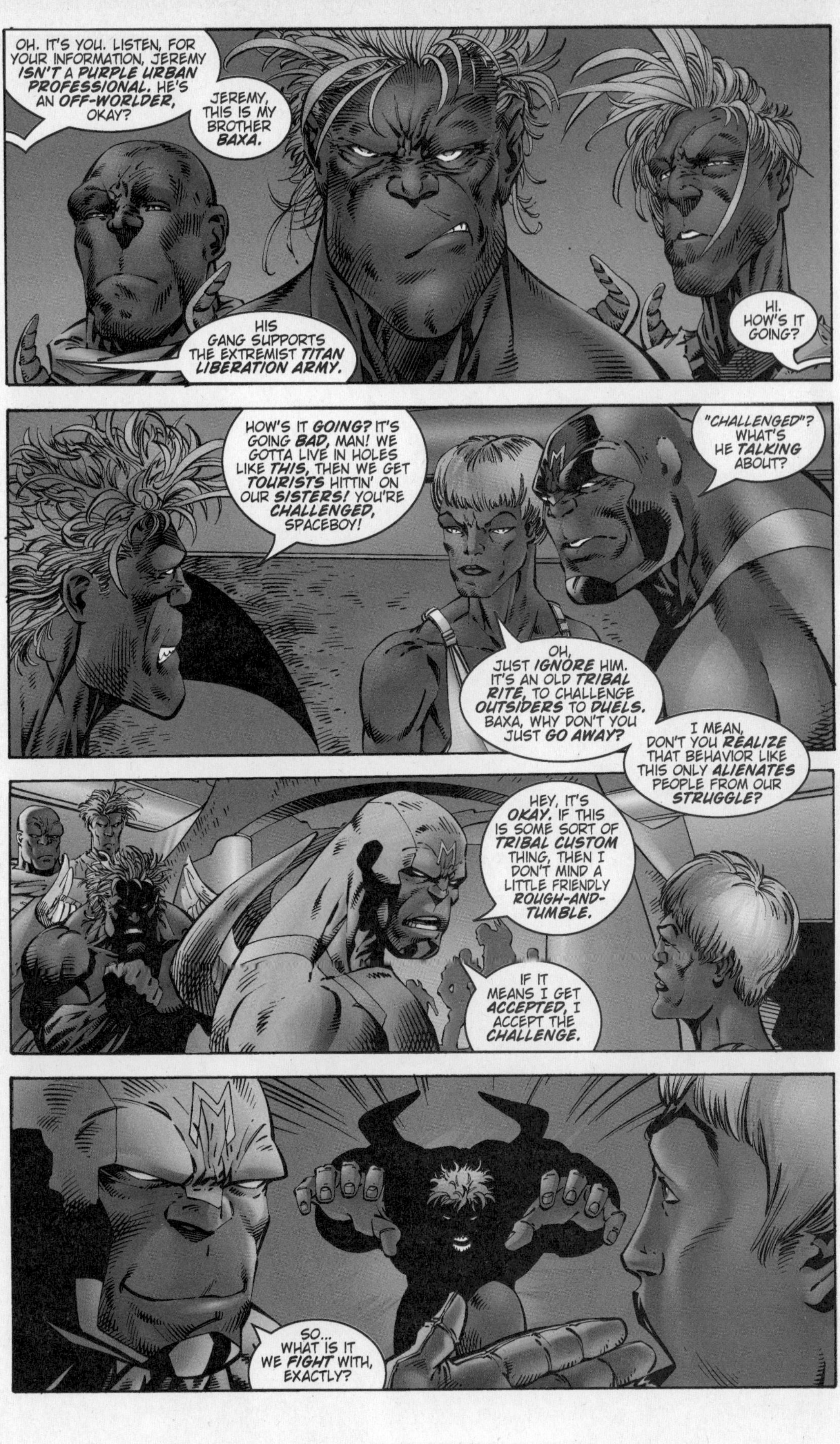
OH. IT'S YOU. LISTEN, FOR YOUR INFORMATION, JEREMY ISN'T A PURPLE URBAN PROFESSIONAL. HE'S AN OFF-WORLDER, OKAY?
JEREMY, THIS IS MY BROTHER BAXA.
HIS GANG SUPPORTS THE EXTREMIST TITAN LIBERATION ARMY.
HI. HOW'S IT GOING?
HOW'S IT GOING? IT'S GOING BAD, MAN! WE GOTTA LIVE IN HOLES LIKE THIS, THEN WE GET TOURISTS HITTIN' ON OUR SISTERS! YOU'RE CHALLENGED, SPACEBOY!
"CHALLENGED"? WHAT'S HE TALKING ABOUT?
OH, JUST IGNORE HIM. IT'S AN OLD TRIBAL RITE, TO CHALLENGE OUTSIDERS TO DUELS. BAXA, WHY DON'T YOU JUST GO AWAY?
I MEAN, DON'T YOU REALIZE THAT BEHAVIOR LIKE THIS ONLY ALIENATES PEOPLE FROM OUR STRUGGLE?
HEY, IT'S OKAY. IF THIS IS SOME SORT OF TRIBAL CUSTOM THING, THEN I DON'T MIND A LITTLE FRIENDLY ROUGH-AND-TUMBLE.
IF IT MEANS I GET ACCEPTED, I ACCEPT THE CHALLENGE.
SO... WHAT IS IT WE FIGHT WITH, EXACTLY?

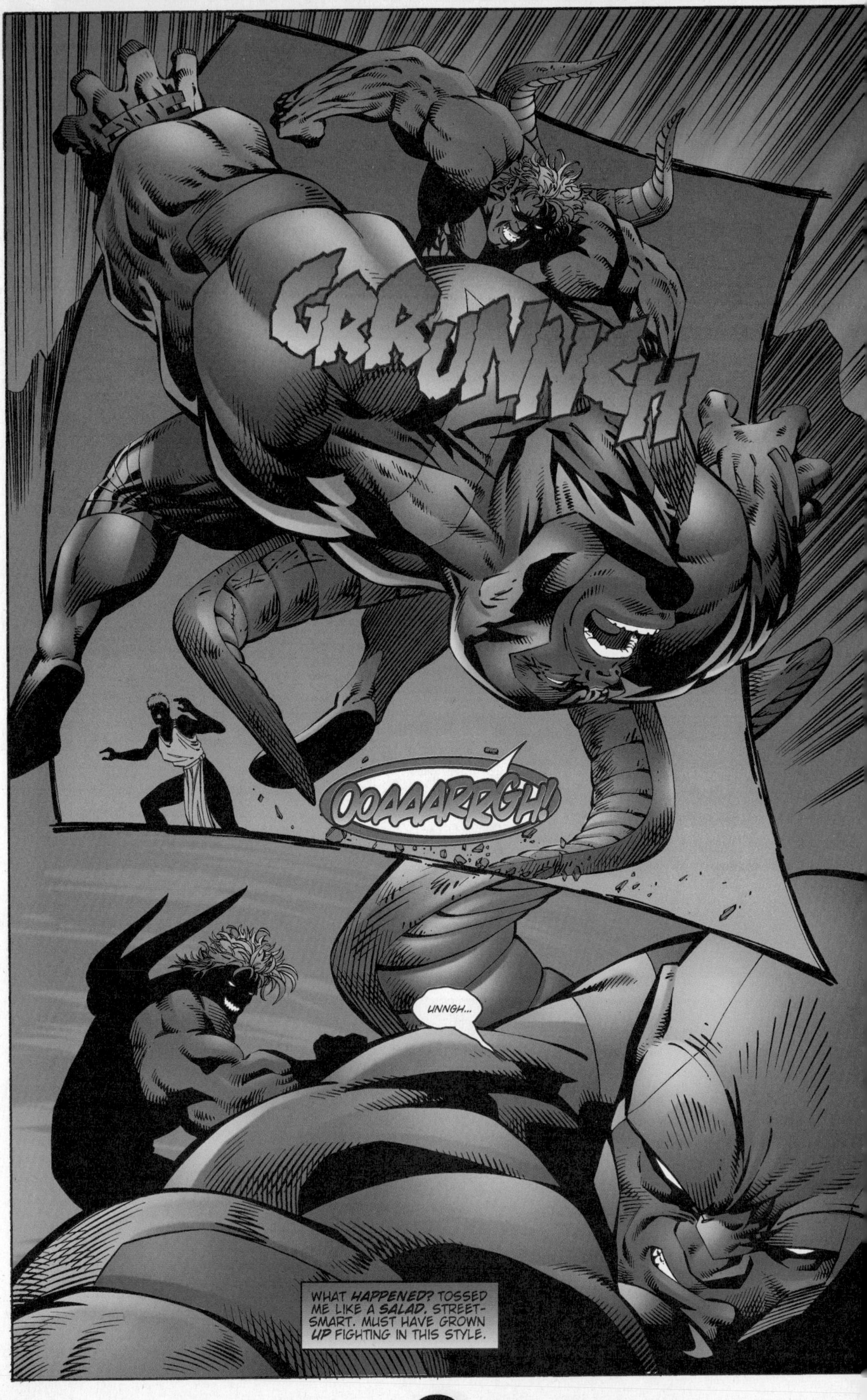
GRRUNNCH
OOAAARRRGH!
UNNGH...
WHAT HAPPENED? TOSSED ME LIKE A SALAD. STREET-SMART. MUST HAVE GROWN UP FIGHTING IN THIS STYLE.

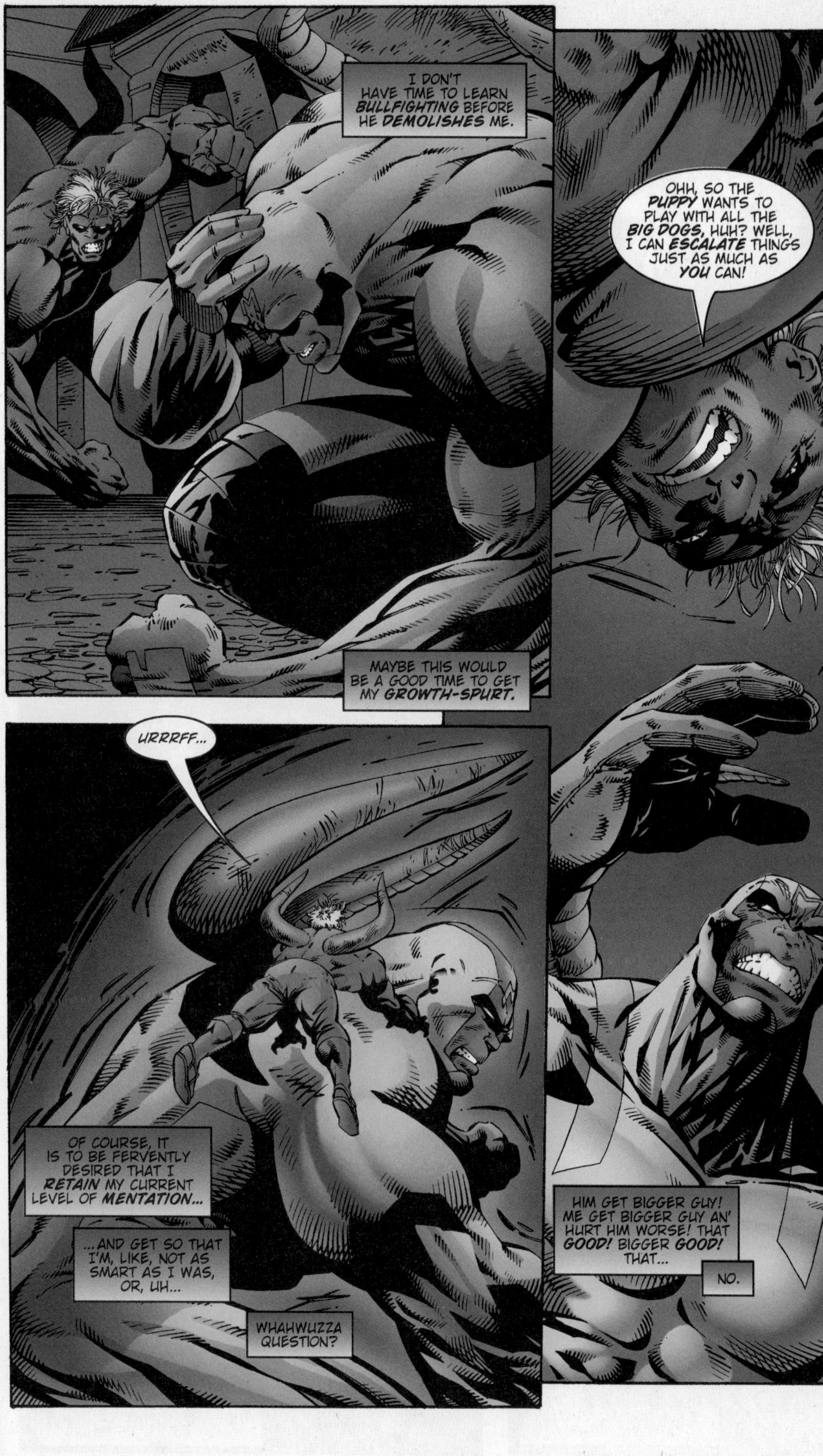

I DON'T HAVE TIME TO LEARN **BULLFIGHTING** BEFORE HE **DEMOLISHES** ME.
MAYBE THIS WOULD BE A GOOD TIME TO GET MY **GROWTH-SPURT.**
OHH, SO THE **PUPPY** WANTS TO PLAY WITH ALL THE **BIG DOGS**, HUH? WELL, I CAN **ESCALATE** THINGS JUST AS MUCH AS **YOU** CAN!
URRRFF...
OF COURSE, IT IS TO BE FERVENTLY DESIRED THAT I **RETAIN** MY CURRENT LEVEL OF **MENTATION...**
...AND GET SO THAT I'M, LIKE, NOT AS SMART AS I WAS, OR, UH...
WHAHWUZZA QUESTION?
HIM GET BIGGER GUY! ME GET BIGGER GUY AN' HURT HIM WORSE! THAT **GOOD!** BIGGER **GOOD!** THAT...
NO.

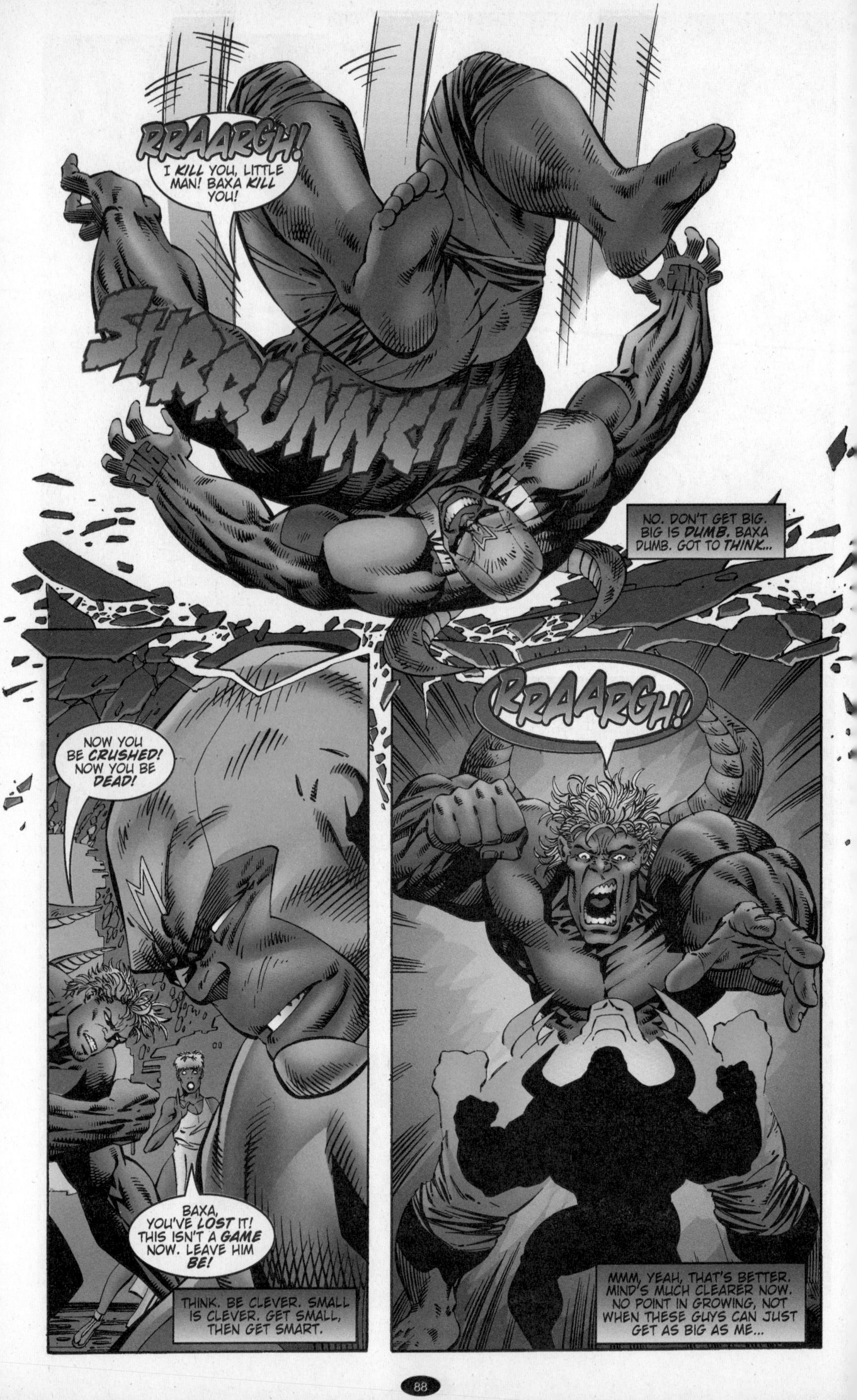
RRAARGH! I KILL YOU, LITTLE MAN! BAXA KILL YOU!
SHRRUNNCH!
NO. DON'T GET BIG. BIG IS DUMB. BAXA DUMB. GOT TO THINK...
NOW YOU BE CRUSHED! NOW YOU BE DEAD!
BAXA, YOU'VE LOST IT! THIS ISN'T A GAME NOW. LEAVE HIM BE!
THINK. BE CLEVER. SMALL IS CLEVER. GET SMALL, THEN GET SMART.
RRAARGH!
MMM, YEAH, THAT'S BETTER. MIND'S MUCH CLEARER NOW. NO POINT IN GROWING, NOT WHEN THESE GUYS CAN JUST GET AS BIG AS ME...

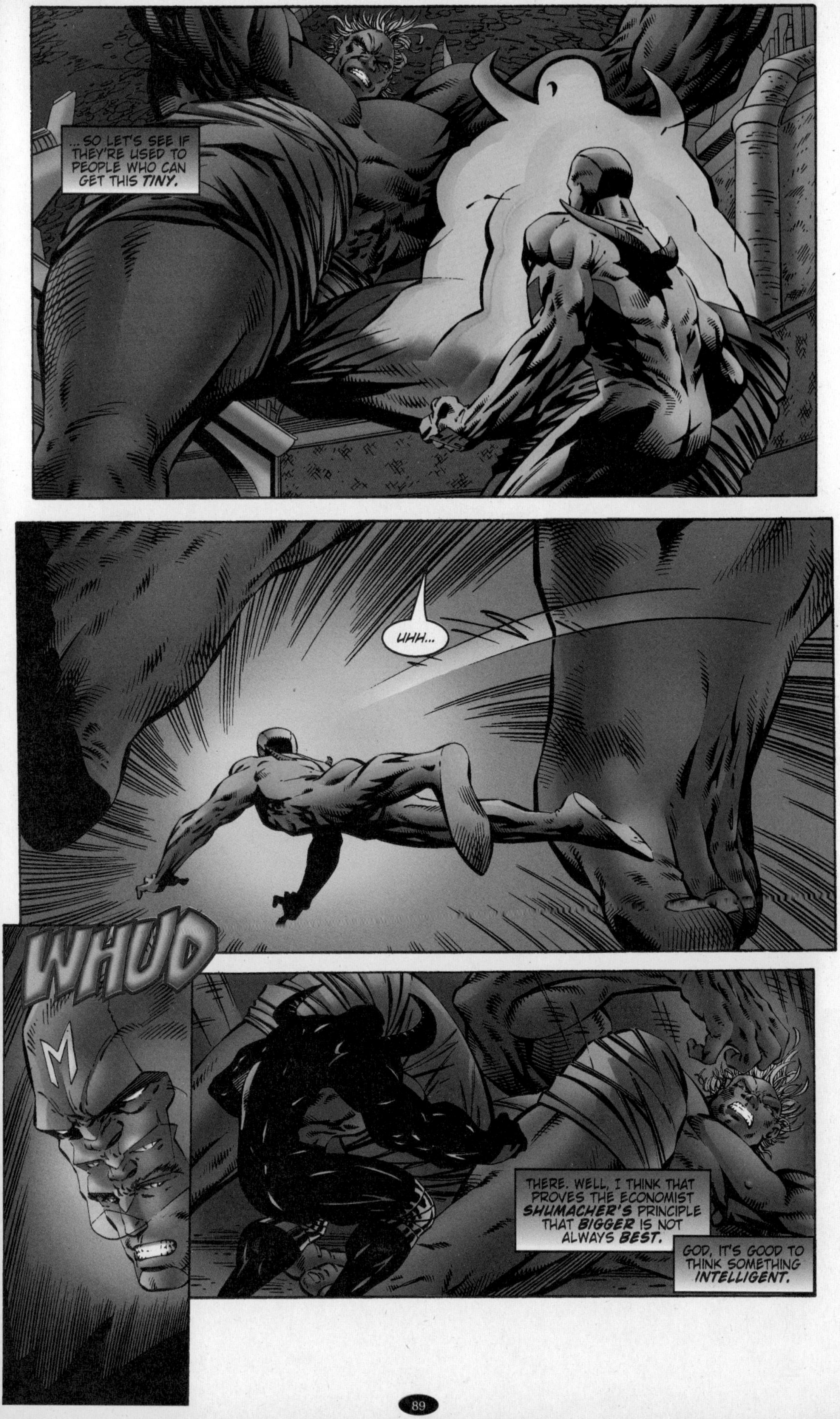
...SO LET'S SEE IF THEY'RE USED TO PEOPLE WHO CAN GET THIS *TINY.*
UHH...
WHUD
THERE. WELL, I THINK THAT PROVES THE ECONOMIST **SHUMACHER'S** PRINCIPLE THAT **BIGGER** IS NOT ALWAYS **BEST.**
GOD, IT'S GOOD TO THINK SOMETHING *INTELLIGENT.*

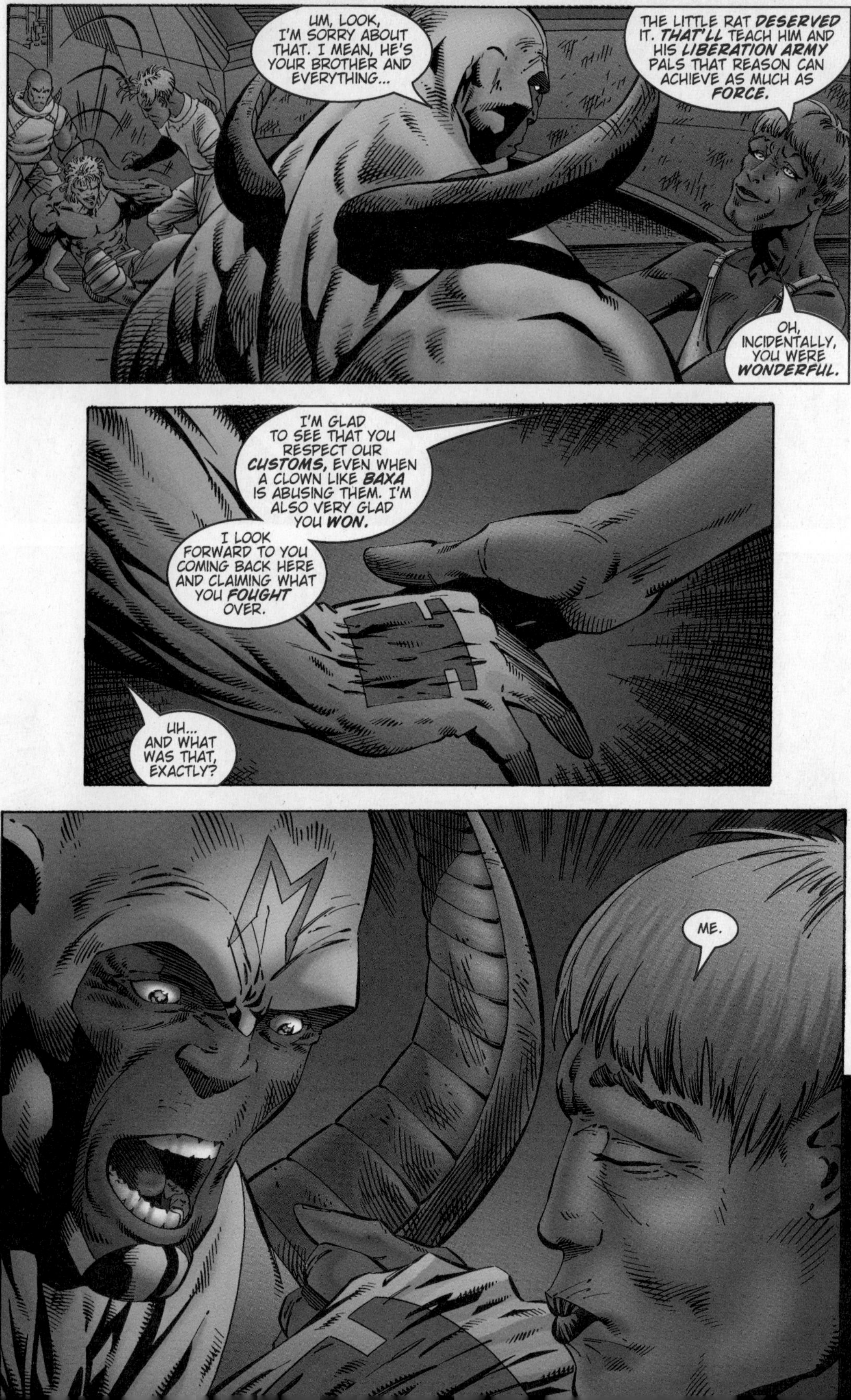
UM, LOOK, I'M SORRY ABOUT THAT. I MEAN, HE'S YOUR BROTHER AND EVERYTHING...
THE LITTLE RAT DESERVED IT. THAT'LL TEACH HIM AND HIS LIBERATION ARMY PALS THAT REASON CAN ACHIEVE AS MUCH AS FORCE.
OH, INCIDENTALLY, YOU WERE WONDERFUL.
I'M GLAD TO SEE THAT YOU RESPECT OUR CUSTOMS, EVEN WHEN A CLOWN LIKE BAXA IS ABUSING THEM. I'M ALSO VERY GLAD YOU WON.
I LOOK FORWARD TO YOU COMING BACK HERE AND CLAIMING WHAT YOU FOUGHT OVER.
UH... AND WHAT WAS THAT, EXACTLY?
ME.

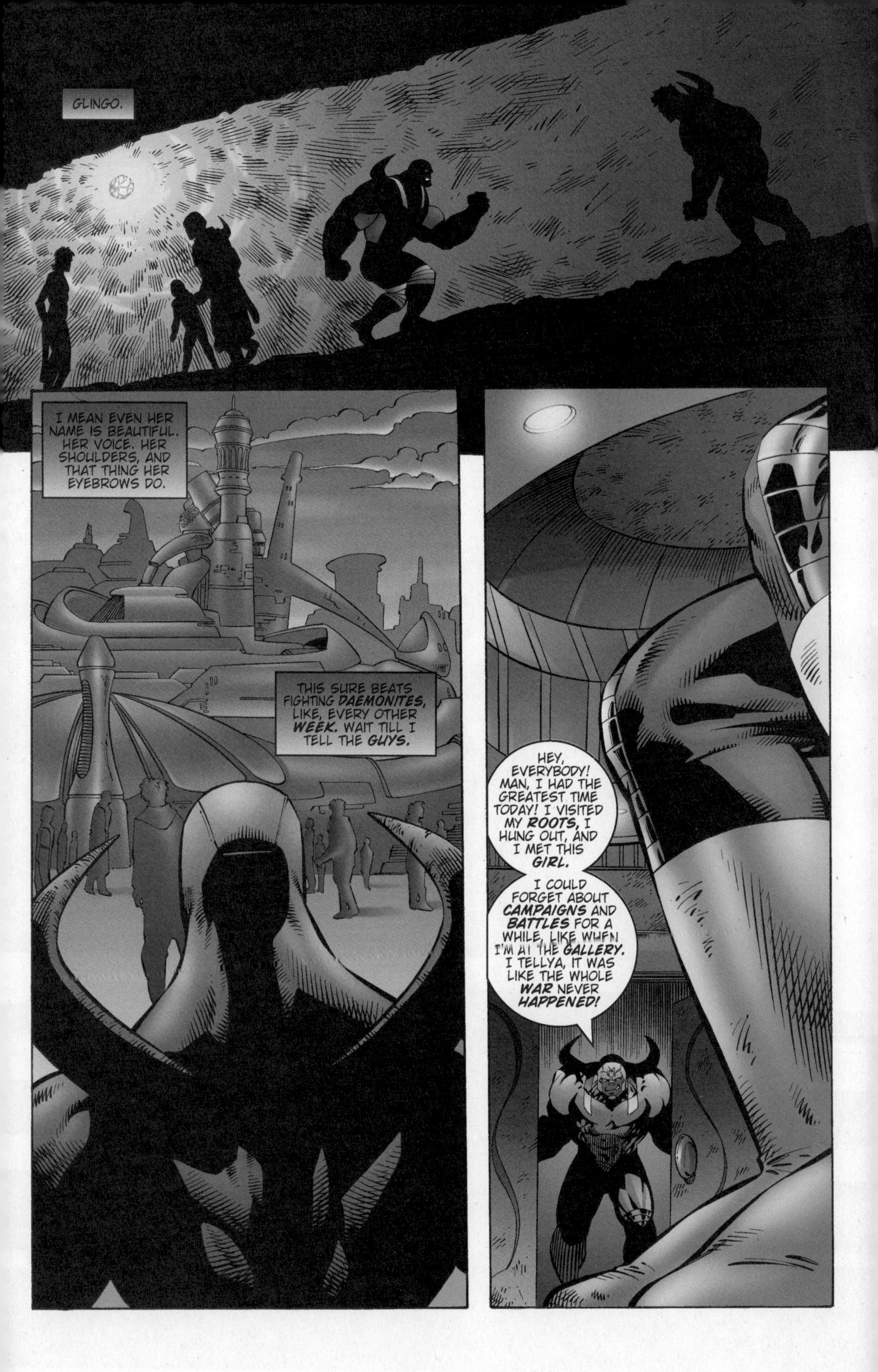
GLINGO.
I MEAN EVEN HER NAME IS BEAUTIFUL. HER VOICE. HER SHOULDERS, AND THAT THING HER EYEBROWS DO.
THIS SURE BEATS FIGHTING DAEMONITES, LIKE, EVERY OTHER WEEK. WAIT TILL I TELL THE GUYS.
HEY, EVERYBODY! MAN, I HAD THE GREATEST TIME TODAY! I VISITED MY ROOTS, I HUNG OUT, AND I MET THIS GIRL.
I COULD FORGET ABOUT CAMPAIGNS AND BATTLES FOR A WHILE, LIKE WHEN I'M AT THE GALLERY. I TELLYA, IT WAS LIKE THE WHOLE WAR NEVER HAPPENED!

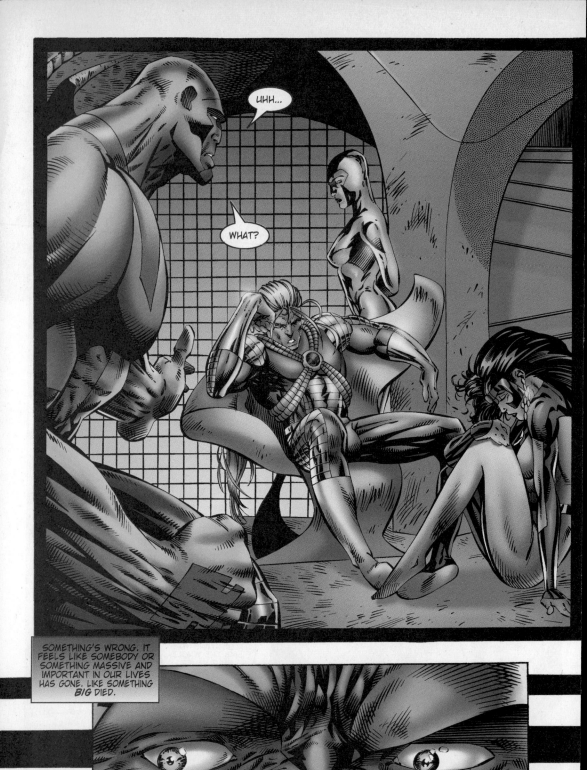

UHH...

WHAT?

SOMETHING'S WRONG. IT FEELS LIKE SOMEBODY OR SOMETHING MASSIVE AND IMPORTANT IN OUR LIVES HAS GONE. LIKE SOMETHING *BIG* DIED.

IT FEELS LIKE A *FUNERAL.*

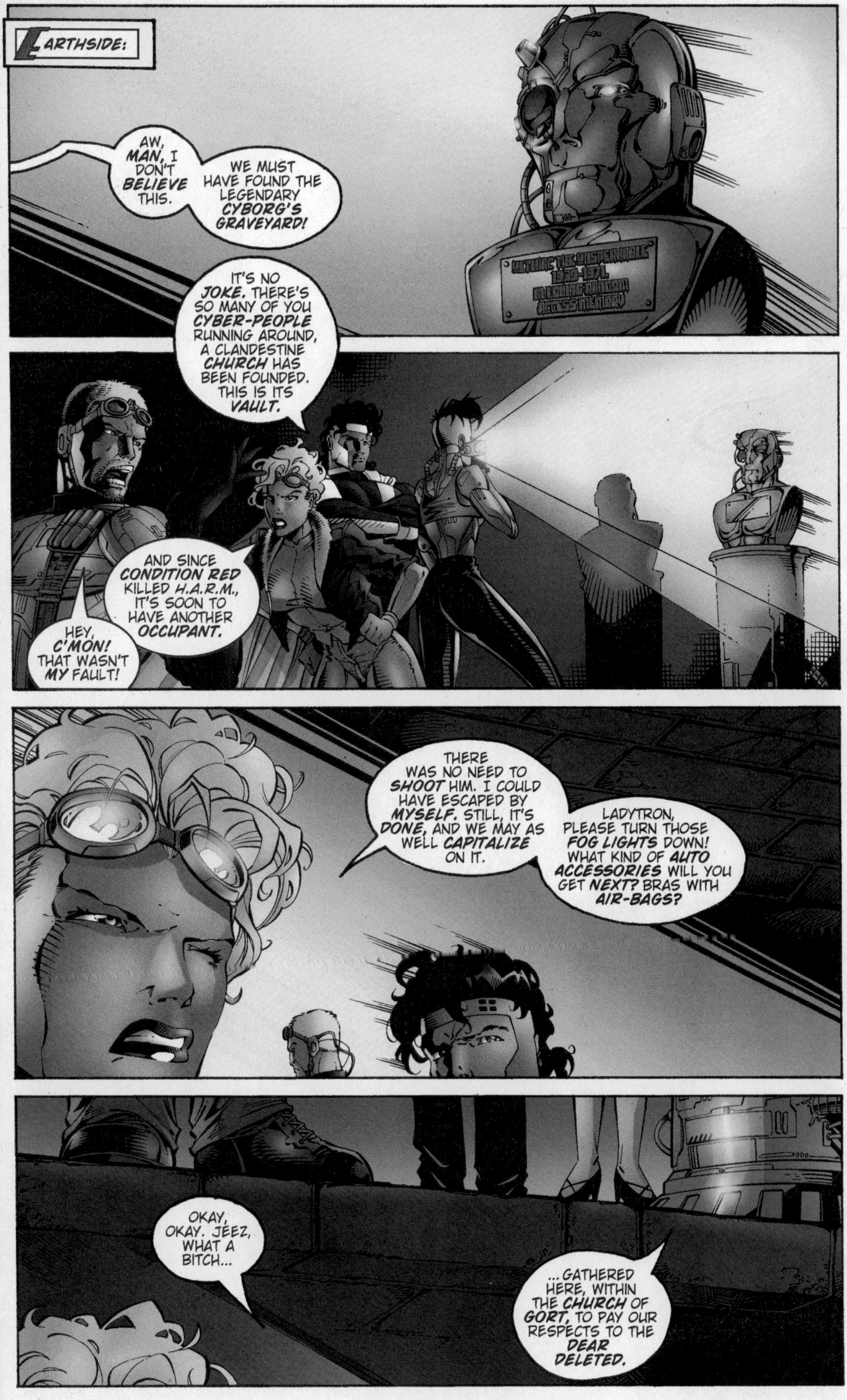
EARTHSIDE:
AW, MAN, I DON'T BELIEVE THIS.
WE MUST HAVE FOUND THE LEGENDARY CYBORG'S GRAVEYARD!
1939-1971
IN LOVING RANDOM
ACCESS MEMORY
IT'S NO JOKE. THERE'S SO MANY OF YOU CYBER-PEOPLE RUNNING AROUND, A CLANDESTINE CHURCH HAS BEEN FOUNDED. THIS IS ITS VAULT.
AND SINCE CONDITION RED KILLED H.A.R.M., IT'S SOON TO HAVE ANOTHER OCCUPANT.
HEY, C'MON! THAT WASN'T MY FAULT!
THERE WAS NO NEED TO SHOOT HIM. I COULD HAVE ESCAPED BY MYSELF. STILL, IT'S DONE, AND WE MAY AS WELL CAPITALIZE ON IT.
LADYTRON, PLEASE TURN THOSE FOG LIGHTS DOWN! WHAT KIND OF AUTO ACCESSORIES WILL YOU GET NEXT? BRAS WITH AIR-BAGS?
OKAY, OKAY. JEEZ, WHAT A BITCH...
...GATHERED HERE, WITHIN THE CHURCH OF GORT, TO PAY OUR RESPECTS TO THE DEAR DELETED.

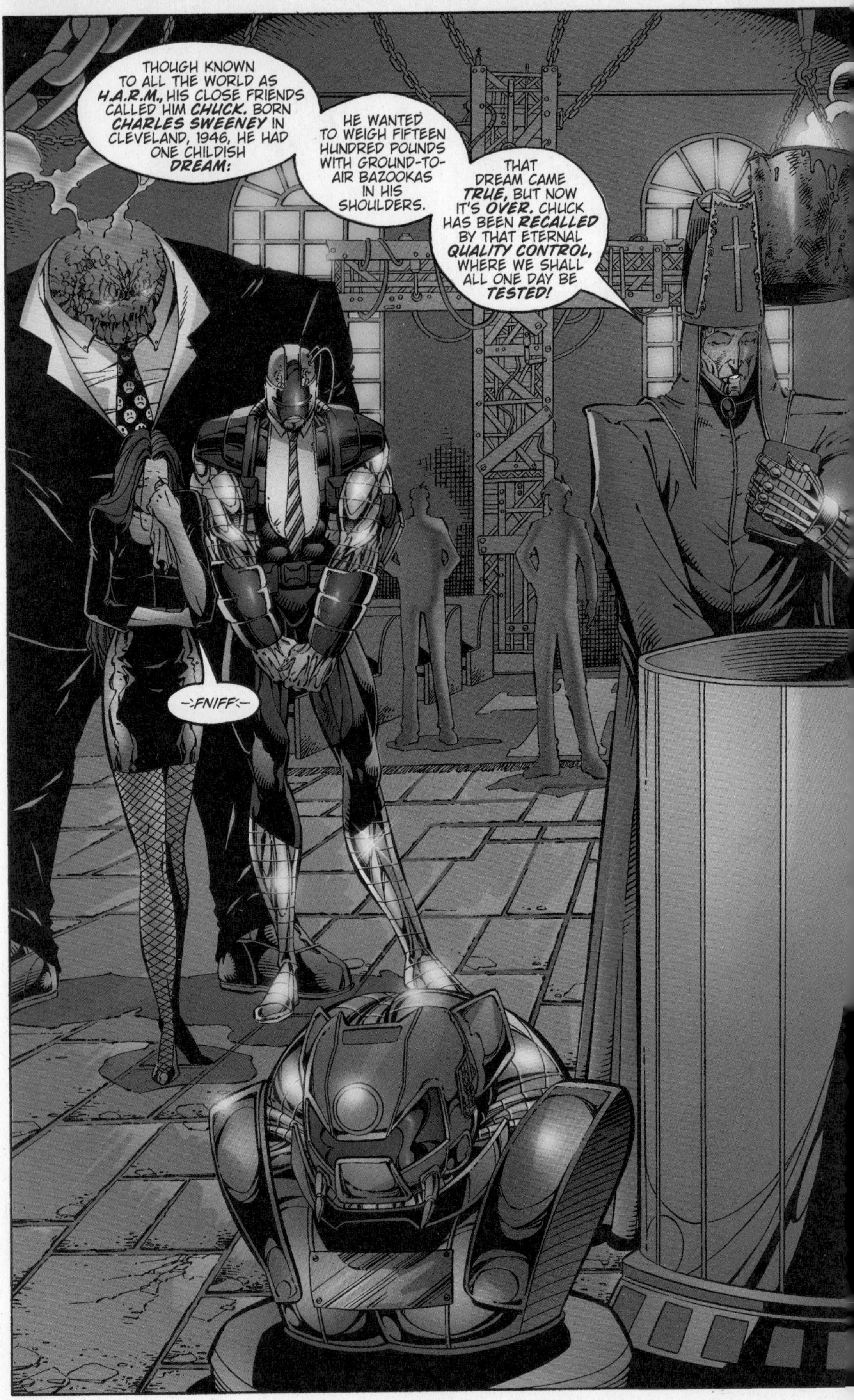
THOUGH KNOWN TO ALL THE WORLD AS H.A.R.M., HIS CLOSE FRIENDS CALLED HIM CHUCK. BORN CHARLES SWEENEY IN CLEVELAND, 1946, HE HAD ONE CHILDISH DREAM:
HE WANTED TO WEIGH FIFTEEN HUNDRED POUNDS WITH GROUND-TO-AIR BAZOOKAS IN HIS SHOULDERS.
THAT DREAM CAME TRUE, BUT NOW IT'S OVER. CHUCK HAS BEEN RECALLED BY THAT ETERNAL QUALITY CONTROL, WHERE WE SHALL ALL ONE DAY BE TESTED!
-FNIFF-

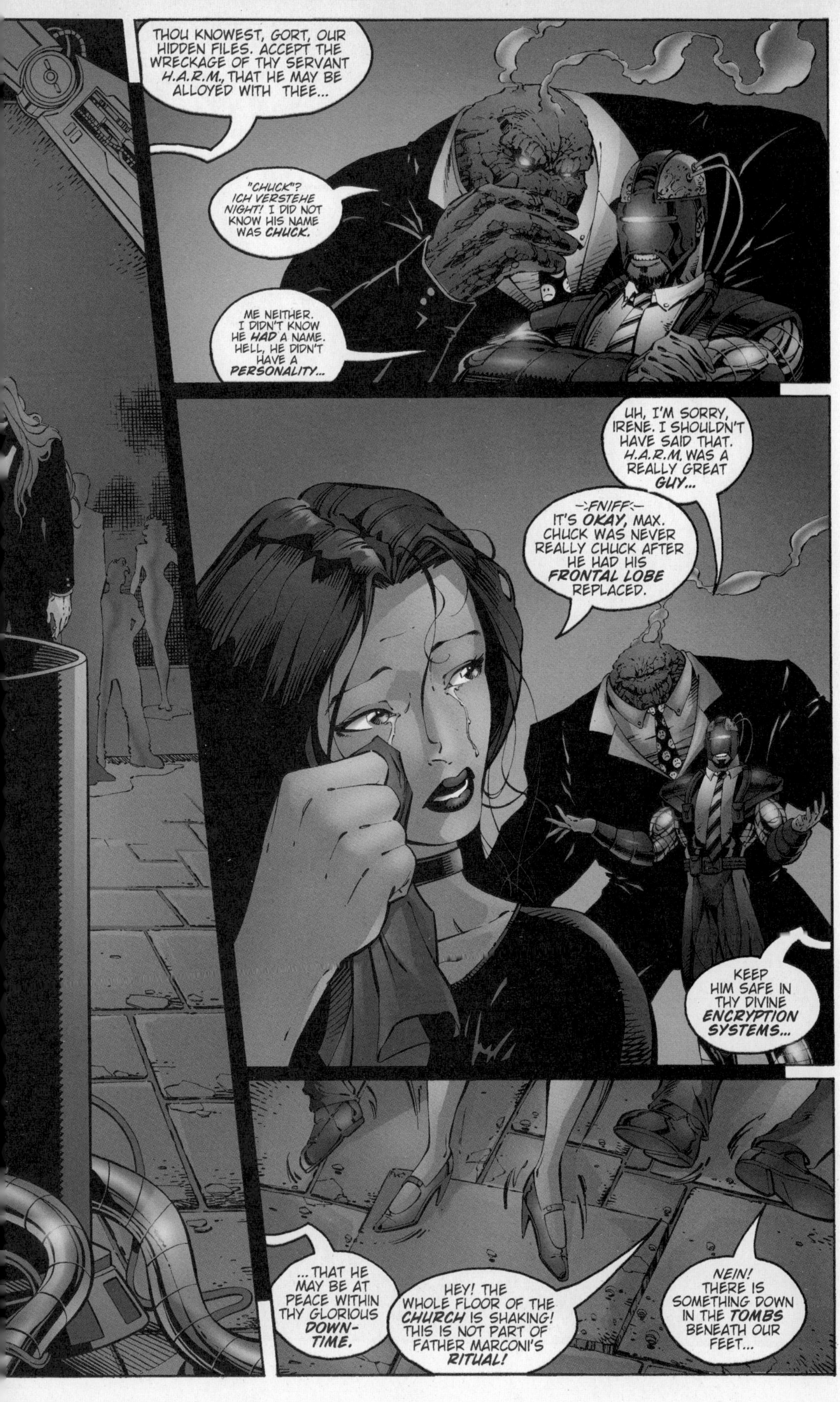

THOU KNOWEST, GORT, OUR HIDDEN FILES. ACCEPT THE WRECKAGE OF THY SERVANT H.A.R.M., THAT HE MAY BE ALLOYED WITH THEE...
"CHUCK"? ICH VERSTEHE NIGHT! I DID NOT KNOW HIS NAME WAS CHUCK.
ME NEITHER. I DIDN'T KNOW HE HAD A NAME. HELL, HE DIDN'T HAVE A PERSONALITY...
UH, I'M SORRY, IRENE. I SHOULDN'T HAVE SAID THAT. H.A.R.M. WAS A REALLY GREAT GUY...
-FNIFF- IT'S OKAY, MAX. CHUCK WAS NEVER REALLY CHUCK AFTER HE HAD HIS FRONTAL LOBE REPLACED.
KEEP HIM SAFE IN THY DIVINE ENCRYPTION SYSTEMS...
...THAT HE MAY BE AT PEACE WITHIN THY GLORIOUS DOWN-TIME.
HEY! THE WHOLE FLOOR OF THE CHURCH IS SHAKING! THIS IS NOT PART OF FATHER MARCONI'S RITUAL!
NEIN! THERE IS SOMETHING DOWN IN THE TOMBS BENEATH OUR FEET...

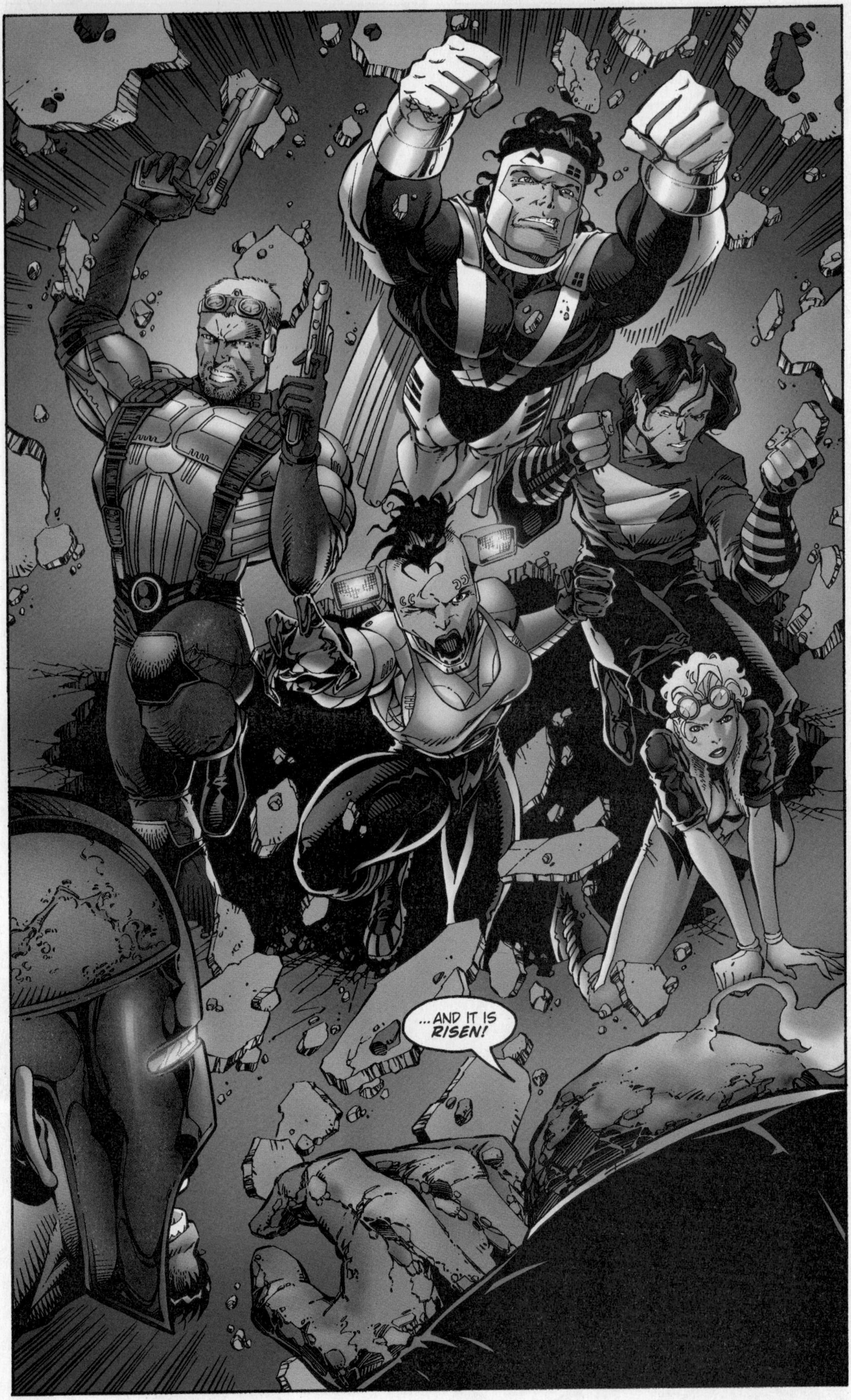
...AND IT IS *RISEN!*

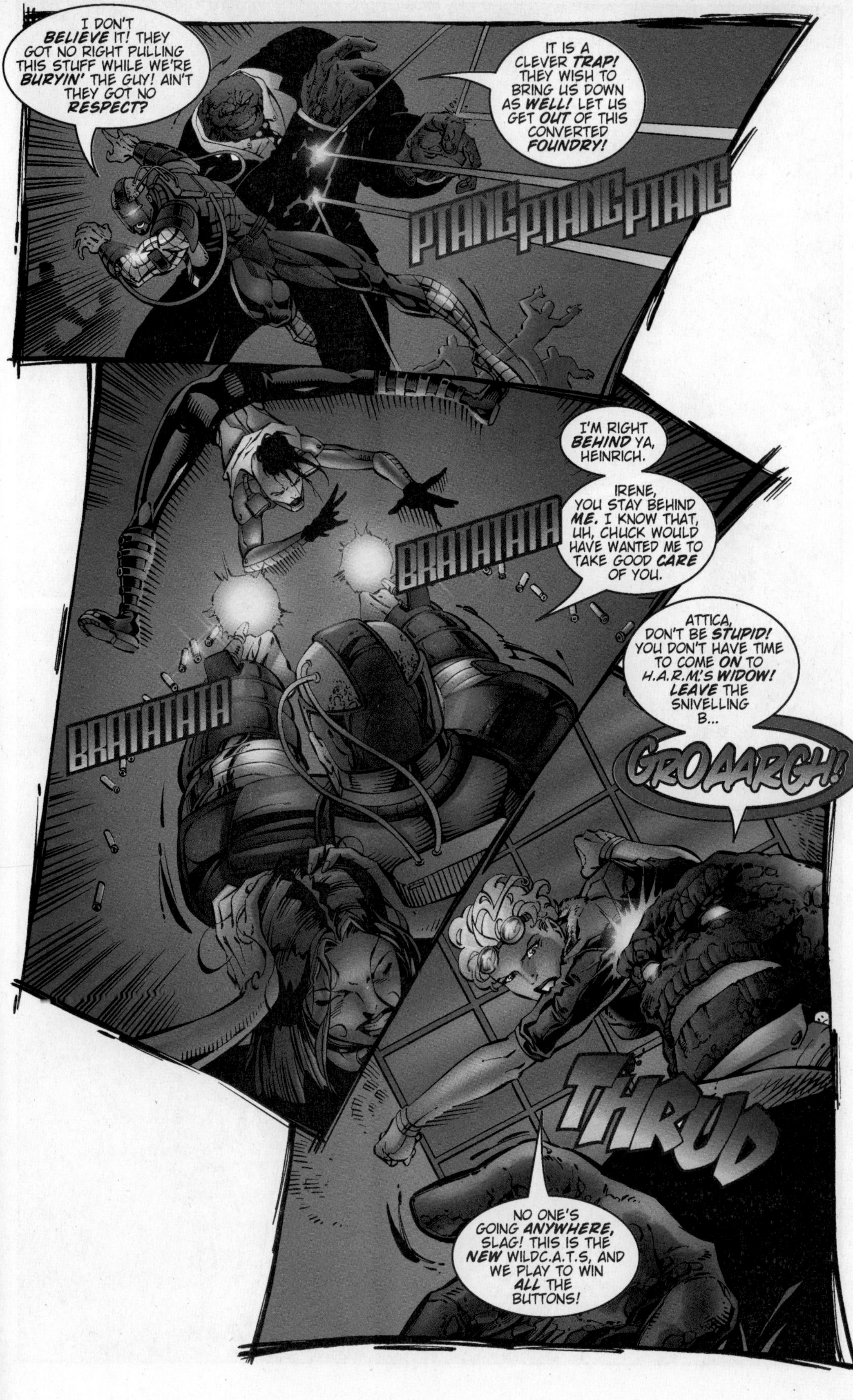
I DON'T BELIEVE IT! THEY GOT NO RIGHT PULLING THIS STUFF WHILE WE'RE BURYIN' THE GUY! AIN'T THEY GOT NO RESPECT?
IT IS A CLEVER TRAP! THEY WISH TO BRING US DOWN AS WELL! LET US GET OUT OF THIS CONVERTED FOUNDRY!
PTANG PTANG PTANG
BRATATATA
I'M RIGHT BEHIND YA, HEINRICH.
IRENE, YOU STAY BEHIND ME. I KNOW THAT, UH, CHUCK WOULD HAVE WANTED ME TO TAKE GOOD CARE OF YOU.
BRATATATA
ATTICA, DON'T BE STUPID! YOU DON'T HAVE TIME TO COME ON TO H.A.R.M.'S WIDOW! LEAVE THE SNIVELLING B...
GROAARGH!
THRUD
NO ONE'S GOING ANYWHERE, SLAG! THIS IS THE NEW WILDC.A.T.S, AND WE PLAY TO WIN ALL THE BUTTONS!

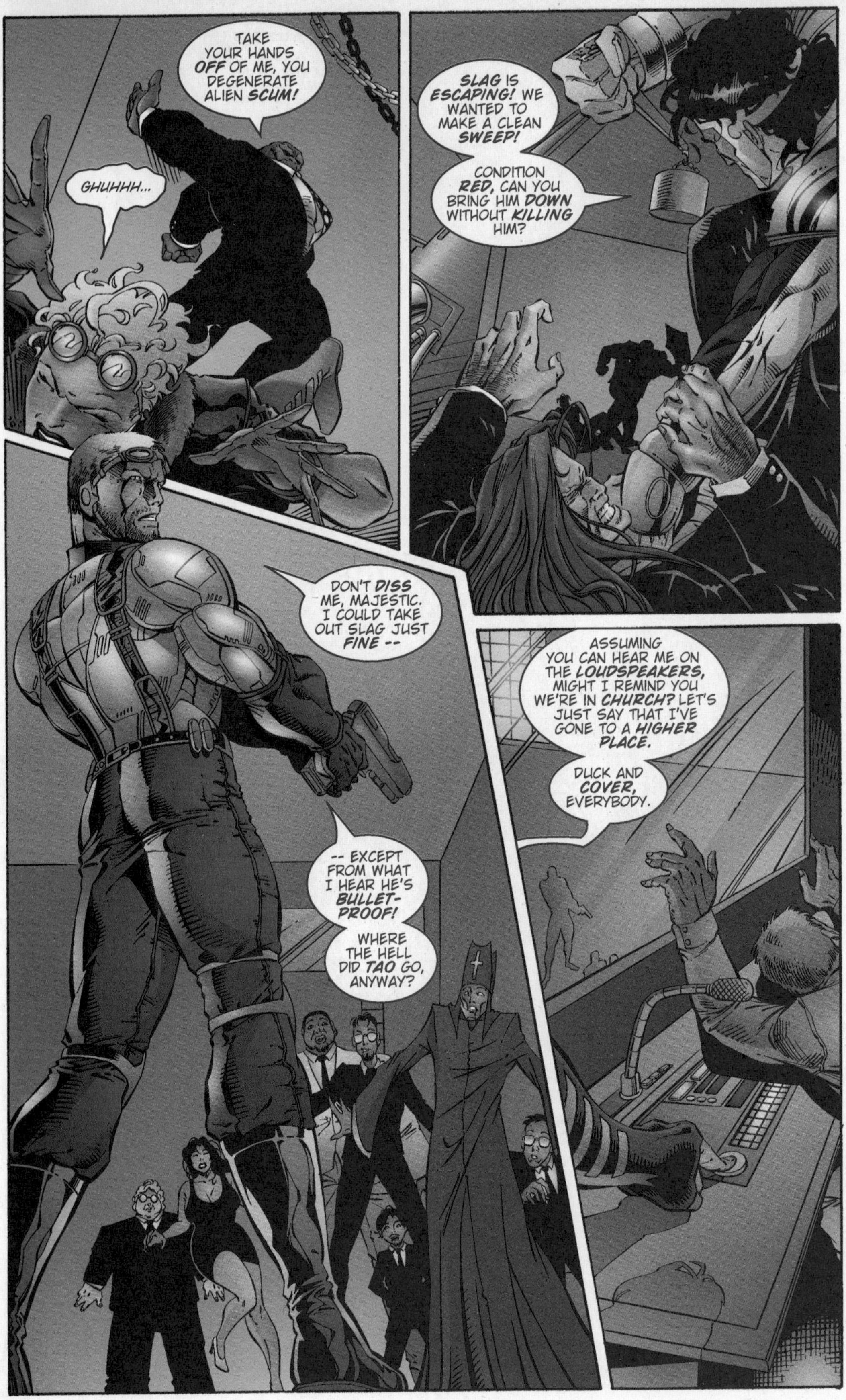

TAKE YOUR HANDS OFF OF ME, YOU DEGENERATE ALIEN SCUM!
GHUHHH...
SLAG IS ESCAPING! WE WANTED TO MAKE A CLEAN SWEEP!
CONDITION RED, CAN YOU BRING HIM DOWN WITHOUT KILLING HIM?
DON'T DISS ME, MAJESTIC. I COULD TAKE OUT SLAG JUST FINE --
-- EXCEPT FROM WHAT I HEAR HE'S BULLET-PROOF!
WHERE THE HELL DID TAO GO, ANYWAY?
ASSUMING YOU CAN HEAR ME ON THE LOUDSPEAKERS, MIGHT I REMIND YOU WE'RE IN CHURCH? LET'S JUST SAY THAT I'VE GONE TO A HIGHER PLACE.
DUCK AND COVER, EVERYBODY.

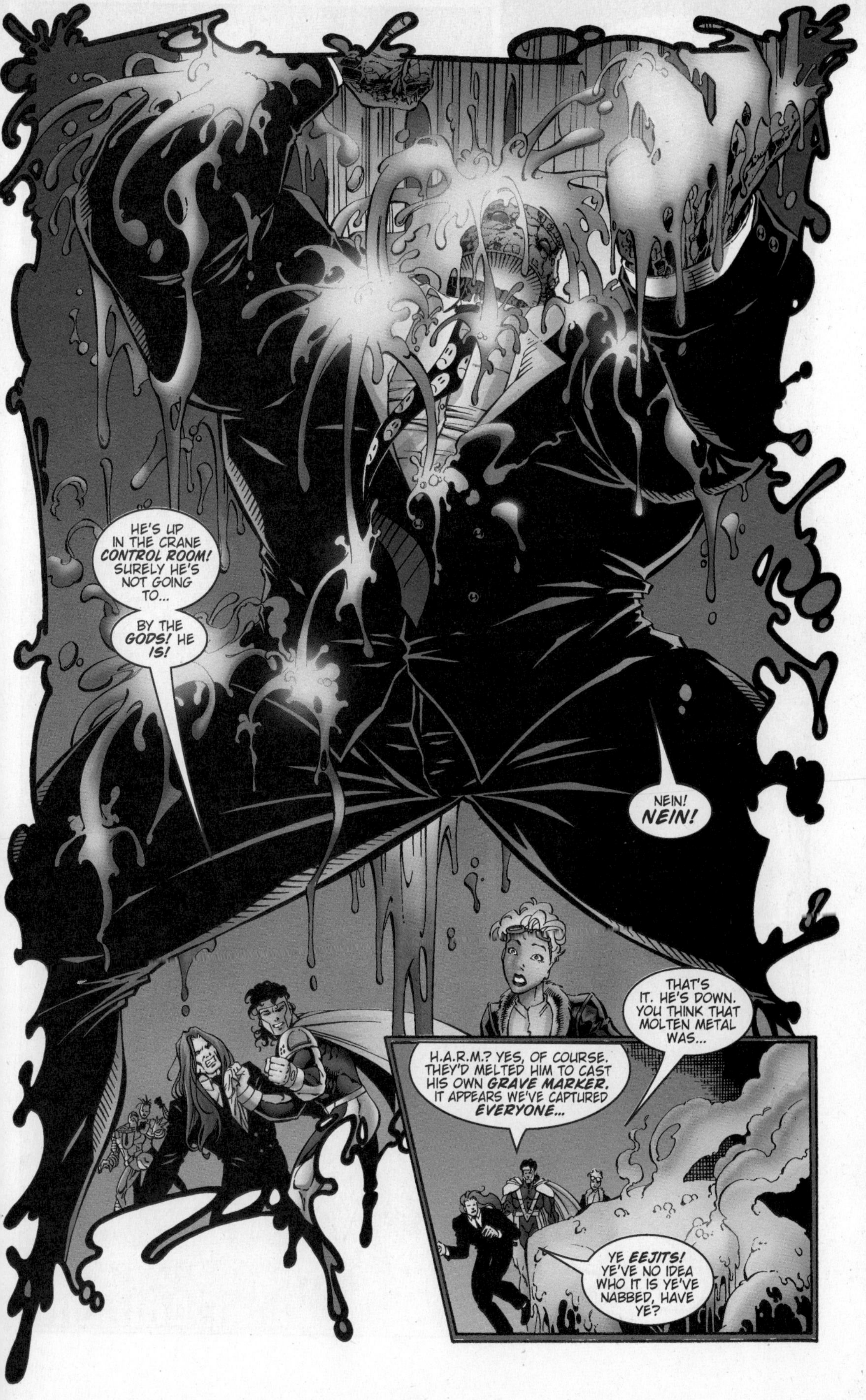
HE'S UP IN THE CRANE CONTROL ROOM! SURELY HE'S NOT GOING TO...
BY THE GODS! HE IS!
NEIN! NEIN!
THAT'S IT. HE'S DOWN. YOU THINK THAT MOLTEN METAL WAS...
H.A.R.M.? YES, OF COURSE. THEY'D MELTED HIM TO CAST HIS OWN GRAVE MARKER. IT APPEARS WE'VE CAPTURED EVERYONE...
YE EEJITS! YE'VE NO IDEA WHO IT IS YE'VE NABBED, HAVE YE?

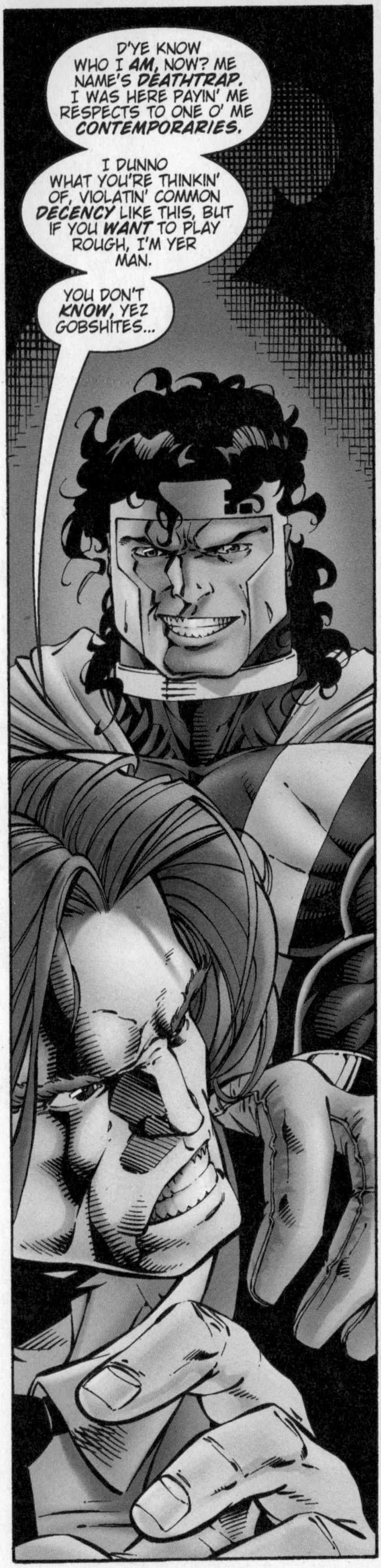
D'YE KNOW WHO I **AM**, NOW? ME NAME'S ***DEATHTRAP.*** I WAS HERE PAYIN' ME RESPECTS TO ONE O' ME ***CONTEMPORARIES.***
I DUNNO WHAT YOU'RE THINKIN' OF, VIOLATIN' COMMON ***DECENCY*** LIKE THIS, BUT IF YOU ***WANT*** TO PLAY ROUGH, I'M YER MAN.
YOU DON'T ***KNOW,*** YEZ GOBSHITES...
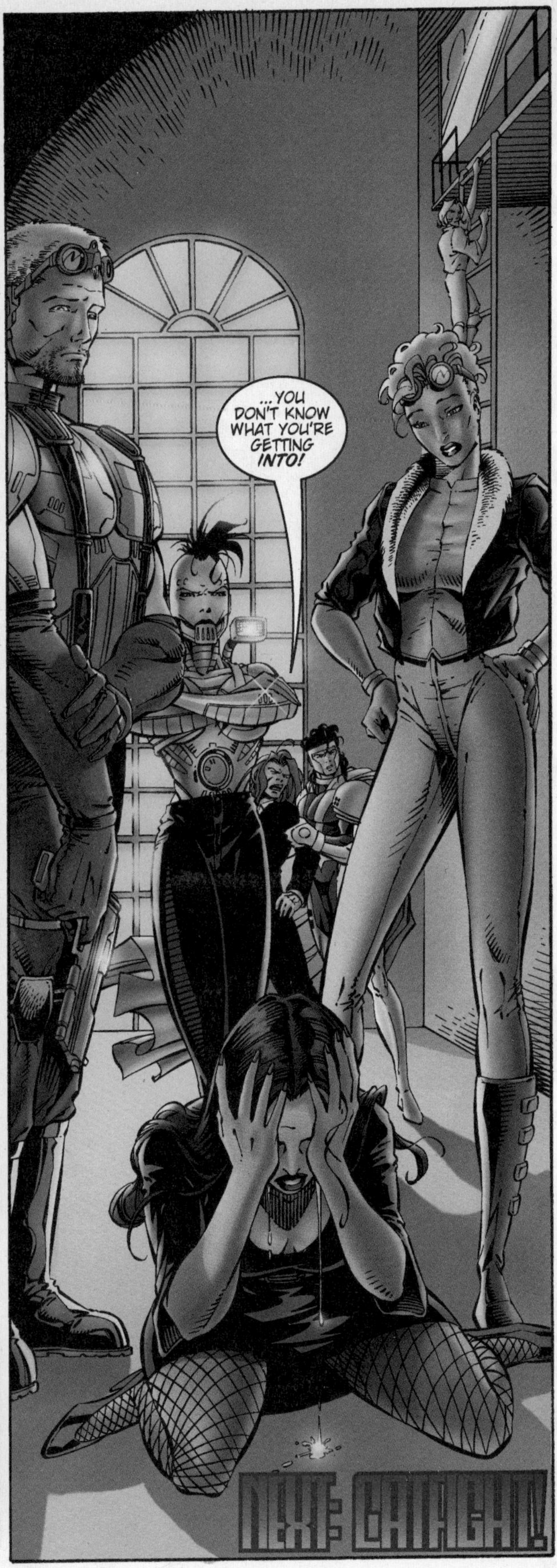
...YOU DON'T KNOW WHAT YOU'RE GETTING ***INTO!***

SPARTAN PINUP

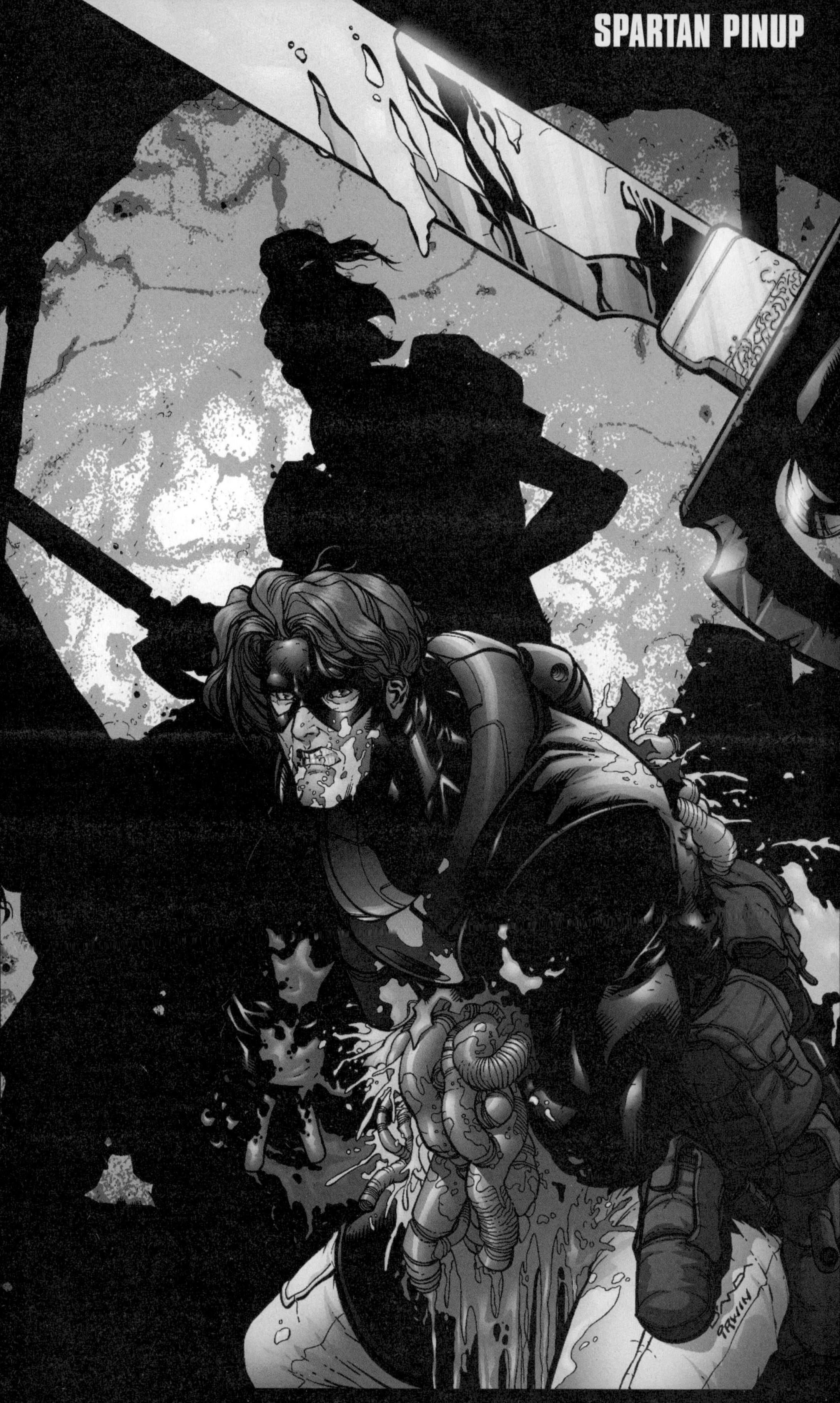

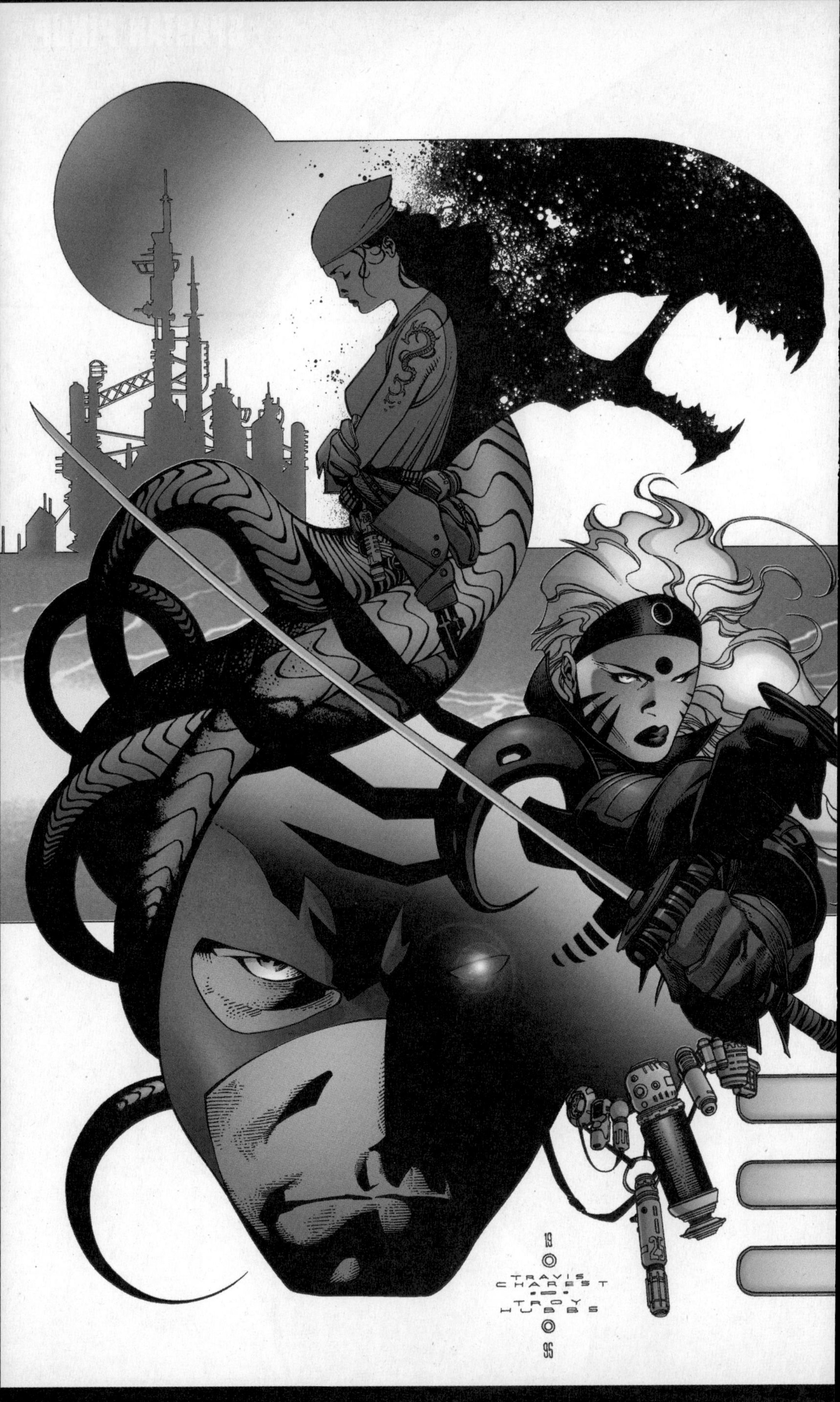
19
TRAVIS
CHAREST
TROY
HUBBS
95

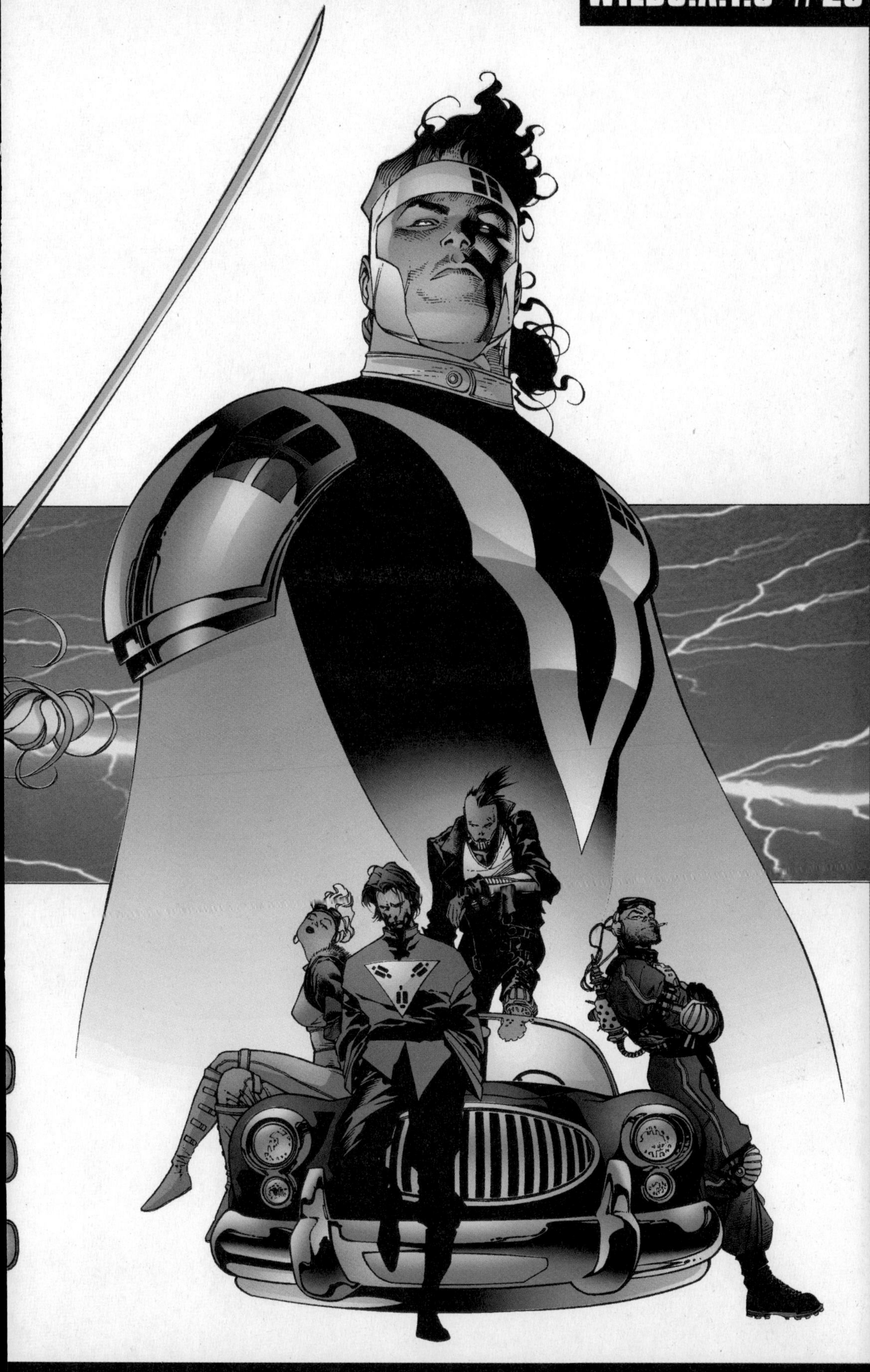

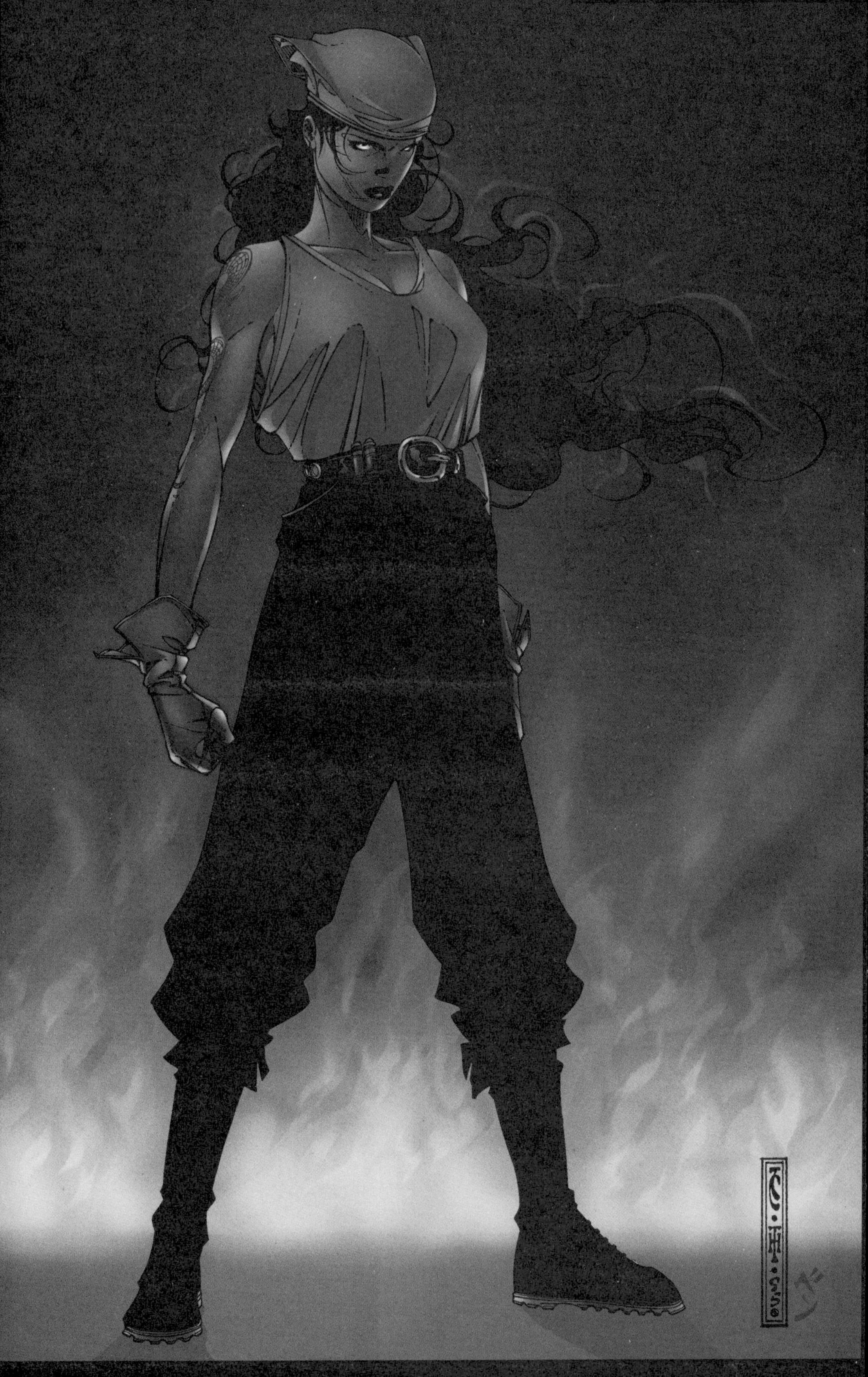

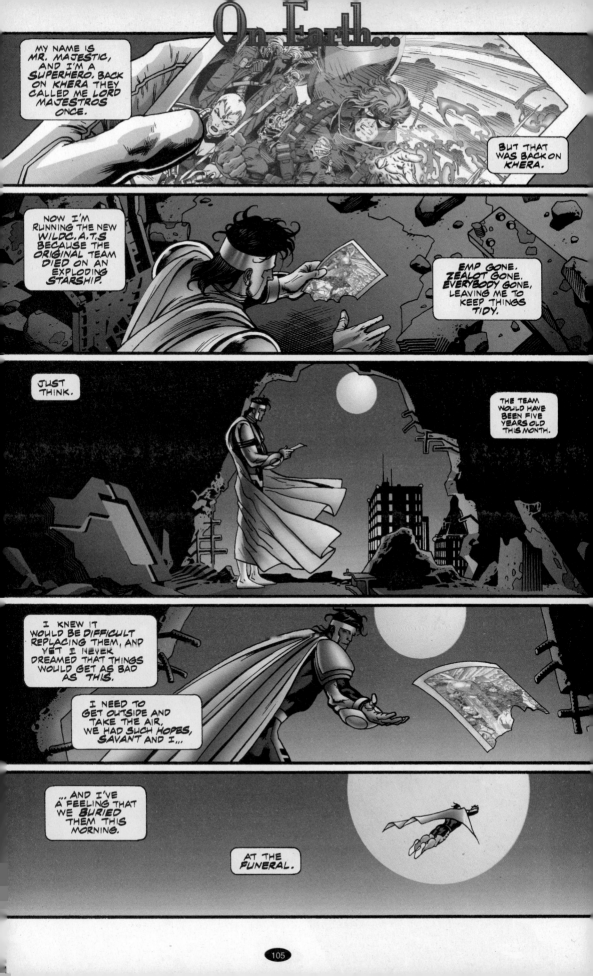

MY NAME IS MR. MAJESTIC, AND I'M A SUPERHERO. BACK ON KHERA THEY CALLED ME LORD MAJESTROS ONCE.

BUT THAT WAS BACK ON KHERA.

NOW I'M RUNNING THE NEW W.I.L.D.C.A.T.S BECAUSE THE ORIGINAL TEAM DIED ON AN EXPLODING STARSHIP.

EMP GONE. ZEALOT GONE. EVERYBODY GONE, LEAVING ME TO KEEP THINGS TIDY.

JUST THINK.

THE TEAM WOULD HAVE BEEN FIVE YEARS OLD THIS MONTH.

I KNEW IT WOULD BE DIFFICULT REPLACING THEM, AND YET I NEVER DREAMED THAT THINGS WOULD GET AS BAD AS THIS.

I NEED TO GET OUTSIDE AND TAKE THE AIR. WE HAD SUCH HOPES, SAVANT AND I...

...AND I'VE A FEELING THAT WE BURIED THEM THIS MORNING.

AT THE FUNERAL.

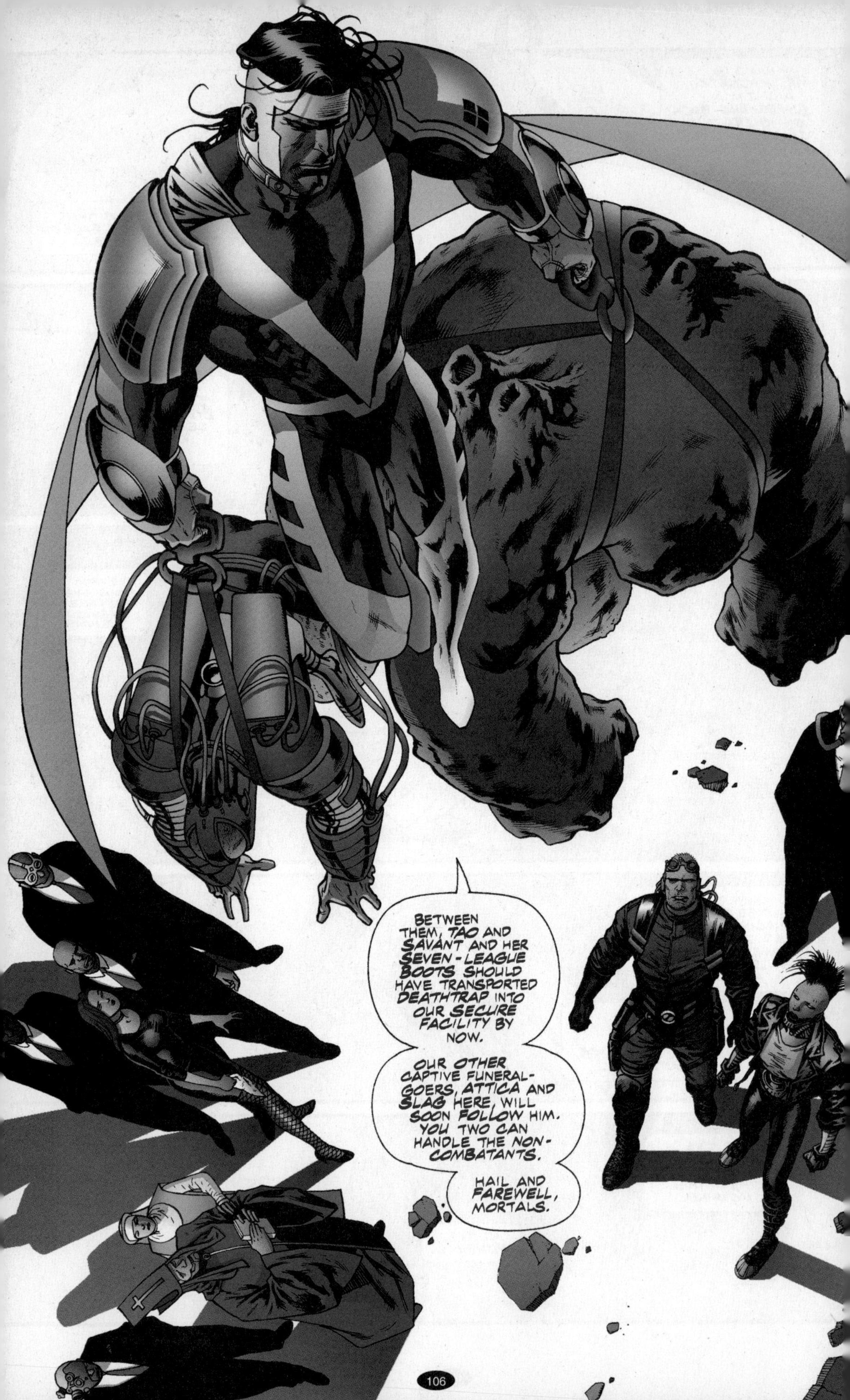
BETWEEN THEM, TAO AND SAVANT AND HER SEVEN-LEAGUE BOOTS SHOULD HAVE TRANSPORTED DEATHTRAP INTO OUR SECURE FACILITY BY NOW.
OUR OTHER CAPTIVE FUNERAL-GOERS, ATTICA AND SLAG HERE, WILL SOON FOLLOW HIM. YOU TWO CAN HANDLE THE NON-COMBATANTS.
HAIL AND FAREWELL, MORTALS.

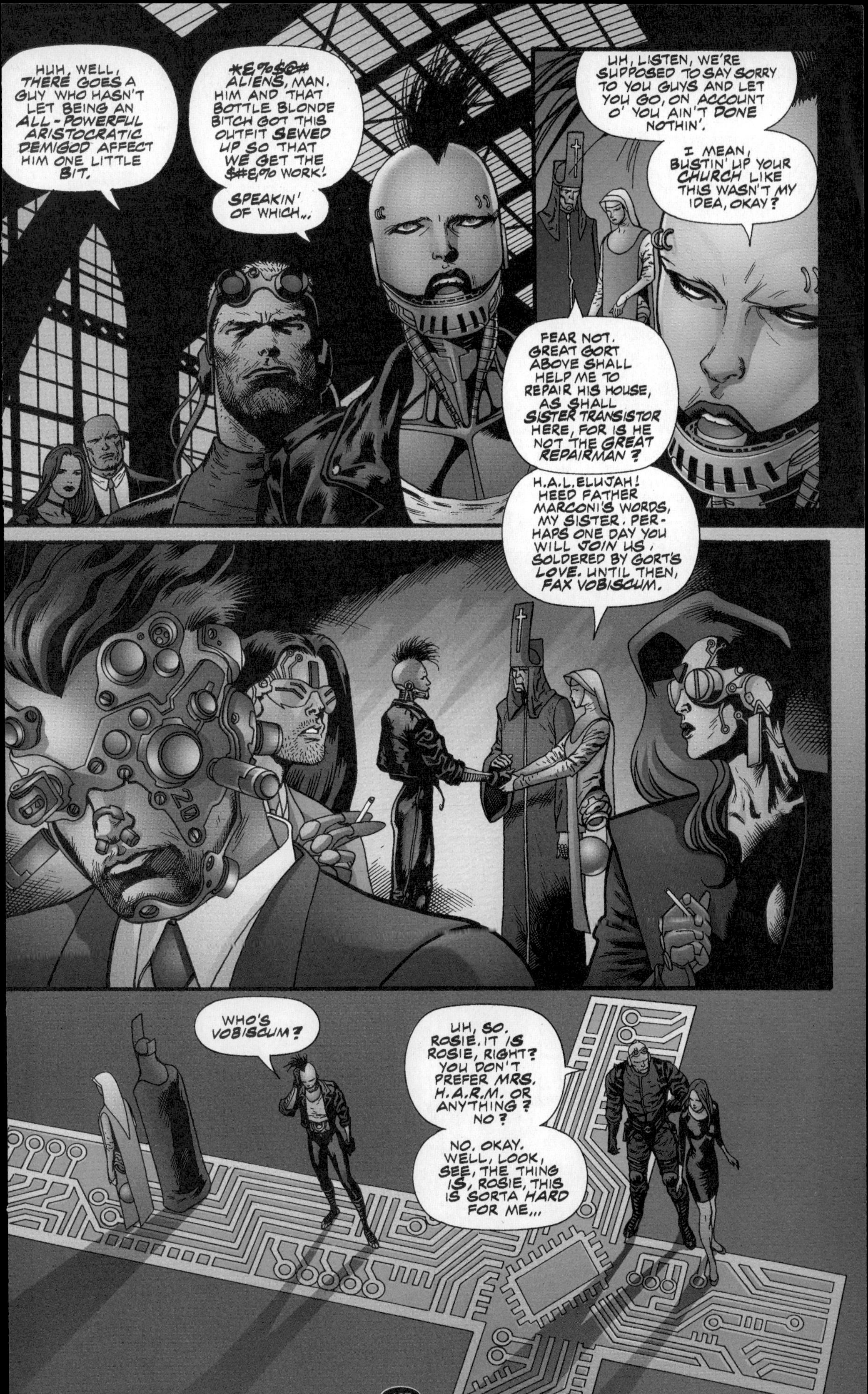
HUH, WELL, THERE GOES A GUY WHO HASN'T LET BEING AN ALL-POWERFUL ARISTOCRATIC DEMIGOD AFFECT HIM ONE LITTLE BIT.
*£%$@# ALIENS, MAN. HIM AND THAT BOTTLE BLONDE BITCH GOT THIS OUTFIT SEWED UP SO THAT WE GET THE $#£% WORK!
SPEAKIN' OF WHICH...
UH, LISTEN, WE'RE SUPPOSED TO SAY SORRY TO YOU GUYS AND LET YOU GO, ON ACCOUNT O' YOU AIN'T DONE NOTHIN'.
I MEAN, BUSTIN' UP YOUR CHURCH LIKE THIS WASN'T MY IDEA, OKAY?
FEAR NOT. GREAT GORT ABOVE SHALL HELP ME TO REPAIR HIS HOUSE, AS SHALL SISTER TRANSISTOR HERE, FOR IS HE NOT THE GREAT REPAIRMAN?
H.A.L.ELUJAH! HEED FATHER MARCONI'S WORDS, MY SISTER. PERHAPS ONE DAY YOU WILL JOIN US, SOLDERED BY GORT'S LOVE. UNTIL THEN, FAX VOBISCUM.
WHO'S VOBISCUM?
UH, SO. ROSIE. IT IS ROSIE, RIGHT? YOU DON'T PREFER MRS. H.A.R.M. OR ANYTHING? NO?
NO. OKAY. WELL, LOOK, SEE, THE THING IS, ROSIE, THIS IS SORTA HARD FOR ME...

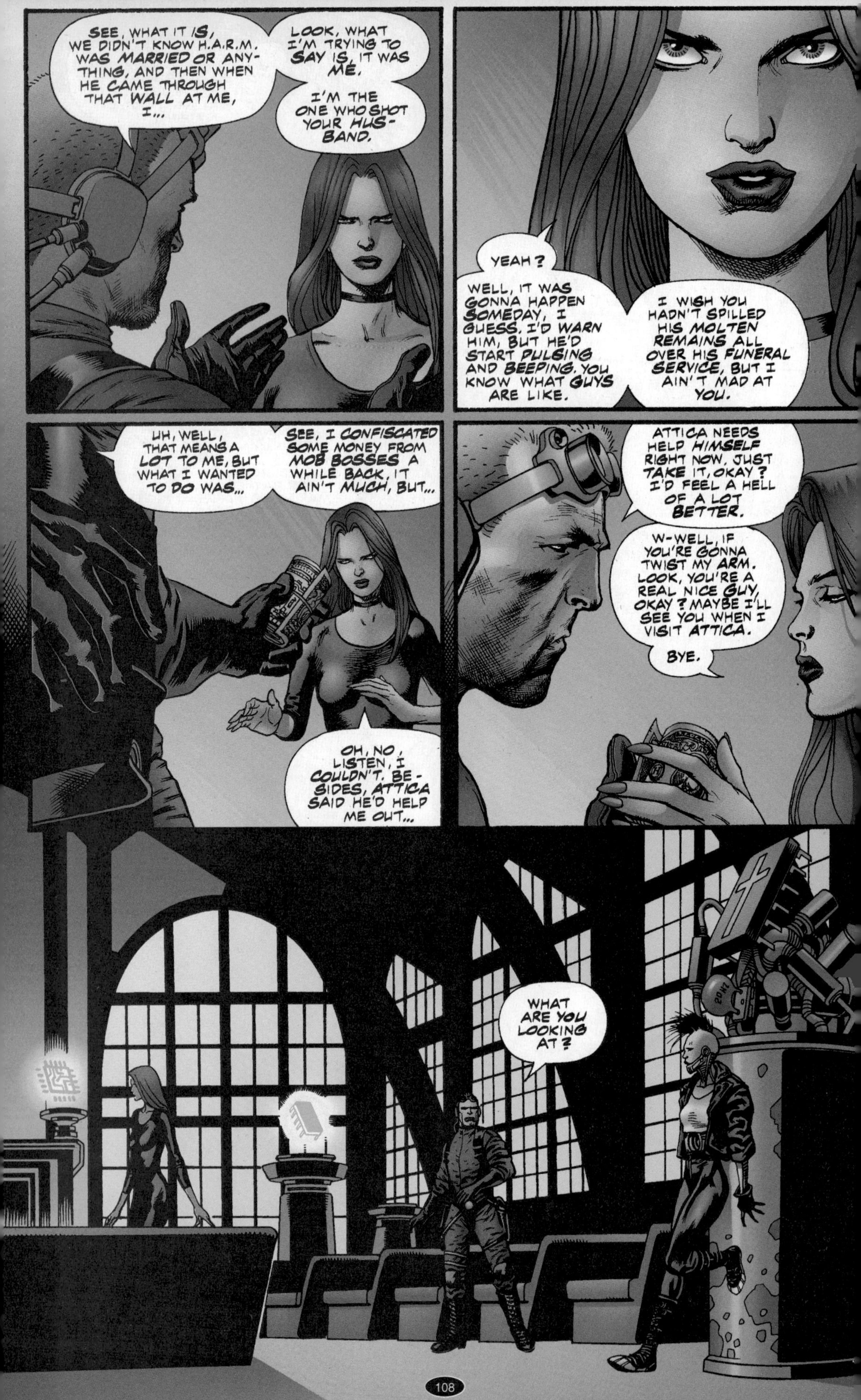

SEE, WHAT IT IS, WE DIDN'T KNOW H.A.R.M. WAS MARRIED OR ANY-THING, AND THEN WHEN HE CAME THROUGH THAT WALL AT ME, I...
LOOK, WHAT I'M TRYING TO SAY IS, IT WAS ME.
I'M THE ONE WHO SHOT YOUR HUS-BAND.
YEAH?
WELL, IT WAS GONNA HAPPEN SOMEDAY, I GUESS. I'D WARN HIM, BUT HE'D START PULSING AND BEEPING. YOU KNOW WHAT GUYS ARE LIKE.
I WISH YOU HADN'T SPILLED HIS MOLTEN REMAINS ALL OVER HIS FUNERAL SERVICE, BUT I AIN'T MAD AT YOU.
UH, WELL, THAT MEANS A LOT TO ME, BUT WHAT I WANTED TO DO WAS...
SEE, I CONFISCATED SOME MONEY FROM MOB BOSSES A WHILE BACK, IT AIN'T MUCH, BUT...
OH, NO, LISTEN, I COULDN'T. BE-SIDES, ATTICA SAID HE'D HELP ME OUT...
ATTICA NEEDS HELP HIMSELF RIGHT NOW. JUST TAKE IT, OKAY? I'D FEEL A HELL OF A LOT BETTER.
W-WELL, IF YOU'RE GONNA TWIST MY ARM. LOOK, YOU'RE A REAL NICE GUY, OKAY? MAYBE I'LL SEE YOU WHEN I VISIT ATTICA.
BYE.
WHAT ARE YOU LOOKING AT?

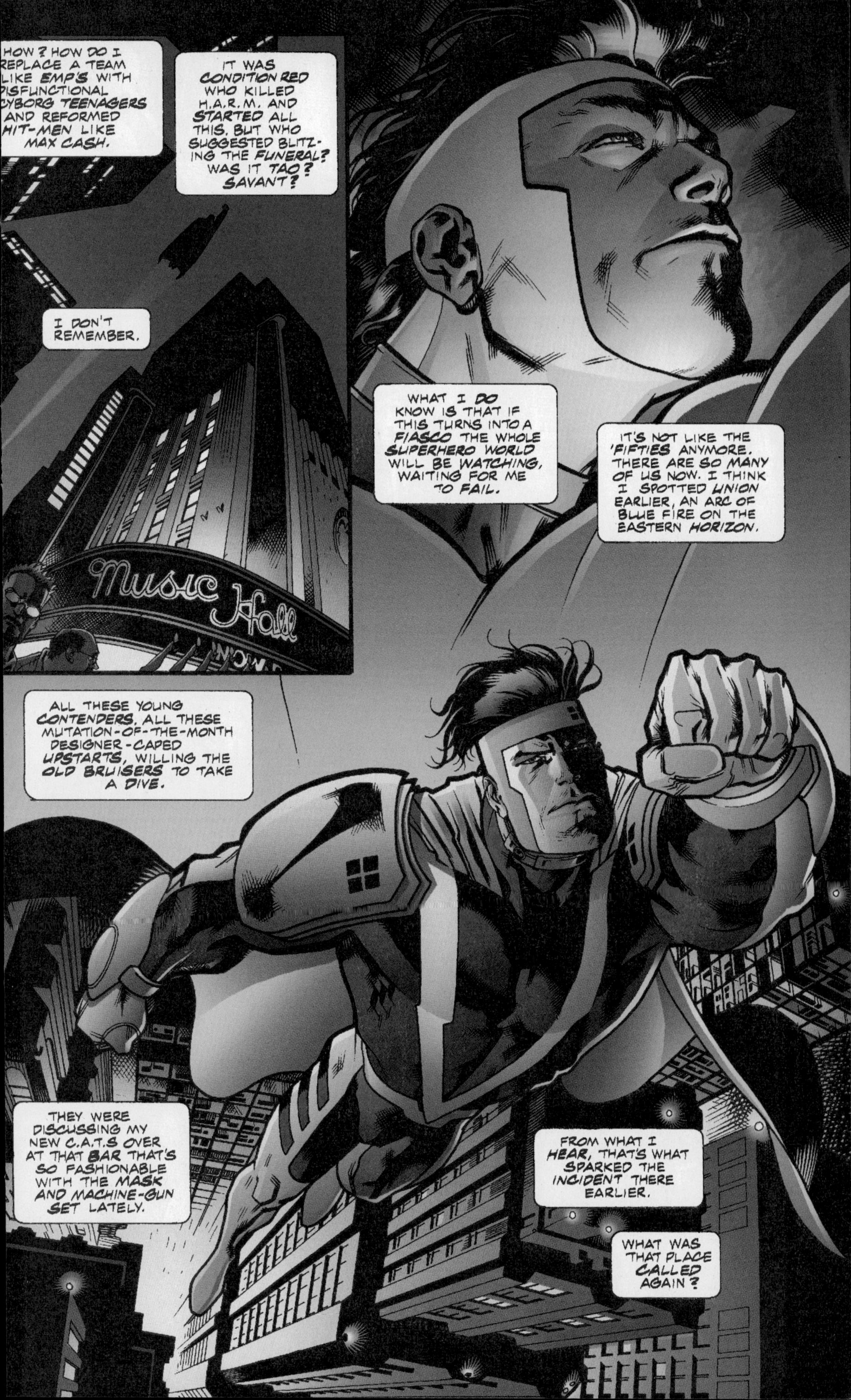
HOW? HOW DO I REPLACE A TEAM LIKE EMP'S WITH DISFUNCTIONAL CYBORG TEENAGERS AND REFORMED HIT-MEN LIKE MAX CASH.
IT WAS CONDITION RED WHO KILLED H.A.R.M. AND STARTED ALL THIS. BUT WHO SUGGESTED BLITZ-ING THE FUNERAL? WAS IT TAO? SAVANT?
I DON'T REMEMBER.
Music Hall
WHAT I DO KNOW IS THAT IF THIS TURNS INTO A FIASCO THE WHOLE SUPERHERO WORLD WILL BE WATCHING, WAITING FOR ME TO FAIL.
IT'S NOT LIKE THE 'FIFTIES ANYMORE. THERE ARE SO MANY OF US NOW. I THINK I SPOTTED UNION EARLIER, AN ARC OF BLUE FIRE ON THE EASTERN HORIZON.
ALL THESE YOUNG CONTENDERS. ALL THESE MUTATION-OF-THE-MONTH DESIGNER-CAPED UPSTARTS, WILLING THE OLD BRUISERS TO TAKE A DIVE.
THEY WERE DISCUSSING MY NEW C.A.T.S OVER AT THAT BAR THAT'S SO FASHIONABLE WITH THE MASK AND MACHINE-GUN SET LATELY.
FROM WHAT I HEAR, THAT'S WHAT SPARKED THE INCIDENT THERE EARLIER.
WHAT WAS THAT PLACE CALLED AGAIN?

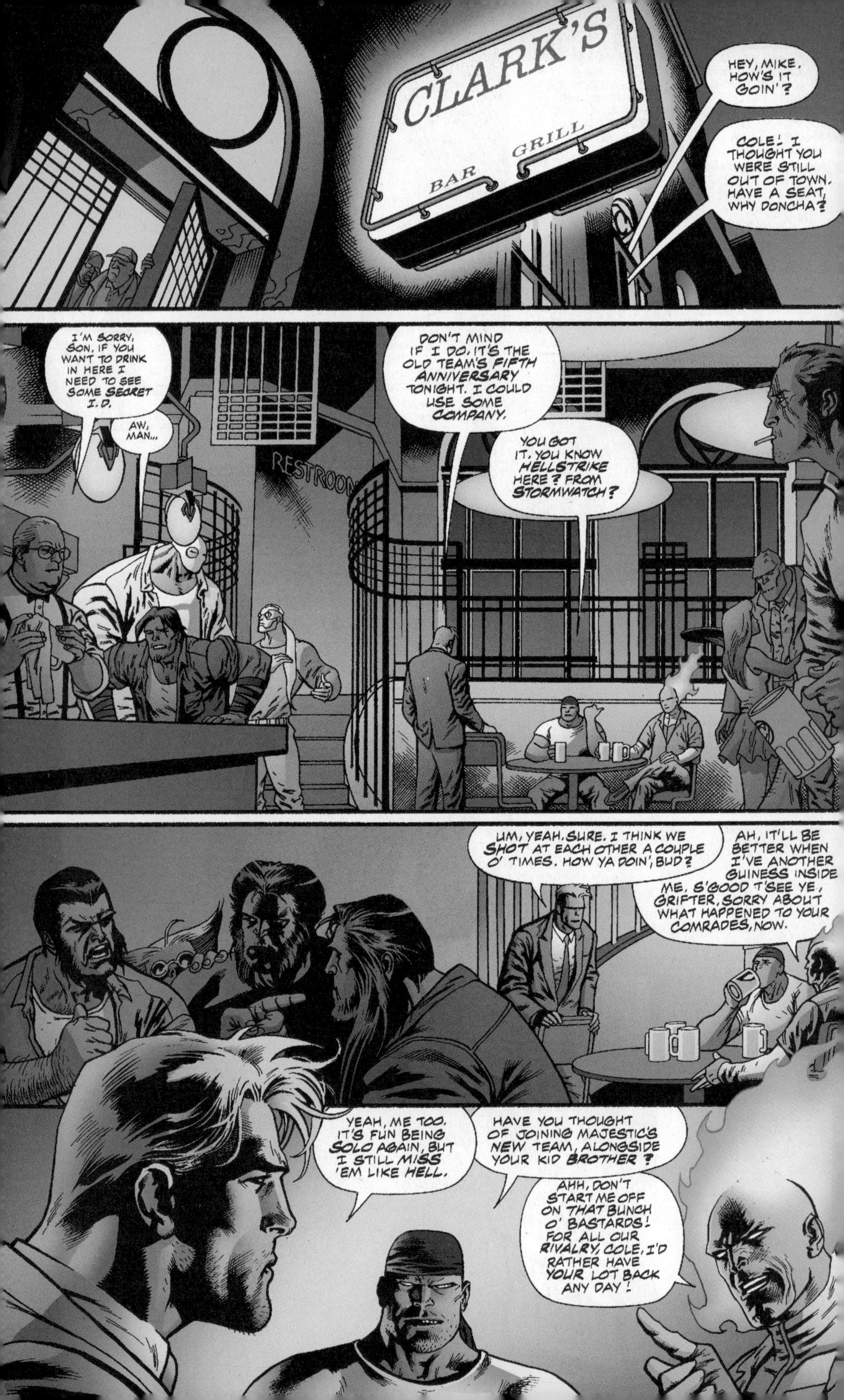
CLARK'S
BAR GRILL
HEY, MIKE. HOW'S IT GOIN'?
COLE! I THOUGHT YOU WERE STILL OUT OF TOWN. HAVE A SEAT, WHY DONCHA?
I'M SORRY, SON, IF YOU WANT TO DRINK IN HERE I NEED TO SEE SOME SECRET I.D.
AW, MAN...
RESTROOM
DON'T MIND IF I DO. IT'S THE OLD TEAM'S FIFTH ANNIVERSARY TONIGHT. I COULD USE SOME COMPANY.
YOU GOT IT. YOU KNOW HELLSTRIKE HERE? FROM STORMWATCH?
UM, YEAH. SURE. I THINK WE SHOT AT EACH OTHER A COUPLE O' TIMES. HOW YA DOIN', BUD?
AH, IT'LL BE BETTER WHEN I'VE ANOTHER GUINESS INSIDE ME. S'GOOD T'SEE YE, GRIFTER. SORRY ABOUT WHAT HAPPENED TO YOUR COMRADES, NOW.
YEAH, ME TOO. IT'S FUN BEING SOLO AGAIN, BUT I STILL MISS 'EM LIKE HELL.
HAVE YOU THOUGHT OF JOINING MAJESTIC'S NEW TEAM, ALONGSIDE YOUR KID BROTHER?
AHH, DON'T START ME OFF ON THAT BUNCH O' BASTARDS! FOR ALL OUR RIVALRY, COLE, I'D RATHER HAVE YOUR LOT BACK ANY DAY!

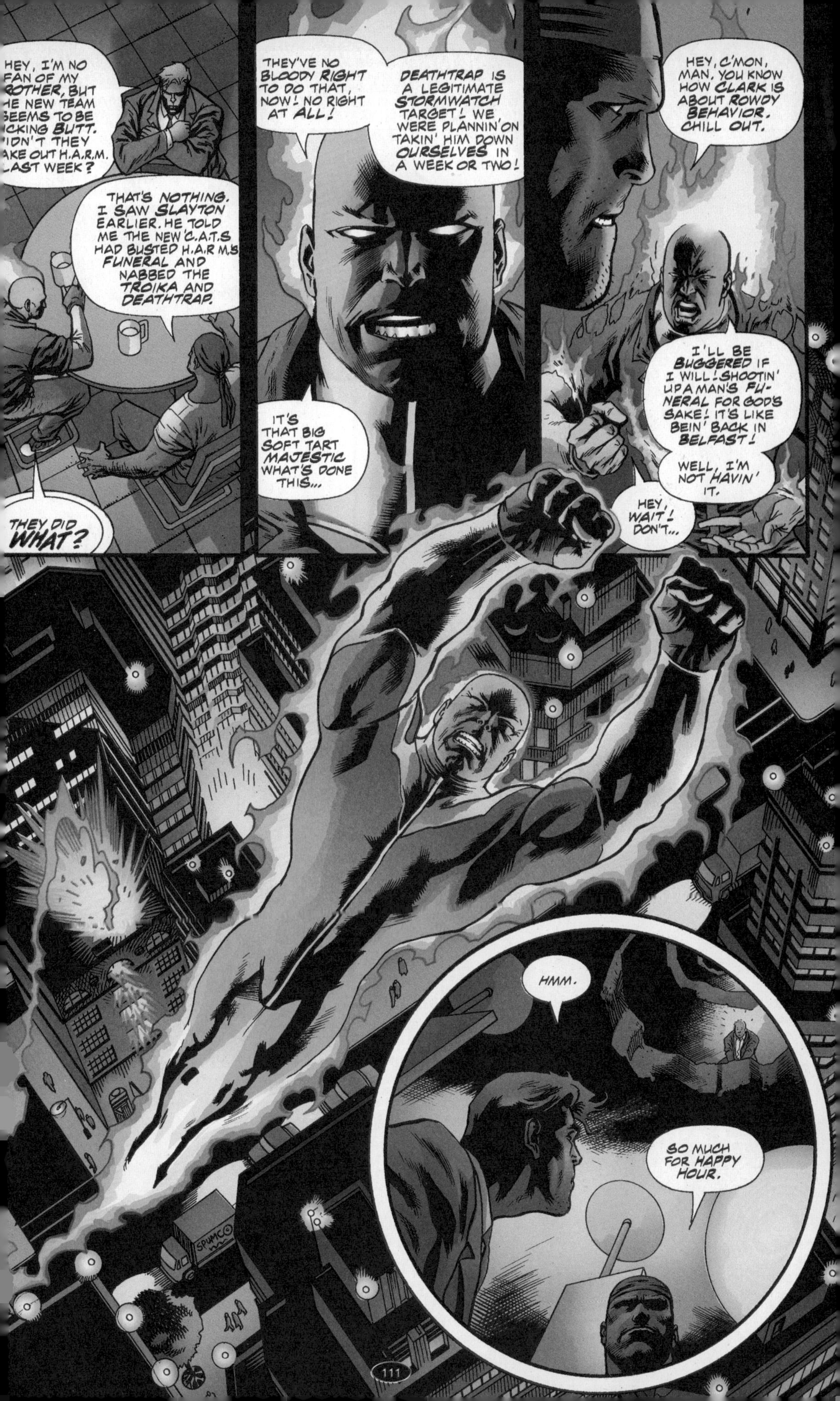

HEY, I'M NO FAN OF MY ROTHER, BUT HE NEW TEAM SEEMS TO BE ICKING BUTT. DIDN'T THEY AKE OUT H.A.R.M. LAST WEEK?
THAT'S NOTHING. I SAW SLAYTON EARLIER. HE TOLD ME THE NEW C.A.T.S HAD BUSTED H.A.R.M.'S FUNERAL AND NABBED THE TROIKA AND DEATHTRAP.
THEY DID WHAT?
THEY'VE NO BLOODY RIGHT TO DO THAT, NOW! NO RIGHT AT ALL!
DEATHTRAP IS A LEGITIMATE STORMWATCH TARGET! WE WERE PLANNIN' ON TAKIN' HIM DOWN OURSELVES IN A WEEK OR TWO!
IT'S THAT BIG SOFT TART MAJESTIC WHAT'S DONE THIS...
HEY, C'MON, MAN. YOU KNOW HOW CLARK IS ABOUT ROWDY BEHAVIOR. CHILL OUT.
I'LL BE BUGGERED IF I WILL! SHOOTIN' UP A MAN'S FUNERAL FOR GOD'S SAKE! IT'S LIKE BEIN' BACK IN BELFAST!
WELL, I'M NOT HAVIN' IT.
HEY, WAIT! DON'T...
HMM.
SO MUCH FOR HAPPY HOUR.

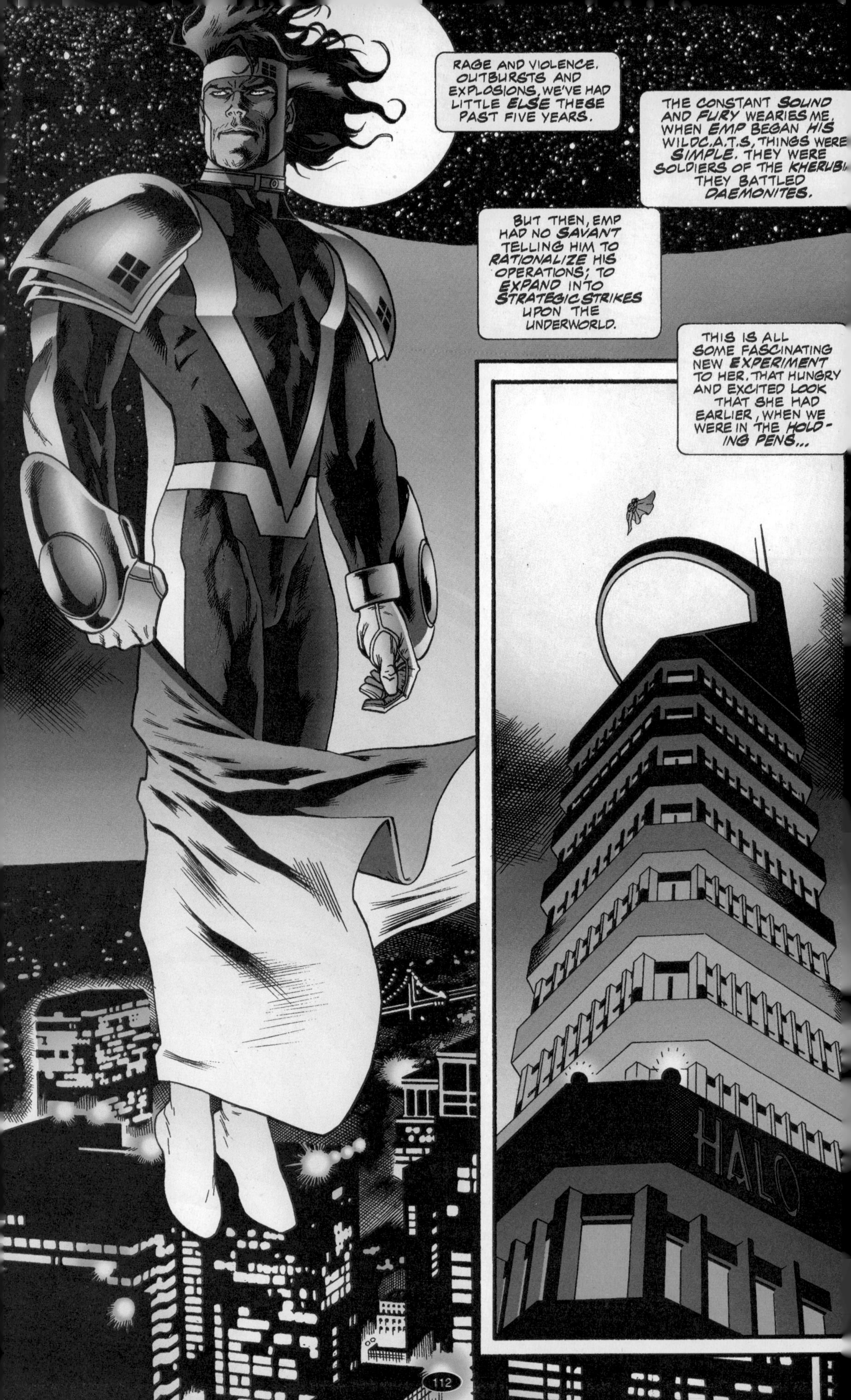

RAGE AND VIOLENCE. OUTBURSTS AND EXPLOSIONS, WE'VE HAD LITTLE ELSE THESE PAST FIVE YEARS.
THE CONSTANT SOUND AND FURY WEARIES ME. WHEN EMP BEGAN HIS WILDC.A.T.S, THINGS WERE SIMPLE. THEY WERE SOLDIERS OF THE KHERUBI THEY BATTLED DAEMONITES.
BUT THEN, EMP HAD NO SAVANT TELLING HIM TO RATIONALIZE HIS OPERATIONS; TO EXPAND INTO STRATEGIC STRIKES UPON THE UNDERWORLD.
THIS IS ALL SOME FASCINATING NEW EXPERIMENT TO HER. THAT HUNGRY AND EXCITED LOOK THAT SHE HAD EARLIER, WHEN WE WERE IN THE HOLDING PENS...
HALO

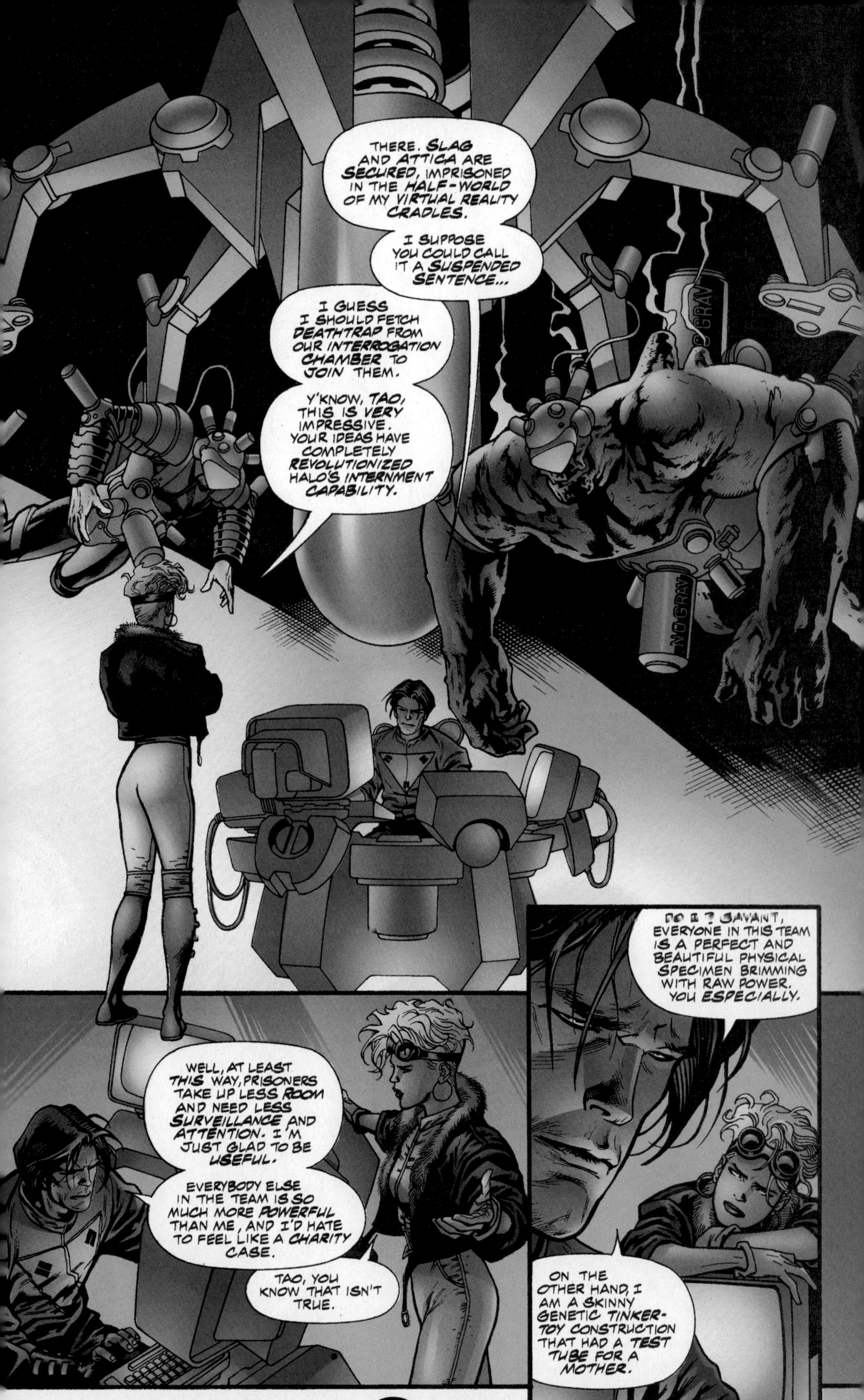
THERE. SLAG AND ATTICA ARE SECURED, IMPRISONED IN THE HALF-WORLD OF MY VIRTUAL REALITY CRADLES.
I SUPPOSE YOU COULD CALL IT A SUSPENDED SENTENCE...
I GUESS I SHOULD FETCH DEATHTRAP FROM OUR INTERROGATION CHAMBER TO JOIN THEM.
Y'KNOW, TAO, THIS IS VERY IMPRESSIVE. YOUR IDEAS HAVE COMPLETELY REVOLUTIONIZED HALO'S INTERNMENT CAPABILITY.
NO-GRAV
NO-GRAV
WELL, AT LEAST THIS WAY, PRISONERS TAKE UP LESS ROOM AND NEED LESS SURVEILLANCE AND ATTENTION. I'M JUST GLAD TO BE USEFUL.
EVERYBODY ELSE IN THE TEAM IS SO MUCH MORE POWERFUL THAN ME, AND I'D HATE TO FEEL LIKE A CHARITY CASE.
TAO, YOU KNOW THAT ISN'T TRUE.
DO I? GAVANT, EVERYONE IN THIS TEAM IS A PERFECT AND BEAUTIFUL PHYSICAL SPECIMEN BRIMMING WITH RAW POWER. YOU ESPECIALLY.
ON THE OTHER HAND, I AM A SKINNY GENETIC TINKER-TOY CONSTRUCTION THAT HAD A TEST TUBE FOR A MOTHER.

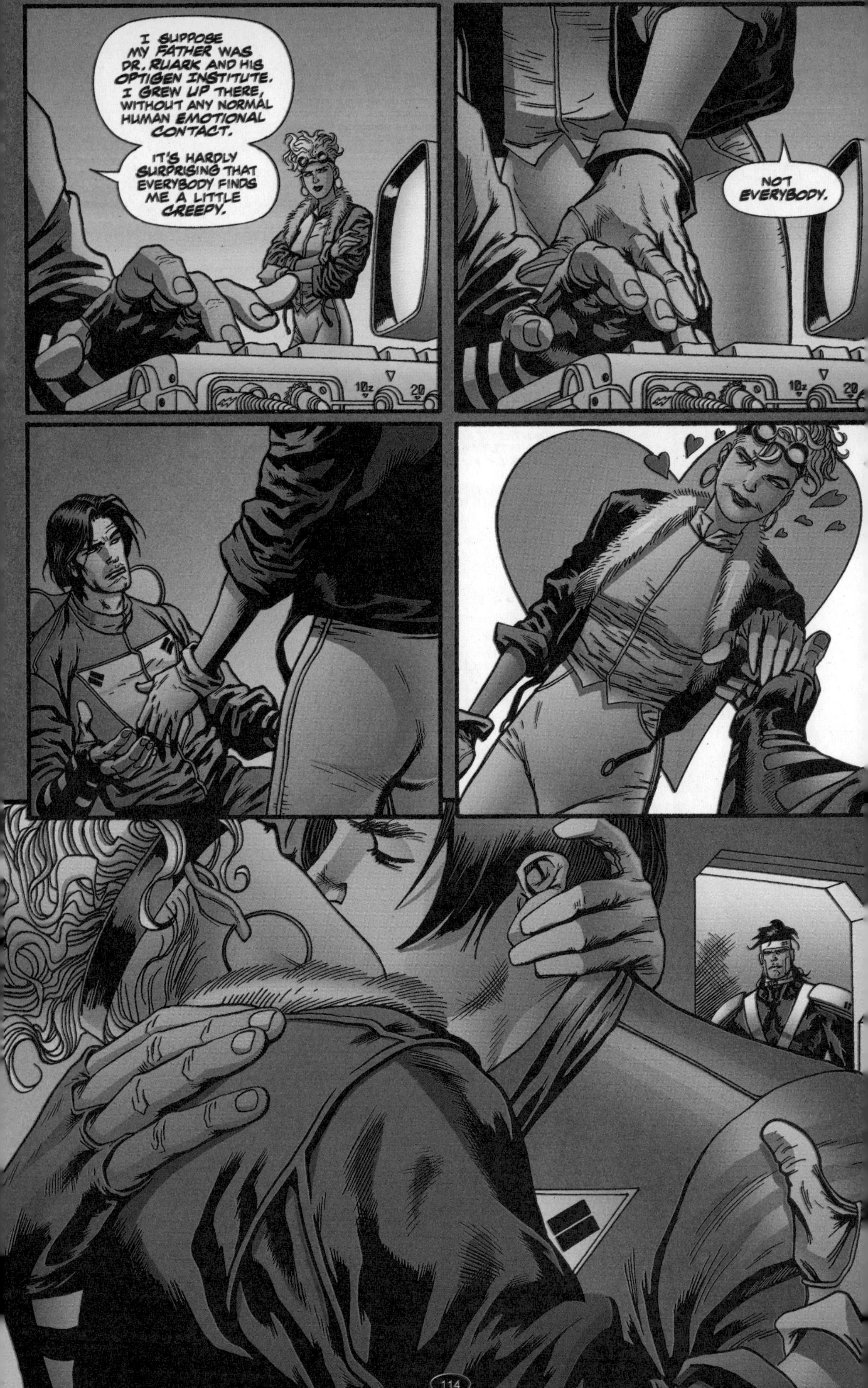
I SUPPOSE MY FATHER WAS DR. RUARK AND HIS OPTIGEN INSTITUTE. I GREW UP THERE, WITHOUT ANY NORMAL HUMAN EMOTIONAL CONTACT.
IT'S HARDLY SURPRISING THAT EVERYBODY FINDS ME A LITTLE CREEPY.
NOT EVERYBODY.

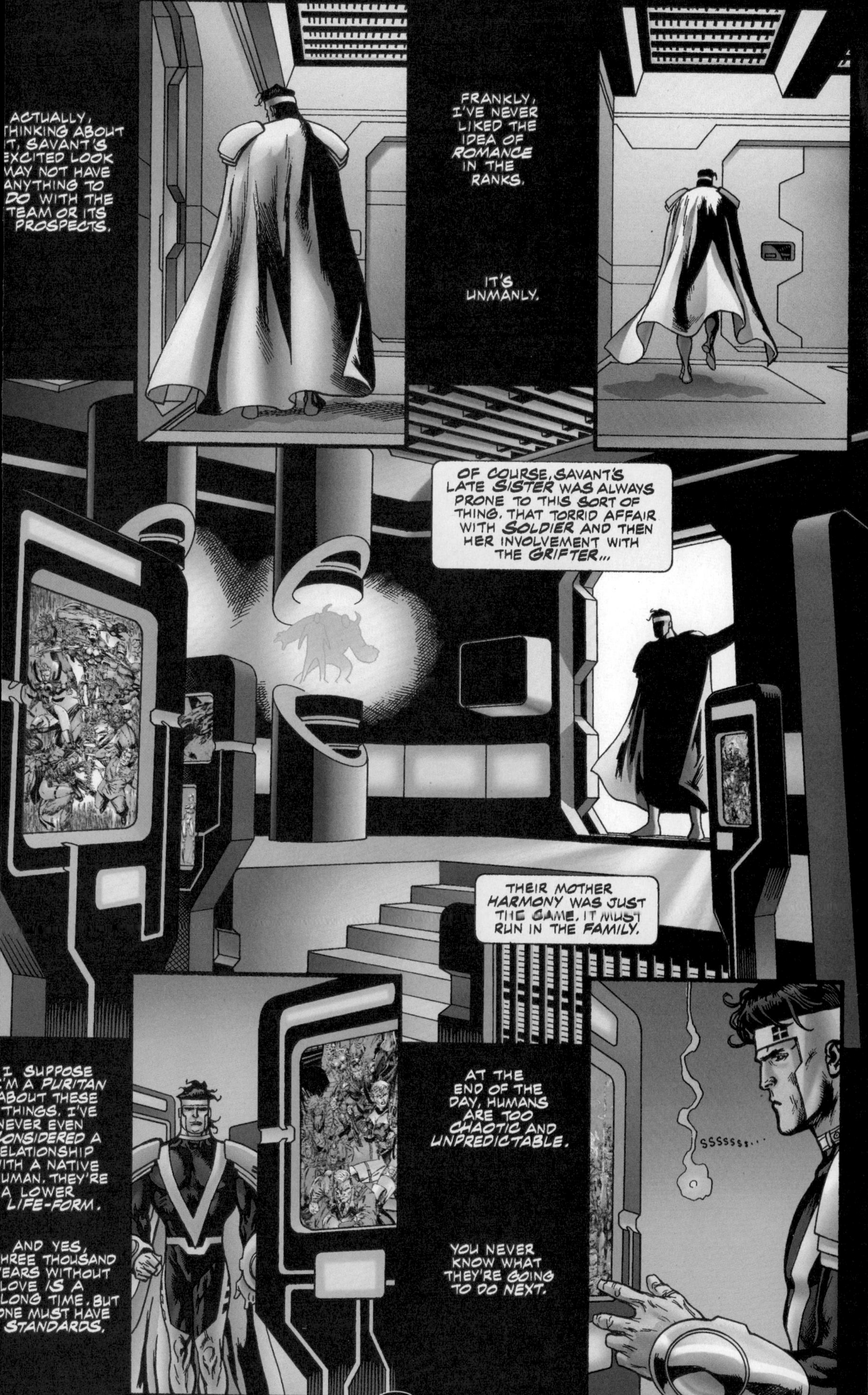
ACTUALLY, THINKING ABOUT IT, SAVANT'S EXCITED LOOK MAY NOT HAVE ANYTHING TO DO WITH THE TEAM OR ITS PROSPECTS.
FRANKLY, I'VE NEVER LIKED THE IDEA OF ROMANCE IN THE RANKS.
IT'S UNMANLY.
OF COURSE, SAVANT'S LATE SISTER WAS ALWAYS PRONE TO THIS SORT OF THING. THAT TORRID AFFAIR WITH SOLDIER AND THEN HER INVOLVEMENT WITH THE GRIFTER...
THEIR MOTHER HARMONY WAS JUST THE SAME. IT MUST RUN IN THE FAMILY.
I SUPPOSE I'M A PURITAN ABOUT THESE THINGS. I'VE NEVER EVEN CONSIDERED A RELATIONSHIP WITH A NATIVE HUMAN. THEY'RE A LOWER LIFE-FORM.
AND YES, THREE THOUSAND YEARS WITHOUT LOVE IS A LONG TIME. BUT ONE MUST HAVE STANDARDS.
AT THE END OF THE DAY, HUMANS ARE TOO CHAOTIC AND UNPREDICTABLE.
YOU NEVER KNOW WHAT THEY'RE GOING TO DO NEXT.
SSSSSSS...

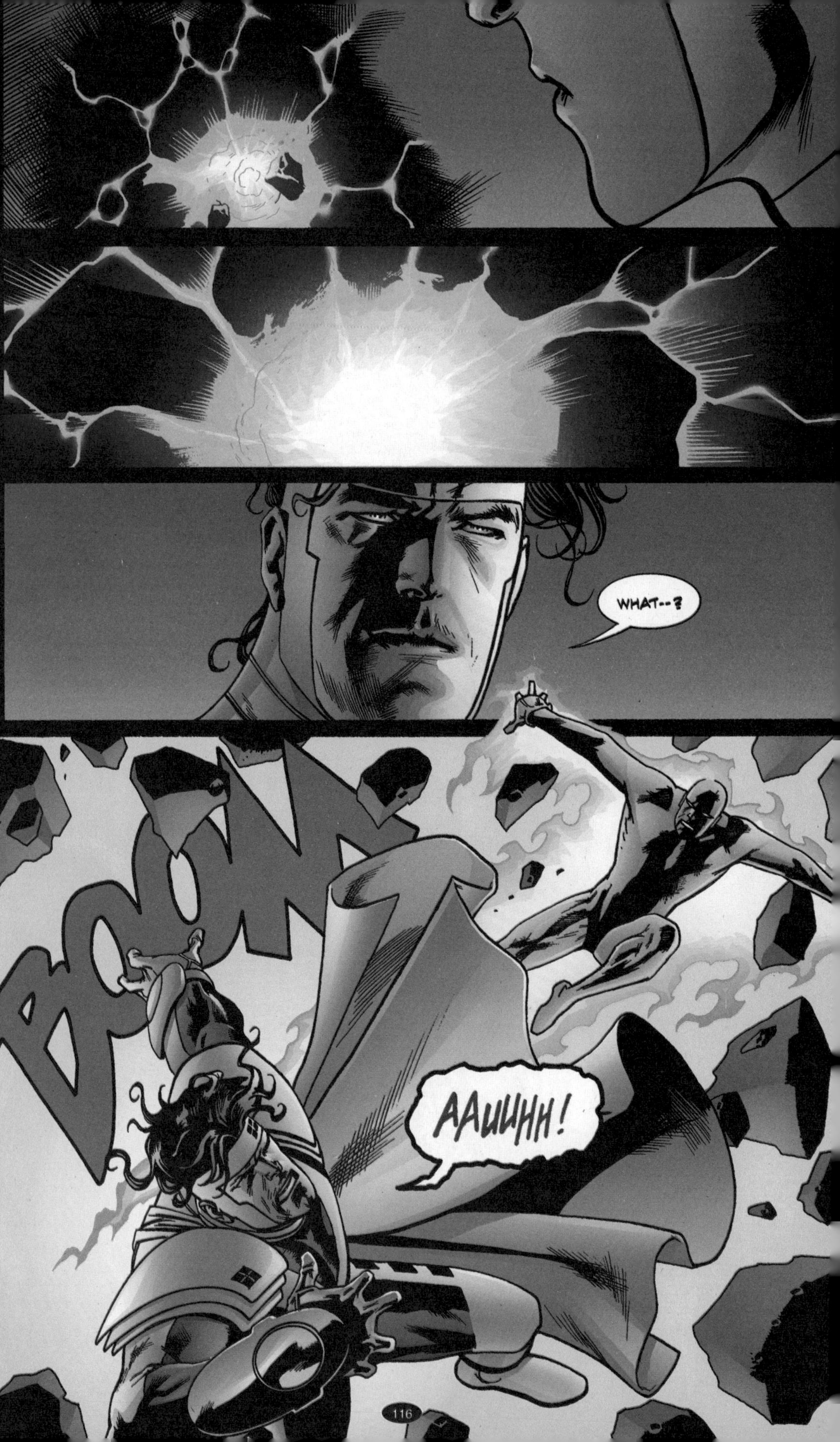
WHAT--?
BOOM
AAUUHH!

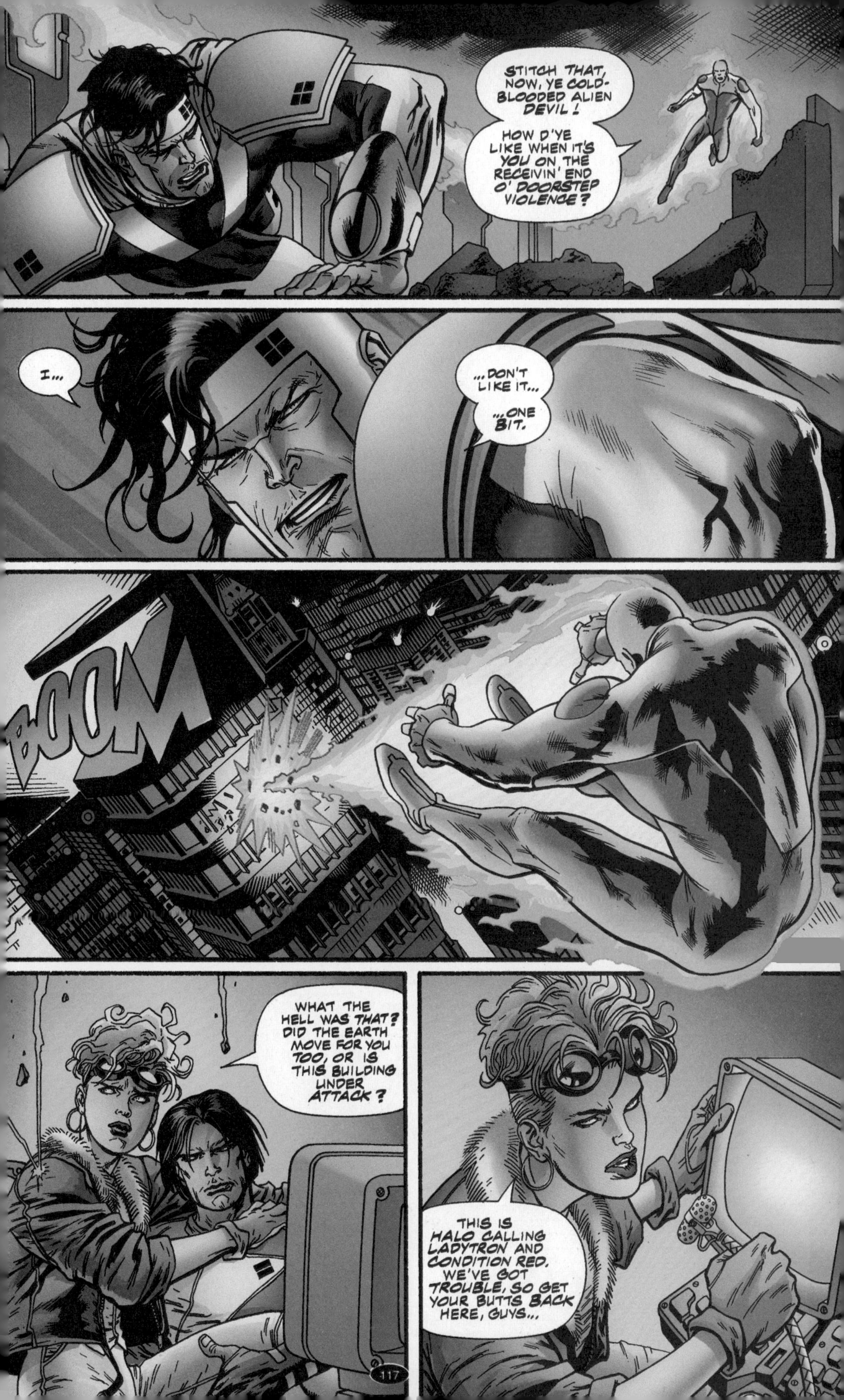
STITCH THAT, NOW, YE COLD-BLOODED ALIEN DEVIL!
HOW D'YE LIKE WHEN IT'S YOU ON THE RECEIVIN' END O' DOORSTEP VIOLENCE?
I...
...DON'T LIKE IT...
...ONE BIT.
BOOM
WHAT THE HELL WAS THAT? DID THE EARTH MOVE FOR YOU TOO, OR IS THIS BUILDING UNDER ATTACK?
THIS IS HALO CALLING LADYTRON AND CONDITION RED. WE'VE GOT TROUBLE, SO GET YOUR BUTTS BACK HERE, GUYS...

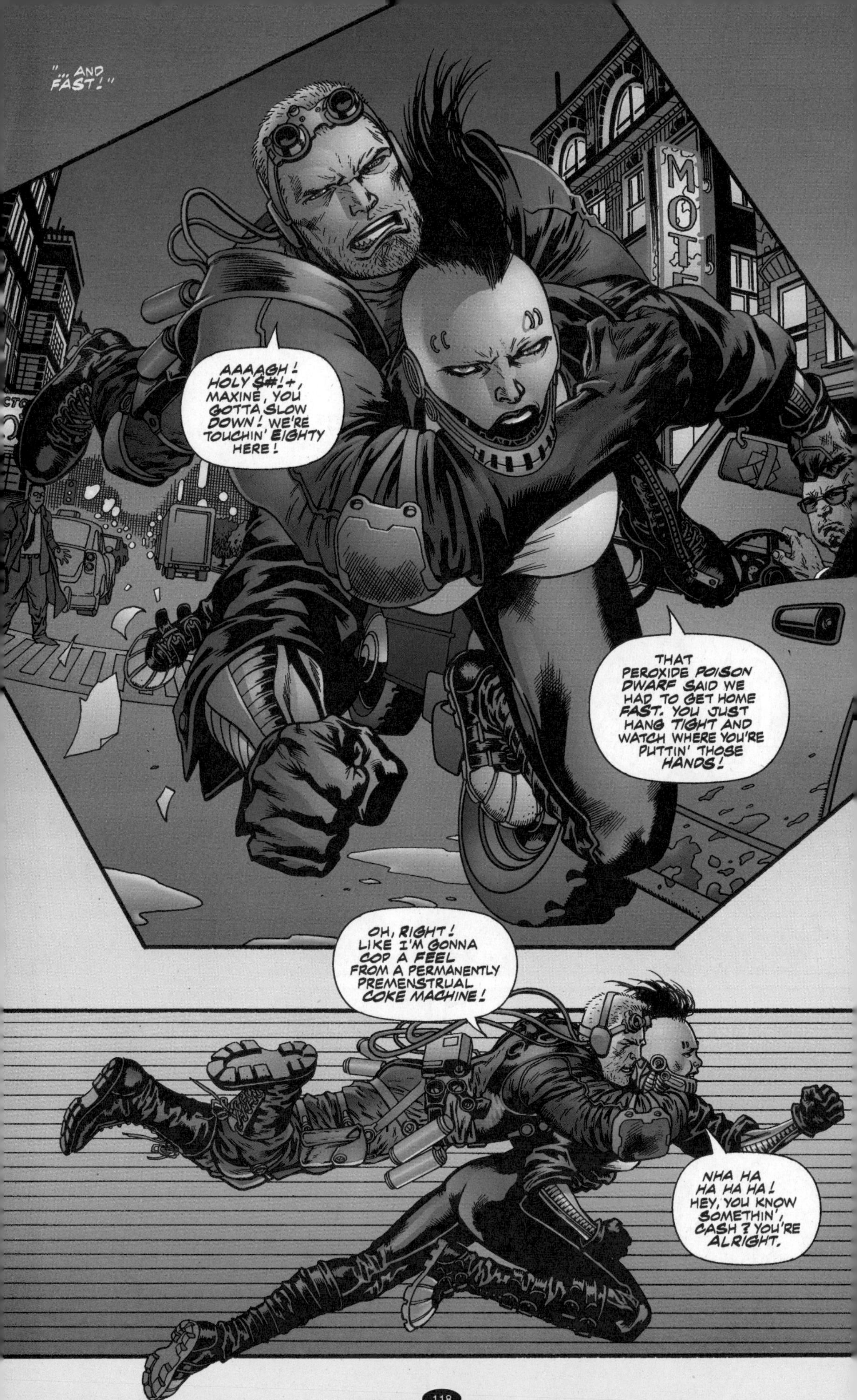
"... AND FAST!"
AAAAGH! HOLY $#!+, MAXINE, YOU GOTTA SLOW DOWN! WE'RE TOUCHIN' EIGHTY HERE!
MOTEL
THAT PEROXIDE POISON DWARF SAID WE HAD TO GET HOME FAST. YOU JUST HANG TIGHT AND WATCH WHERE YOU'RE PUTTIN' THOSE HANDS!
OH, RIGHT! LIKE I'M GONNA COP A FEEL FROM A PERMANENTLY PREMENSTRUAL COKE MACHINE!
NHA HA HA HA HA! HEY, YOU KNOW SOMETHIN', CASH? YOU'RE ALRIGHT.

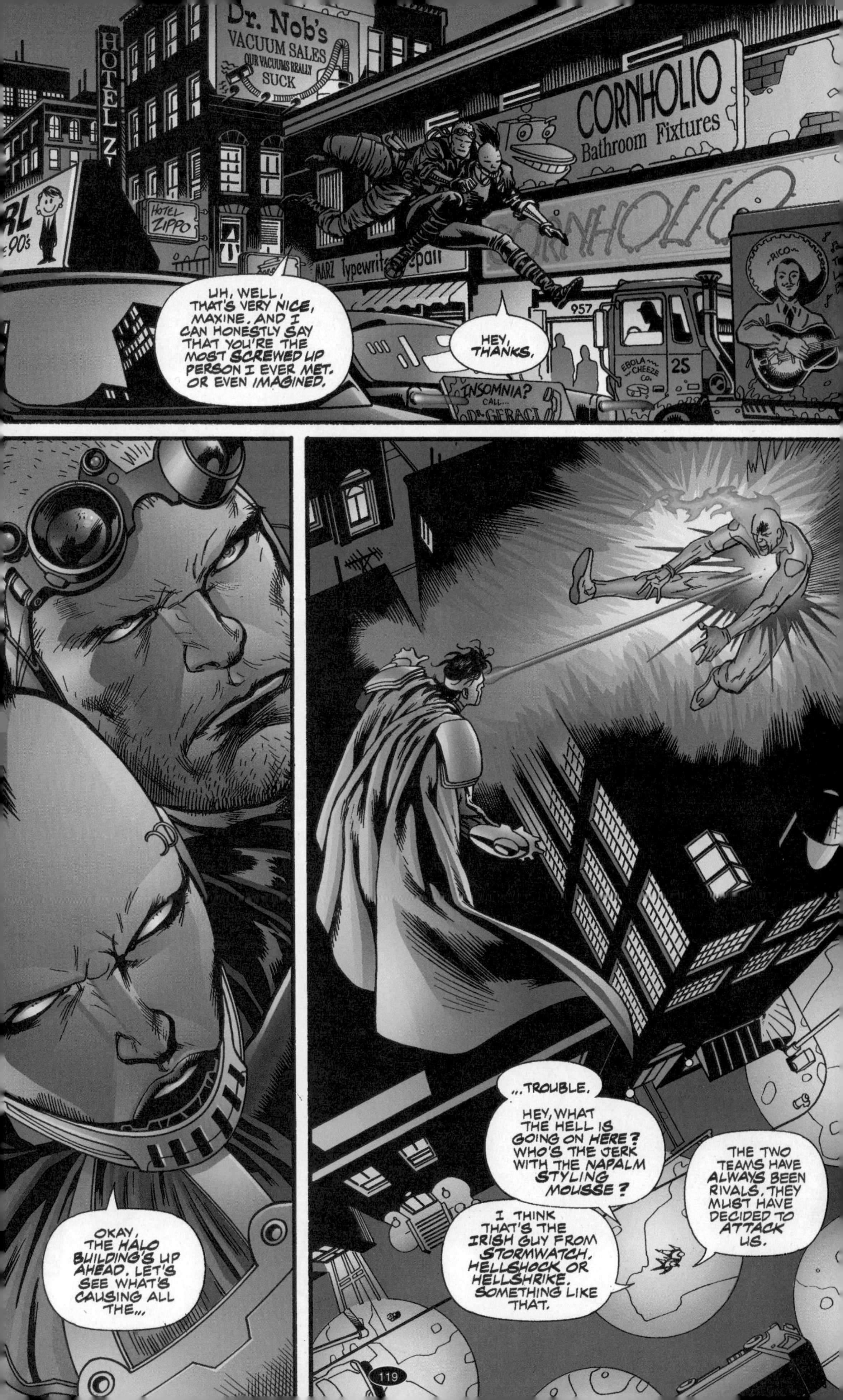
Dr. Nob's
VACUUM SALES
OUR VACUUMS REALLY SUCK
HOTEL Z
CORNHOLIO
Bathroom Fixtures
HOTEL ZIPPO
MARZ Typewrit
epair
UH, WELL, THAT'S VERY NICE, MAXINE. AND I CAN HONESTLY SAY THAT YOU'RE THE MOST SCREWED UP PERSON I EVER MET. OR EVEN IMAGINED.
HEY, THANKS.
957
EBOLA CHEEZE CO.
25
RICO
INSOMNIA? CALL... DR. GERACI
OKAY, THE HALO BUILDING'S UP AHEAD. LET'S SEE WHAT'S CAUSING ALL THE...
...TROUBLE.
HEY, WHAT THE HELL IS GOING ON HERE? WHO'S THE JERK WITH THE NAPALM STYLING MOUSSE?
I THINK THAT'S THE IRISH GUY FROM STORMWATCH. HELLSHOCK OR HELLSHRIKE. SOMETHING LIKE THAT.
THE TWO TEAMS HAVE ALWAYS BEEN RIVALS. THEY MUST HAVE DECIDED TO ATTACK US.

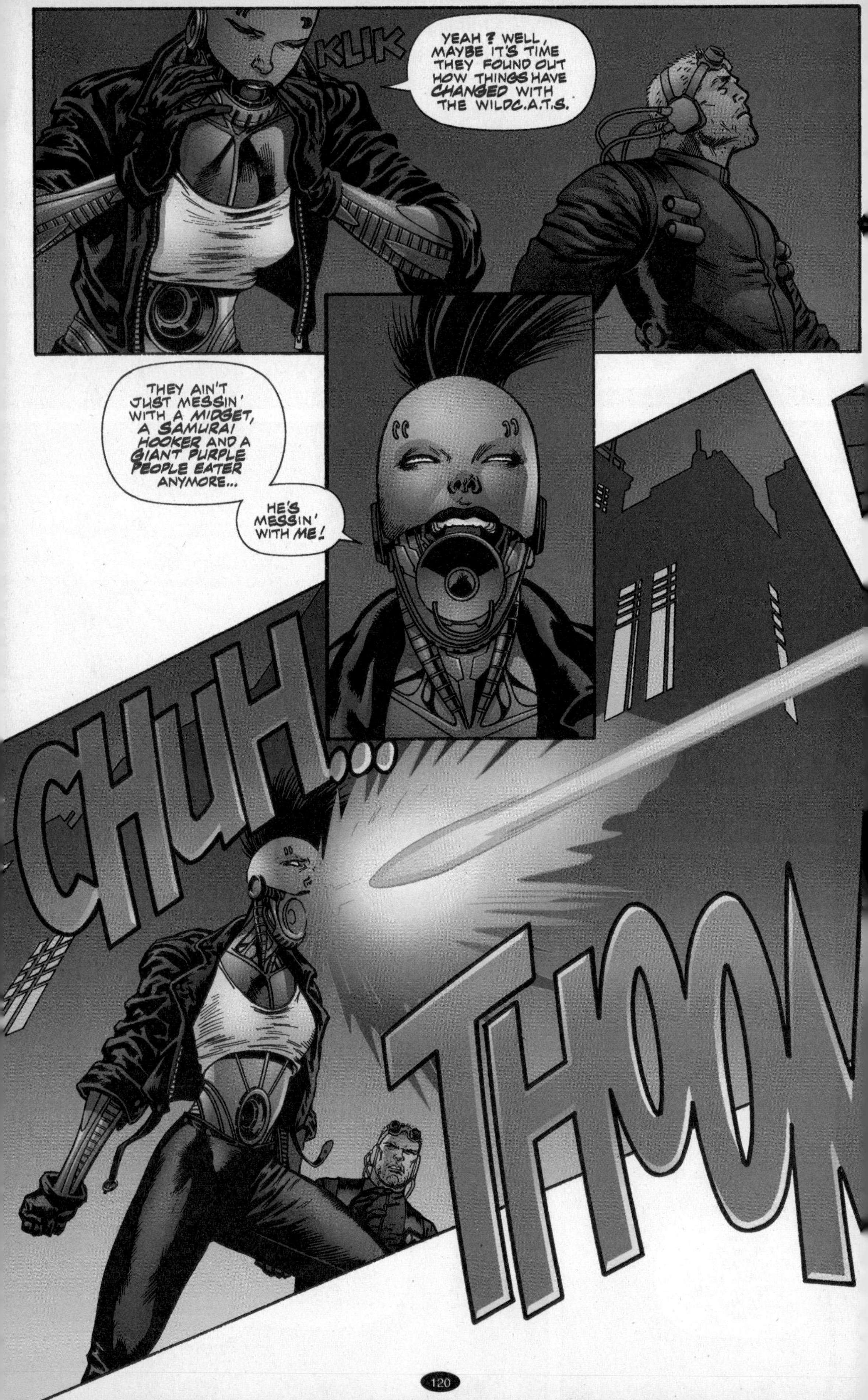
KLIK
YEAH ? WELL, MAYBE IT'S TIME THEY FOUND OUT HOW THINGS HAVE CHANGED WITH THE WILDC.A.T.S.
THEY AIN'T JUST MESSIN' WITH A MIDGET, A SAMURAI HOOKER AND A GIANT PURPLE PEOPLE EATER ANYMORE...
HE'S MESSIN' WITH ME!
CHUH...
THOO

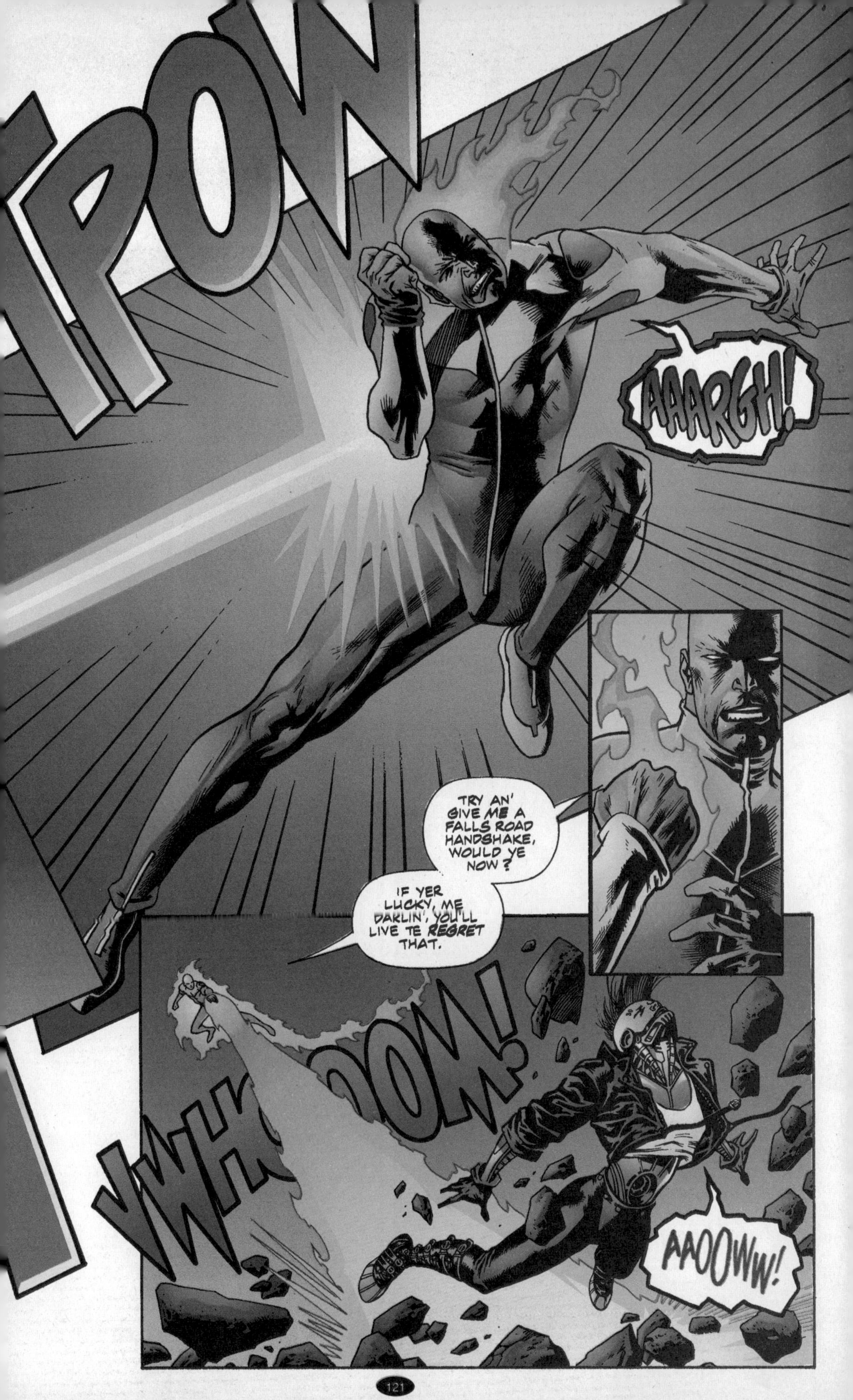
POW
AAARGH!
TRY AN' GIVE ME A FALLS ROAD HANDSHAKE, WOULD YE NOW?
IF YER LUCKY, ME DARLIN', YOU'LL LIVE TE REGRET THAT.
WHOOM!
AAOOWW!

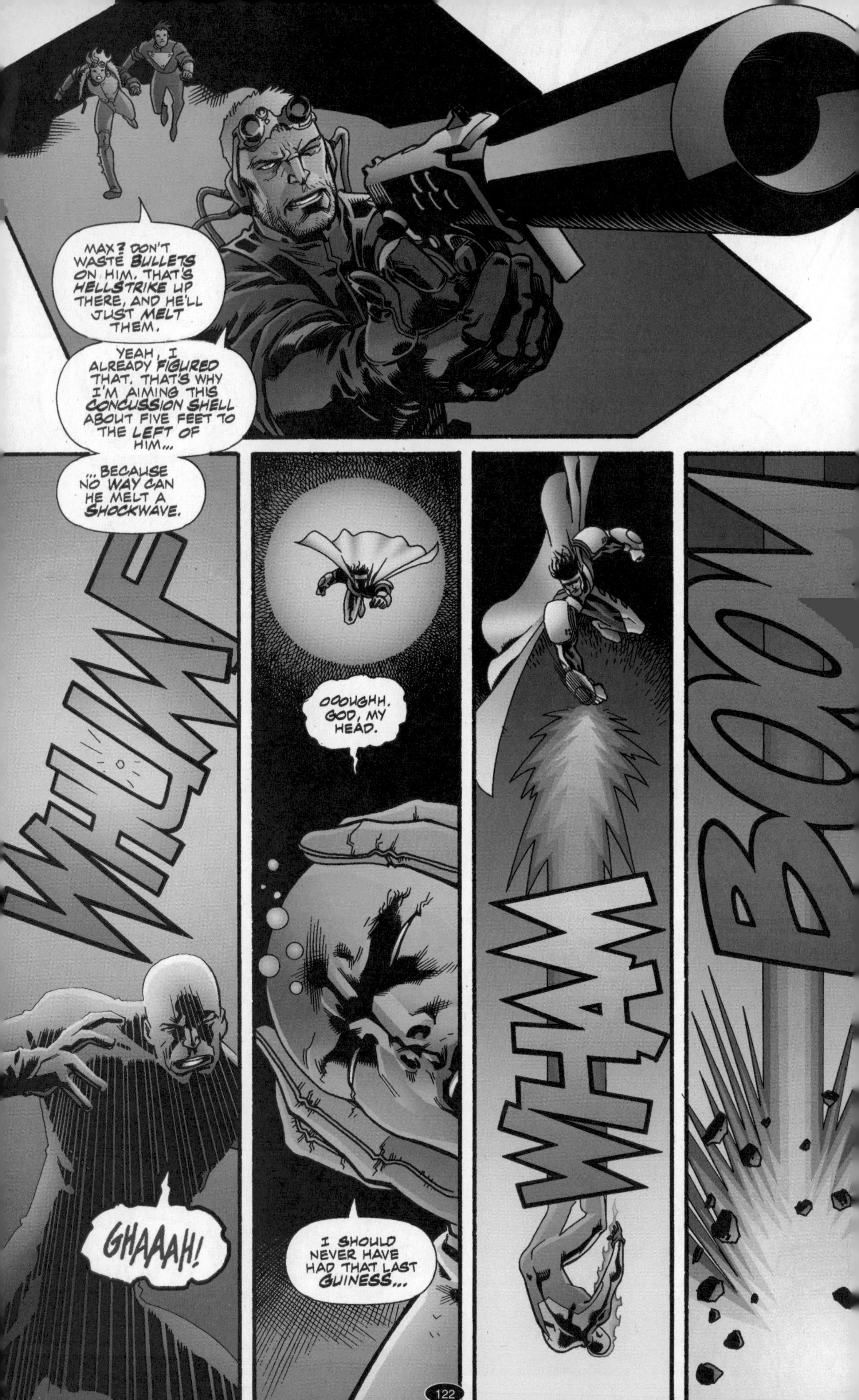
MAX? DON'T WASTE BULLETS ON HIM. THAT'S HELLSTRIKE UP THERE, AND HE'LL JUST MELT THEM.
YEAH, I ALREADY FIGURED THAT. THAT'S WHY I'M AIMING THIS CONCUSSION SHELL ABOUT FIVE FEET TO THE LEFT OF HIM...
...BECAUSE NO WAY CAN HE MELT A SHOCKWAVE.
WHUMF
GHAAAH!
OOOUGHH. GOD, MY HEAD.
I SHOULD NEVER HAVE HAD THAT LAST GUINESS...
WHAM
BOOM

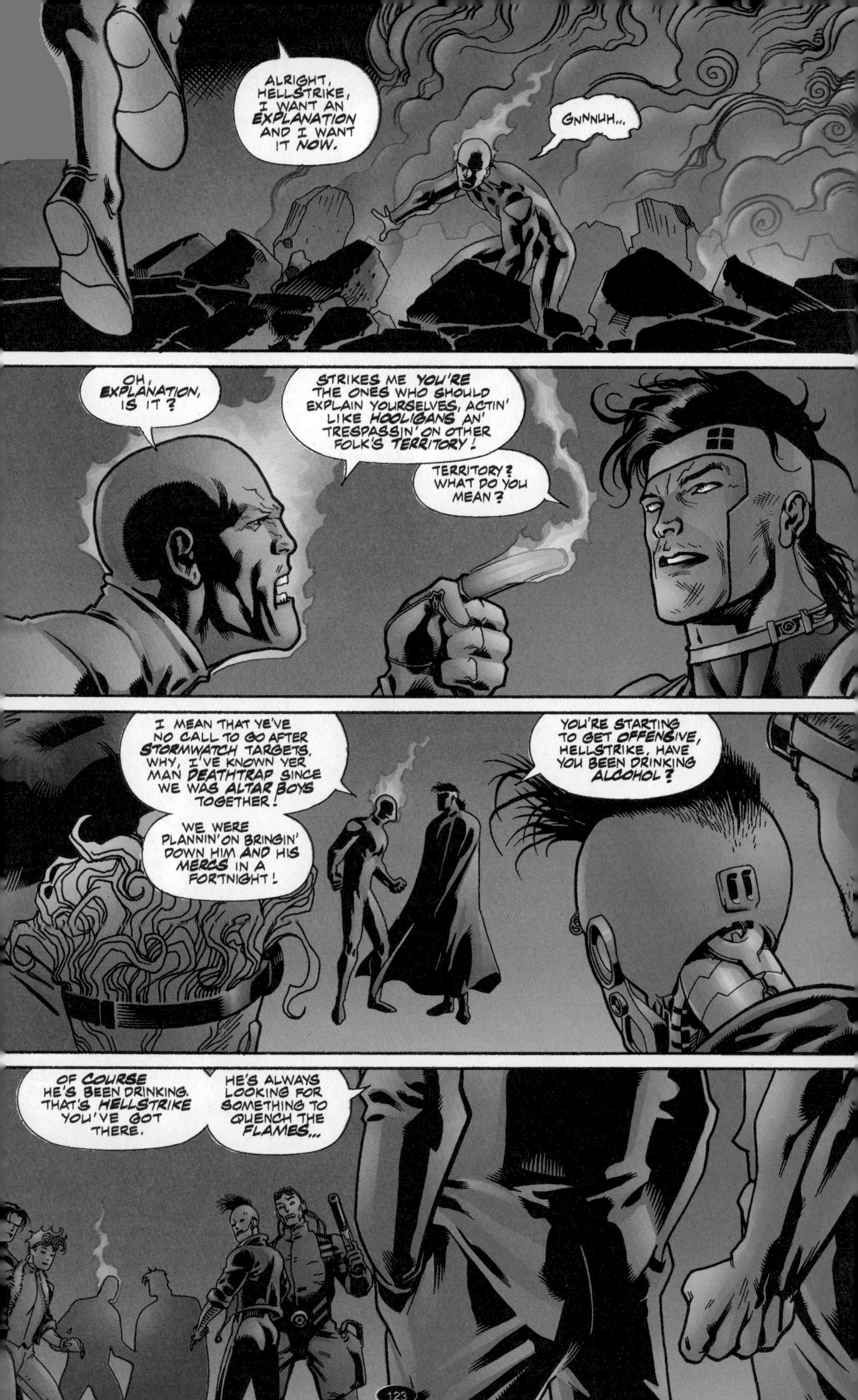
ALRIGHT, HELLSTRIKE, I WANT AN EXPLANATION AND I WANT IT NOW.
GNNNUH...
OH, EXPLANATION, IS IT?
STRIKES ME YOU'RE THE ONES WHO SHOULD EXPLAIN YOURSELVES, ACTIN' LIKE HOOLIGANS AN' TRESPASSIN' ON OTHER FOLK'S TERRITORY!
TERRITORY? WHAT DO YOU MEAN?
I MEAN THAT YE'VE NO CALL TO GO AFTER STORMWATCH TARGETS. WHY, I'VE KNOWN YER MAN DEATHTRAP SINCE WE WAS ALTAR BOYS TOGETHER!
WE WERE PLANNIN' ON BRINGIN' DOWN HIM AND HIS MERCS IN A FORTNIGHT!
YOU'RE STARTING TO GET OFFENSIVE, HELLSTRIKE, HAVE YOU BEEN DRINKING ALCOHOL?
OF COURSE HE'S BEEN DRINKING. THAT'S HELLSTRIKE YOU'VE GOT THERE.
HE'S ALWAYS LOOKING FOR SOMETHING TO QUENCH THE FLAMES...

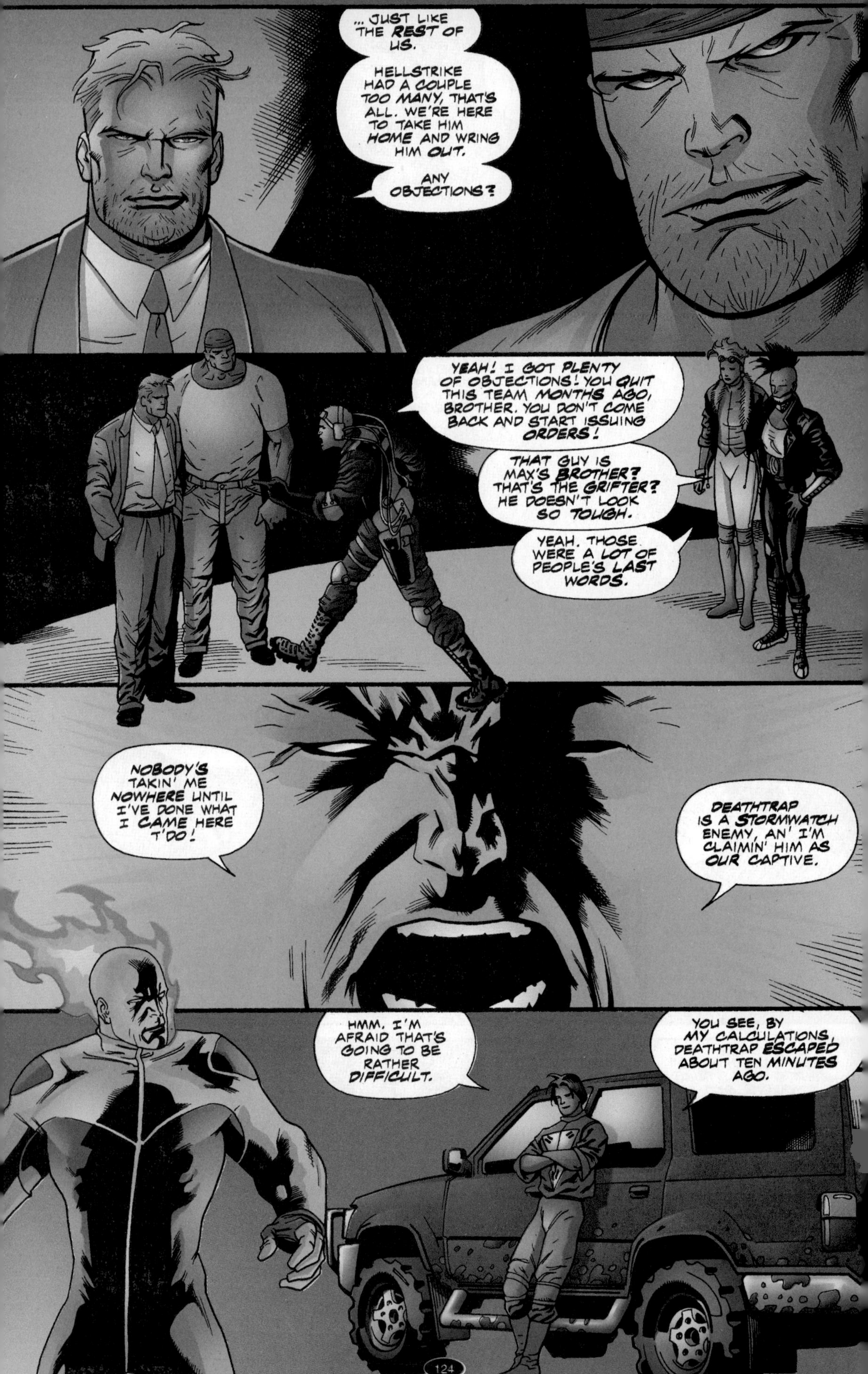

...JUST LIKE THE REST OF US.
HELLSTRIKE HAD A COUPLE TOO MANY, THAT'S ALL. WE'RE HERE TO TAKE HIM HOME AND WRING HIM OUT.
ANY OBJECTIONS?
YEAH! I GOT PLENTY OF OBJECTIONS! YOU QUIT THIS TEAM MONTHS AGO, BROTHER. YOU DON'T COME BACK AND START ISSUING ORDERS!
THAT GUY IS MAX'S BROTHER? THAT'S THE GRIFTER? HE DOESN'T LOOK SO TOUGH.
YEAH. THOSE WERE A LOT OF PEOPLE'S LAST WORDS.
NOBODY'S TAKIN' ME NOWHERE UNTIL I'VE DONE WHAT I CAME HERE T'DO!
DEATHTRAP IS A STORMWATCH ENEMY, AN' I'M CLAIMIN' HIM AS OUR CAPTIVE.
HMM. I'M AFRAID THAT'S GOING TO BE RATHER DIFFICULT.
YOU SEE, BY MY CALCULATIONS, DEATHTRAP ESCAPED ABOUT TEN MINUTES AGO.

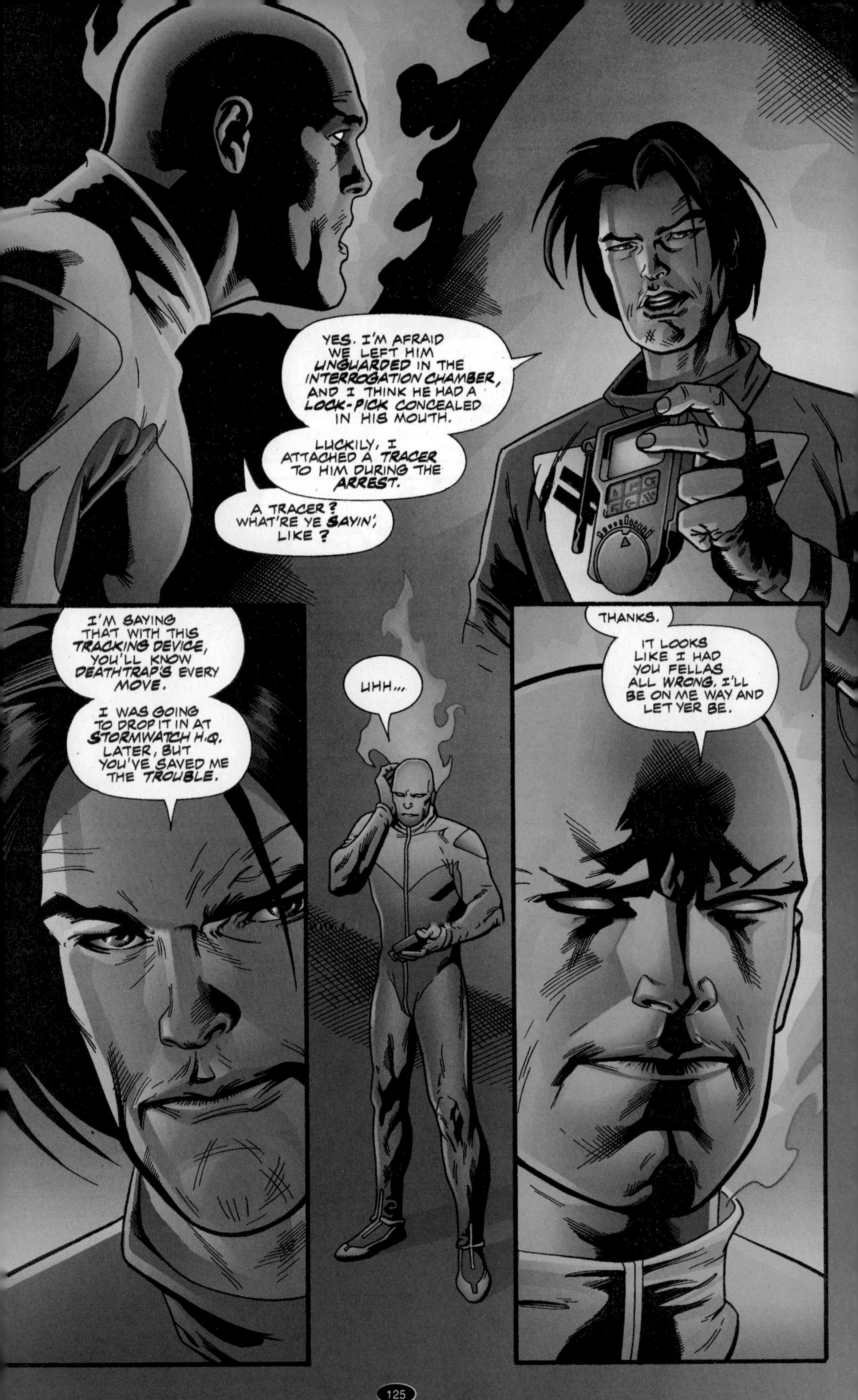
YES. I'M AFRAID WE LEFT HIM UNGUARDED IN THE INTERROGATION CHAMBER, AND I THINK HE HAD A LOCK-PICK CONCEALED IN HIS MOUTH.
LUCKILY, I ATTACHED A TRACER TO HIM DURING THE ARREST.
A TRACER? WHAT'RE YE SAYIN', LIKE?
I'M SAYING THAT WITH THIS TRACKING DEVICE, YOU'LL KNOW DEATHTRAP'S EVERY MOVE.
I WAS GOING TO DROP IT IN AT STORMWATCH H.Q. LATER, BUT YOU'VE SAVED ME THE TROUBLE.
UHH...
THANKS.
IT LOOKS LIKE I HAD YOU FELLAS ALL WRONG. I'LL BE ON ME WAY AND LET YER BE.

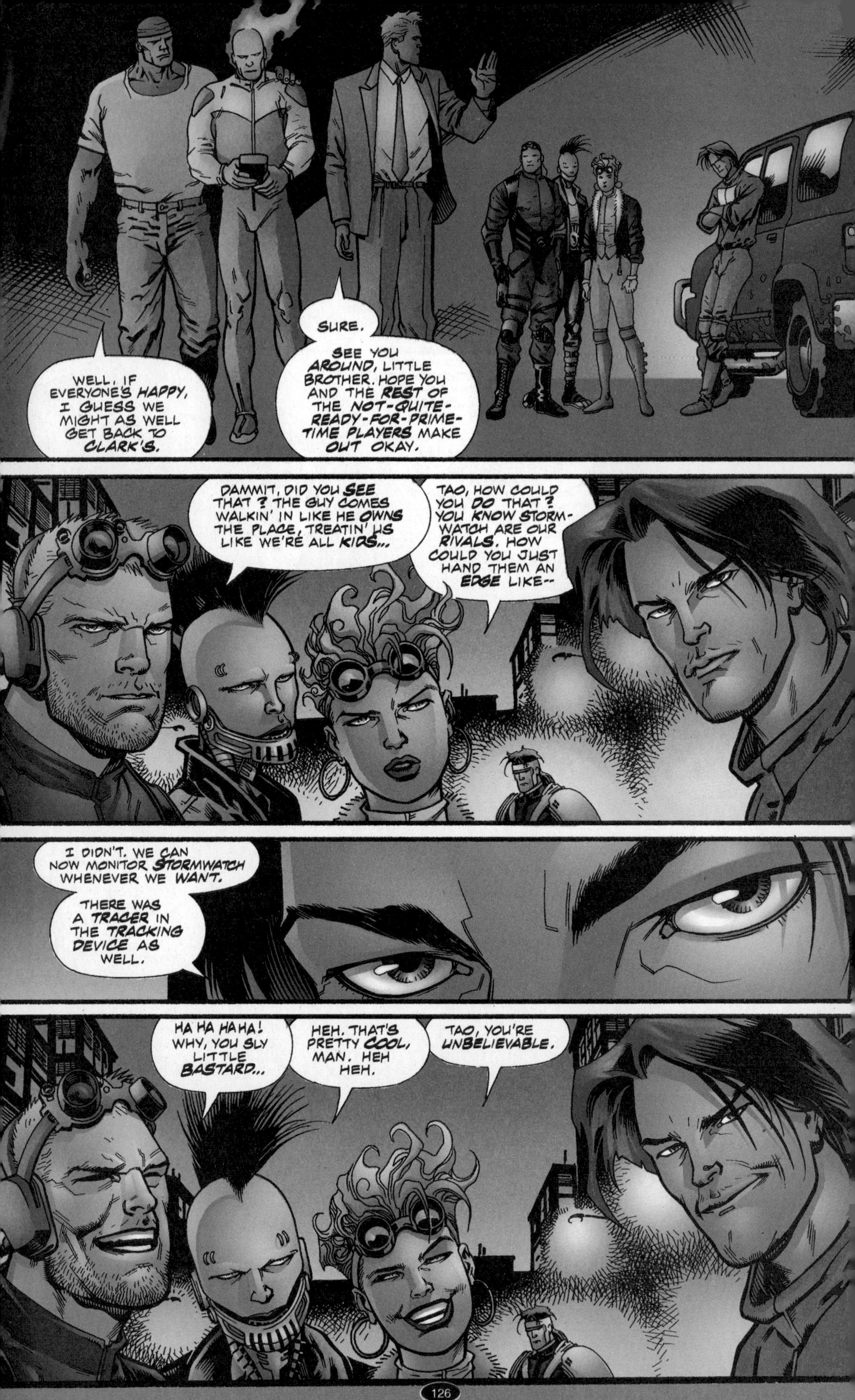
WELL, IF EVERYONE'S HAPPY, I GUESS WE MIGHT AS WELL GET BACK TO CLARK'S.
SURE.
SEE YOU AROUND, LITTLE BROTHER. HOPE YOU AND THE REST OF THE NOT-QUITE-READY-FOR-PRIME-TIME PLAYERS MAKE OUT OKAY.
DAMMIT, DID YOU SEE THAT? THE GUY COMES WALKIN' IN LIKE HE OWNS THE PLACE, TREATIN' US LIKE WE'RE ALL KIDS...
TAO, HOW COULD YOU DO THAT? YOU KNOW STORMWATCH ARE OUR RIVALS. HOW COULD YOU JUST HAND THEM AN EDGE LIKE--
I DIDN'T. WE CAN NOW MONITOR STORMWATCH WHENEVER WE WANT.
THERE WAS A TRACER IN THE TRACKING DEVICE AS WELL.
HA HA HA HA! WHY, YOU SLY LITTLE BASTARD...
HEH. THAT'S PRETTY COOL, MAN. HEH HEH.
TAO, YOU'RE UNBELIEVABLE.

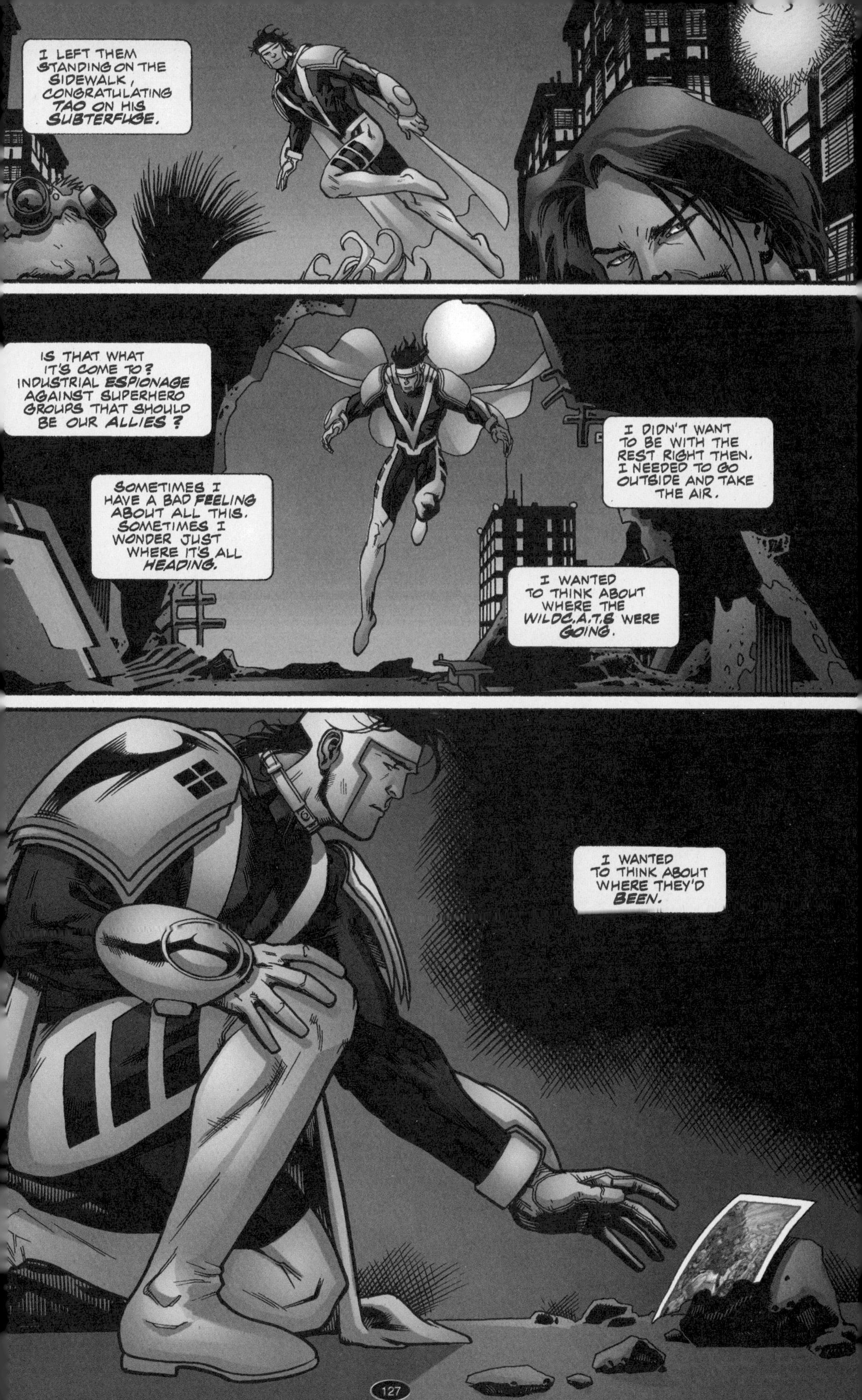
I LEFT THEM STANDING ON THE SIDEWALK, CONGRATULATING TAO ON HIS SUBTERFUGE.
IS THAT WHAT IT'S COME TO? INDUSTRIAL ESPIONAGE AGAINST SUPERHERO GROUPS THAT SHOULD BE OUR ALLIES?
SOMETIMES I HAVE A BAD FEELING ABOUT ALL THIS. SOMETIMES I WONDER JUST WHERE IT'S ALL HEADING.
I DIDN'T WANT TO BE WITH THE REST RIGHT THEN. I NEEDED TO GO OUTSIDE AND TAKE THE AIR.
I WANTED TO THINK ABOUT WHERE THE WILDC.A.T.S WERE GOING.
I WANTED TO THINK ABOUT WHERE THEY'D BEEN.

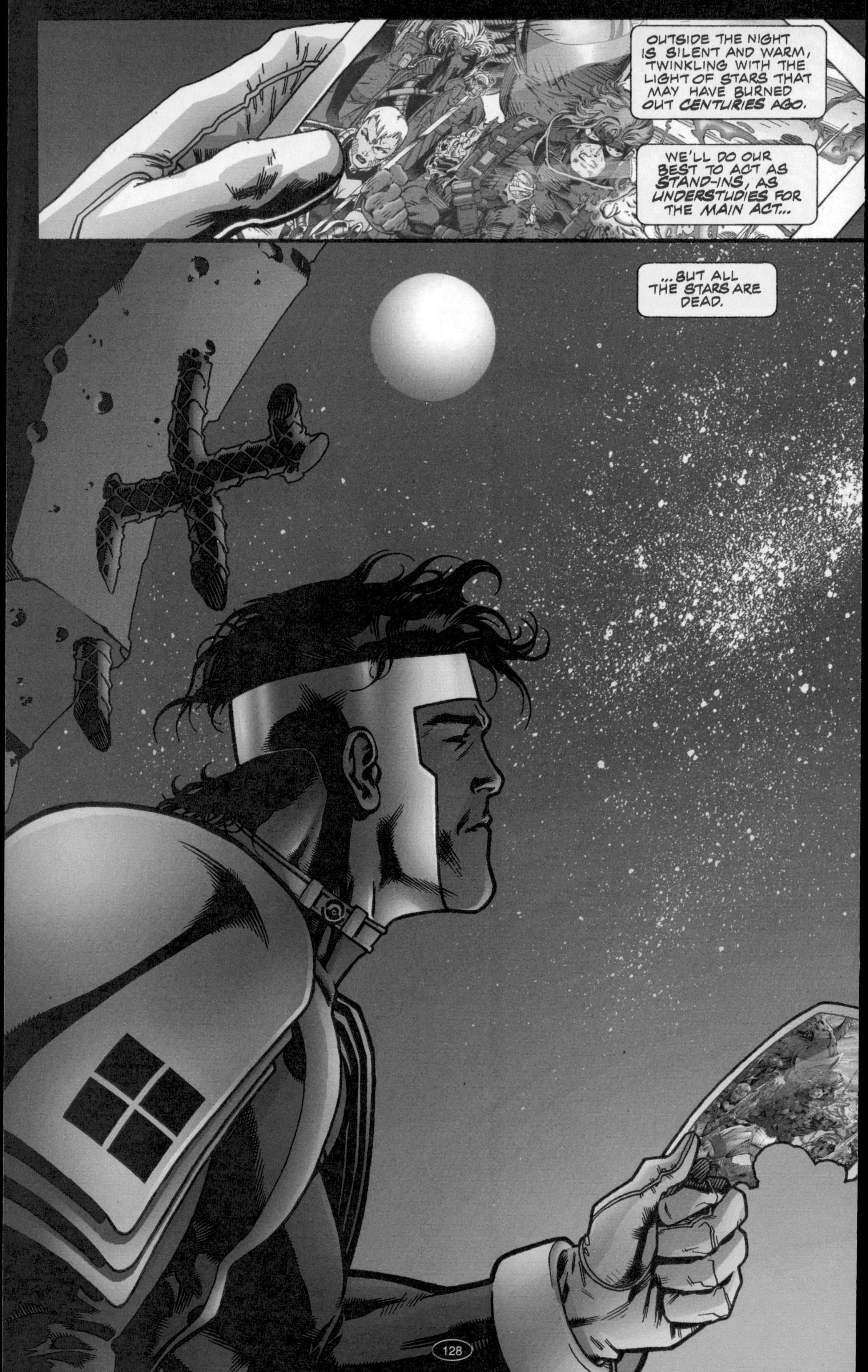
OUTSIDE THE NIGHT IS SILENT AND WARM, TWINKLING WITH THE LIGHT OF STARS THAT MAY HAVE BURNED OUT CENTURIES AGO.
WE'LL DO OUR BEST TO ACT AS STAND-INS, AS UNDERSTUDIES FOR THE MAIN ACT...
...BUT ALL THE STARS ARE DEAD.

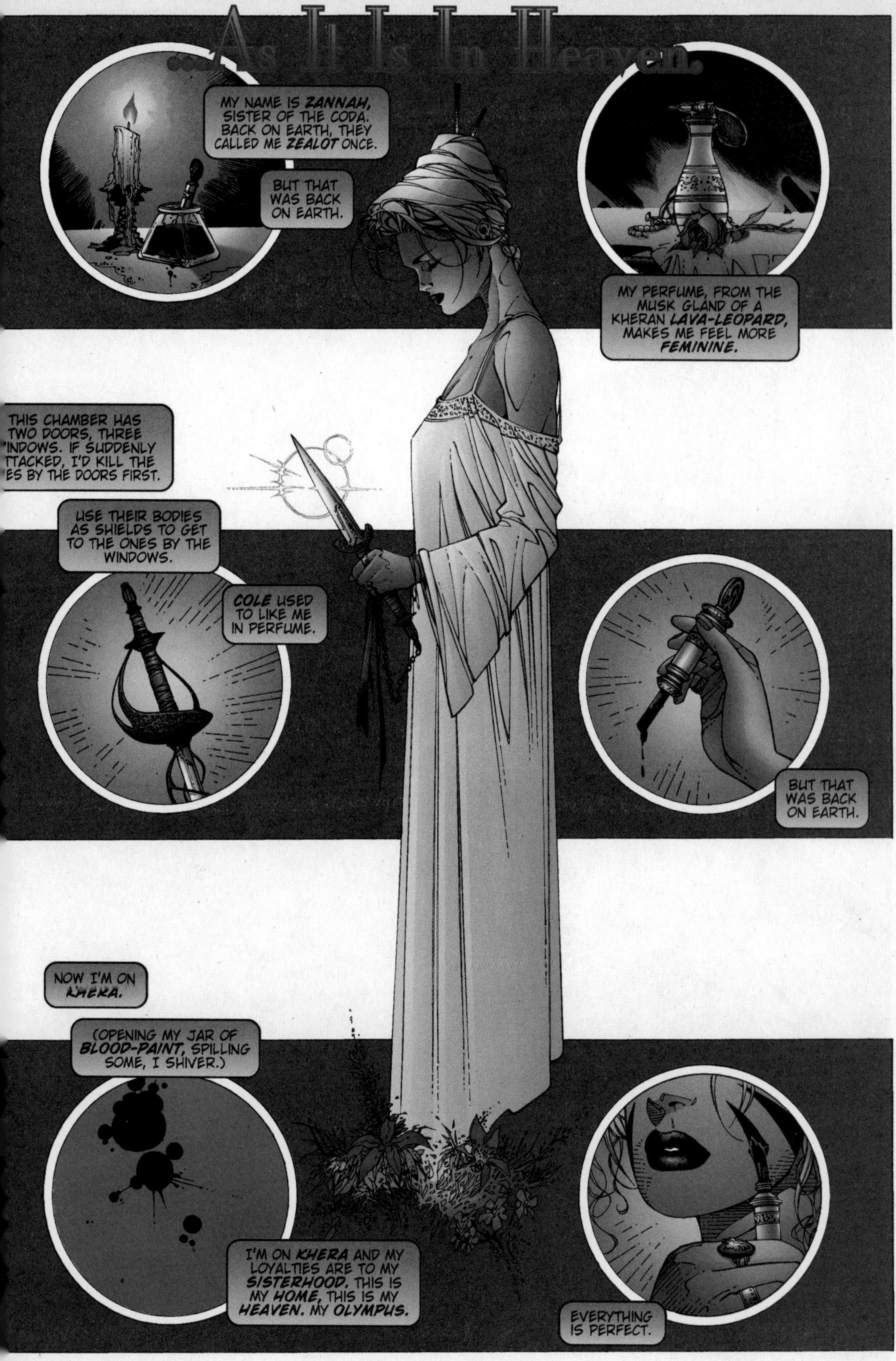
...As It Is In Heaven.
MY NAME IS ZANNAH, SISTER OF THE CODA. BACK ON EARTH, THEY CALLED ME ZEALOT ONCE.
BUT THAT WAS BACK ON EARTH.
MY PERFUME, FROM THE MUSK GLAND OF A KHERAN LAVA-LEOPARD, MAKES ME FEEL MORE FEMININE.
THIS CHAMBER HAS TWO DOORS, THREE INDOWS. IF SUDDENLY TTACKED, I'D KILL THE ES BY THE DOORS FIRST.
USE THEIR BODIES AS SHIELDS TO GET TO THE ONES BY THE WINDOWS.
COLE USED TO LIKE ME IN PERFUME.
BUT THAT WAS BACK ON EARTH.
NOW I'M ON KHERA.
(OPENING MY JAR OF BLOOD-PAINT, SPILLING SOME, I SHIVER.)
I'M ON KHERA AND MY LOYALTIES ARE TO MY SISTERHOOD. THIS IS MY HOME, THIS IS MY HEAVEN. MY OLYMPUS.
EVERYTHING IS PERFECT.

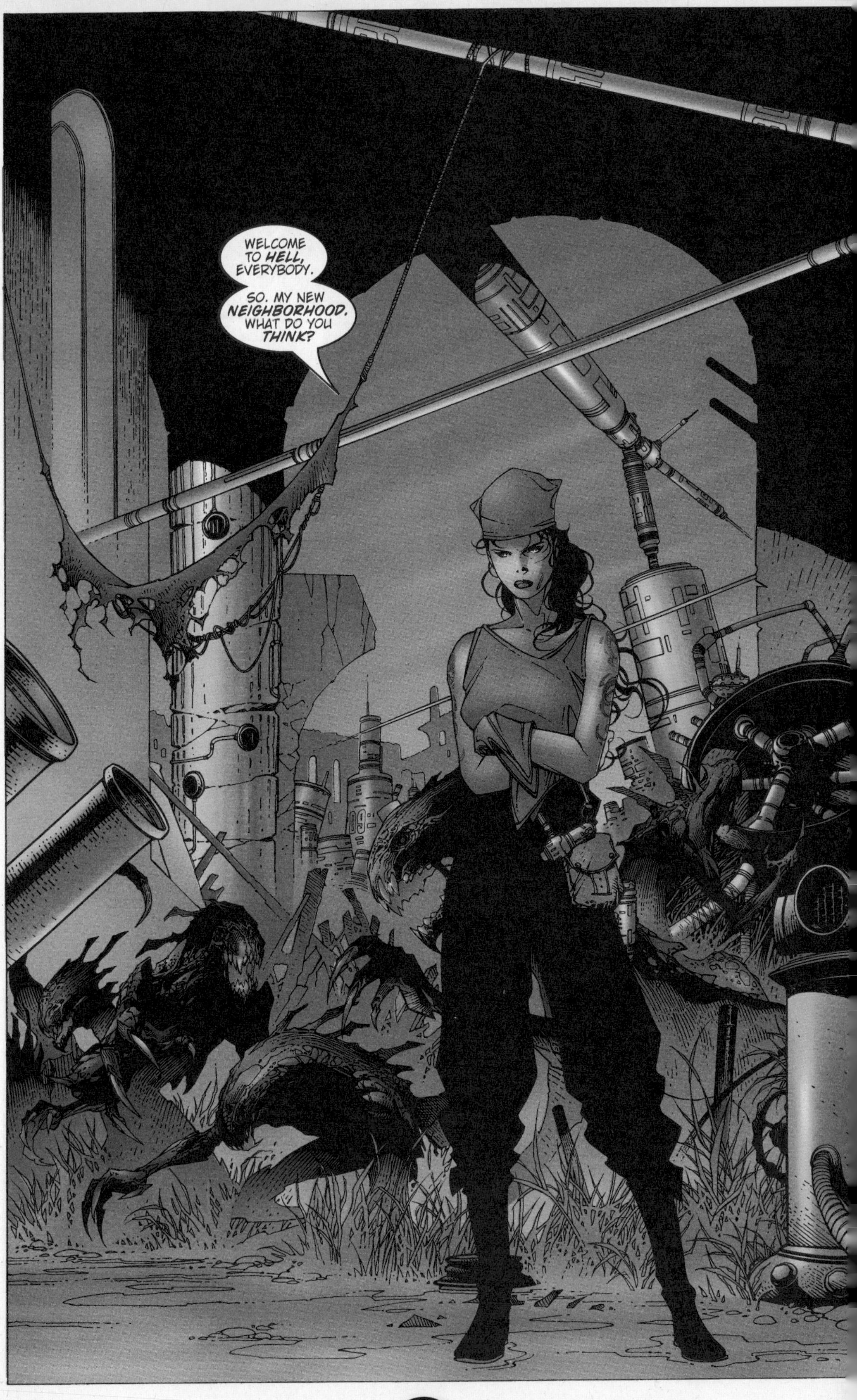
WELCOME TO HELL, EVERYBODY.
SO. MY NEW NEIGHBORHOOD. WHAT DO YOU THINK?

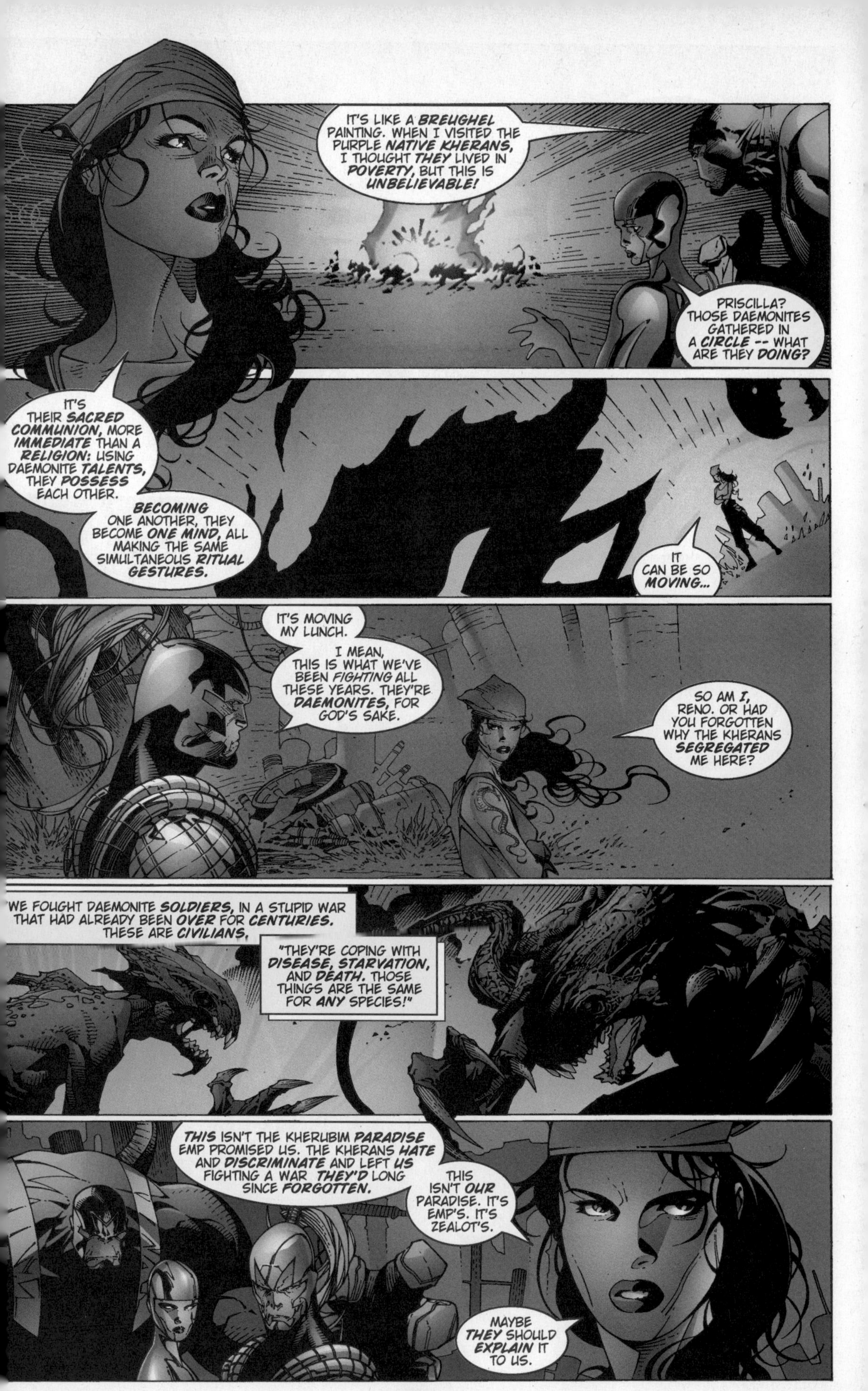
IT'S LIKE A BREUGHEL PAINTING. WHEN I VISITED THE PURPLE NATIVE KHERANS, I THOUGHT THEY LIVED IN POVERTY, BUT THIS IS UNBELIEVABLE!
PRISCILLA? THOSE DAEMONITES GATHERED IN A CIRCLE -- WHAT ARE THEY DOING?
IT'S THEIR SACRED COMMUNION, MORE IMMEDIATE THAN A RELIGION: USING DAEMONITE TALENTS, THEY POSSESS EACH OTHER.
BECOMING ONE ANOTHER, THEY BECOME ONE MIND, ALL MAKING THE SAME SIMULTANEOUS RITUAL GESTURES.
IT CAN BE SO MOVING...
IT'S MOVING MY LUNCH.
I MEAN, THIS IS WHAT WE'VE BEEN FIGHTING ALL THESE YEARS. THEY'RE DAEMONITES, FOR GOD'S SAKE.
SO AM I, RENO. OR HAD YOU FORGOTTEN WHY THE KHERANS SEGREGATED ME HERE?
WE FOUGHT DAEMONITE SOLDIERS, IN A STUPID WAR THAT HAD ALREADY BEEN OVER FOR CENTURIES. THESE ARE CIVILIANS.
"THEY'RE COPING WITH DISEASE, STARVATION, AND DEATH. THOSE THINGS ARE THE SAME FOR ANY SPECIES!"
THIS ISN'T THE KHERUBIM PARADISE EMP PROMISED US. THE KHERANS HATE AND DISCRIMINATE AND LEFT US FIGHTING A WAR THEY'D LONG SINCE FORGOTTEN.
THIS ISN'T OUR PARADISE. IT'S EMP'S. IT'S ZEALOT'S.
MAYBE THEY SHOULD EXPLAIN IT TO US.

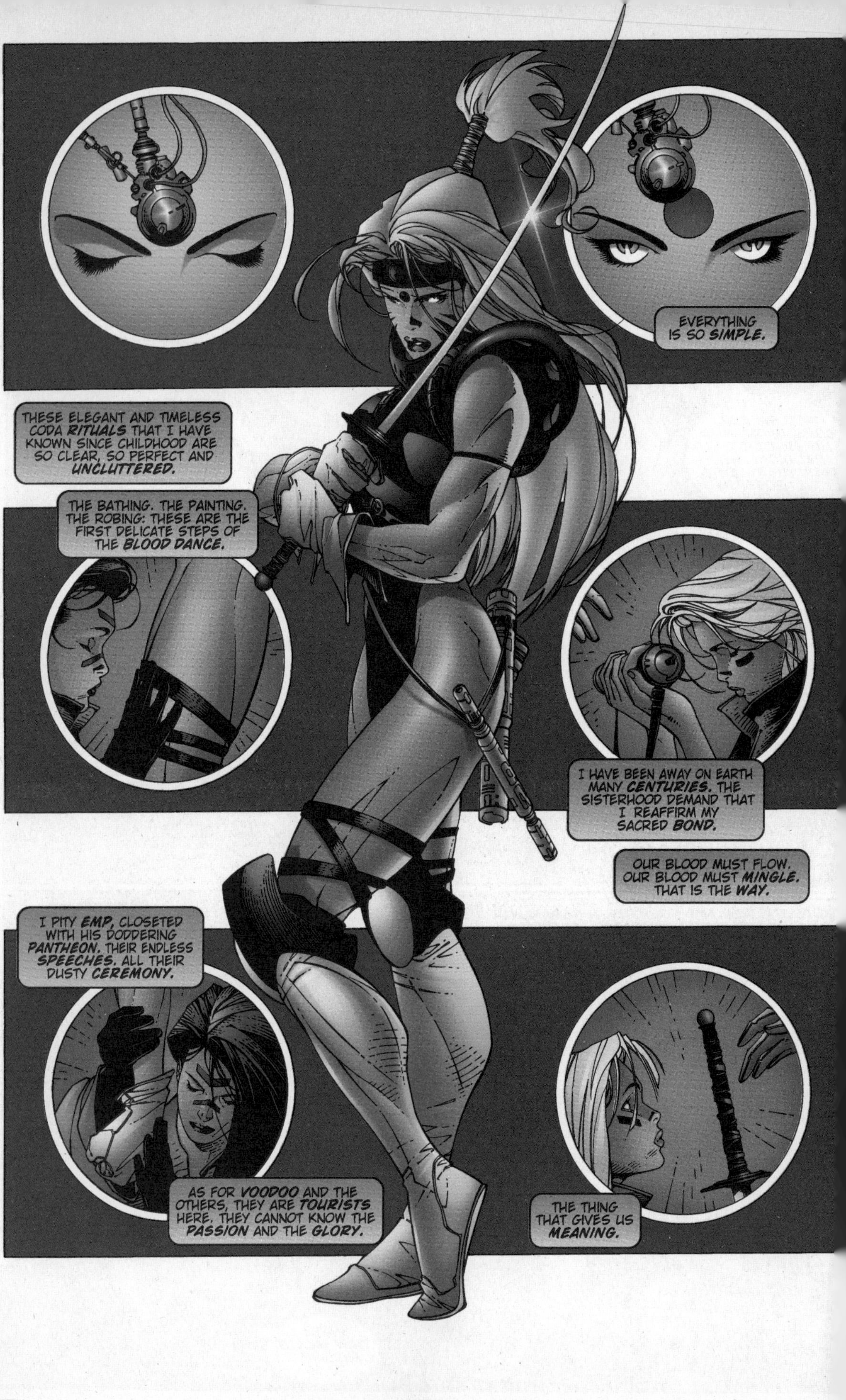
EVERYTHING IS SO SIMPLE.
THESE ELEGANT AND TIMELESS CODA RITUALS THAT I HAVE KNOWN SINCE CHILDHOOD ARE SO CLEAR, SO PERFECT AND UNCLUTTERED.
THE BATHING. THE PAINTING. THE ROBING: THESE ARE THE FIRST DELICATE STEPS OF THE BLOOD DANCE.
I HAVE BEEN AWAY ON EARTH MANY CENTURIES. THE SISTERHOOD DEMAND THAT I REAFFIRM MY SACRED BOND.
OUR BLOOD MUST FLOW. OUR BLOOD MUST MINGLE. THAT IS THE WAY.
I PITY EMP, CLOSETED WITH HIS DODDERING PANTHEON. THEIR ENDLESS SPEECHES. ALL THEIR DUSTY CEREMONY.
AS FOR VOODOO AND THE OTHERS, THEY ARE TOURISTS HERE. THEY CANNOT KNOW THE PASSION AND THE GLORY.
THE THING THAT GIVES US MEANING.

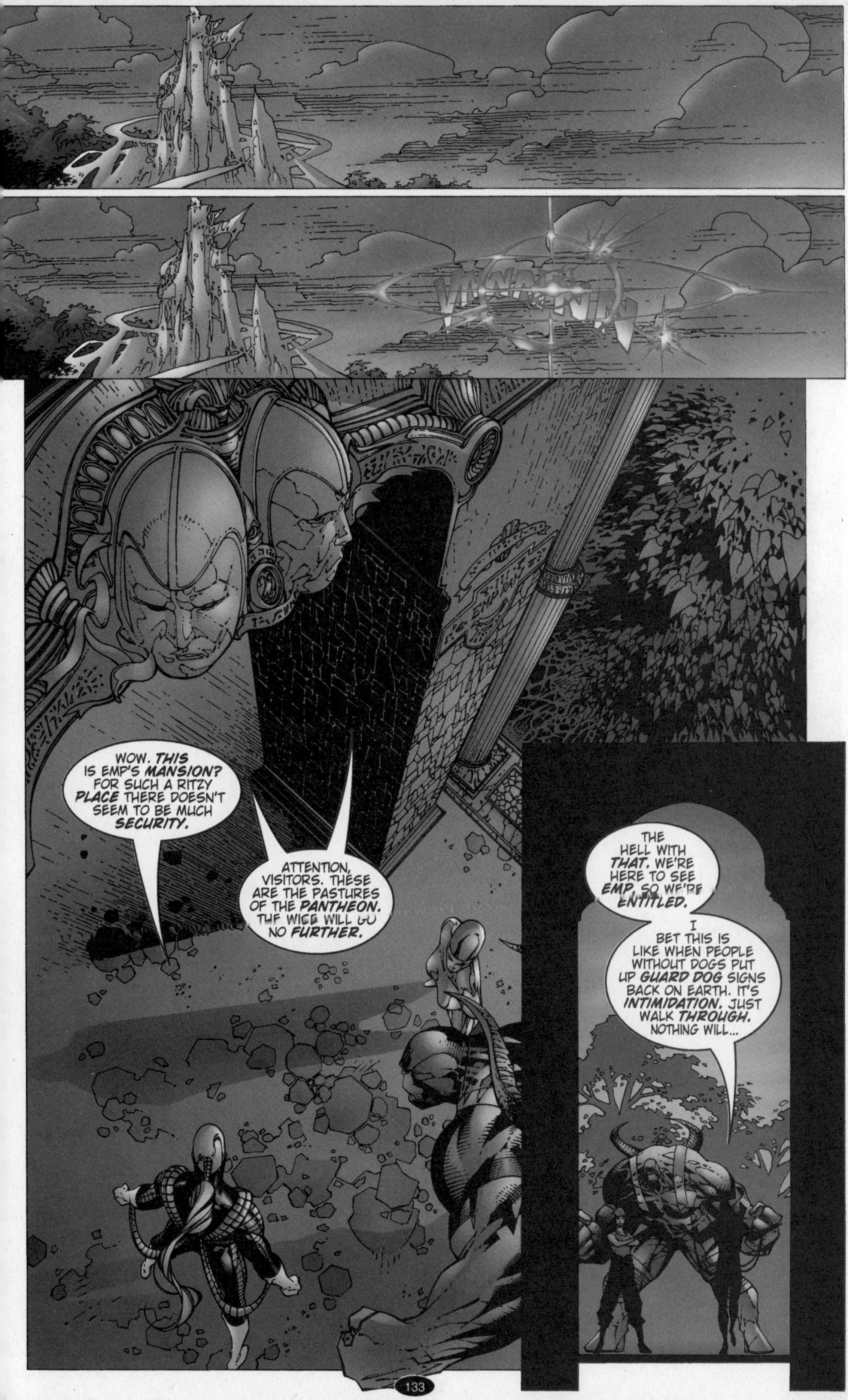
WOW. THIS IS EMP'S MANSION? FOR SUCH A RITZY PLACE THERE DOESN'T SEEM TO BE MUCH SECURITY.
ATTENTION, VISITORS. THESE ARE THE PASTURES OF THE PANTHEON. THE WISE WILL GO NO FURTHER.
THE HELL WITH THAT. WE'RE HERE TO SEE EMP, SO WE'RE ENTITLED.
I BET THIS IS LIKE WHEN PEOPLE WITHOUT DOGS PUT UP GUARD DOG SIGNS BACK ON EARTH. IT'S INTIMIDATION. JUST WALK THROUGH. NOTHING WILL...

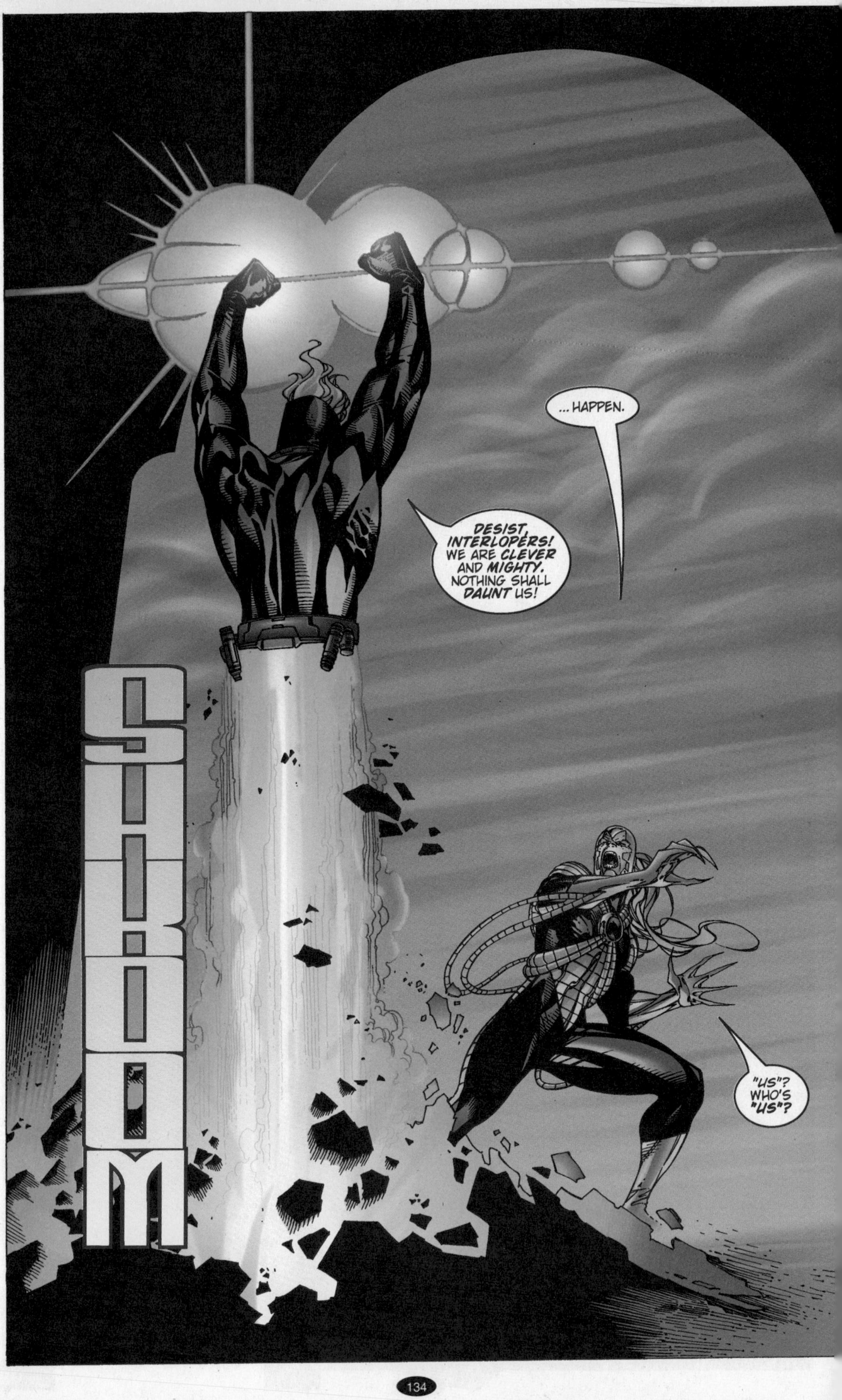
... HAPPEN.
DESIST, INTERLOPERS! WE ARE CLEVER AND MIGHTY. NOTHING SHALL DAUNT US!
"US"? WHO'S "US"?

THERE'S *ANOTHER* ONE OVER HERE, RENO!

H-HADRIAN? I-IS THAT *YOU?*

NO. I'M NOT *HADRIAN.*

I'M *INNOCENT.*

SWAK

~UNNNGHH~

STAY *AWAY* FROM HER!

JEREMY, THIS IS LOOKING *SERIOUS!* THESE GUYS ARE ALL LIKE *IMPROVED VERSIONS* OF HADRIAN!

I *KNOW.* THEY'RE THE PANTHEON'S *SPARTAN GUARDS.* ALL I CAN THINK OF TO *DO* IS GET *MASSIVE* ENOUGH TO STOMP THEM *DEAD.*

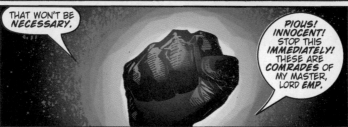

THAT WON'T BE *NECESSARY.*

PIOUS! INNOCENT! STOP THIS *IMMEDIATELY!* THESE ARE *COMRADES* OF MY MASTER, LORD *EMP.*

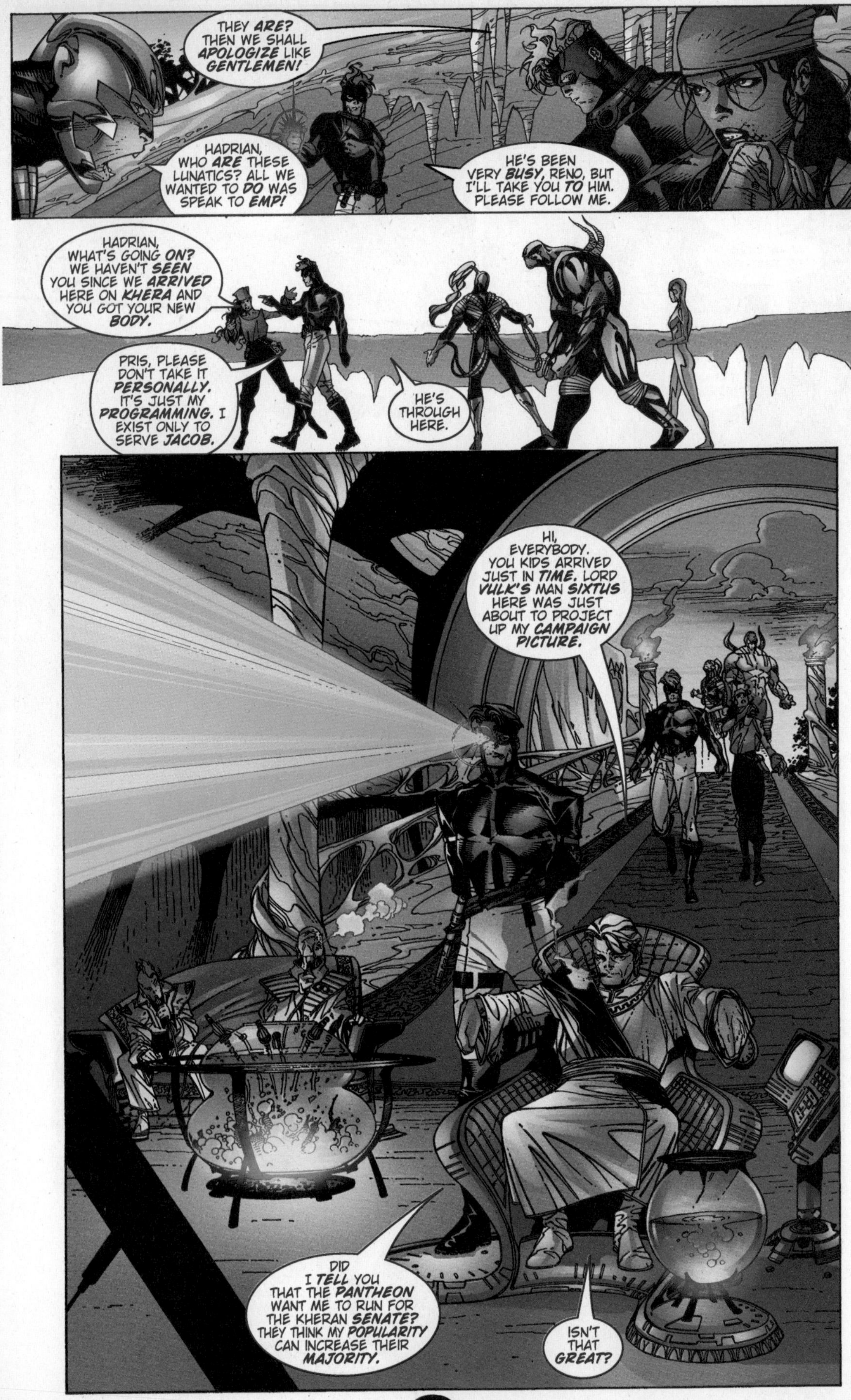
THEY ARE? THEN WE SHALL APOLOGIZE LIKE GENTLEMEN!
HADRIAN, WHO ARE THESE LUNATICS? ALL WE WANTED TO DO WAS SPEAK TO EMP!
HE'S BEEN VERY BUSY, RENO, BUT I'LL TAKE YOU TO HIM. PLEASE FOLLOW ME.
HADRIAN, WHAT'S GOING ON? WE HAVEN'T SEEN YOU SINCE WE ARRIVED HERE ON KHERA AND YOU GOT YOUR NEW BODY.
PRIS, PLEASE DON'T TAKE IT PERSONALLY. IT'S JUST MY PROGRAMMING. I EXIST ONLY TO SERVE JACOB.
HE'S THROUGH HERE.
HI, EVERYBODY. YOU KIDS ARRIVED JUST IN TIME. LORD VULK'S MAN SIXTUS HERE WAS JUST ABOUT TO PROJECT UP MY CAMPAIGN PICTURE.
DID I TELL YOU THAT THE PANTHEON WANT ME TO RUN FOR THE KHERAN SENATE? THEY THINK MY POPULARITY CAN INCREASE THEIR MAJORITY.
ISN'T THAT GREAT?

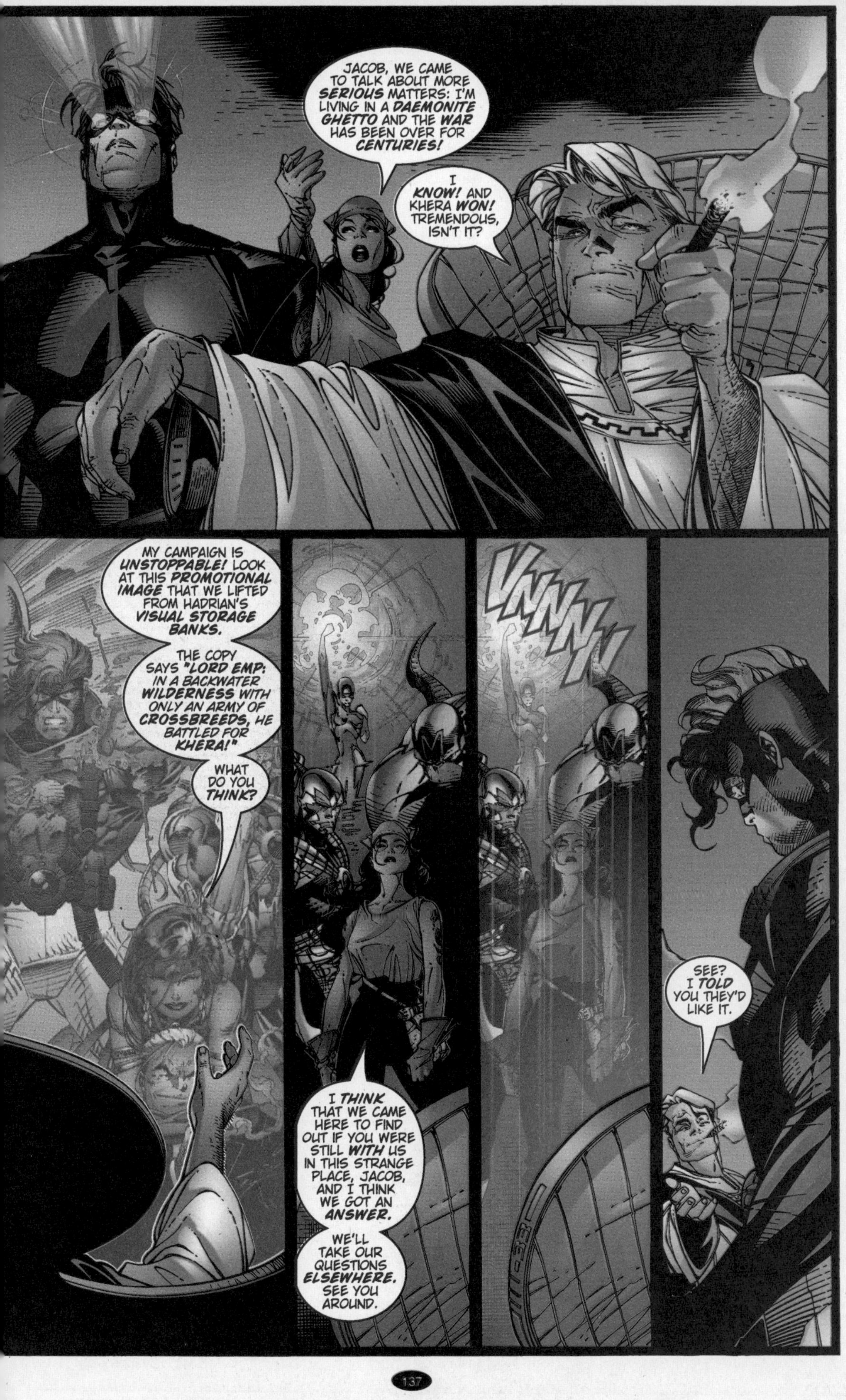
JACOB, WE CAME TO TALK ABOUT MORE SERIOUS MATTERS: I'M LIVING IN A DAEMONITE GHETTO AND THE WAR HAS BEEN OVER FOR CENTURIES!
I KNOW! AND KHERA WON! TREMENDOUS, ISN'T IT?
MY CAMPAIGN IS UNSTOPPABLE! LOOK AT THIS PROMOTIONAL IMAGE THAT WE LIFTED FROM HADRIAN'S VISUAL STORAGE BANKS.
THE COPY SAYS "LORD EMP: IN A BACKWATER WILDERNESS WITH ONLY AN ARMY OF CROSSBREEDS, HE BATTLED FOR KHERA!"
WHAT DO YOU THINK?
I THINK THAT WE CAME HERE TO FIND OUT IF YOU WERE STILL WITH US IN THIS STRANGE PLACE, JACOB, AND I THINK WE GOT AN ANSWER.
WE'LL TAKE OUR QUESTIONS ELSEWHERE. SEE YOU AROUND.
VNNNN
SEE? I TOLD YOU THEY'D LIKE IT.

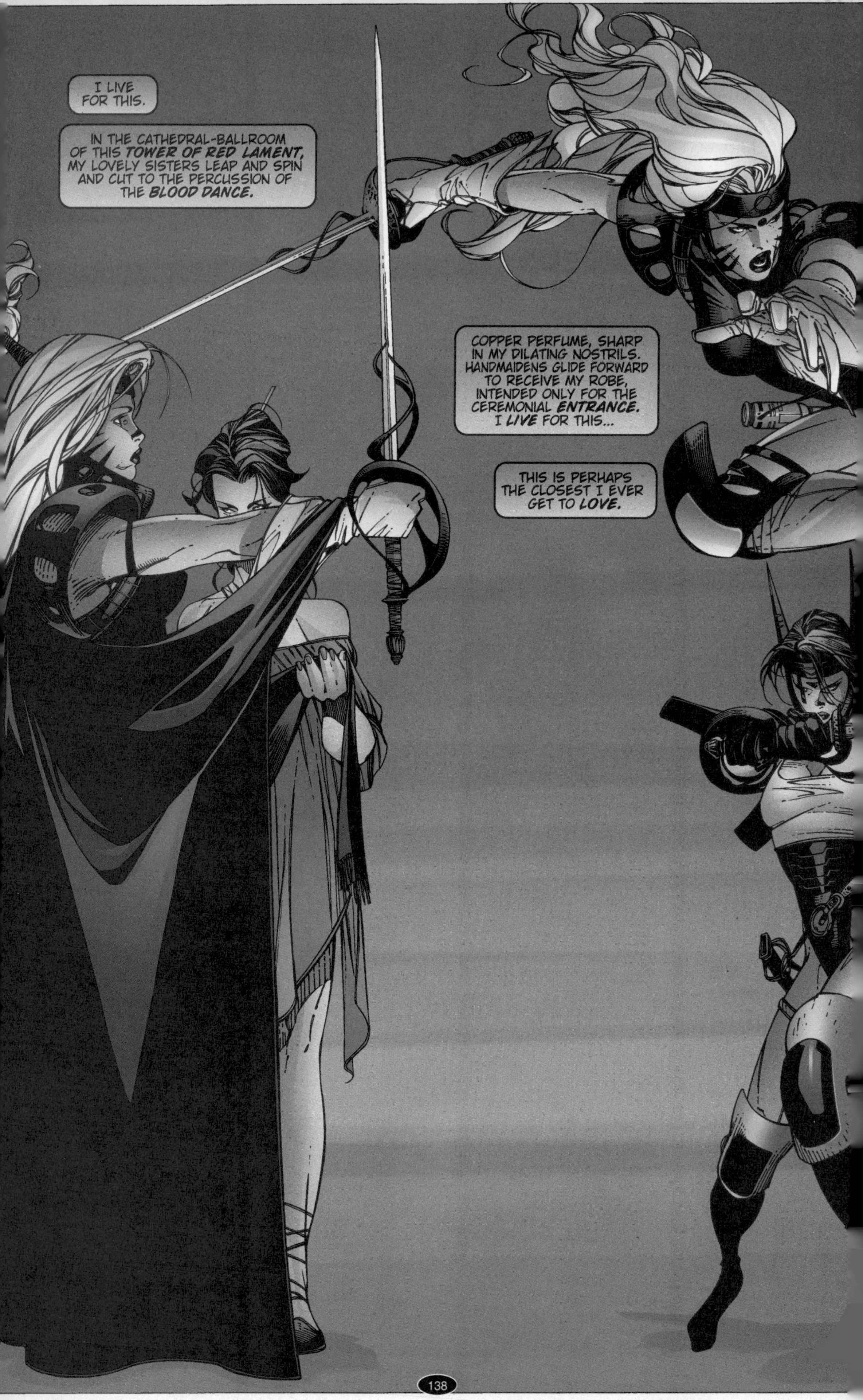
I LIVE FOR THIS.
IN THE CATHEDRAL-BALLROOM OF THIS TOWER OF RED LAMENT, MY LOVELY SISTERS LEAP AND SPIN AND CUT TO THE PERCUSSION OF THE BLOOD DANCE.
COPPER PERFUME, SHARP IN MY DILATING NOSTRILS. HANDMAIDENS GLIDE FORWARD TO RECEIVE MY ROBE, INTENDED ONLY FOR THE CEREMONIAL ENTRANCE. I LIVE FOR THIS...
THIS IS PERHAPS THE CLOSEST I EVER GET TO LOVE.

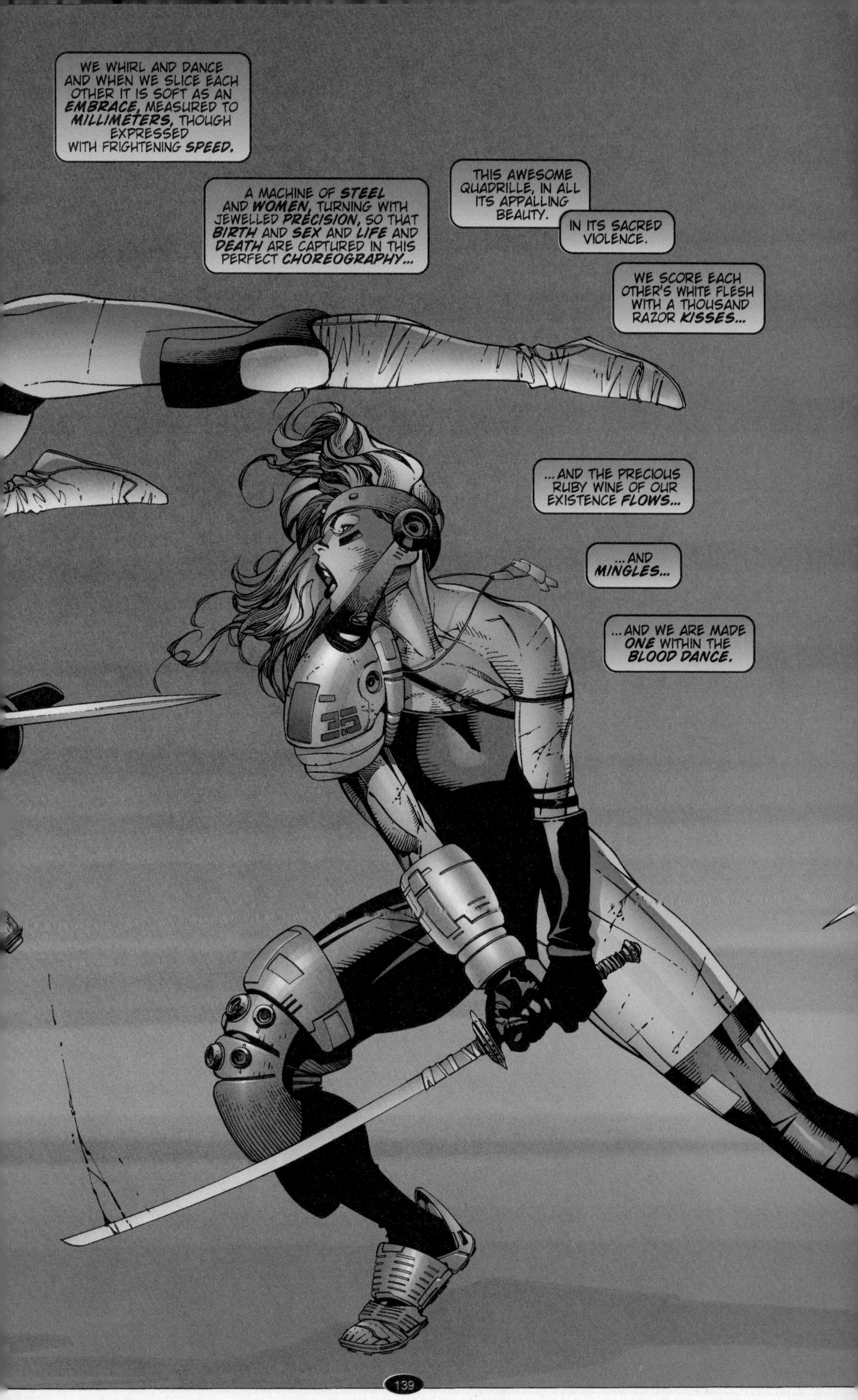
WE WHIRL AND DANCE AND WHEN WE SLICE EACH OTHER IT IS SOFT AS AN *EMBRACE,* MEASURED TO *MILLIMETERS,* THOUGH EXPRESSED WITH FRIGHTENING *SPEED.*
A MACHINE OF *STEEL* AND *WOMEN,* TURNING WITH JEWELLED *PRECISION,* SO THAT *BIRTH* AND *SEX* AND *LIFE* AND *DEATH* ARE CAPTURED IN THIS PERFECT *CHOREOGRAPHY...*
THIS AWESOME QUADRILLE, IN ALL ITS APPALLING BEAUTY.
IN ITS SACRED VIOLENCE.
WE SCORE EACH OTHER'S WHITE FLESH WITH A THOUSAND RAZOR *KISSES...*
...AND THE PRECIOUS RUBY WINE OF OUR EXISTENCE *FLOWS...*
...AND *MINGLES...*
...AND WE ARE MADE *ONE* WITHIN THE *BLOOD DANCE.*

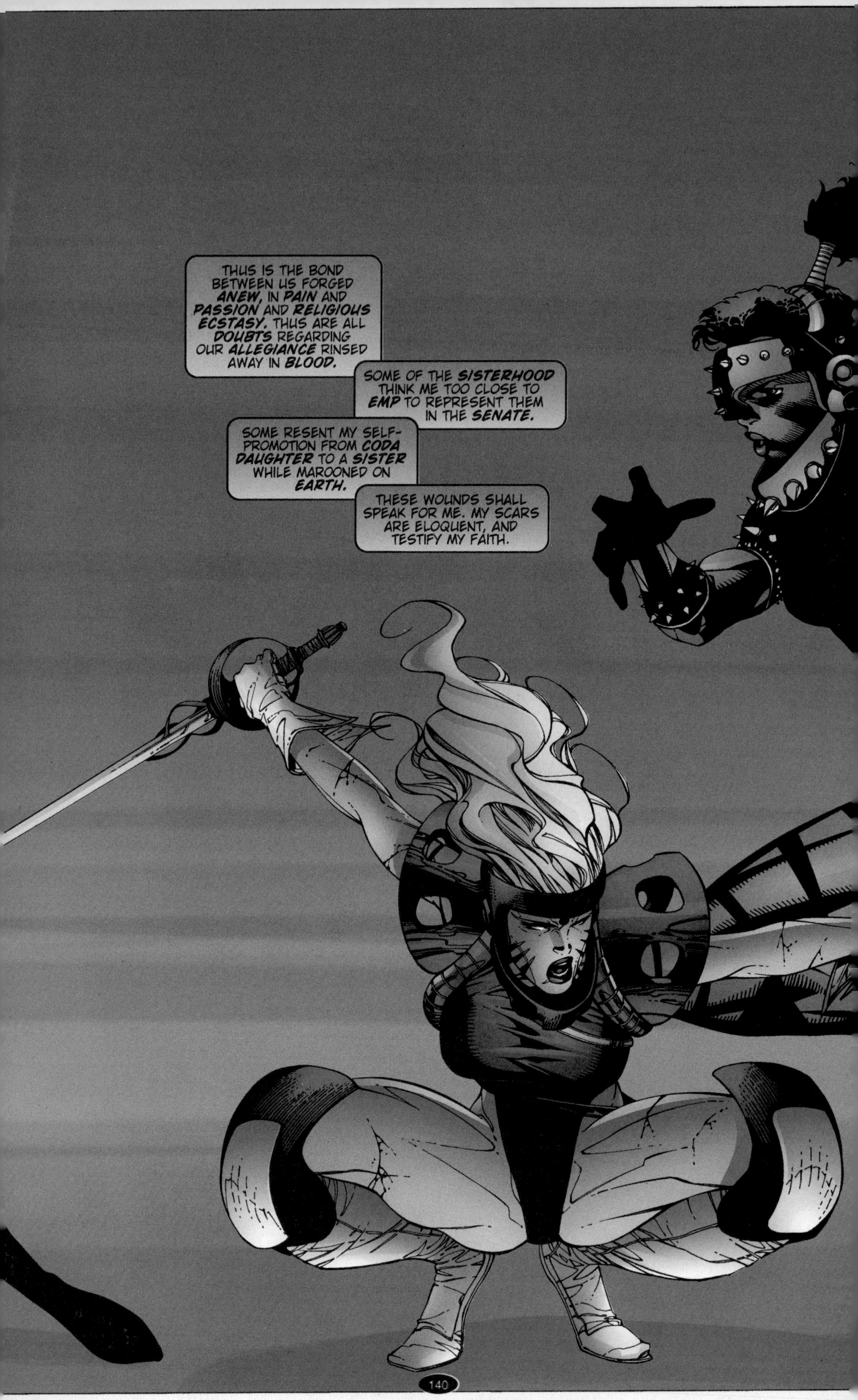
THUS IS THE BOND BETWEEN US FORGED ANEW, IN PAIN AND PASSION AND RELIGIOUS ECSTASY. THUS ARE ALL DOUBTS REGARDING OUR ALLEGIANCE RINSED AWAY IN BLOOD.
SOME OF THE SISTERHOOD THINK ME TOO CLOSE TO EMP TO REPRESENT THEM IN THE SENATE.
SOME RESENT MY SELF-PROMOTION FROM CODA DAUGHTER TO A SISTER WHILE MAROONED ON EARTH.
THESE WOUNDS SHALL SPEAK FOR ME. MY SCARS ARE ELOQUENT, AND TESTIFY MY FAITH.

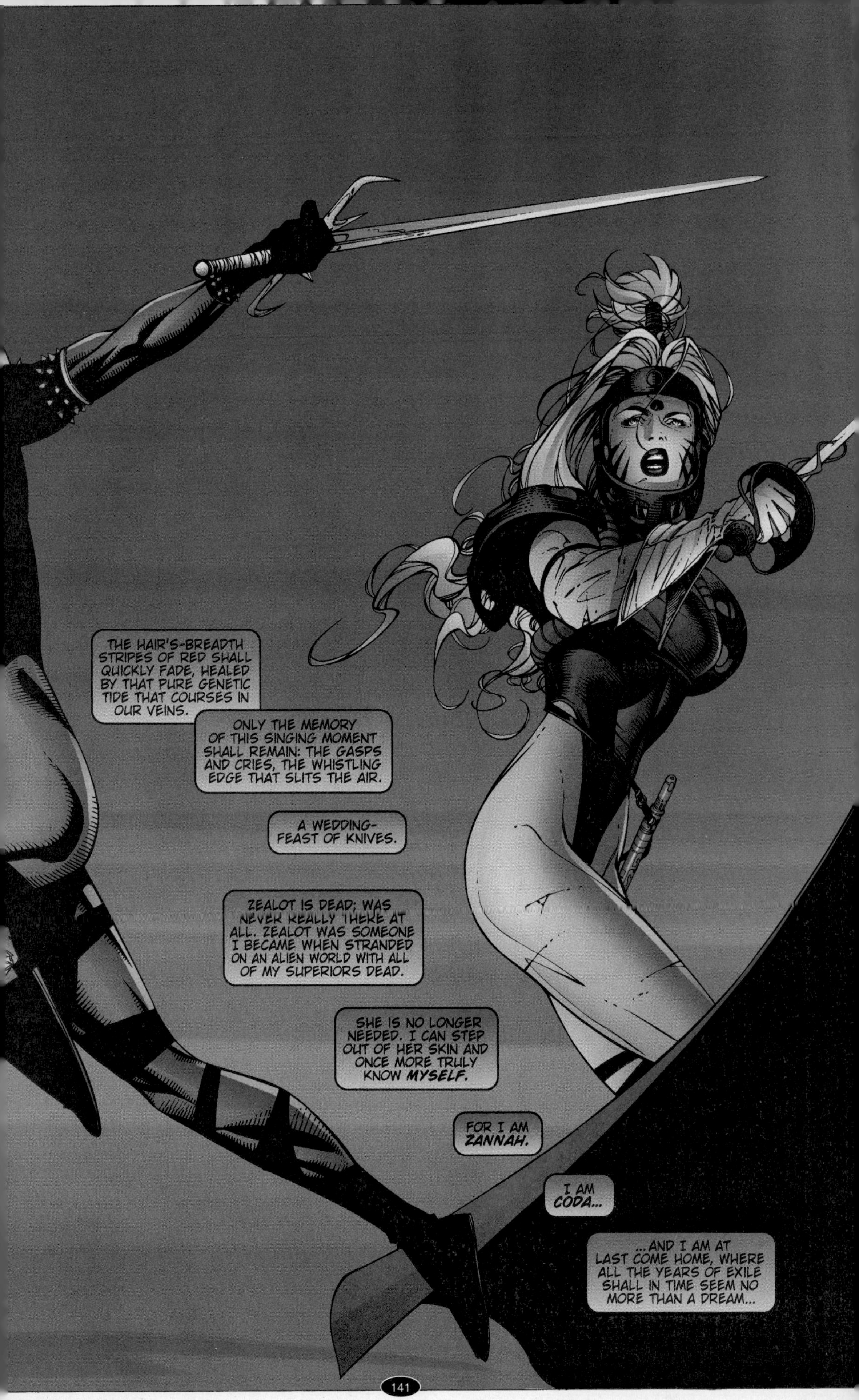
THE HAIR'S-BREADTH STRIPES OF RED SHALL QUICKLY FADE, HEALED BY THAT PURE GENETIC TIDE THAT COURSES IN OUR VEINS.
ONLY THE MEMORY OF THIS SINGING MOMENT SHALL REMAIN: THE GASPS AND CRIES, THE WHISTLING EDGE THAT SLITS THE AIR.
A WEDDING-FEAST OF KNIVES.
ZEALOT IS DEAD; WAS NEVER REALLY THERE AT ALL. ZEALOT WAS SOMEONE I BECAME WHEN STRANDED ON AN ALIEN WORLD WITH ALL OF MY SUPERIORS DEAD.
SHE IS NO LONGER NEEDED. I CAN STEP OUT OF HER SKIN AND ONCE MORE TRULY KNOW *MYSELF.*
FOR I AM *ZANNAH.*
I AM *CODA...*
...AND I AM AT LAST COME HOME, WHERE ALL THE YEARS OF EXILE SHALL IN TIME SEEM NO MORE THAN A DREAM...

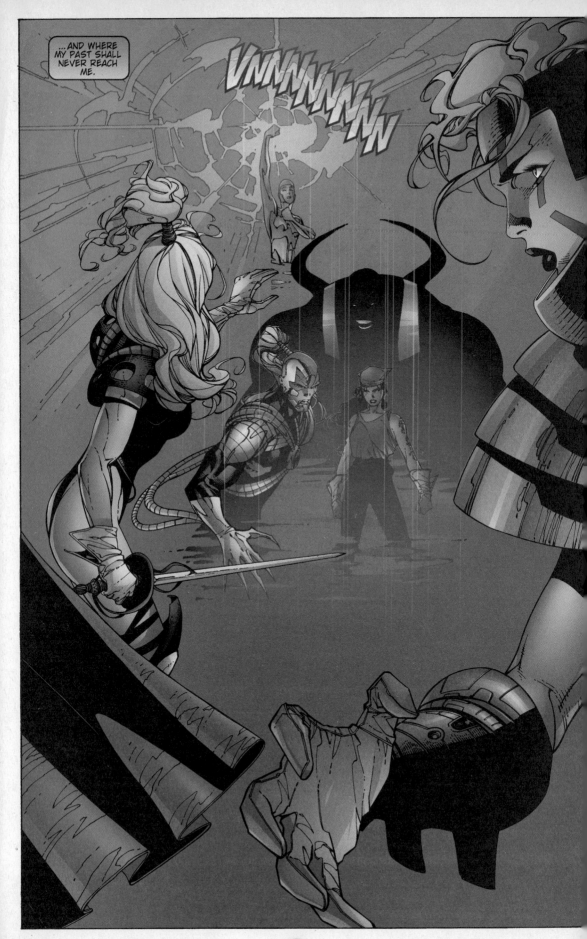

...AND WHERE MY PAST SHALL NEVER REACH ME.

VNNNNNNNN

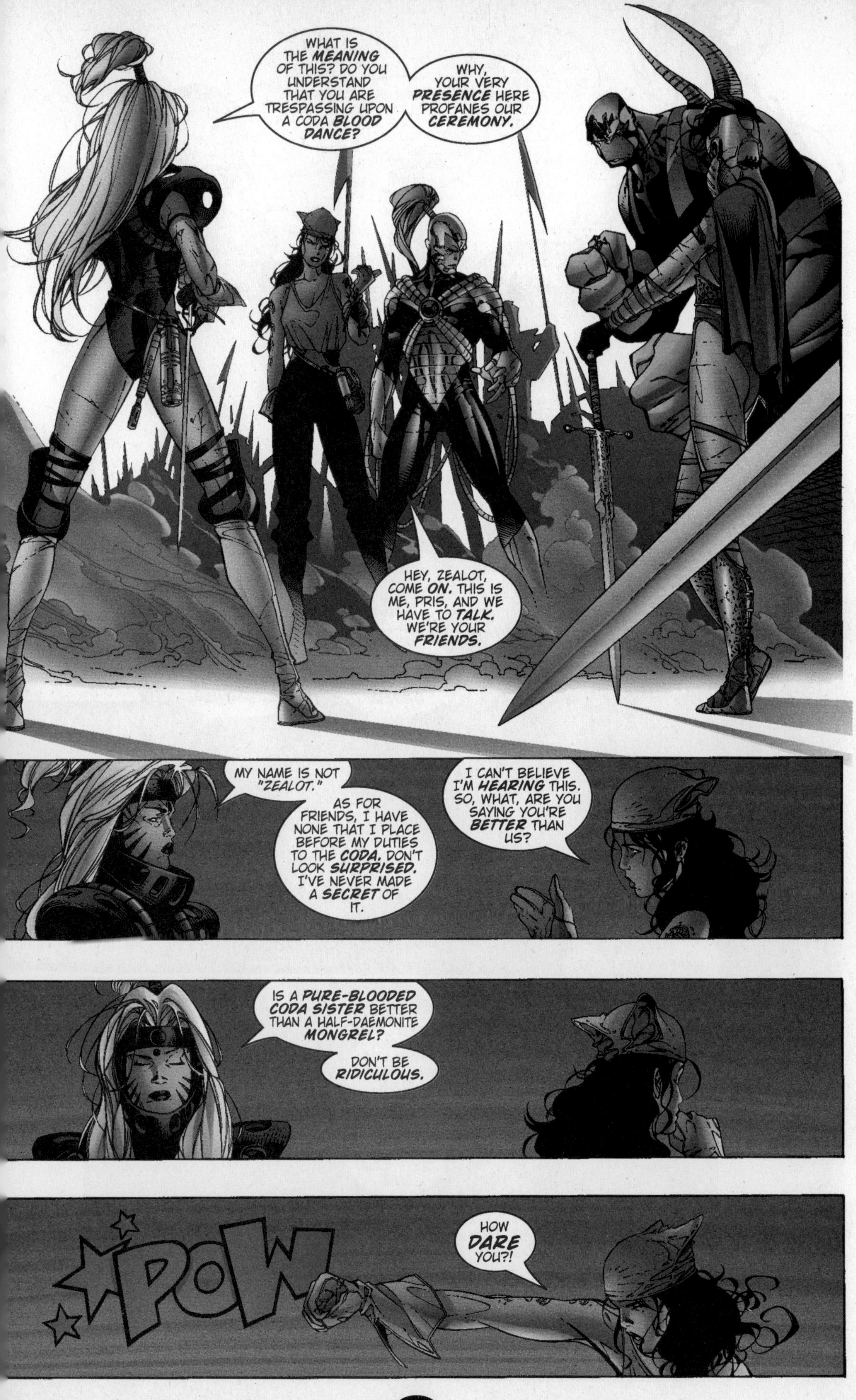
WHAT IS THE MEANING OF THIS? DO YOU UNDERSTAND THAT YOU ARE TRESPASSING UPON A CODA BLOOD DANCE?
WHY, YOUR VERY PRESENCE HERE PROFANES OUR CEREMONY.
HEY, ZEALOT, COME ON. THIS IS ME, PRIS, AND WE HAVE TO TALK. WE'RE YOUR FRIENDS.
MY NAME IS NOT "ZEALOT."
AS FOR FRIENDS, I HAVE NONE THAT I PLACE BEFORE MY DUTIES TO THE CODA. DON'T LOOK SURPRISED. I'VE NEVER MADE A SECRET OF IT.
I CAN'T BELIEVE I'M HEARING THIS. SO, WHAT, ARE YOU SAYING YOU'RE BETTER THAN US?
IS A PURE-BLOODED CODA SISTER BETTER THAN A HALF-DAEMONITE MONGREL?
DON'T BE RIDICULOUS.
POW
HOW DARE YOU?!

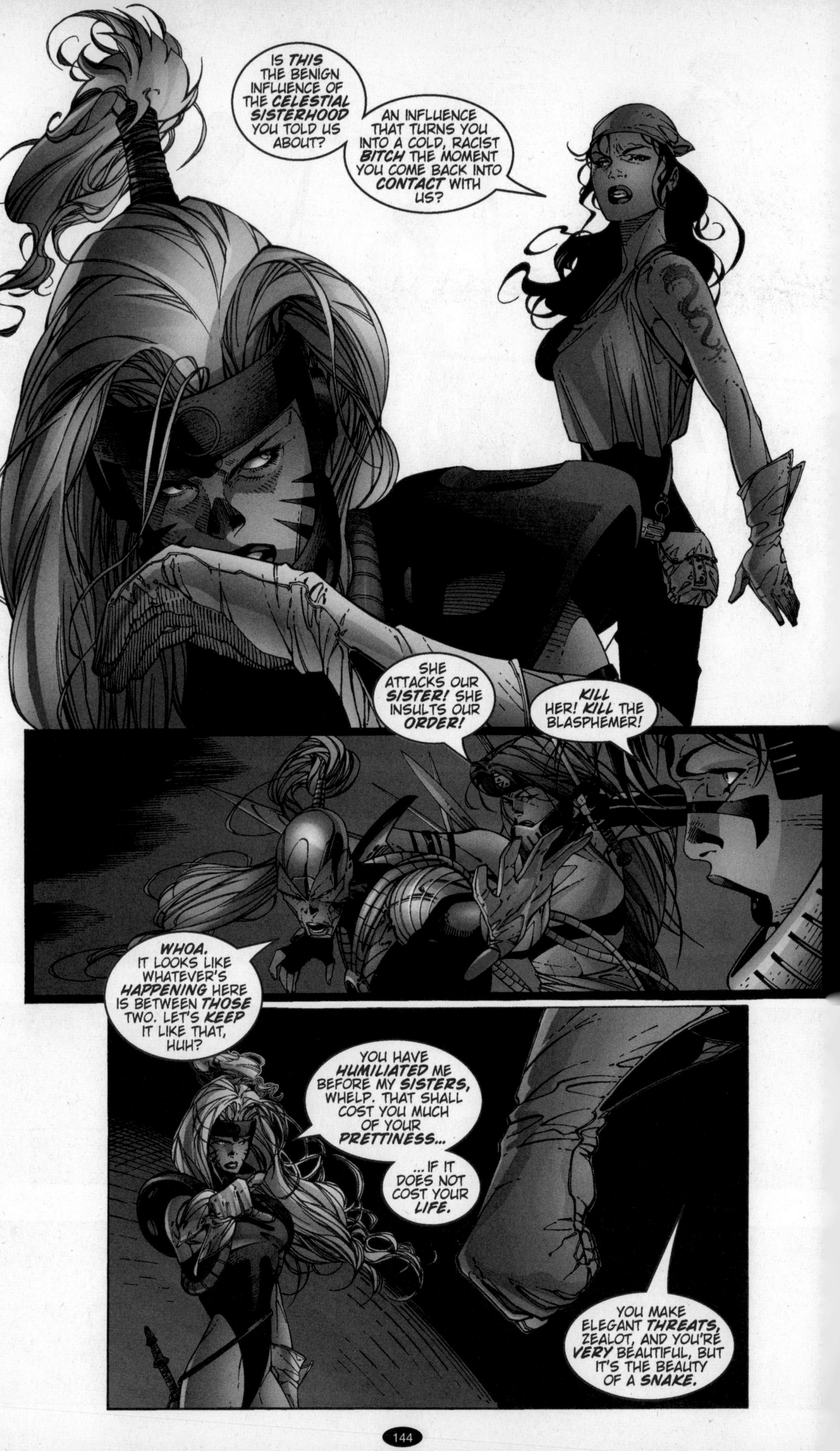

IS THIS THE BENIGN INFLUENCE OF THE CELESTIAL SISTERHOOD YOU TOLD US ABOUT?
AN INFLUENCE THAT TURNS YOU INTO A COLD, RACIST BITCH THE MOMENT YOU COME BACK INTO CONTACT WITH US?
SHE ATTACKS OUR SISTER! SHE INSULTS OUR ORDER!
KILL HER! KILL THE BLASPHEMER!
WHOA. IT LOOKS LIKE WHATEVER'S HAPPENING HERE IS BETWEEN THOSE TWO. LET'S KEEP IT LIKE THAT, HUH?
YOU HAVE HUMILIATED ME BEFORE MY SISTERS, WHELP. THAT SHALL COST YOU MUCH OF YOUR PRETTINESS...
...IF IT DOES NOT COST YOUR LIFE.
YOU MAKE ELEGANT THREATS, ZEALOT, AND YOU'RE VERY BEAUTIFUL, BUT IT'S THE BEAUTY OF A SNAKE.

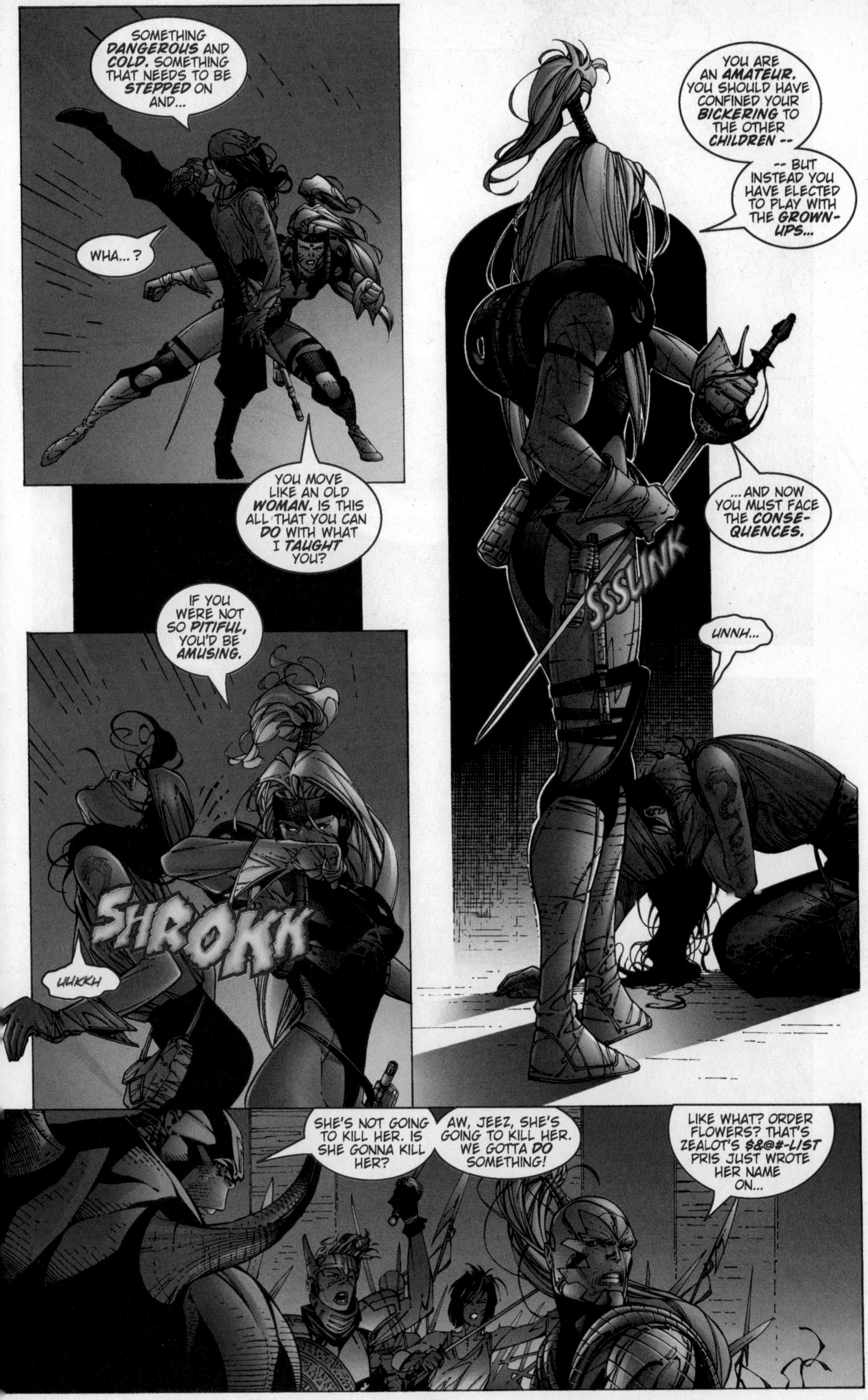
SOMETHING DANGEROUS AND COLD. SOMETHING THAT NEEDS TO BE STEPPED ON AND...
WHA...?
YOU MOVE LIKE AN OLD WOMAN. IS THIS ALL THAT YOU CAN DO WITH WHAT I TAUGHT YOU?
IF YOU WERE NOT SO PITIFUL, YOU'D BE AMUSING.
SHROKK
UUKKH
YOU ARE AN AMATEUR. YOU SHOULD HAVE CONFINED YOUR BICKERING TO THE OTHER CHILDREN --
-- BUT INSTEAD YOU HAVE ELECTED TO PLAY WITH THE GROWN-UPS...
...AND NOW YOU MUST FACE THE CONSE-QUENCES.
SSSLINK
UNNH...
SHE'S NOT GOING TO KILL HER. IS SHE GONNA KILL HER?
AW, JEEZ, SHE'S GOING TO KILL HER. WE GOTTA DO SOMETHING!
LIKE WHAT? ORDER FLOWERS? THAT'S ZEALOT'S $&@#-LIST PRIS JUST WROTE HER NAME ON...

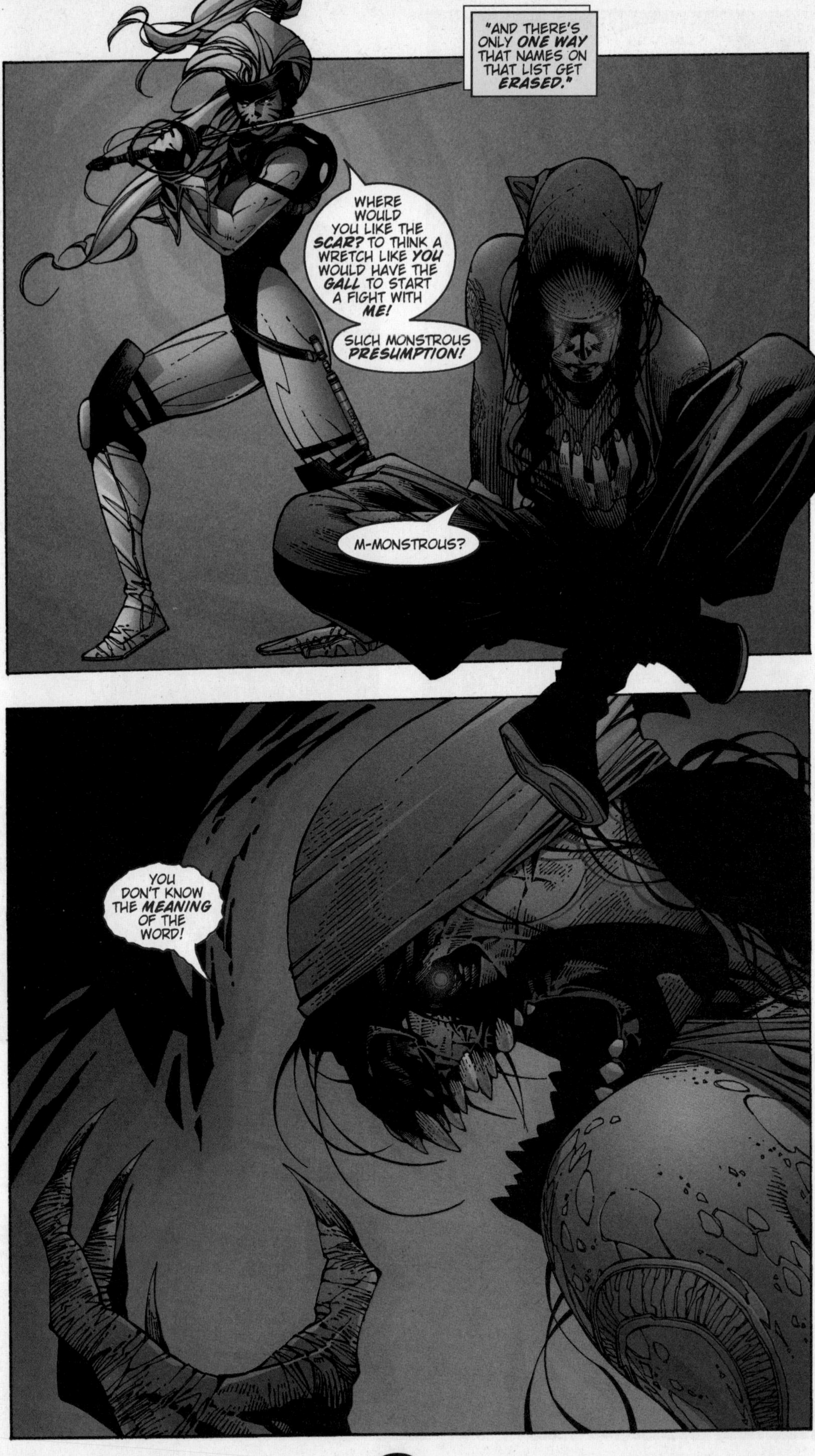
"AND THERE'S ONLY ONE WAY THAT NAMES ON THAT LIST GET ERASED."
WHERE WOULD YOU LIKE THE SCAR? TO THINK A WRETCH LIKE YOU WOULD HAVE THE GALL TO START A FIGHT WITH ME!
SUCH MONSTROUS PRESUMPTION!
M-MONSTROUS?
YOU DON'T KNOW THE MEANING OF THE WORD!

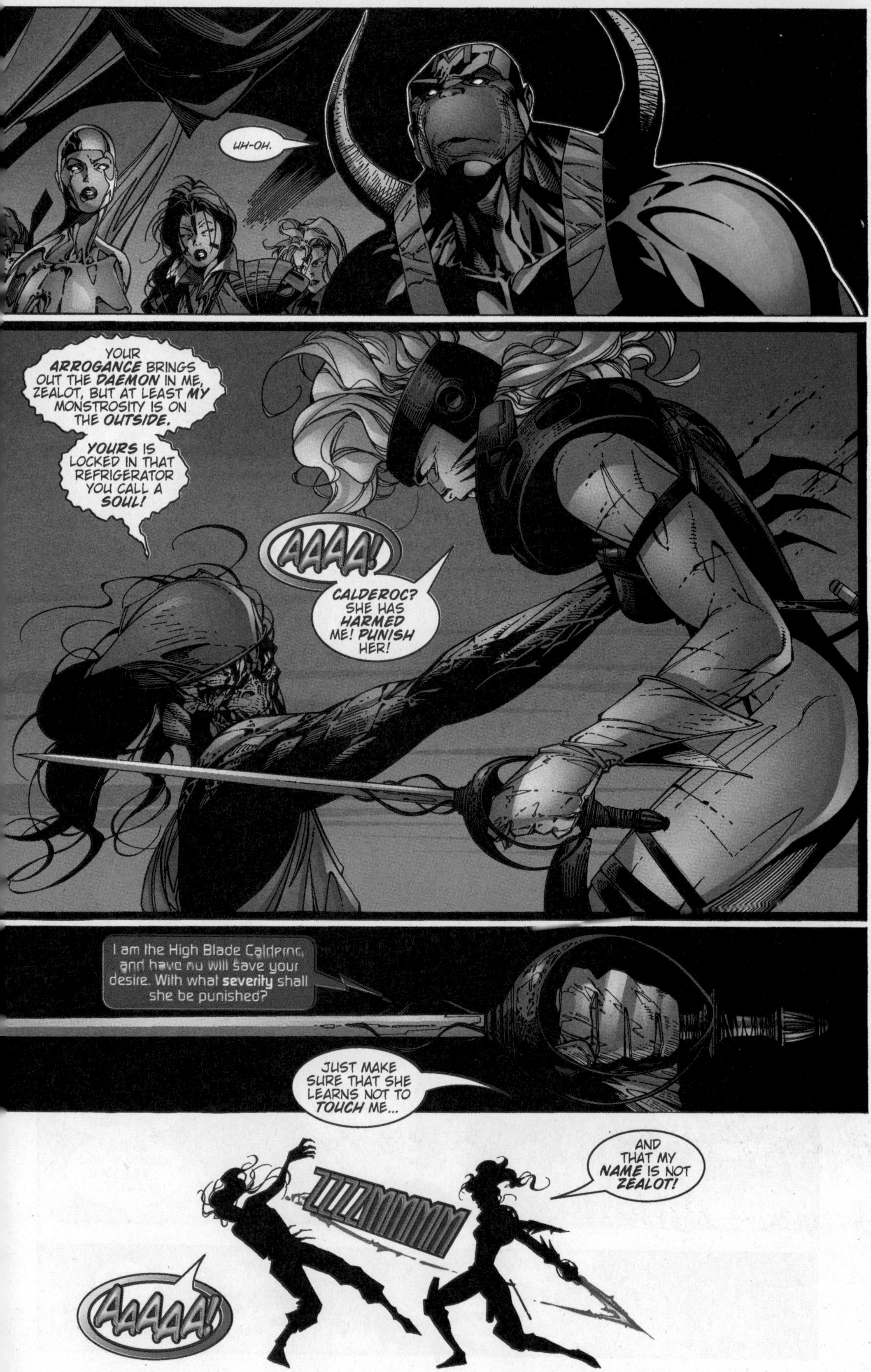
UH-OH.
YOUR **ARROGANCE** BRINGS OUT THE **DAEMON** IN ME, ZEALOT, BUT AT LEAST **MY** MONSTROSITY IS ON THE **OUTSIDE.**
YOURS IS LOCKED IN THAT REFRIGERATOR YOU CALL A **SOUL!**
AAAA!
CALDEROC? SHE HAS **HARMED** ME! **PUNISH** HER!
I am the High Blade Calderoc, and have no will save your desire. With what **severity** shall she be punished?
JUST MAKE SURE THAT SHE LEARNS NOT TO **TOUCH** ME...
ZZZZMMMMM
AND THAT MY **NAME** IS NOT **ZEALOT!**
AAAAA!

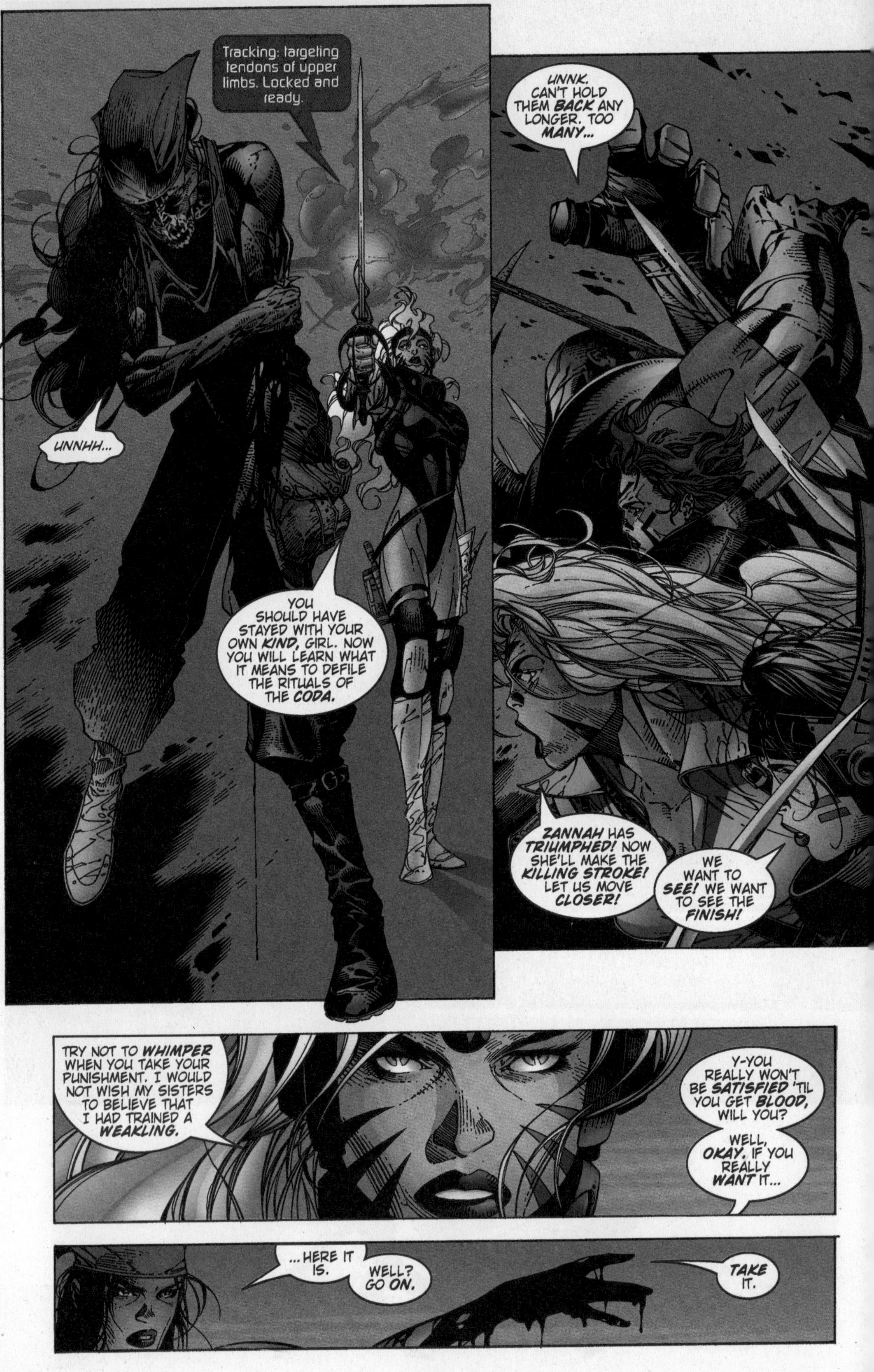
Tracking: targeting tendons of upper limbs. Locked and ready.
UNNHH...
YOU SHOULD HAVE STAYED WITH YOUR OWN KIND, GIRL. NOW YOU WILL LEARN WHAT IT MEANS TO DEFILE THE RITUALS OF THE CODA.
UNNK. CAN'T HOLD THEM BACK ANY LONGER. TOO MANY...
ZANNAH HAS TRIUMPHED! NOW SHE'LL MAKE THE KILLING STROKE! LET US MOVE CLOSER!
WE WANT TO SEE! WE WANT TO SEE THE FINISH!
TRY NOT TO WHIMPER WHEN YOU TAKE YOUR PUNISHMENT. I WOULD NOT WISH MY SISTERS TO BELIEVE THAT I HAD TRAINED A WEAKLING.
Y-YOU REALLY WON'T BE SATISFIED 'TIL YOU GET BLOOD, WILL YOU?
WELL, OKAY. IF YOU REALLY WANT IT...
...HERE IT IS.
WELL? GO ON.
TAKE IT.

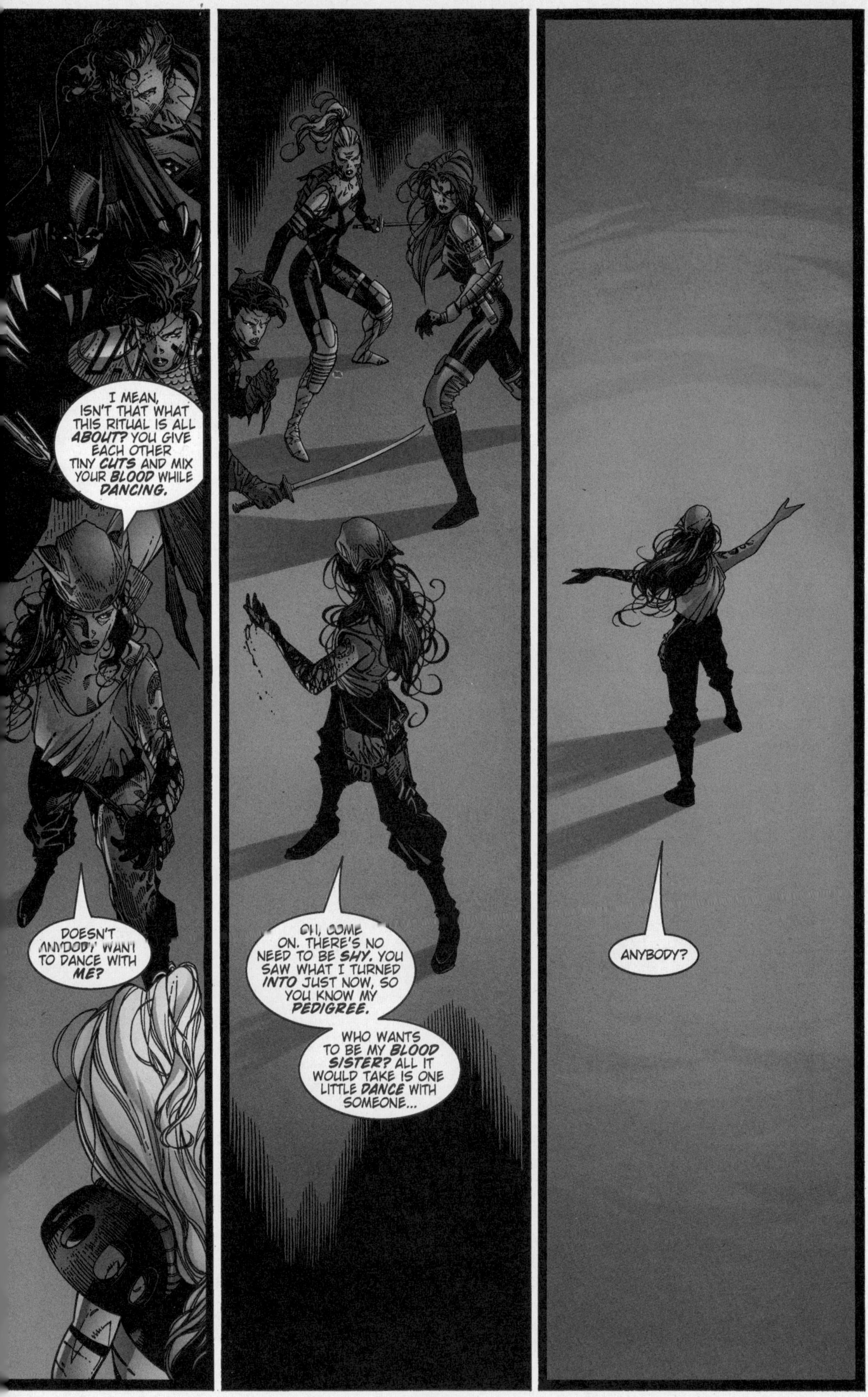
I MEAN, ISN'T THAT WHAT THIS RITUAL IS ALL ABOUT? YOU GIVE EACH OTHER TINY CUTS AND MIX YOUR BLOOD WHILE DANCING.
DOESN'T ANYBODY WANT TO DANCE WITH ME?
OH, COME ON. THERE'S NO NEED TO BE SHY. YOU SAW WHAT I TURNED INTO JUST NOW, SO YOU KNOW MY PEDIGREE.
WHO WANTS TO BE MY BLOOD SISTER? ALL IT WOULD TAKE IS ONE LITTLE DANCE WITH SOMEONE...
ANYBODY?

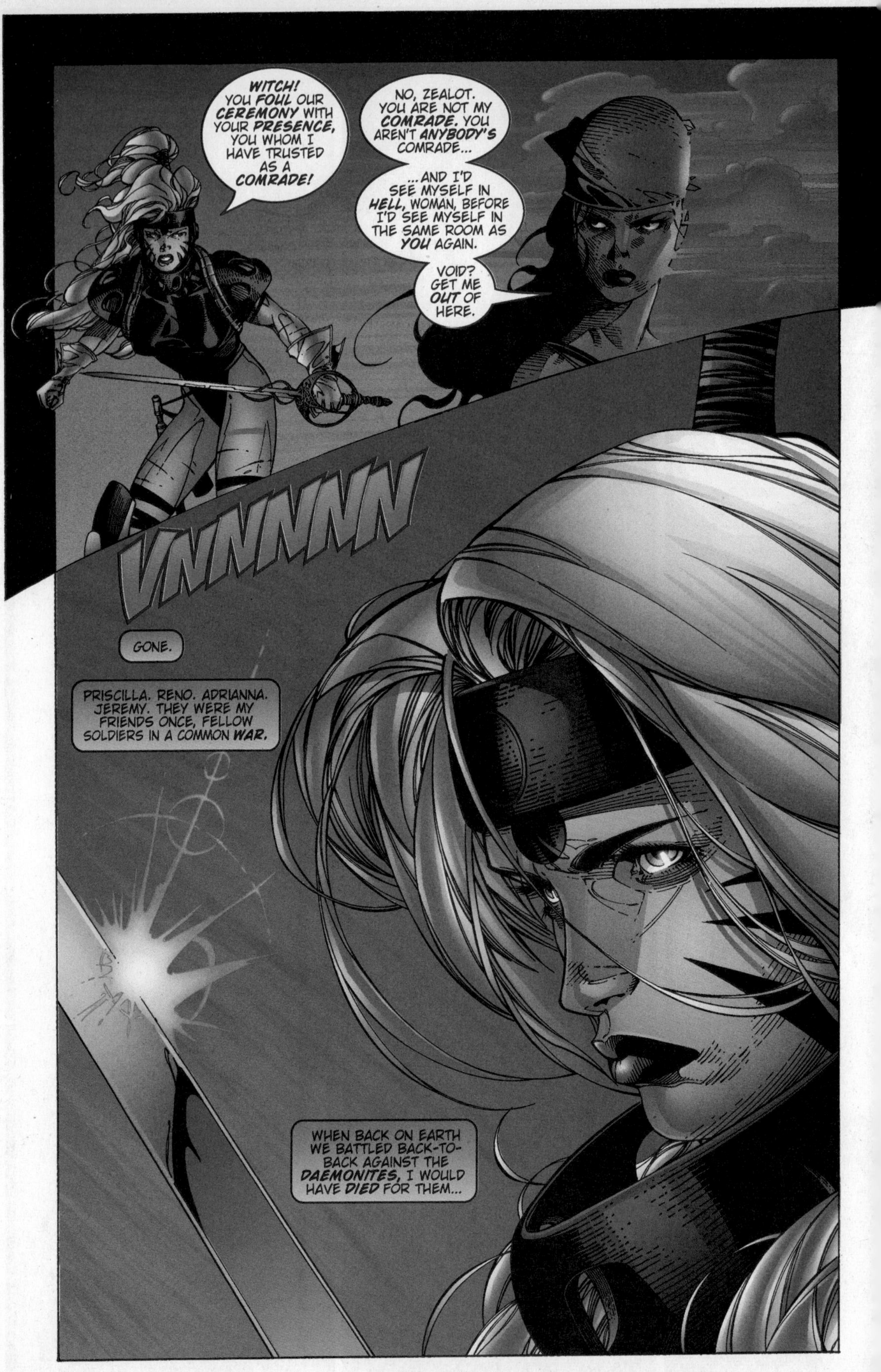
WITCH! YOU FOUL OUR CEREMONY WITH YOUR PRESENCE, YOU WHOM I HAVE TRUSTED AS A COMRADE!
NO, ZEALOT. YOU ARE NOT MY COMRADE. YOU AREN'T ANYBODY'S COMRADE...
...AND I'D SEE MYSELF IN HELL, WOMAN, BEFORE I'D SEE MYSELF IN THE SAME ROOM AS YOU AGAIN.
VOID? GET ME OUT OF HERE.
VNNNNN
GONE.
PRISCILLA. RENO. ADRIANNA. JEREMY. THEY WERE MY FRIENDS ONCE, FELLOW SOLDIERS IN A COMMON WAR.
WHEN BACK ON EARTH WE BATTLED BACK-TO-BACK AGAINST THE DAEMONITES, I WOULD HAVE DIED FOR THEM...

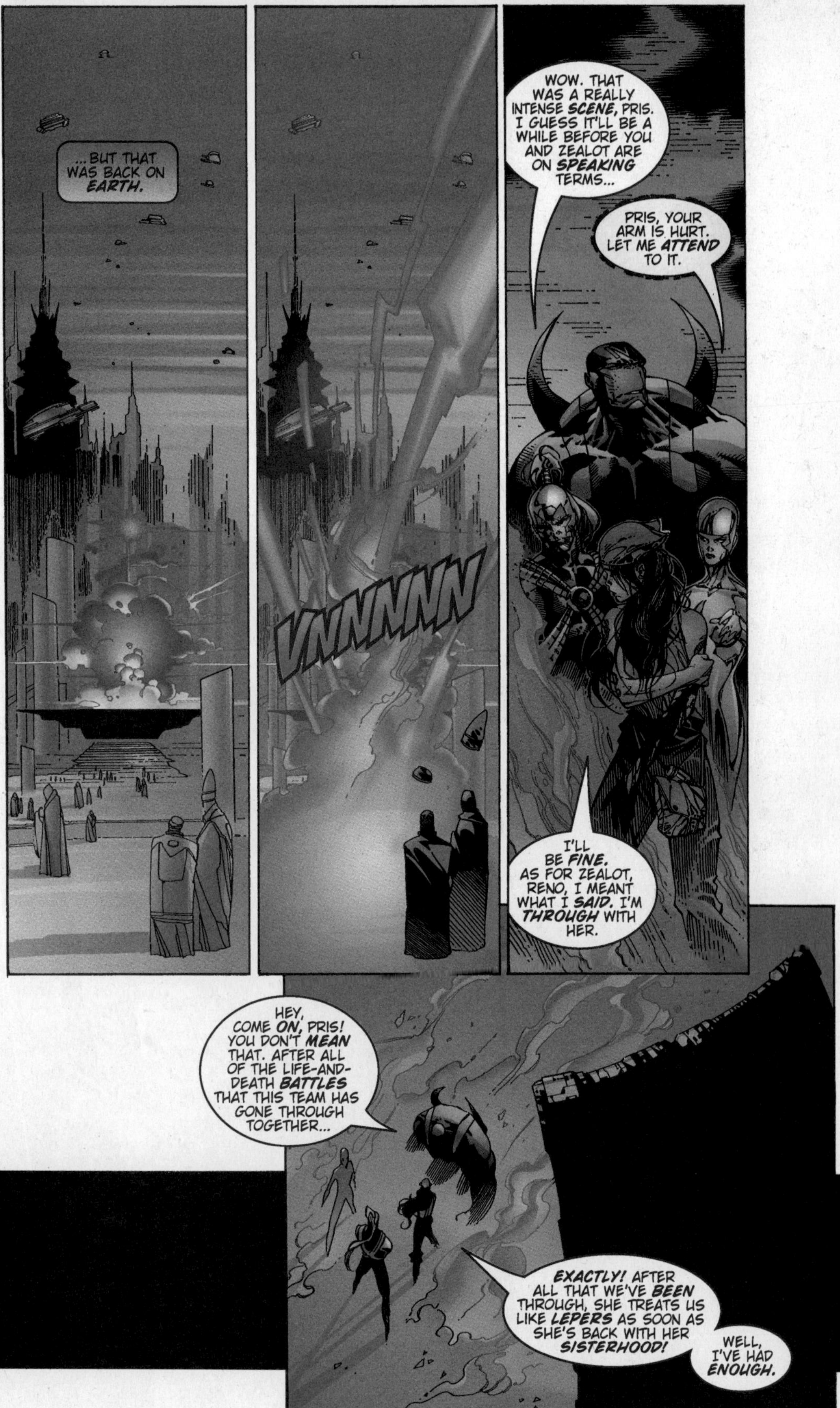
...BUT THAT WAS BACK ON EARTH.
VNNNNN
WOW. THAT WAS A REALLY INTENSE SCENE, PRIS. I GUESS IT'LL BE A WHILE BEFORE YOU AND ZEALOT ARE ON SPEAKING TERMS...
PRIS, YOUR ARM IS HURT. LET ME ATTEND TO IT.
I'LL BE FINE. AS FOR ZEALOT, RENO, I MEANT WHAT I SAID. I'M THROUGH WITH HER.
HEY, COME ON, PRIS! YOU DON'T MEAN THAT. AFTER ALL OF THE LIFE-AND-DEATH BATTLES THAT THIS TEAM HAS GONE THROUGH TOGETHER...
EXACTLY! AFTER ALL THAT WE'VE BEEN THROUGH, SHE TREATS US LIKE LEPERS AS SOON AS SHE'S BACK WITH HER SISTERHOOD!
WELL, I'VE HAD ENOUGH.

I'VE HAD ENOUGH OF EMP AND ZEALOT AND THEIR PHONY WAR. AFTER THESE LAST TWO YEARS, I'VE HAD ENOUGH OF WILDC.A.T.S.
THIS IS WHERE WE REACH THE END OF THE ROAD, HERE ON KHERA.
IT'S ALL OVER.
NEXT: CAT'SPAWS

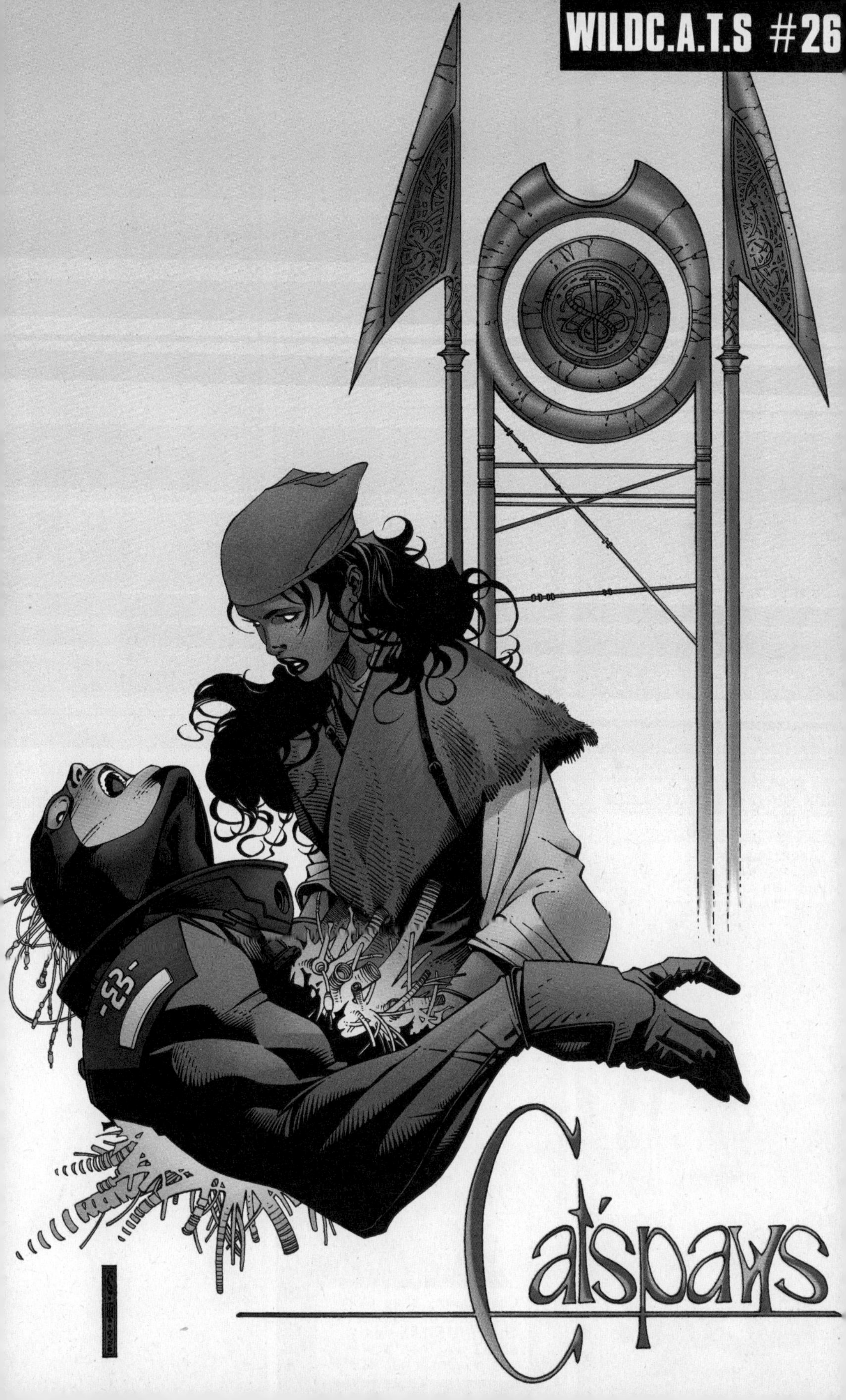
WILDC.A.T.S #26
-53-
Cat's paws

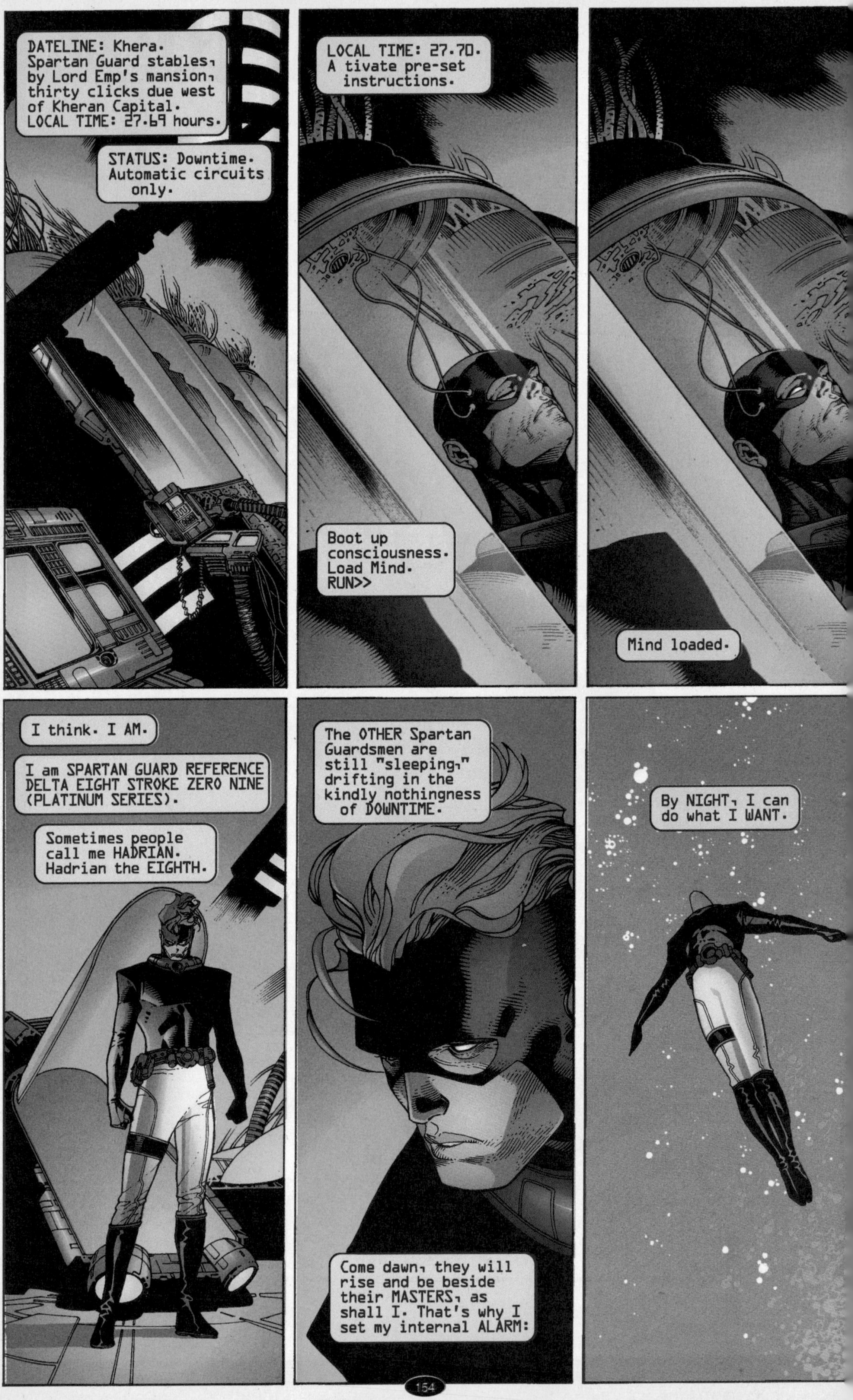
DATELINE: Khera. Spartan Guard stables, by Lord Emp's mansion, thirty clicks due west of Kheran Capital. LOCAL TIME: 27.69 hours.
STATUS: Downtime. Automatic circuits only.
LOCAL TIME: 27.70. A tivate pre-set instructions.
Boot up consciousness. Load Mind. RUN>>
Mind loaded.
I think. I AM.
I am SPARTAN GUARD REFERENCE DELTA EIGHT STROKE ZERO NINE (PLATINUM SERIES).
Sometimes people call me HADRIAN. Hadrian the EIGHTH.
The OTHER Spartan Guardsmen are still "sleeping," drifting in the kindly nothingness of DOWNTIME.
Come dawn, they will rise and be beside their MASTERS, as shall I. That's why I set my internal ALARM:
By NIGHT, I can do what I WANT.

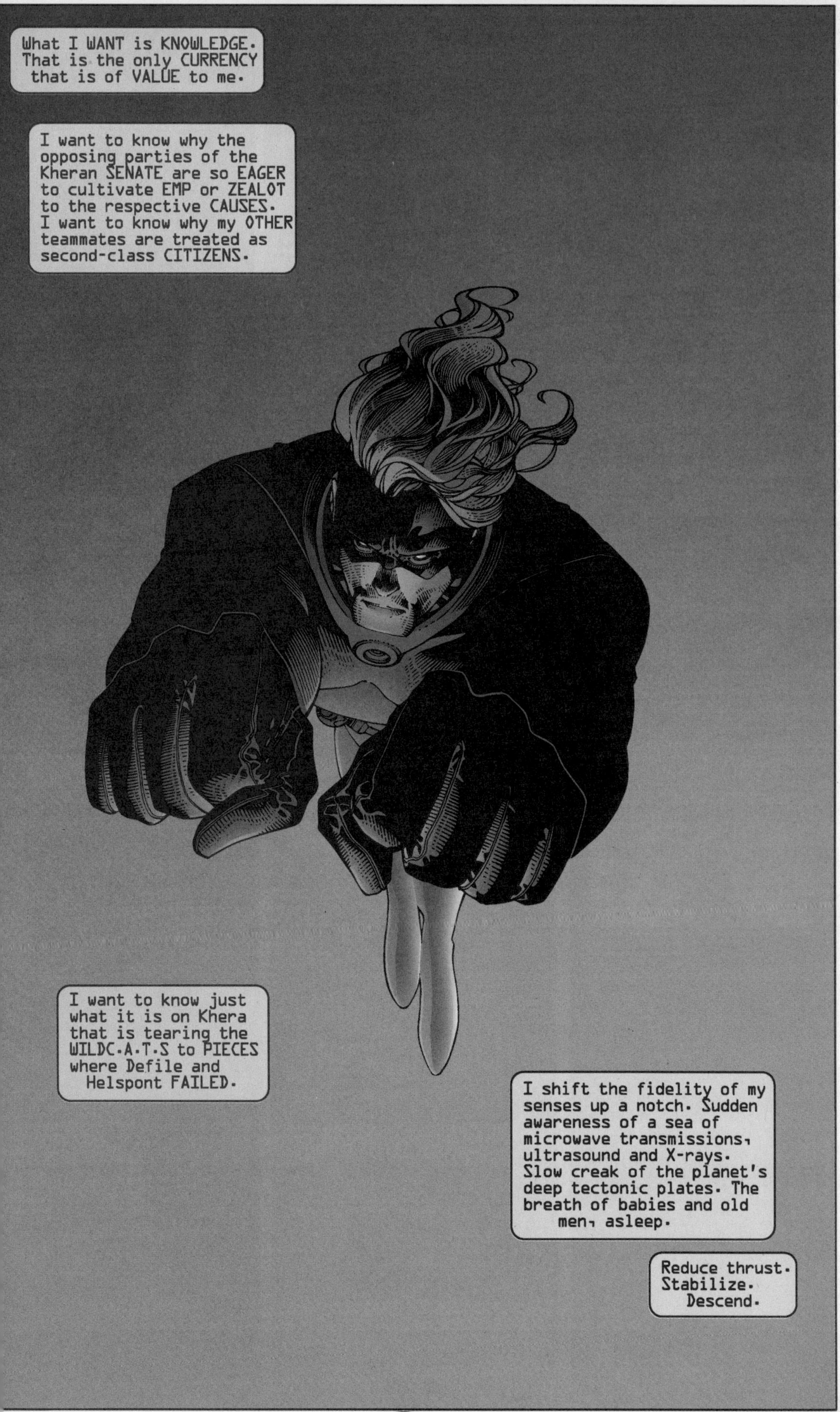
What I WANT is KNOWLEDGE. That is the only CURRENCY that is of VALUE to me.
I want to know why the opposing parties of the Kheran SENATE are so EAGER to cultivate EMP or ZEALOT to the respective CAUSES. I want to know why my OTHER teammates are treated as second-class CITIZENS.
I want to know just what it is on Khera that is tearing the WILDC.A.T.S to PIECES where Defile and Helspont FAILED.
I shift the fidelity of my senses up a notch. Sudden awareness of a sea of microwave transmissions, ultrasound and X-rays. Slow creak of the planet's deep tectonic plates. The breath of babies and old men, asleep.
Reduce thrust. Stabilize. Descend.

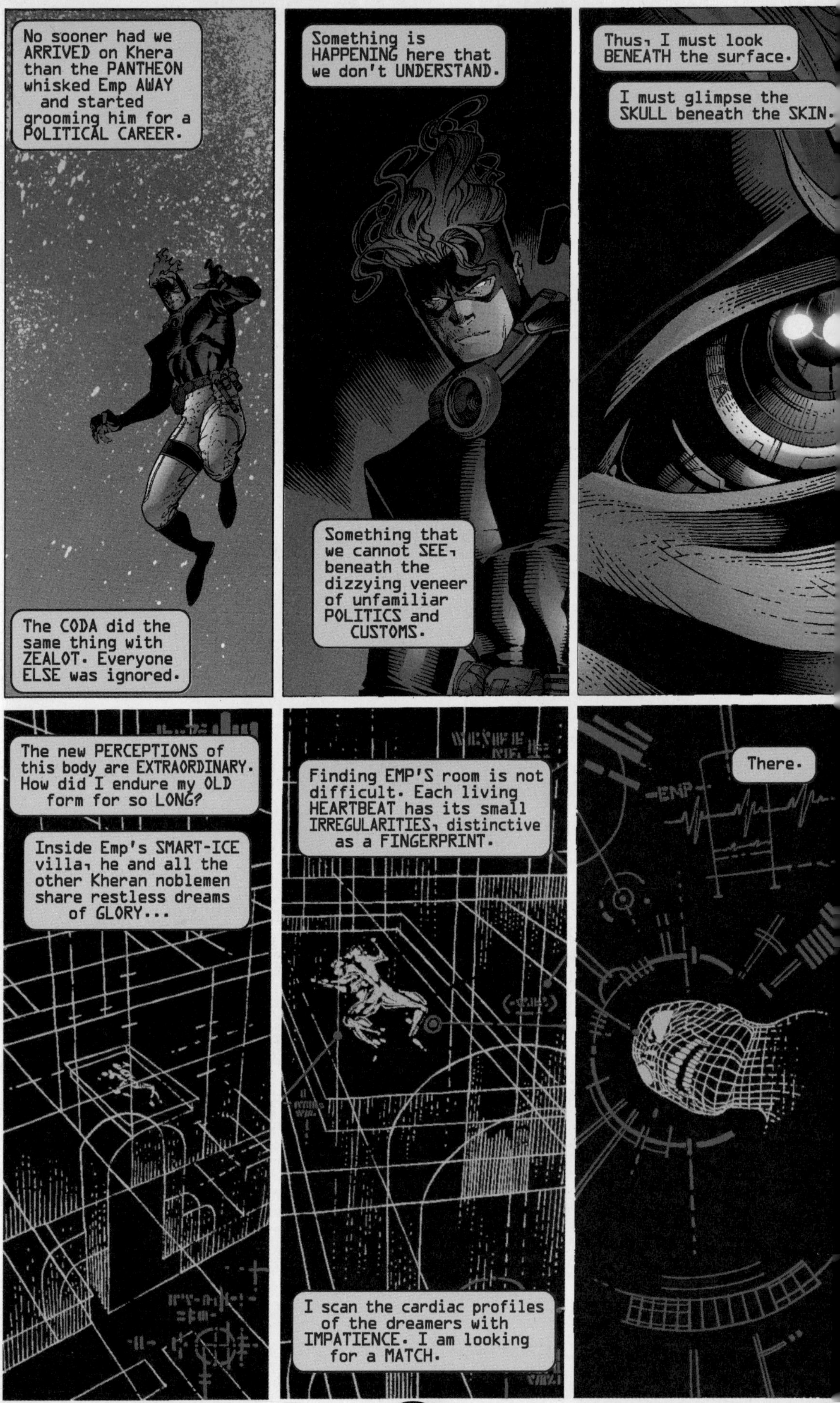
No sooner had we ARRIVED on Khera than the PANTHEON whisked Emp AWAY and started grooming him for a POLITICAL CAREER.
The CODA did the same thing with ZEALOT. Everyone ELSE was ignored.
Something is HAPPENING here that we don't UNDERSTAND.
Something that we cannot SEE, beneath the dizzying veneer of unfamiliar POLITICS and CUSTOMS.
Thus, I must look BENEATH the surface.
I must glimpse the SKULL beneath the SKIN.
The new PERCEPTIONS of this body are EXTRAORDINARY. How did I endure my OLD form for so LONG?
Inside Emp's SMART-ICE villa, he and all the other Kheran noblemen share restless dreams of GLORY...
Finding EMP'S room is not difficult. Each living HEARTBEAT has its small IRREGULARITIES, distinctive as a FINGERPRINT.
I scan the cardiac profiles of the dreamers with IMPATIENCE. I am looking for a MATCH.
EMP
There.

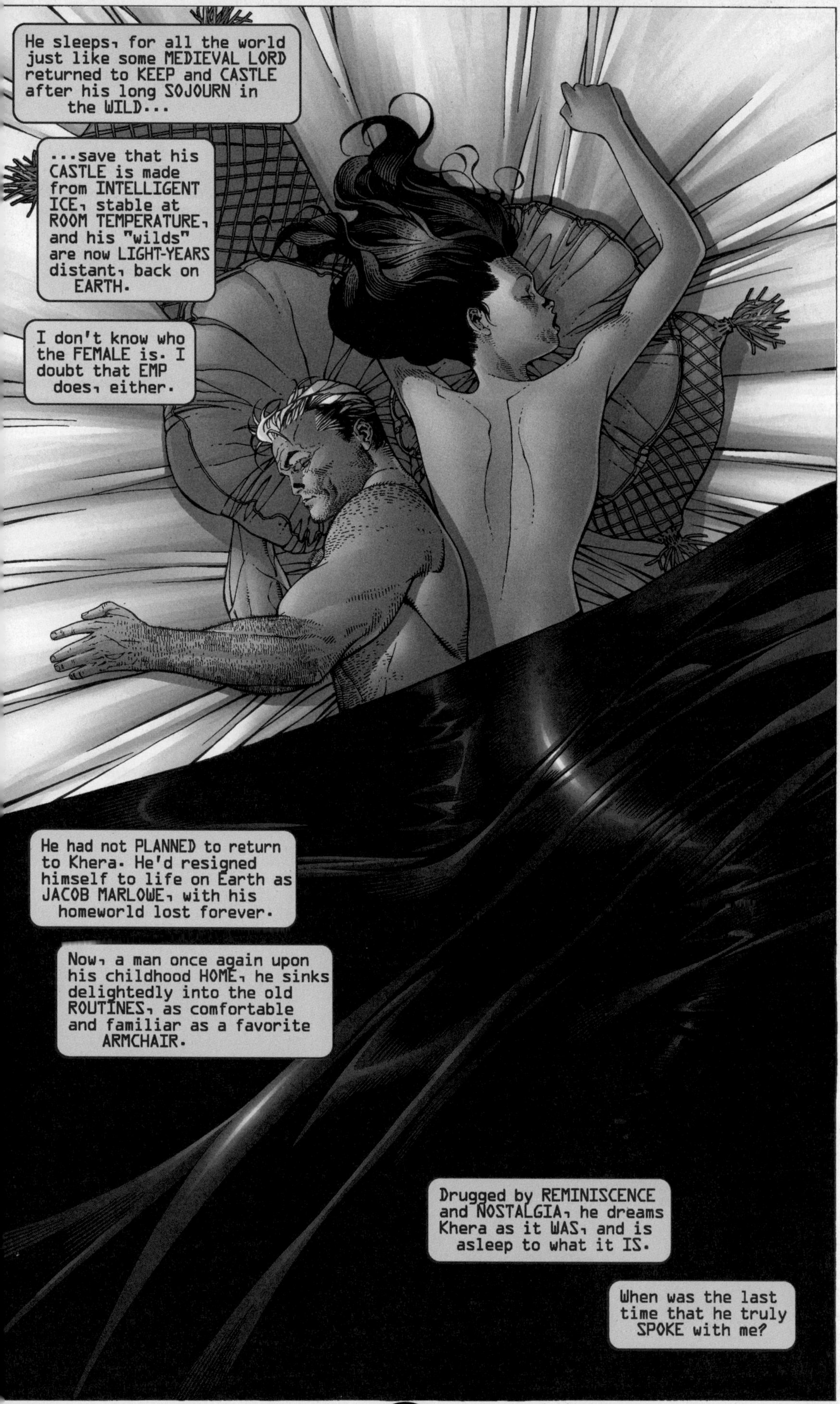
He sleeps, for all the world just like some MEDIEVAL LORD returned to KEEP and CASTLE after his long SOJOURN in the WILD...
...save that his CASTLE is made from INTELLIGENT ICE, stable at ROOM TEMPERATURE, and his "wilds" are now LIGHT-YEARS distant, back on EARTH.
I don't know who the FEMALE is. I doubt that EMP does, either.
He had not PLANNED to return to Khera. He'd resigned himself to life on Earth as JACOB MARLOWE, with his homeworld lost forever.
Now, a man once again upon his childhood HOME, he sinks delightedly into the old ROUTINES, as comfortable and familiar as a favorite ARMCHAIR.
Drugged by REMINISCENCE and NOSTALGIA, he dreams Khera as it WAS, and is asleep to what it IS.
When was the last time that he truly SPOKE with me?

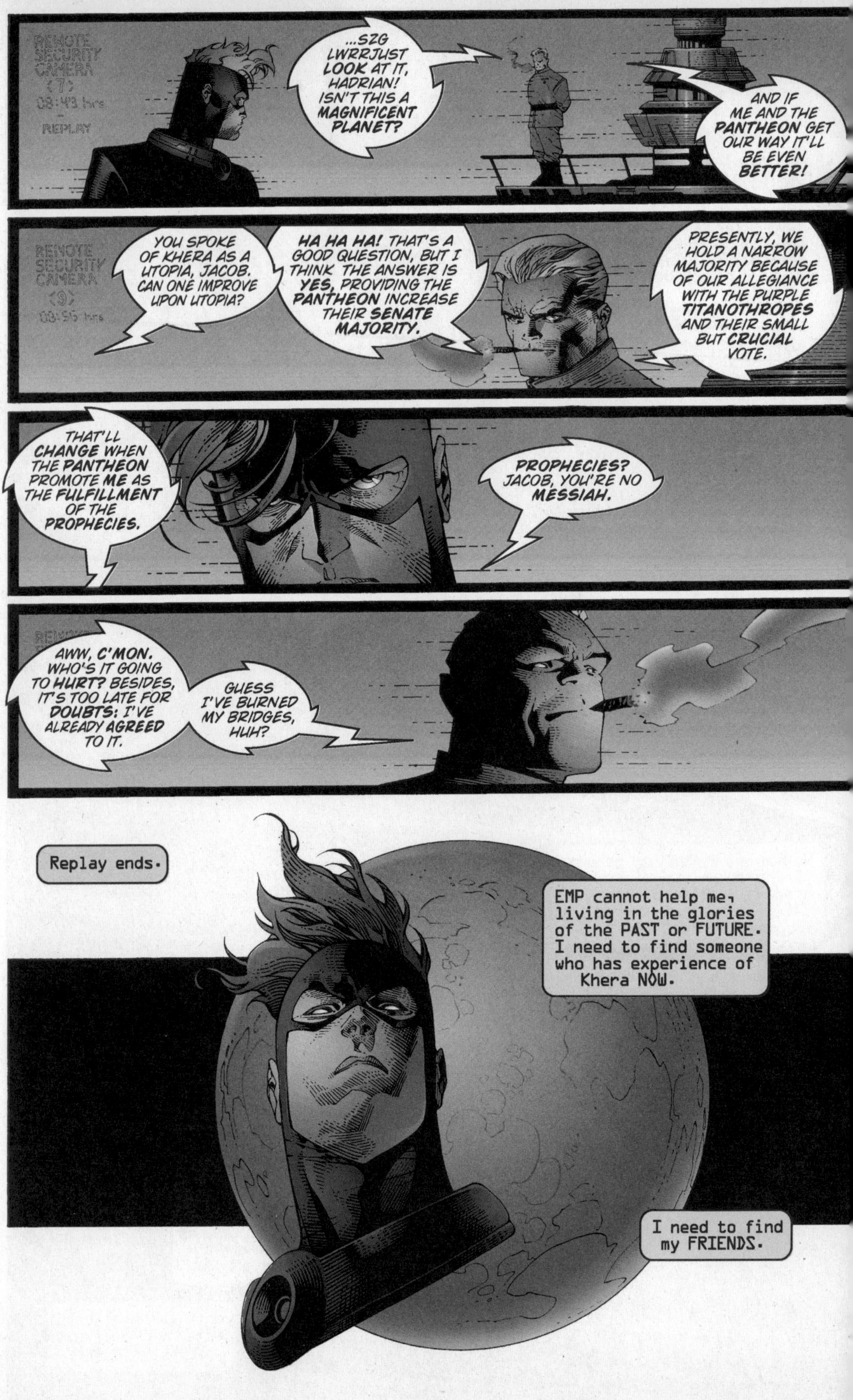
REMOTE SECURITY CAMERA <7> 08:43 hrs REPLAY
...SZG LWRRJUST LOOK AT IT, HADRIAN! ISN'T THIS A MAGNIFICENT PLANET?
AND IF ME AND THE PANTHEON GET OUR WAY IT'LL BE EVEN BETTER!
REMOTE SECURITY CAMERA <9> 08:56 hrs
YOU SPOKE OF KHERA AS A UTOPIA, JACOB. CAN ONE IMPROVE UPON UTOPIA?
HA HA HA! THAT'S A GOOD QUESTION, BUT I THINK THE ANSWER IS YES, PROVIDING THE PANTHEON INCREASE THEIR SENATE MAJORITY.
PRESENTLY, WE HOLD A NARROW MAJORITY BECAUSE OF OUR ALLEGIANCE WITH THE PURPLE TITANOTHROPES AND THEIR SMALL BUT CRUCIAL VOTE.
THAT'LL CHANGE WHEN THE PANTHEON PROMOTE ME AS THE FULFILLMENT OF THE PROPHECIES.
PROPHECIES? JACOB, YOU'RE NO MESSIAH.
AWW, C'MON. WHO'S IT GOING TO HURT? BESIDES, IT'S TOO LATE FOR DOUBTS: I'VE ALREADY AGREED TO IT.
GUESS I'VE BURNED MY BRIDGES, HUH?
Replay ends.
EMP cannot help me, living in the glories of the PAST or FUTURE. I need to find someone who has experience of Khera NOW.
I need to find my FRIENDS.

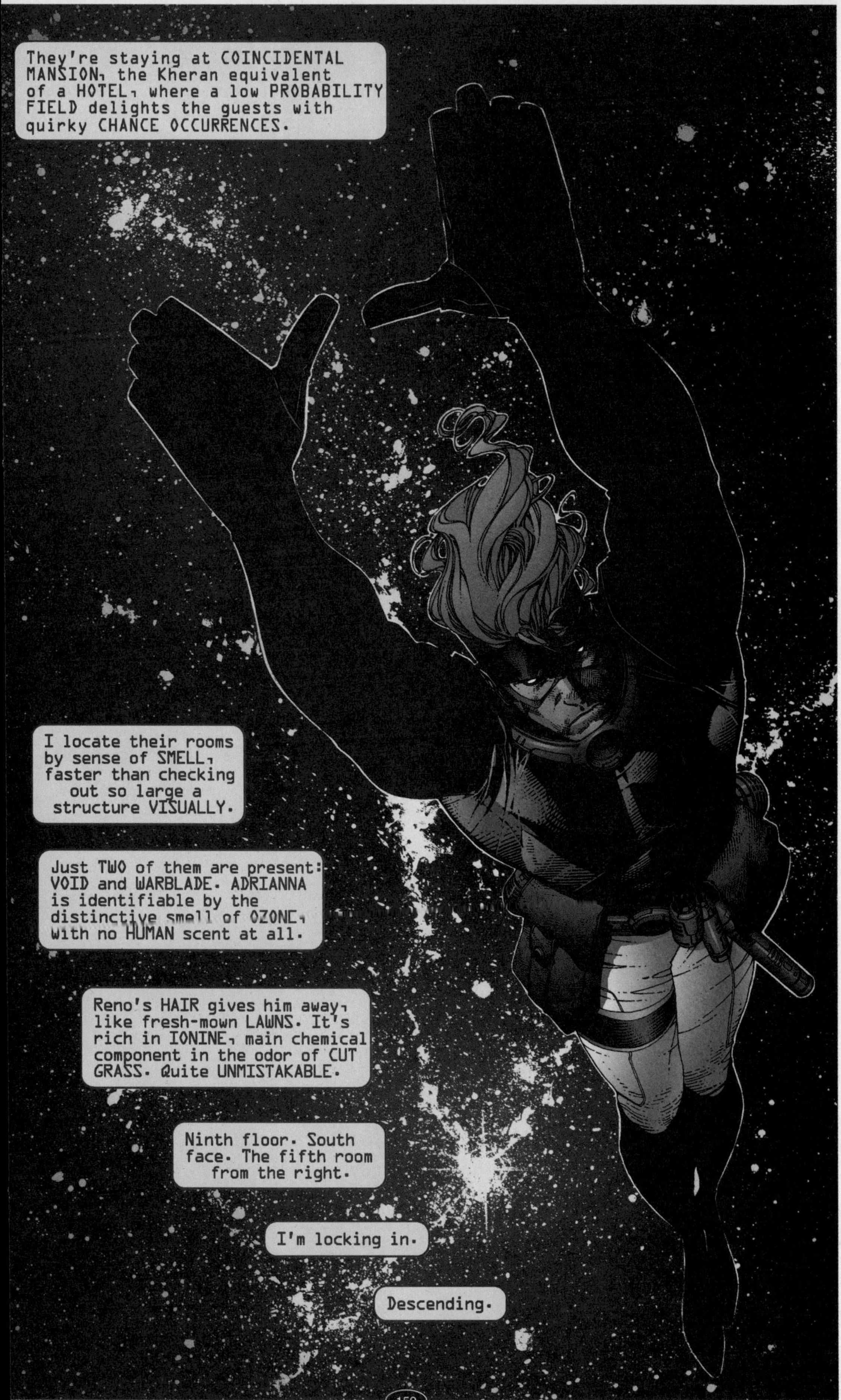
They're staying at COINCIDENTAL MANSION, the Kheran equivalent of a HOTEL, where a low PROBABILITY FIELD delights the guests with quirky CHANCE OCCURRENCES.
I locate their rooms by sense of SMELL, faster than checking out so large a structure VISUALLY.
Just TWO of them are present: VOID and WARBLADE. ADRIANNA is identifiable by the distinctive smell of OZONE, with no HUMAN scent at all.
Reno's HAIR gives him away, like fresh-mown LAWNS. It's rich in IONINE, main chemical component in the odor of CUT GRASS. Quite UNMISTAKABLE.
Ninth floor. South face. The fifth room from the right.
I'm locking in.
Descending.

Panel 2: HI. I WONDERED HOW LONG IT WOULD TAKE YOU TO SHOW UP.

Panel 3: I CAME AS SOON AS I COULD DO SO WITHOUT *OVERRIDING* MY PROGRAMMED LOYALTY TO *EMP.* WHERE ARE THE *OTHERS?*

WELL, *PRIS* QUIT THE *TEAM. MAUL* WENT TO *DOWN-TOWN* TO DROWN HIS *SORROWS.*

OTHER THAN THAT, EVERYBODY'S *FINE.*

Panel 4: PRIS *QUIT?*

HADRIAN, THE GIRL'S BEEN LIVING IN A *DAEMONITE GHETTO!*

YEAH. PLUS SHE GOT IN A FIGHT WITH *ZEALOT* OR *ZANNAH* OR WHATEVER SHE'S CALLING HERSELF NOW. THINGS GOT *UGLY.*

Panel 5: I DON'T *UNDERSTAND.* NO *ENEMY* THREATENS US, YET WE'RE *DISINTEGRATING.* WHAT *HAPPENED?*

KHERA HAPPENED. OUR DREAMS CAME *TRUE,* AND THEY'RE *DESTROYING* US.

LOOK, WE'RE PRETTY *LOW* RIGHT NOW. MAYBE YOU SHOULD GO FIND *MAUL...*

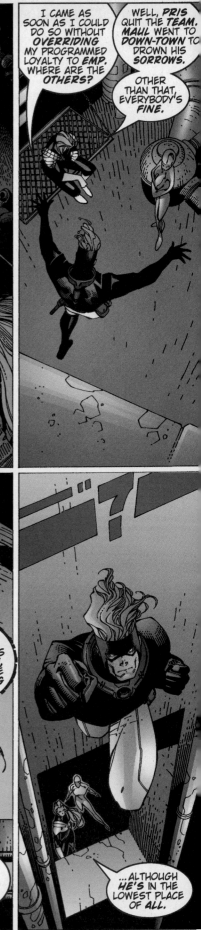

Panel 6: ...ALTHOUGH *HE'S* IN THE LOWEST PLACE OF *ALL.*

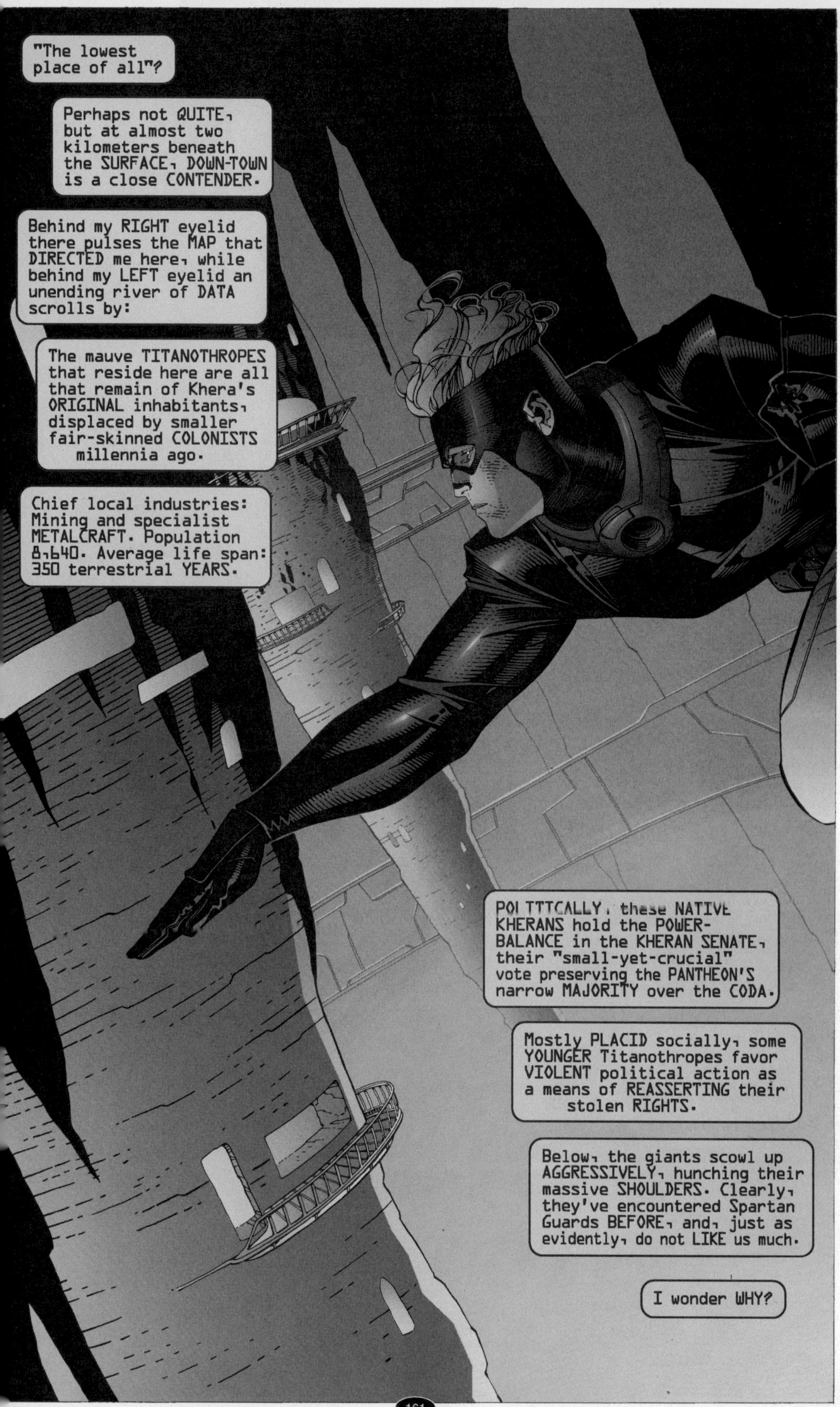
"The lowest place of all"?
Perhaps not QUITE, but at almost two kilometers beneath the SURFACE, DOWN-TOWN is a close CONTENDER.
Behind my RIGHT eyelid there pulses the MAP that DIRECTED me here, while behind my LEFT eyelid an unending river of DATA scrolls by:
The mauve TITANOTHROPES that reside here are all that remain of Khera's ORIGINAL inhabitants, displaced by smaller fair-skinned COLONISTS millennia ago.
Chief local industries: Mining and specialist METALCRAFT. Population 8,640. Average life span: 350 terrestrial YEARS.
POLITICALLY, these NATIVE KHERANS hold the POWER-BALANCE in the KHERAN SENATE, their "small-yet-crucial" vote preserving the PANTHEON'S narrow MAJORITY over the CODA.
Mostly PLACID socially, some YOUNGER Titanothropes favor VIOLENT political action as a means of REASSERTING their stolen RIGHTS.
Below, the giants scowl up AGGRESSIVELY, hunching their massive SHOULDERS. Clearly, they've encountered Spartan Guards BEFORE, and, just as evidently, do not LIKE us much.
I wonder WHY?

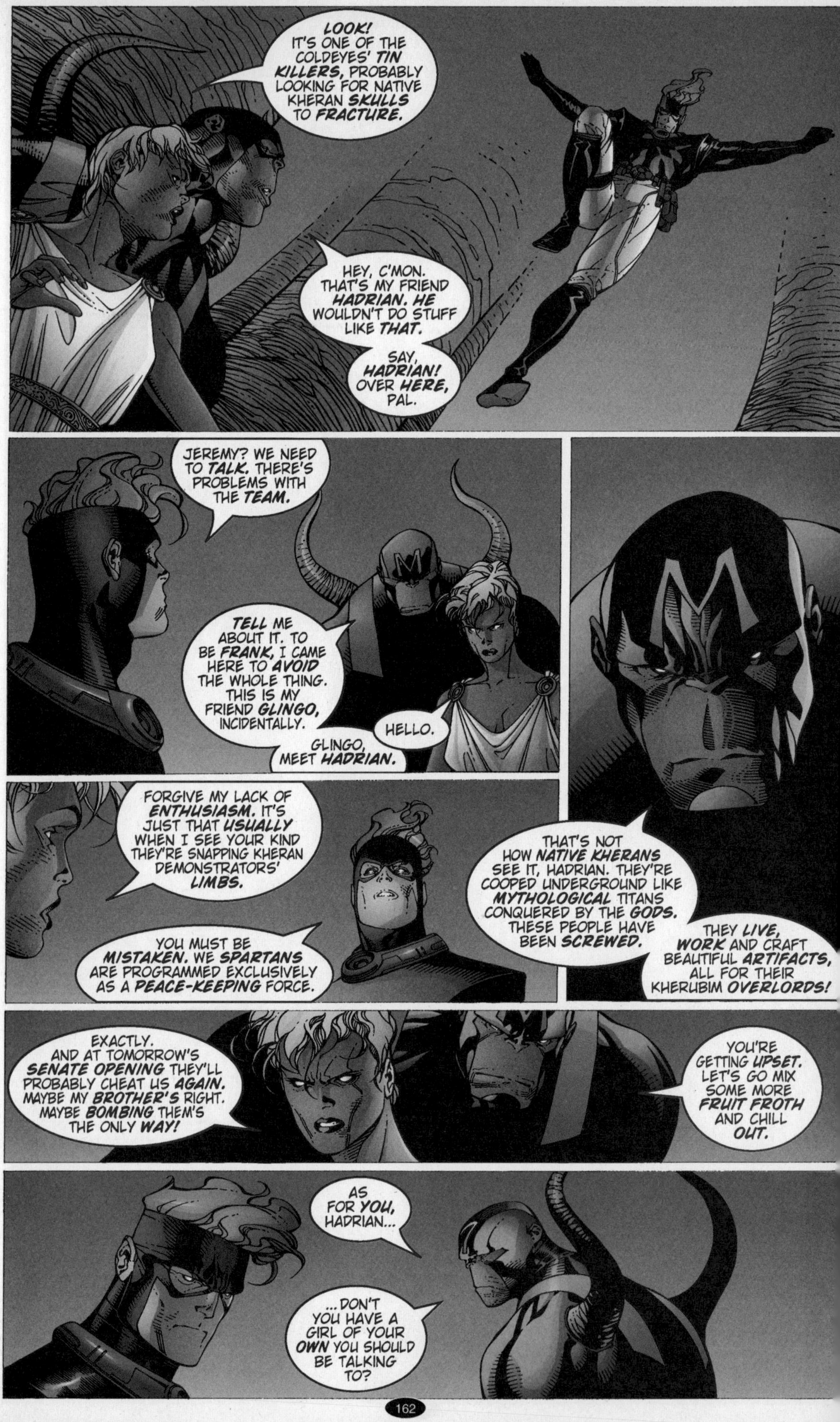
LOOK! IT'S ONE OF THE COLDEYES' TIN KILLERS, PROBABLY LOOKING FOR NATIVE KHERAN SKULLS TO FRACTURE.
HEY, C'MON. THAT'S MY FRIEND HADRIAN. HE WOULDN'T DO STUFF LIKE THAT.
SAY, HADRIAN! OVER HERE, PAL.
JEREMY? WE NEED TO TALK. THERE'S PROBLEMS WITH THE TEAM.
TELL ME ABOUT IT. TO BE FRANK, I CAME HERE TO AVOID THE WHOLE THING. THIS IS MY FRIEND GLINGO, INCIDENTALLY.
HELLO.
GLINGO, MEET HADRIAN.
FORGIVE MY LACK OF ENTHUSIASM. IT'S JUST THAT USUALLY WHEN I SEE YOUR KIND THEY'RE SNAPPING KHERAN DEMONSTRATORS' LIMBS.
YOU MUST BE MISTAKEN. WE SPARTANS ARE PROGRAMMED EXCLUSIVELY AS A PEACE-KEEPING FORCE.
THAT'S NOT HOW NATIVE KHERANS SEE IT, HADRIAN. THEY'RE COOPED UNDERGROUND LIKE MYTHOLOGICAL TITANS CONQUERED BY THE GODS. THESE PEOPLE HAVE BEEN SCREWED.
THEY LIVE, WORK AND CRAFT BEAUTIFUL ARTIFACTS, ALL FOR THEIR KHERUBIM OVERLORDS!
EXACTLY. AND AT TOMORROW'S SENATE OPENING THEY'LL PROBABLY CHEAT US AGAIN. MAYBE MY BROTHER'S RIGHT. MAYBE BOMBING THEM'S THE ONLY WAY!
YOU'RE GETTING UPSET. LET'S GO MIX SOME MORE FRUIT FROTH AND CHILL OUT.
AS FOR YOU, HADRIAN...
...DON'T YOU HAVE A GIRL OF YOUR OWN YOU SHOULD BE TALKING TO?

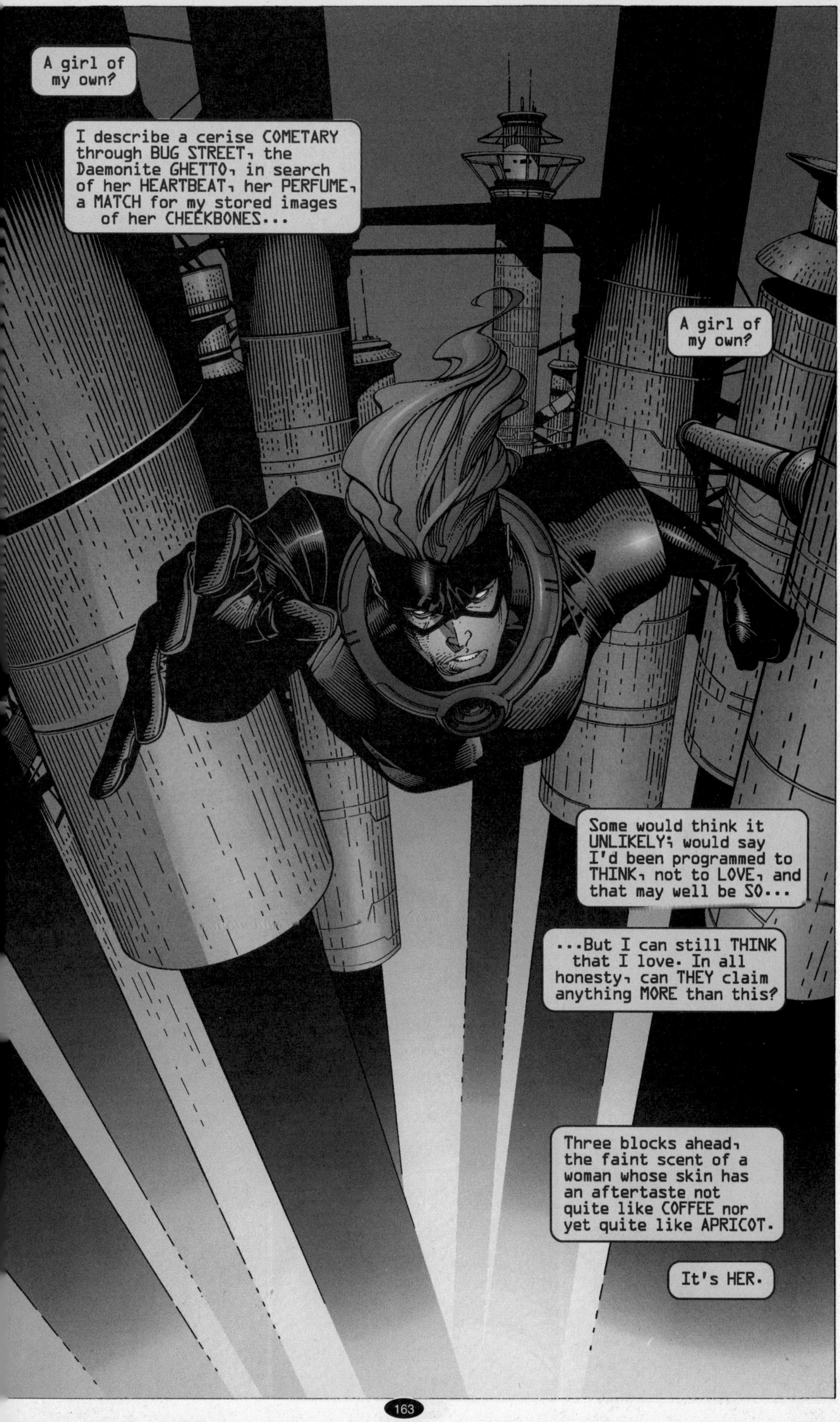
A girl of my own?
I describe a cerise COMETARY through BUG STREET, the Daemonite GHETTO, in search of her HEARTBEAT, her PERFUME, a MATCH for my stored images of her CHEEKBONES...
A girl of my own?
Some would think it UNLIKELY; would say I'd been programmed to THINK, not to LOVE, and that may well be SO...
...But I can still THINK that I love. In all honesty, can THEY claim anything MORE than this?
Three blocks ahead, the faint scent of a woman whose skin has an aftertaste not quite like COFFEE nor yet quite like APRICOT.
It's HER.

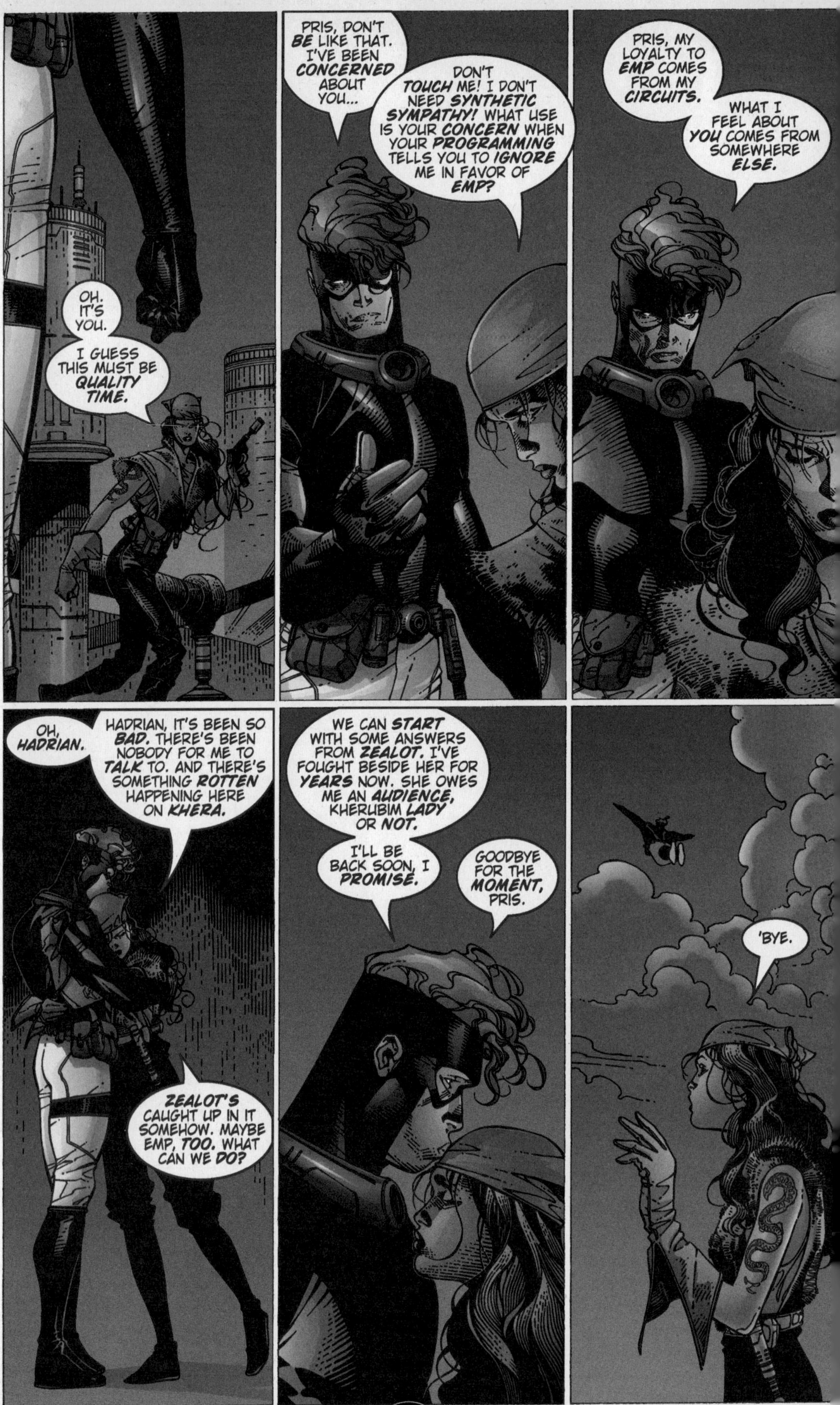
OH. IT'S YOU.
I GUESS THIS MUST BE QUALITY TIME.
PRIS, DON'T BE LIKE THAT. I'VE BEEN CONCERNED ABOUT YOU...
DON'T TOUCH ME! I DON'T NEED SYNTHETIC SYMPATHY! WHAT USE IS YOUR CONCERN WHEN YOUR PROGRAMMING TELLS YOU TO IGNORE ME IN FAVOR OF EMP?
PRIS, MY LOYALTY TO EMP COMES FROM MY CIRCUITS.
WHAT I FEEL ABOUT YOU COMES FROM SOMEWHERE ELSE.
OH, HADRIAN.
HADRIAN, IT'S BEEN SO BAD. THERE'S BEEN NOBODY FOR ME TO TALK TO. AND THERE'S SOMETHING ROTTEN HAPPENING HERE ON KHERA.
ZEALOT'S CAUGHT UP IN IT SOMEHOW. MAYBE EMP, TOO. WHAT CAN WE DO?
WE CAN START WITH SOME ANSWERS FROM ZEALOT. I'VE FOUGHT BESIDE HER FOR YEARS NOW. SHE OWES ME AN AUDIENCE, KHERUBIM LADY OR NOT.
I'LL BE BACK SOON, I PROMISE.
GOODBYE FOR THE MOMENT, PRIS.
'BYE.

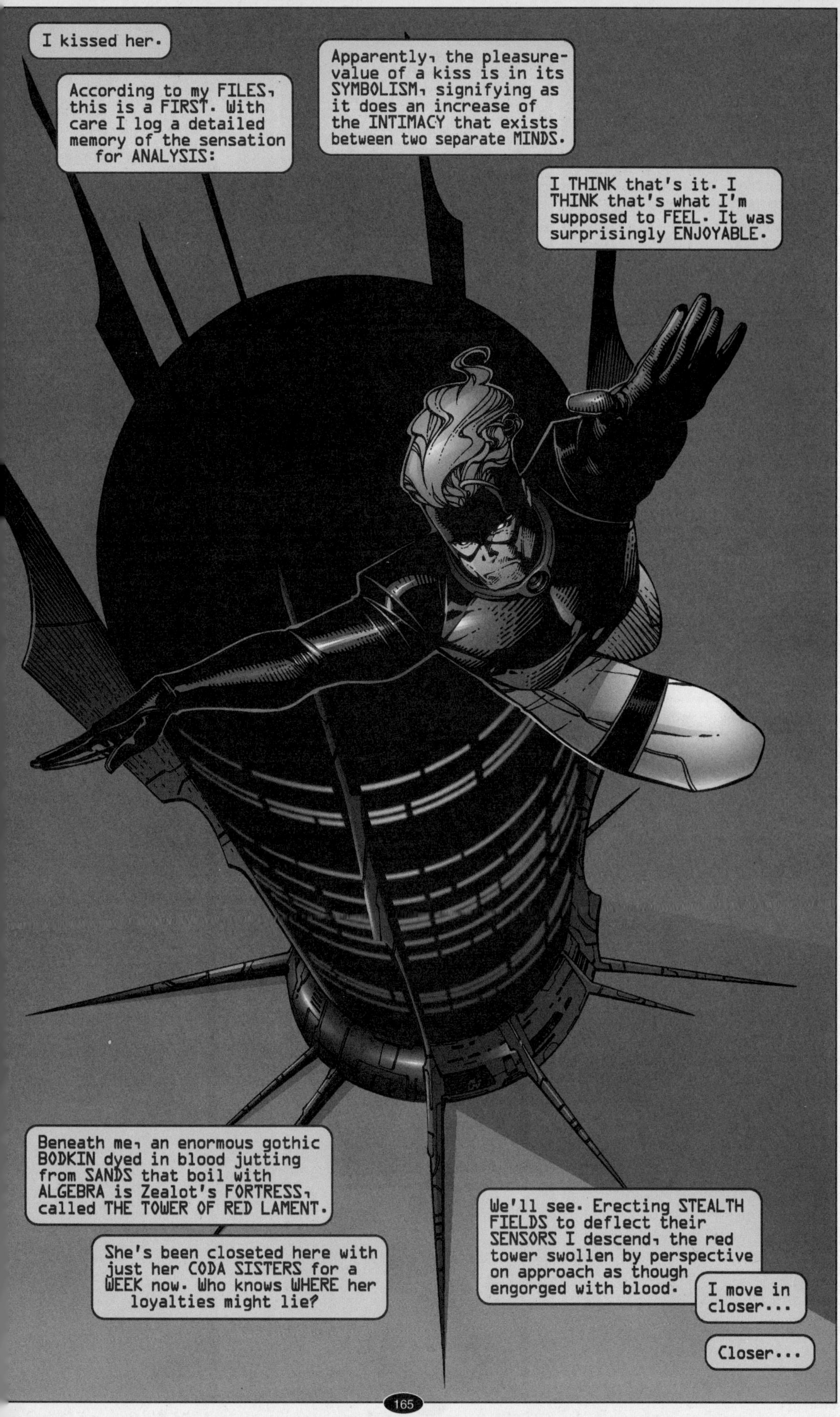
I kissed her.
According to my FILES, this is a FIRST. With care I log a detailed memory of the sensation for ANALYSIS:
Apparently, the pleasure-value of a kiss is in its SYMBOLISM, signifying as it does an increase of the INTIMACY that exists between two separate MINDS.
I THINK that's it. I THINK that's what I'm supposed to FEEL. It was surprisingly ENJOYABLE.
Beneath me, an enormous gothic BODKIN dyed in blood jutting from SANDS that boil with ALGEBRA is Zealot's FORTRESS, called THE TOWER OF RED LAMENT.
She's been closeted here with just her CODA SISTERS for a WEEK now. Who knows WHERE her loyalties might lie?
We'll see. Erecting STEALTH FIELDS to deflect their SENSORS I descend, the red tower swollen by perspective on approach as though engorged with blood.
I move in closer...
Closer...

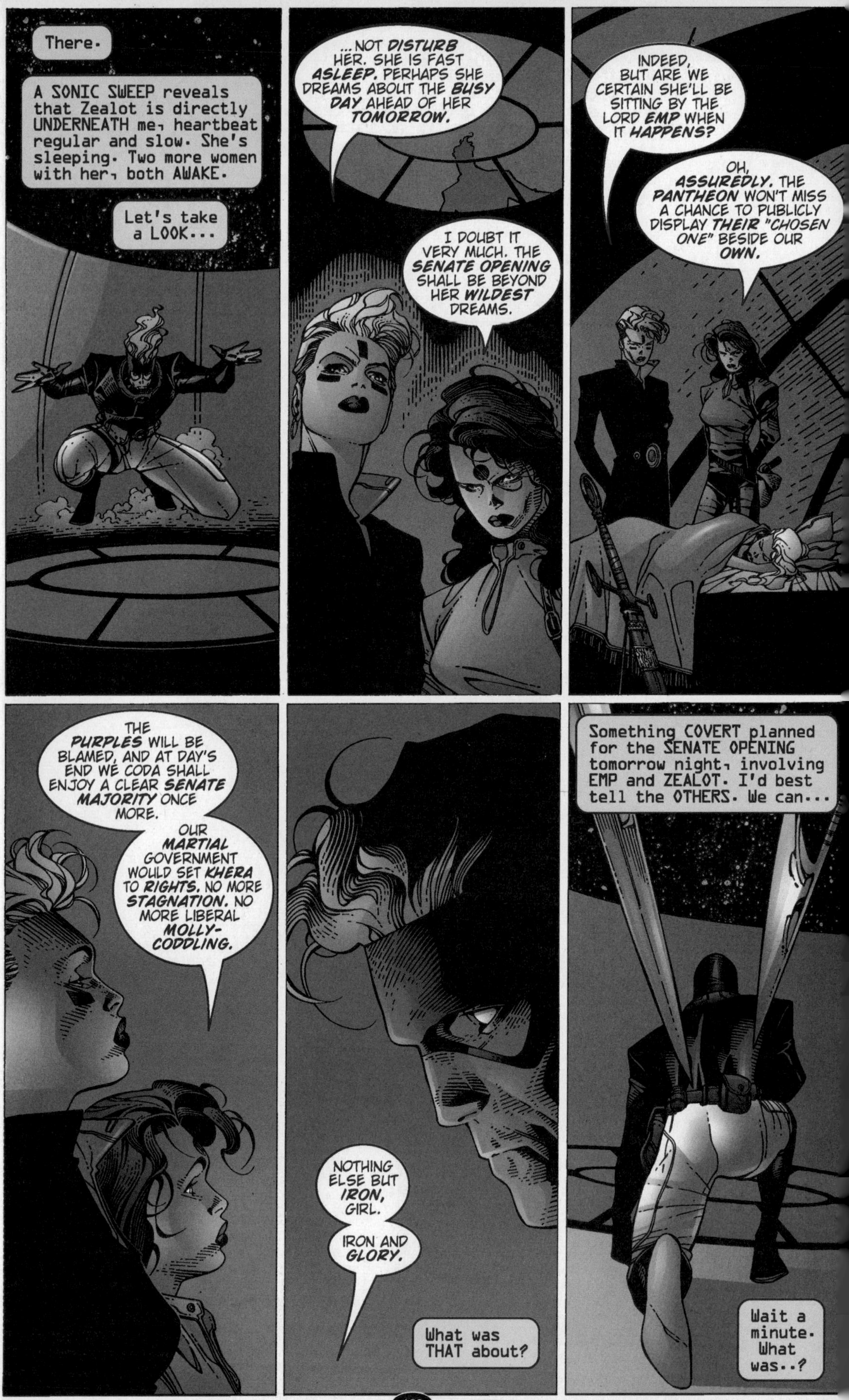
There.
A SONIC SWEEP reveals that Zealot is directly UNDERNEATH me, heartbeat regular and slow. She's sleeping. Two more women with her, both AWAKE.
Let's take a LOOK...
...NOT DISTURB HER. SHE IS FAST ASLEEP. PERHAPS SHE DREAMS ABOUT THE BUSY DAY AHEAD OF HER TOMORROW.
I DOUBT IT VERY MUCH. THE SENATE OPENING SHALL BE BEYOND HER WILDEST DREAMS.
INDEED, BUT ARE WE CERTAIN SHE'LL BE SITTING BY THE LORD EMP WHEN IT HAPPENS?
OH, ASSUREDLY. THE PANTHEON WON'T MISS A CHANCE TO PUBLICLY DISPLAY THEIR "CHOSEN ONE" BESIDE OUR OWN.
THE PURPLES WILL BE BLAMED, AND AT DAY'S END WE CODA SHALL ENJOY A CLEAR SENATE MAJORITY ONCE MORE.
OUR MARTIAL GOVERNMENT WOULD SET KHERA TO RIGHTS. NO MORE STAGNATION. NO MORE LIBERAL MOLLY-CODDLING.
NOTHING ELSE BUT IRON, GIRL.
IRON AND GLORY.
What was THAT about?
Something COVERT planned for the SENATE OPENING tomorrow night, involving EMP and ZEALOT. I'd best tell the OTHERS. We can...
Wait a minute. What was..?

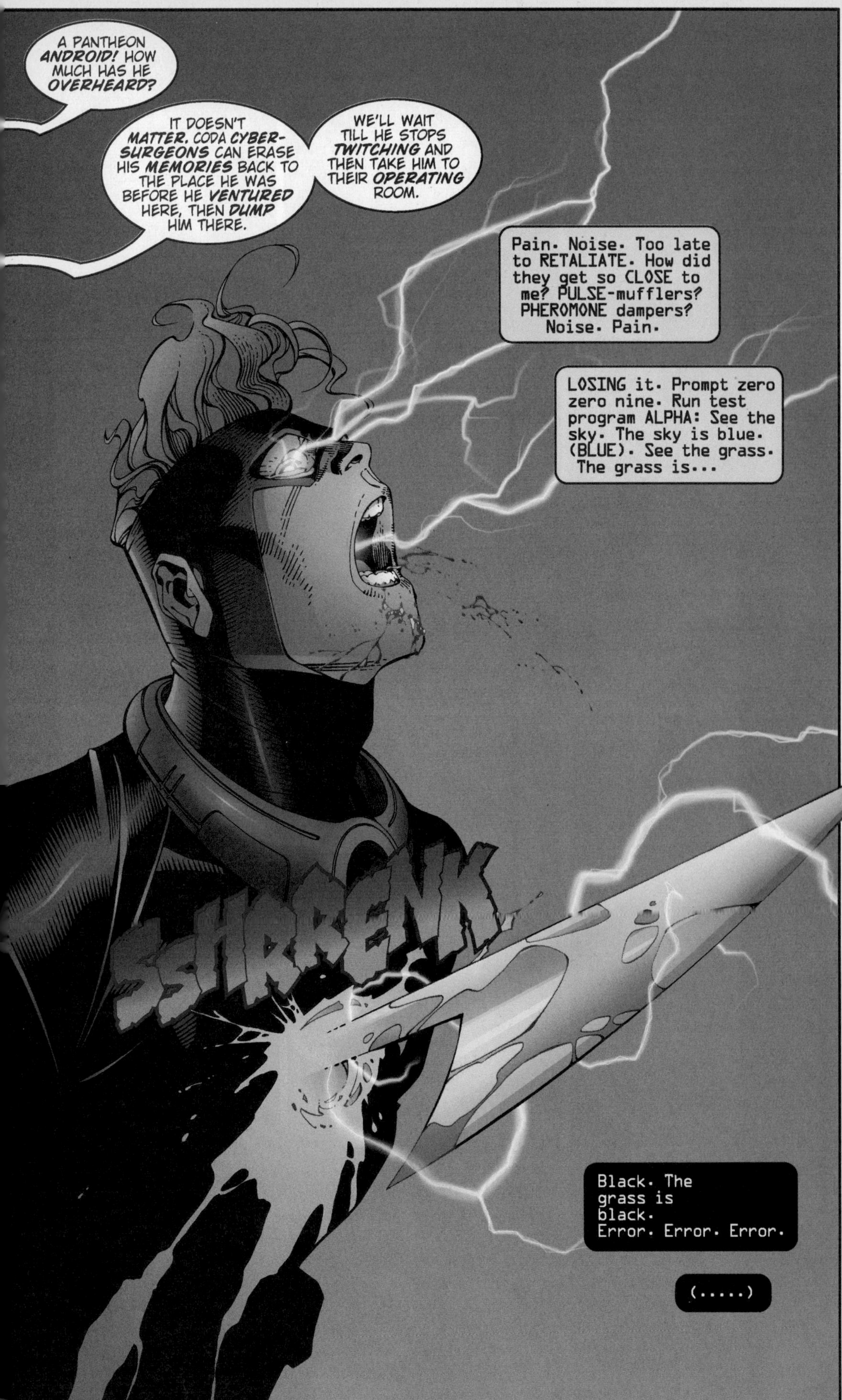
A PANTHEON ANDROID! HOW MUCH HAS HE OVERHEARD?
IT DOESN'T MATTER. CODA CYBER-SURGEONS CAN ERASE HIS MEMORIES BACK TO THE PLACE HE WAS BEFORE HE VENTURED HERE, THEN DUMP HIM THERE.
WE'LL WAIT TILL HE STOPS TWITCHING AND THEN TAKE HIM TO THEIR OPERATING ROOM.
Pain. Noise. Too late to RETALIATE. How did they get so CLOSE to me? PULSE-mufflers? PHEROMONE dampers? Noise. Pain.
LOSING it. Prompt zero zero nine. Run test program ALPHA: See the sky. The sky is blue. (BLUE). See the grass. The grass is...
SSHRRENK
Black. The grass is black. Error. Error. Error.
(.....)

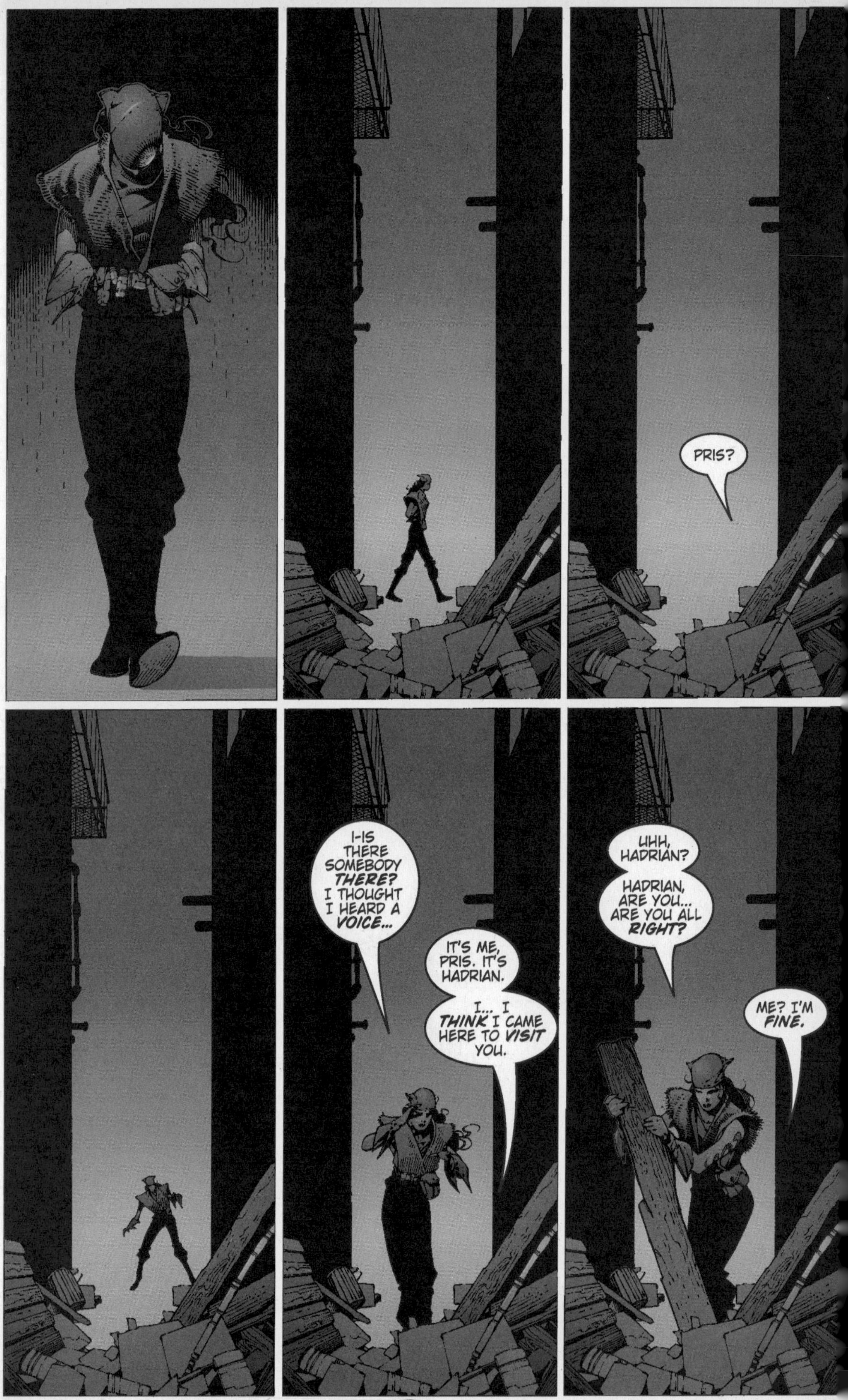
PRIS?
I-IS THERE SOMEBODY *THERE?* I THOUGHT I HEARD A *VOICE...*
IT'S ME, PRIS. IT'S HADRIAN.
I... I *THINK* I CAME HERE TO *VISIT* YOU.
UHH, HADRIAN?
HADRIAN, ARE YOU... ARE YOU ALL *RIGHT?*
ME? I'M *FINE.*

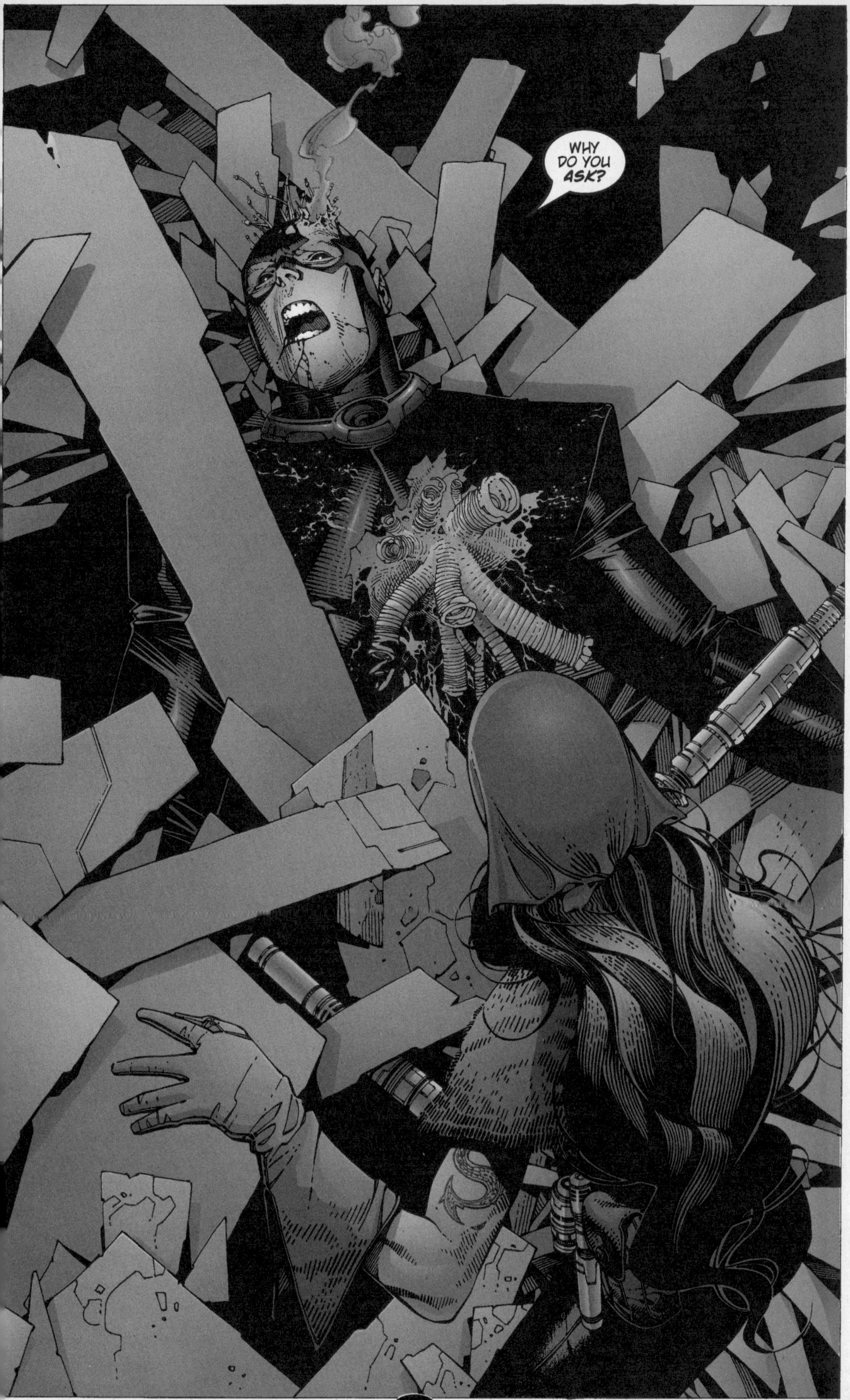
WHY DO YOU ASK?

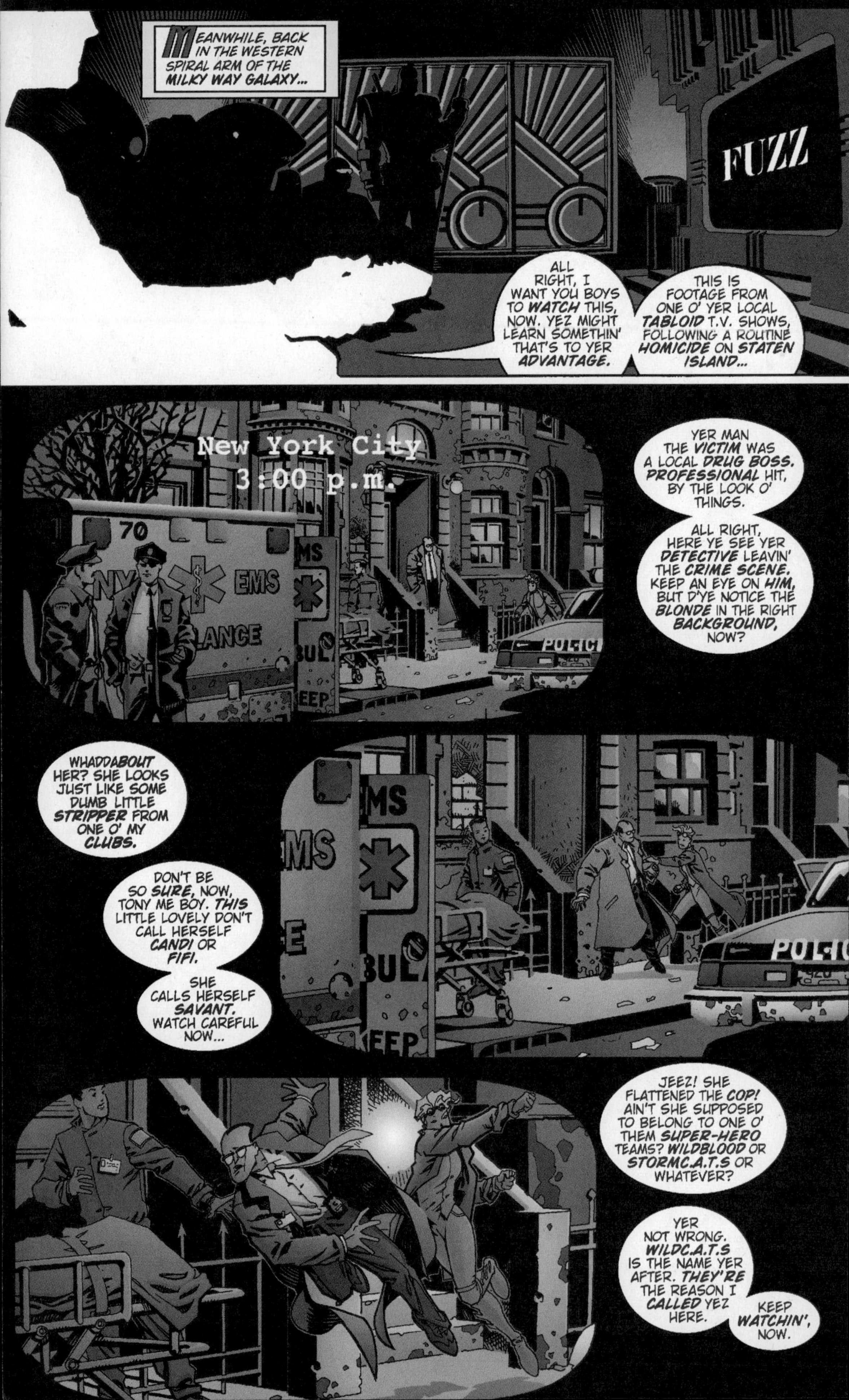
MEANWHILE, BACK IN THE WESTERN SPIRAL ARM OF THE MILKY WAY GALAXY...
FUZZ
ALL RIGHT, I WANT YOU BOYS TO WATCH THIS, NOW. YEZ MIGHT LEARN SOMETHIN' THAT'S TO YER ADVANTAGE.
THIS IS FOOTAGE FROM ONE O' YER LOCAL TABLOID T.V. SHOWS, FOLLOWING A ROUTINE HOMICIDE ON STATEN ISLAND...
New York City
3:00 p.m.
70
NY
EMS
LANCE
MS
BUL
KEEP
POLIC
YER MAN THE VICTIM WAS A LOCAL DRUG BOSS. PROFESSIONAL HIT, BY THE LOOK O' THINGS.
ALL RIGHT, HERE YE SEE YER DETECTIVE LEAVIN' THE CRIME SCENE. KEEP AN EYE ON HIM, BUT D'YE NOTICE THE BLONDE IN THE RIGHT BACKGROUND, NOW?
WHADDABOUT HER? SHE LOOKS JUST LIKE SOME DUMB LITTLE STRIPPER FROM ONE O' MY CLUBS.
DON'T BE SO SURE, NOW, TONY ME BOY. THIS LITTLE LOVELY DON'T CALL HERSELF CANDI OR FIFI.
SHE CALLS HERSELF SAVANT. WATCH CAREFUL NOW...
EMS
EMS
BUL
KEEP
POLIC
JEEZ! SHE FLATTENED THE COP! AIN'T SHE SUPPOSED TO BELONG TO ONE O' THEM SUPER-HERO TEAMS? WILDBLOOD OR STORMC.A.T.S OR WHATEVER?
YER NOT WRONG. WILDC.A.T.S IS THE NAME YER AFTER. THEY'RE THE REASON I CALLED YEZ HERE.
KEEP WATCHIN', NOW.

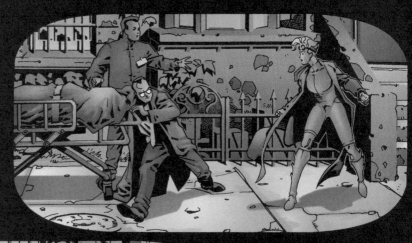

SEE, WHAT THIS IS YER WATCHIN' IS THE *FIRST* FILM I'VE SET *HANDS* ON WITH THE *NEW* WILDC.A.T.S IN *ACTION.*

I'D SAY IT SHOULD GIVE US *ALL* CAUSE FOR *CONCERN.* WATCH *THIS* BIT, NOW. SHE'S RUNNIN' *AFTER* HIM.

I'LL *SLOW* THE *TAPE* SO YE CAN *SEE* IT PROPERLY.

AS SHE *RUNS UP BEHIND* HIM, IT'S LIKE SHE STARTS TO *DISAPPEAR...*

...ONLY TO *REAPPEAR* IN *FRONT* OF HIM. THERE. DID YE *SEE* THAT, NOW?

I'M TOLD IT'S ALL *DOWN* TO A PAIR O' *SEVEN-LEAGUE* BOOTS THAT SHE'S GOT, *BUT* WHO'S TO *SAY?*

THIS IS MY *FAVORITE* BIT, THIS BIT THAT COMES UP *NEXT...*

WHOOAH!

JEEZ, THAT'S GOTTA *HURT...*

WAIT A MINUTE! THAT AIN'T *BLOOD* COMIN' OUT OF HIM...

TWISTELLI'S *RIGHT.* THAT GUY'S NO *COP.* WHAT THE HELL *IS* HE, DEATHTRAP?

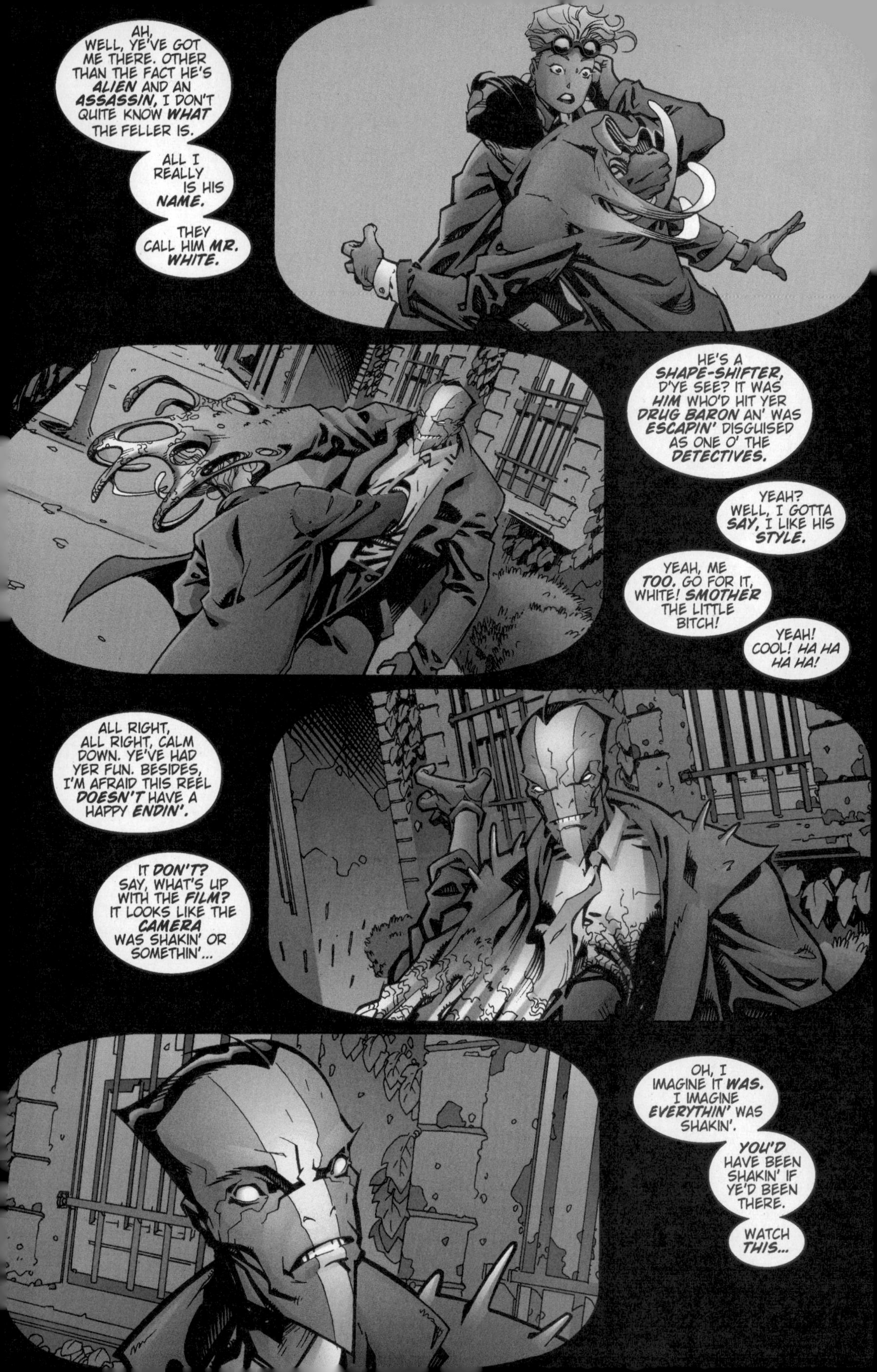
AH, WELL, YE'VE GOT ME THERE. OTHER THAN THE FACT HE'S ALIEN AND AN ASSASSIN, I DON'T QUITE KNOW WHAT THE FELLER IS.
ALL I REALLY IS HIS NAME.
THEY CALL HIM MR. WHITE.
HE'S A SHAPE-SHIFTER, D'YE SEE? IT WAS HIM WHO'D HIT YER DRUG BARON AN' WAS ESCAPIN' DISGUISED AS ONE O' THE DETECTIVES.
YEAH? WELL, I GOTTA SAY, I LIKE HIS STYLE.
YEAH, ME TOO. GO FOR IT, WHITE! SMOTHER THE LITTLE BITCH!
YEAH! COOL! HA HA HA HA!
ALL RIGHT, ALL RIGHT, CALM DOWN. YE'VE HAD YER FUN. BESIDES, I'M AFRAID THIS REEL DOESN'T HAVE A HAPPY ENDIN'.
IT DON'T? SAY, WHAT'S UP WITH THE FILM? IT LOOKS LIKE THE CAMERA WAS SHAKIN' OR SOMETHIN'...
OH, I IMAGINE IT WAS. I IMAGINE EVERYTHIN' WAS SHAKIN'.
YOU'D HAVE BEEN SHAKIN' IF YE'D BEEN THERE.
WATCH THIS...

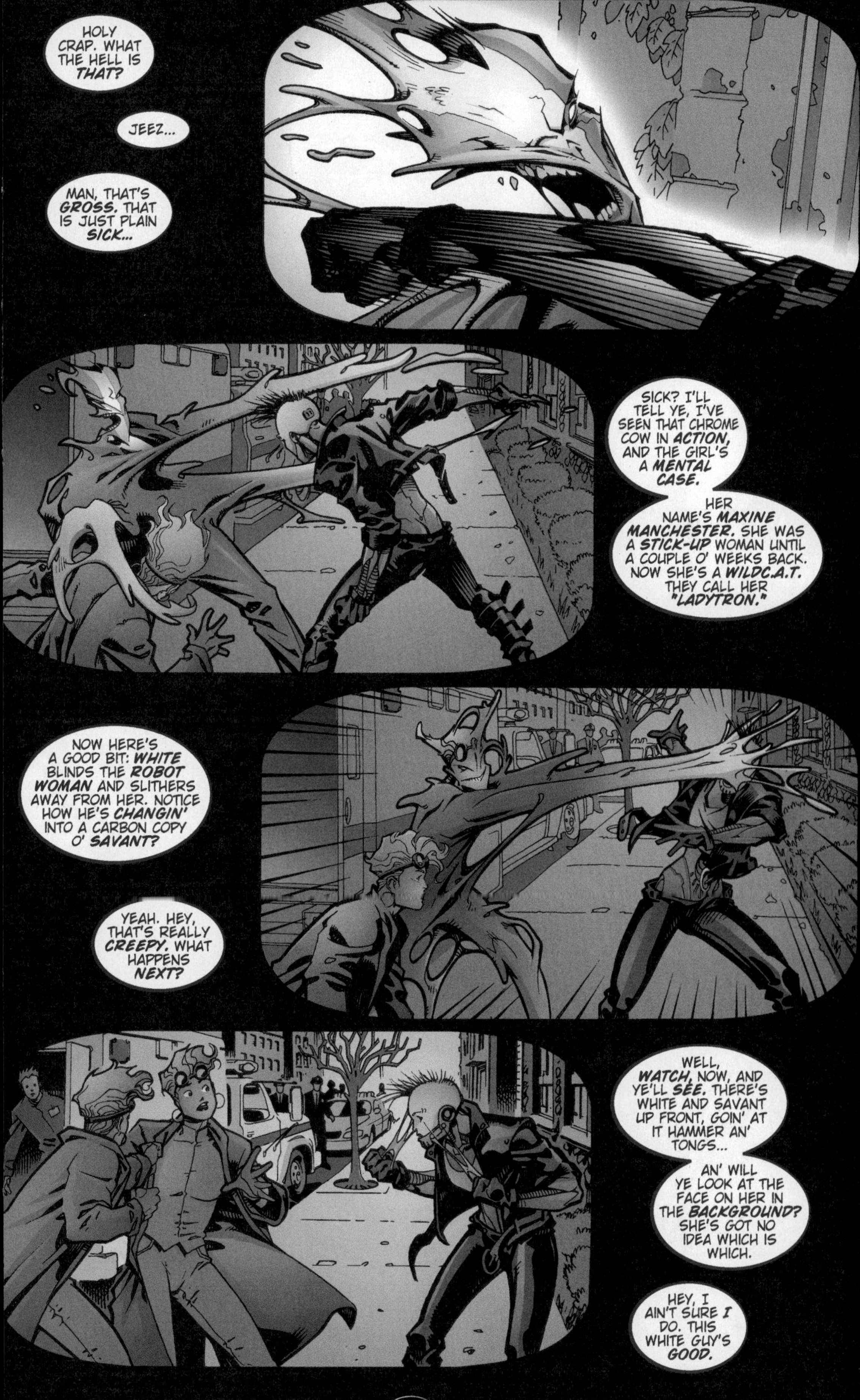
HOLY CRAP. WHAT THE HELL IS THAT?
JEEZ...
MAN, THAT'S GROSS. THAT IS JUST PLAIN SICK...
SICK? I'LL TELL YE, I'VE SEEN THAT CHROME COW IN ACTION, AND THE GIRL'S A MENTAL CASE.
HER NAME'S MAXINE MANCHESTER. SHE WAS A STICK-UP WOMAN UNTIL A COUPLE O' WEEKS BACK. NOW SHE'S A WILDC.A.T. THEY CALL HER "LADYTRON."
NOW HERE'S A GOOD BIT: WHITE BLINDS THE ROBOT WOMAN AND SLITHERS AWAY FROM HER. NOTICE HOW HE'S CHANGIN' INTO A CARBON COPY O' SAVANT?
YEAH. HEY, THAT'S REALLY CREEPY. WHAT HAPPENS NEXT?
WELL, WATCH, NOW, AND YE'LL SEE. THERE'S WHITE AND SAVANT UP FRONT, GOIN' AT IT HAMMER AN' TONGS...
AN' WILL YE LOOK AT THE FACE ON HER IN THE BACKGROUND? SHE'S GOT NO IDEA WHICH IS WHICH.
HEY, I AIN'T SURE I DO. THIS WHITE GUY'S GOOD.

WELL, I'LL TELL YE THIS, IT'S THE *REAL* SAVANT THAT THE ROBOT'S PUNCHIN' OUT *NOW*. I ONLY KNOW THAT 'COS I'VE WATCHED IT *BEFORE*, MIND.

DEATHTRAP, THIS IS ALL VERY *EXCITING*, BUT WHY ARE YOU *SHOWING* US THIS?

WELL, I SUPPOSE YE COULD SAY IT WAS FOR *EDUCATIONAL PURPOSES*: THESE *WILDC.A.T.S* ARE SOMETHIN' *NEW*.

SEE, THEY DON'T WAIT ABOUT FOR ONE OF US TO PULL A *JOB* BEFORE THEY ACT. THEY GO IN *FIRST* AND TAKE US *OUT*...

...WITH EXTREME *PREJUDICE*.

FIRST TIME *OUT*, THEY WENT 'ROUND TO THE PRIVATE ADDRESS OF THE CYBORG *H.A.R.M.* AN' *MURDERED* THE POOR DEVIL. BACK HOME, WE CALL IT *"DOOR-STEPPIN'."*

NEXT, THEY BLITZED HIS *FUNERAL* AND CAPTURED *SLAG* AND *ATTICA.* ME TOO, BUT I *ESCAPED*.

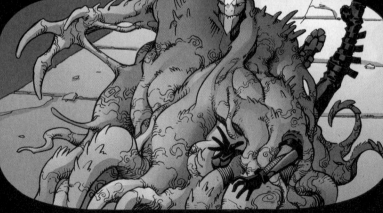

Y'SEE, US *SUPER-PEOPLE* HAVE UNWRITTEN *LAWS,* AND THEY'VE BEEN *BREAKIN'* 'EM. IT'D NOT BE SO BAD IF THEY WERE JUST BRASH, HARMLESS *SECOND STRINGERS*...

...BUT THERE'S *MORE* TO 'EM THAN THAT.

HOLY $*&#! WHERE DID THAT RAY OF *LIGHT* COME FROM? WAS IT...?

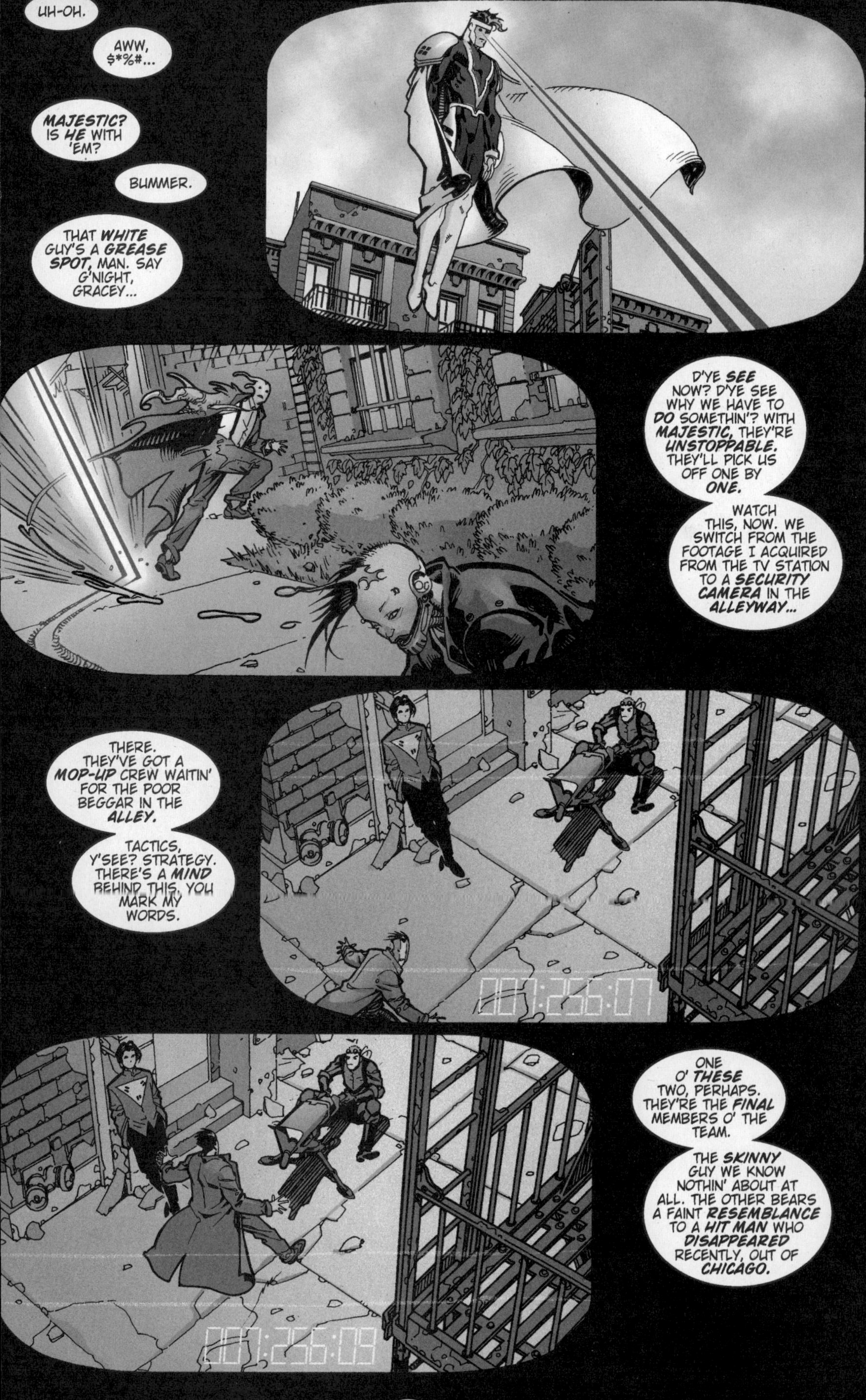
UH-OH.
AWW, $*%#...
MAJESTIC? IS HE WITH 'EM?
BUMMER.
THAT WHITE GUY'S A GREASE SPOT, MAN. SAY G'NIGHT, GRACEY...
D'YE SEE NOW? D'YE SEE WHY WE HAVE TO DO SOMETHIN'? WITH MAJESTIC, THEY'RE UNSTOPPABLE. THEY'LL PICK US OFF ONE BY ONE.
WATCH THIS, NOW. WE SWITCH FROM THE FOOTAGE I ACQUIRED FROM THE TV STATION TO A SECURITY CAMERA IN THE ALLEYWAY...
THERE. THEY'VE GOT A MOP-UP CREW WAITIN' FOR THE POOR BEGGAR IN THE ALLEY.
TACTICS, Y'SEE? STRATEGY. THERE'S A MIND BEHIND THIS, YOU MARK MY WORDS.
007:256:07
ONE O' THESE TWO, PERHAPS. THEY'RE THE FINAL MEMBERS O' THE TEAM.
THE SKINNY GUY WE KNOW NOTHIN' ABOUT AT ALL. THE OTHER BEARS A FAINT RESEMBLANCE TO A HIT MAN WHO DISAPPEARED RECENTLY, OUT OF CHICAGO.
007:256:09

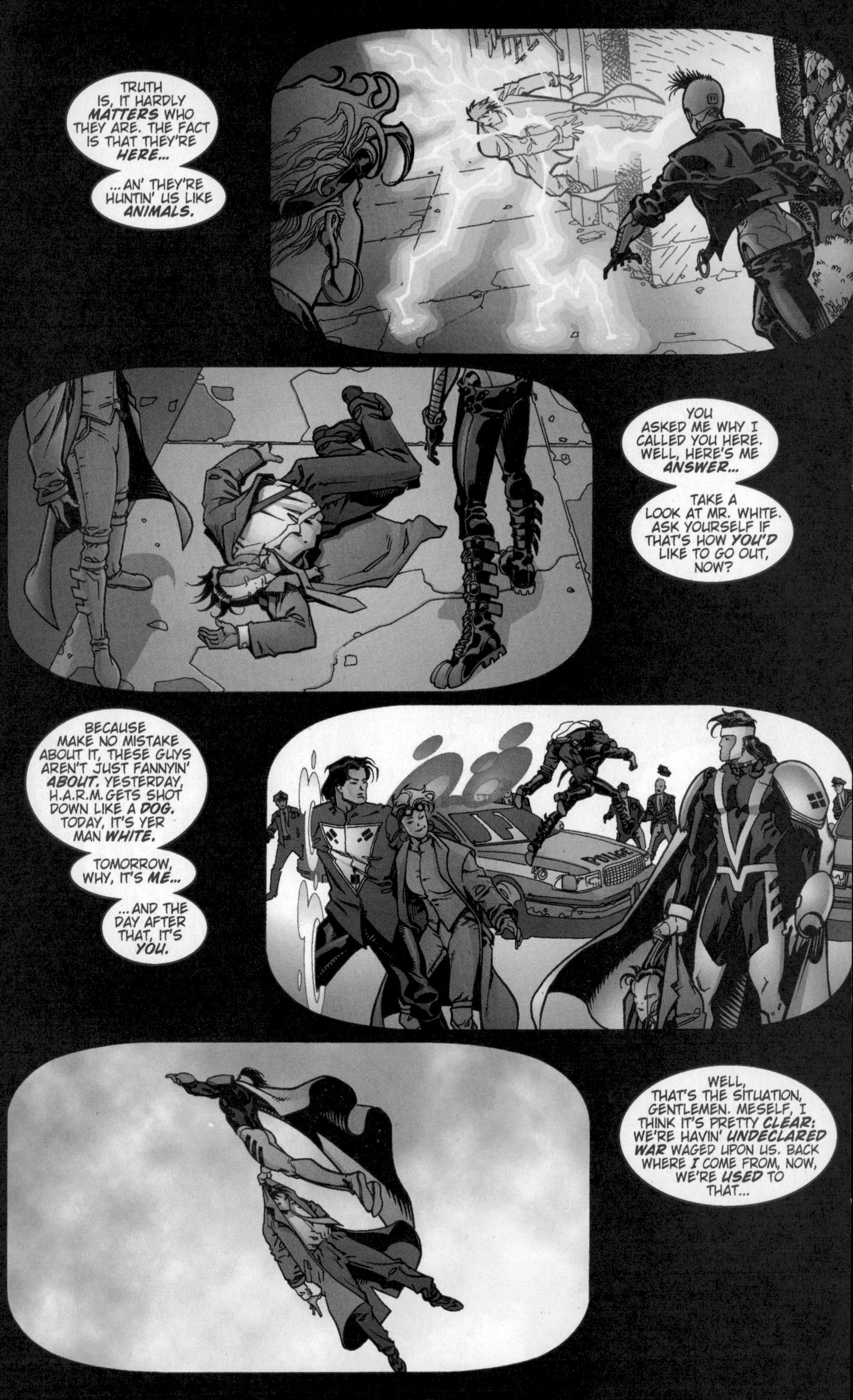

TRUTH IS, IT HARDLY *MATTERS* WHO THEY ARE. THE FACT IS THAT THEY'RE *HERE...*
...AN' THEY'RE HUNTIN' US LIKE *ANIMALS.*
YOU ASKED ME WHY I CALLED YOU HERE. WELL, HERE'S ME *ANSWER...*
TAKE A LOOK AT MR. WHITE. ASK YOURSELF IF THAT'S HOW *YOU'D* LIKE TO GO OUT, NOW?
BECAUSE MAKE NO MISTAKE ABOUT IT, THESE GUYS AREN'T JUST FANNYIN' *ABOUT.* YESTERDAY, H.A.R.M. GETS SHOT DOWN LIKE A *DOG.* TODAY, IT'S YER MAN *WHITE.*
TOMORROW, WHY, IT'S *ME...*
...AND THE DAY AFTER THAT, IT'S *YOU.*
POLICE
WELL, THAT'S THE SITUATION, GENTLEMEN. MESELF, I THINK IT'S PRETTY *CLEAR:* WE'RE HAVIN' *UNDECLARED WAR* WAGED UPON US. BACK WHERE *I* COME FROM, NOW, WE'RE *USED* TO THAT...

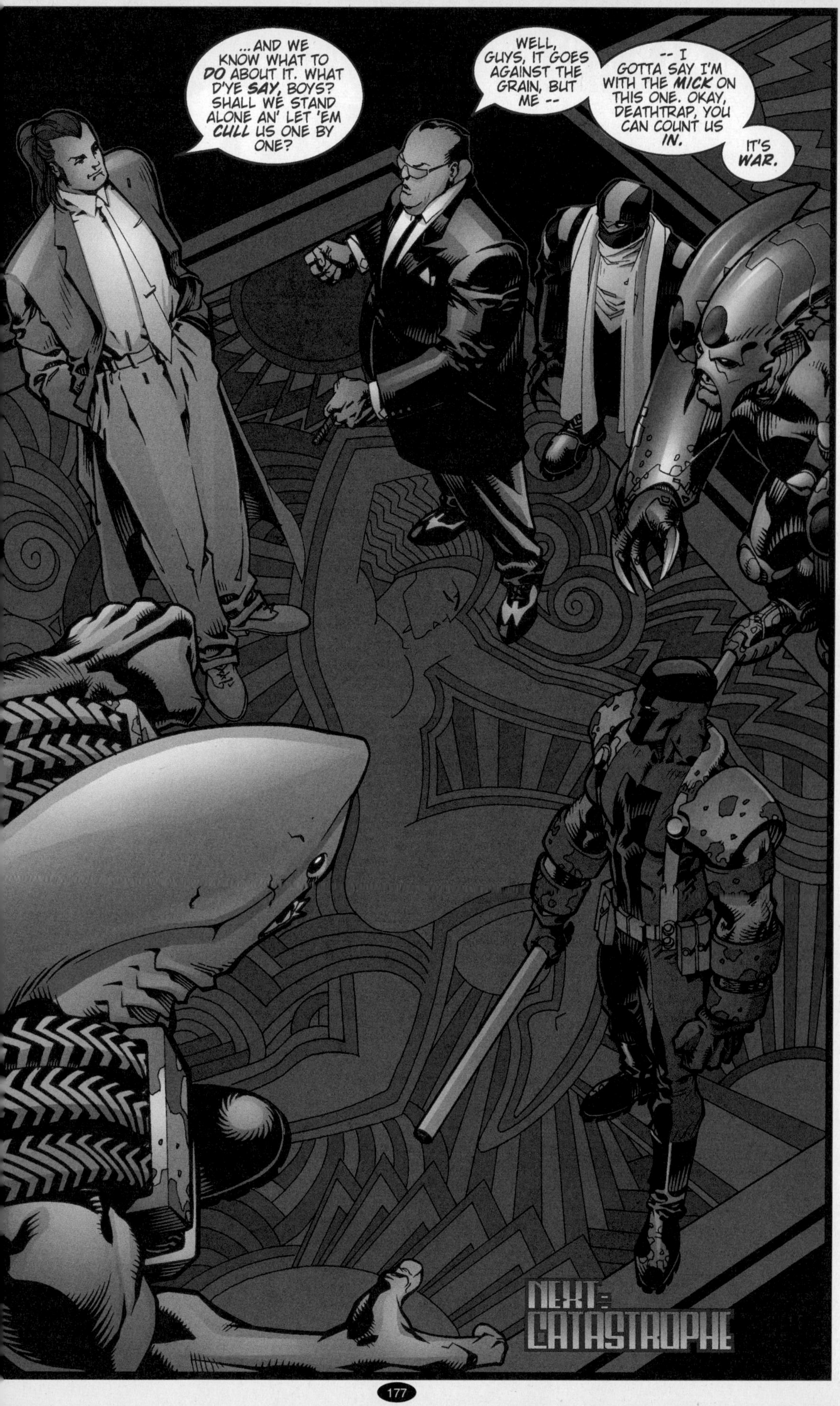
...AND WE KNOW WHAT TO DO ABOUT IT. WHAT D'YE SAY, BOYS? SHALL WE STAND ALONE AN' LET 'EM CULL US ONE BY ONE?
WELL, GUYS, IT GOES AGAINST THE GRAIN, BUT ME --
-- I GOTTA SAY I'M WITH THE MICK ON THIS ONE. OKAY, DEATHTRAP, YOU CAN COUNT US IN.
IT'S WAR.
NEXT: CATASTROPHE

WILDC.A.T.S #27

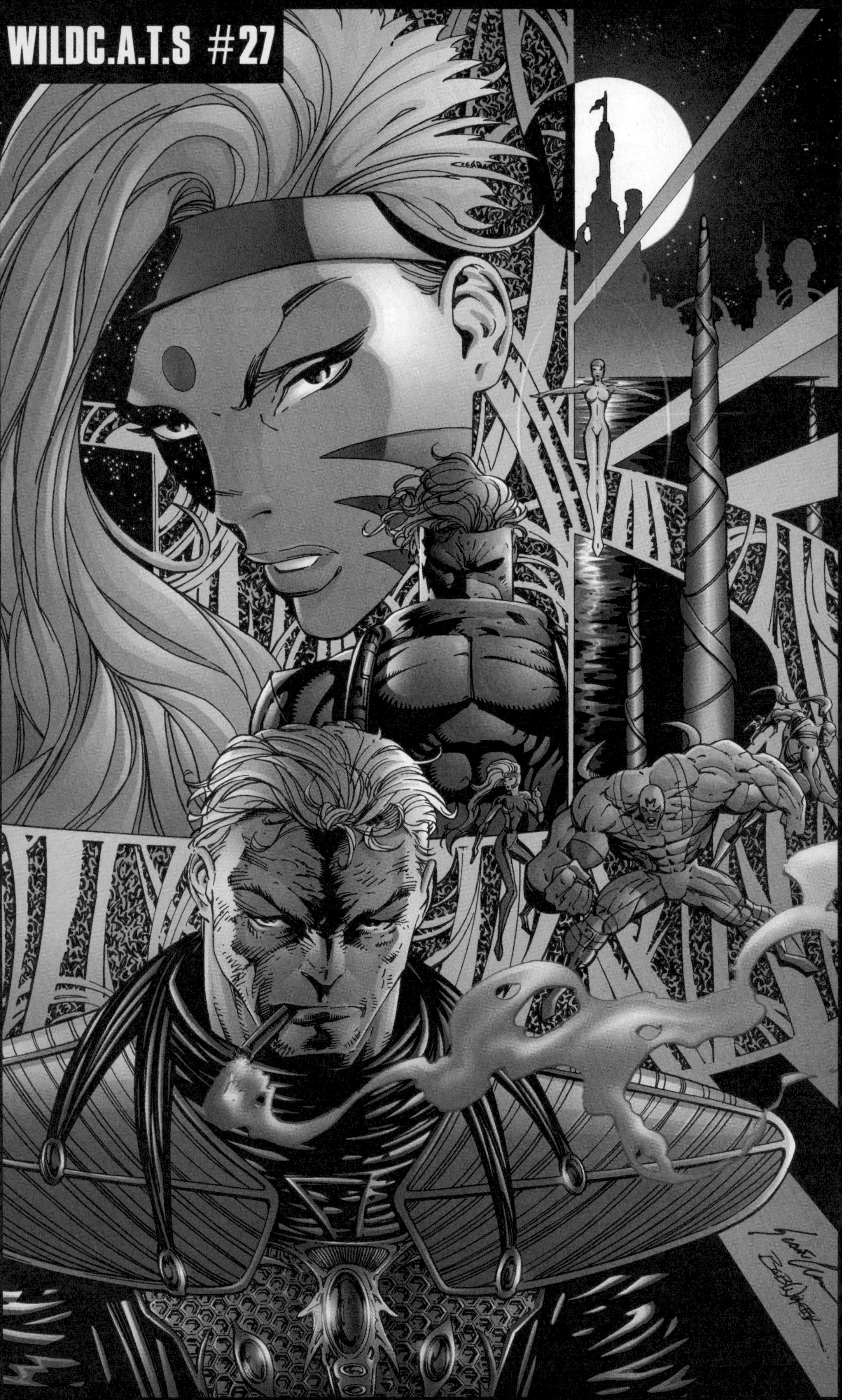

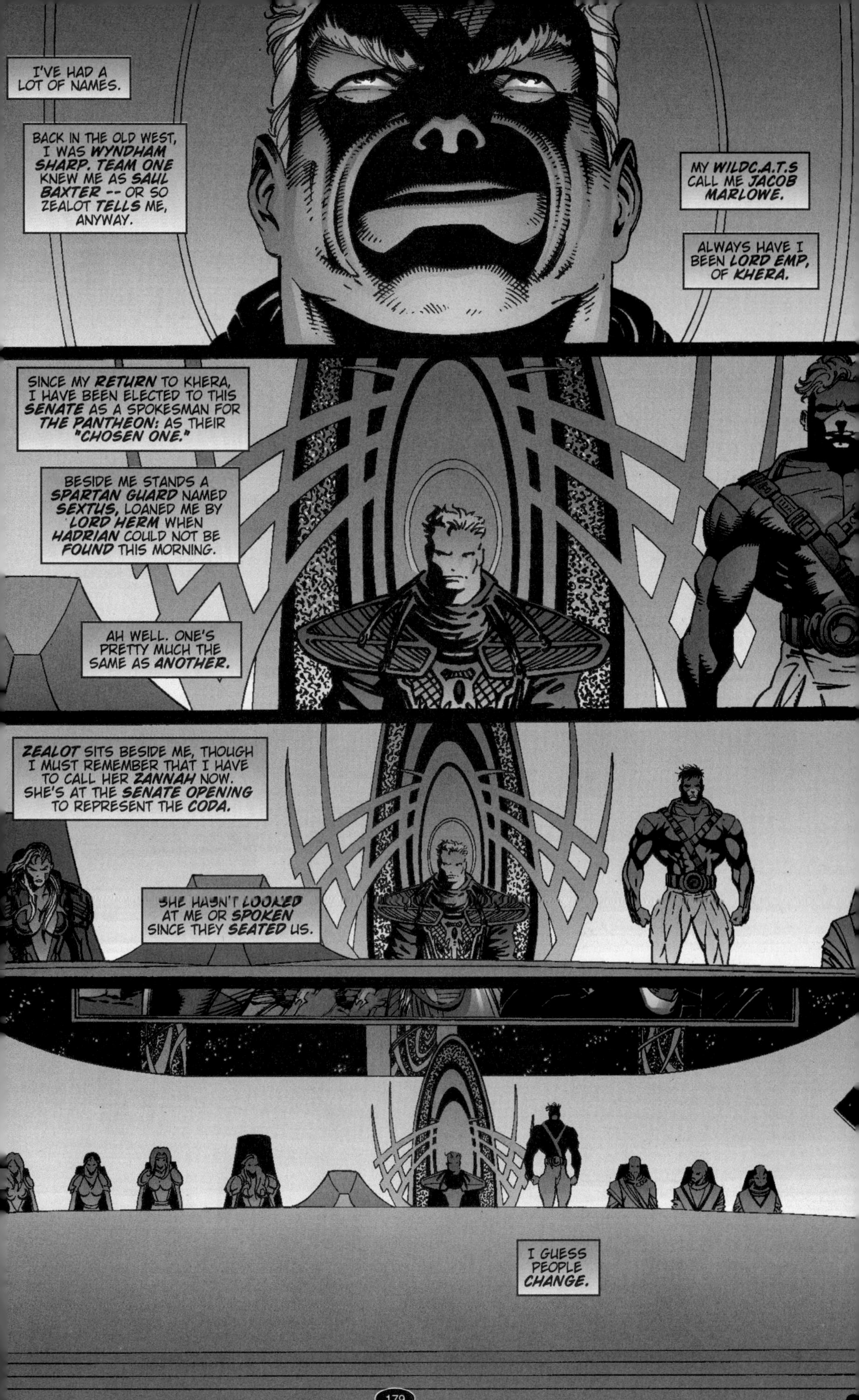
I'VE HAD A LOT OF NAMES.
BACK IN THE OLD WEST, I WAS WYNDHAM SHARP. TEAM ONE KNEW ME AS SAUL BAXTER -- OR SO ZEALOT TELLS ME, ANYWAY.
MY WILDC.A.T.S CALL ME JACOB MARLOWE.
ALWAYS HAVE I BEEN LORD EMP, OF KHERA.
SINCE MY RETURN TO KHERA, I HAVE BEEN ELECTED TO THIS SENATE AS A SPOKESMAN FOR THE PANTHEON: AS THEIR "CHOSEN ONE."
BESIDE ME STANDS A SPARTAN GUARD NAMED SEXTUS, LOANED ME BY LORD HERM WHEN HADRIAN COULD NOT BE FOUND THIS MORNING.
AH WELL. ONE'S PRETTY MUCH THE SAME AS ANOTHER.
ZEALOT SITS BESIDE ME, THOUGH I MUST REMEMBER THAT I HAVE TO CALL HER ZANNAH NOW. SHE'S AT THE SENATE OPENING TO REPRESENT THE CODA.
SHE HASN'T LOOKED AT ME OR SPOKEN SINCE THEY SEATED US.
I GUESS PEOPLE CHANGE.

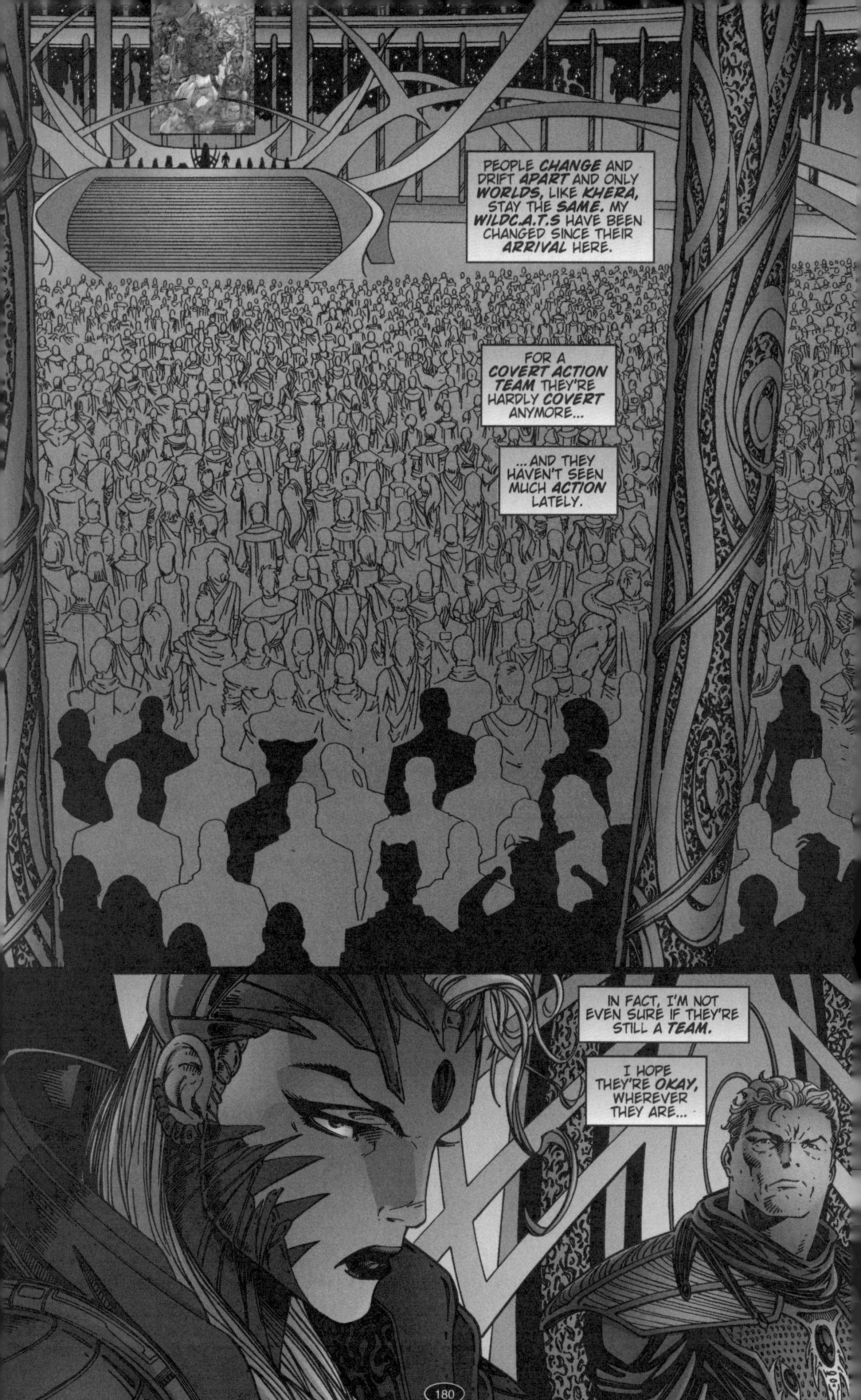
PEOPLE CHANGE AND DRIFT APART AND ONLY WORLDS, LIKE KHERA, STAY THE SAME. MY WILDC.A.T.S HAVE BEEN CHANGED SINCE THEIR ARRIVAL HERE.
FOR A COVERT ACTION TEAM THEY'RE HARDLY COVERT ANYMORE...
...AND THEY HAVEN'T SEEN MUCH ACTION LATELY.
IN FACT, I'M NOT EVEN SURE IF THEY'RE STILL A TEAM.
I HOPE THEY'RE OKAY, WHEREVER THEY ARE...

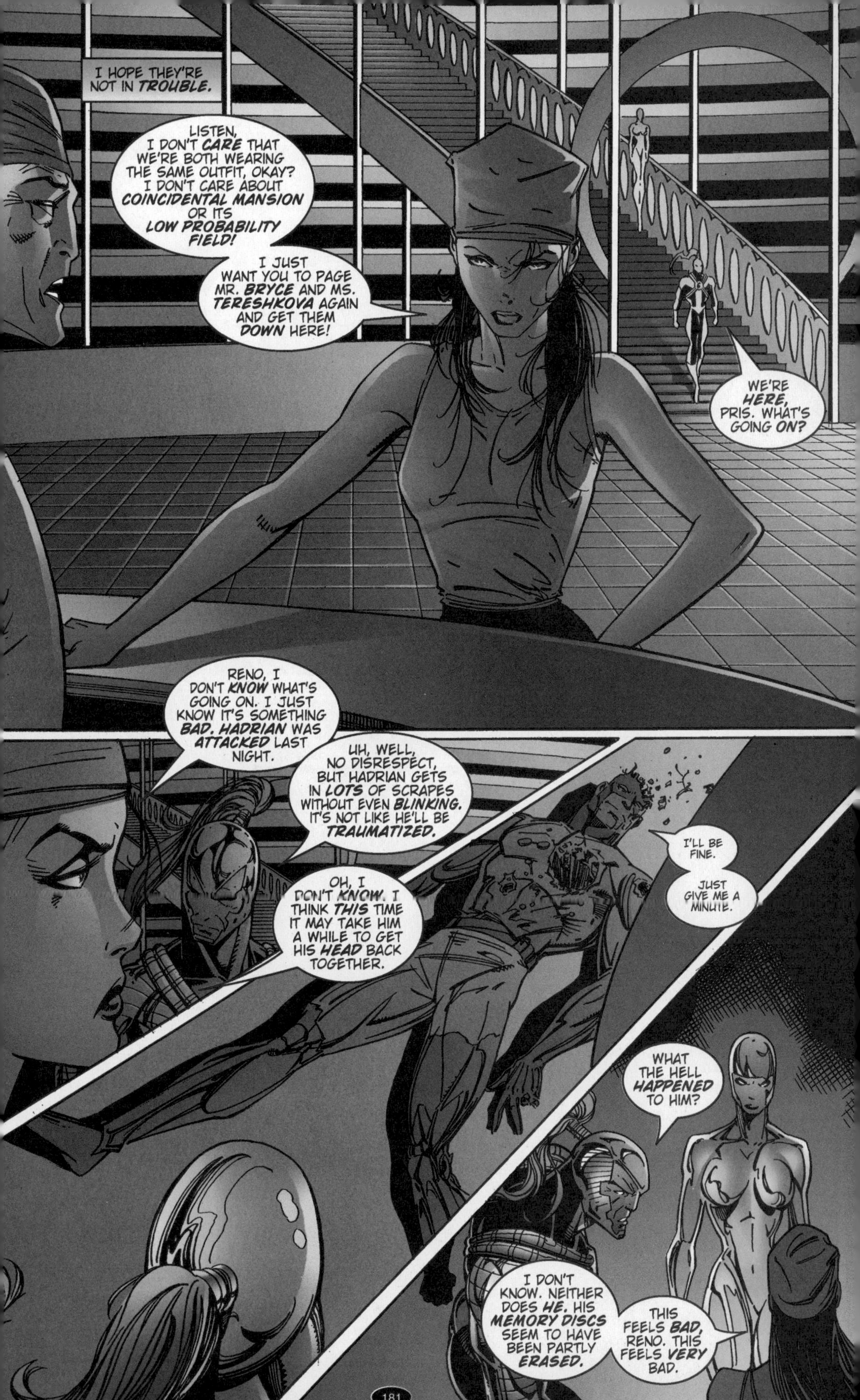
I HOPE THEY'RE NOT IN TROUBLE.
LISTEN, I DON'T CARE THAT WE'RE BOTH WEARING THE SAME OUTFIT, OKAY? I DON'T CARE ABOUT COINCIDENTAL MANSION OR ITS LOW PROBABILITY FIELD!
I JUST WANT YOU TO PAGE MR. BRYCE AND MS. TERESHKOVA AGAIN AND GET THEM DOWN HERE!
WE'RE HERE, PRIS. WHAT'S GOING ON?
RENO, I DON'T KNOW WHAT'S GOING ON. I JUST KNOW IT'S SOMETHING BAD. HADRIAN WAS ATTACKED LAST NIGHT.
UH, WELL, NO DISRESPECT, BUT HADRIAN GETS IN LOTS OF SCRAPES WITHOUT EVEN BLINKING. IT'S NOT LIKE HE'LL BE TRAUMATIZED.
OH, I DON'T KNOW. I THINK THIS TIME IT MAY TAKE HIM A WHILE TO GET HIS HEAD BACK TOGETHER.
I'LL BE FINE.
JUST GIVE ME A MINUTE.
WHAT THE HELL HAPPENED TO HIM?
I DON'T KNOW. NEITHER DOES HE. HIS MEMORY DISCS SEEM TO HAVE BEEN PARTLY ERASED.
THIS FEELS BAD, RENO. THIS FEELS VERY BAD.

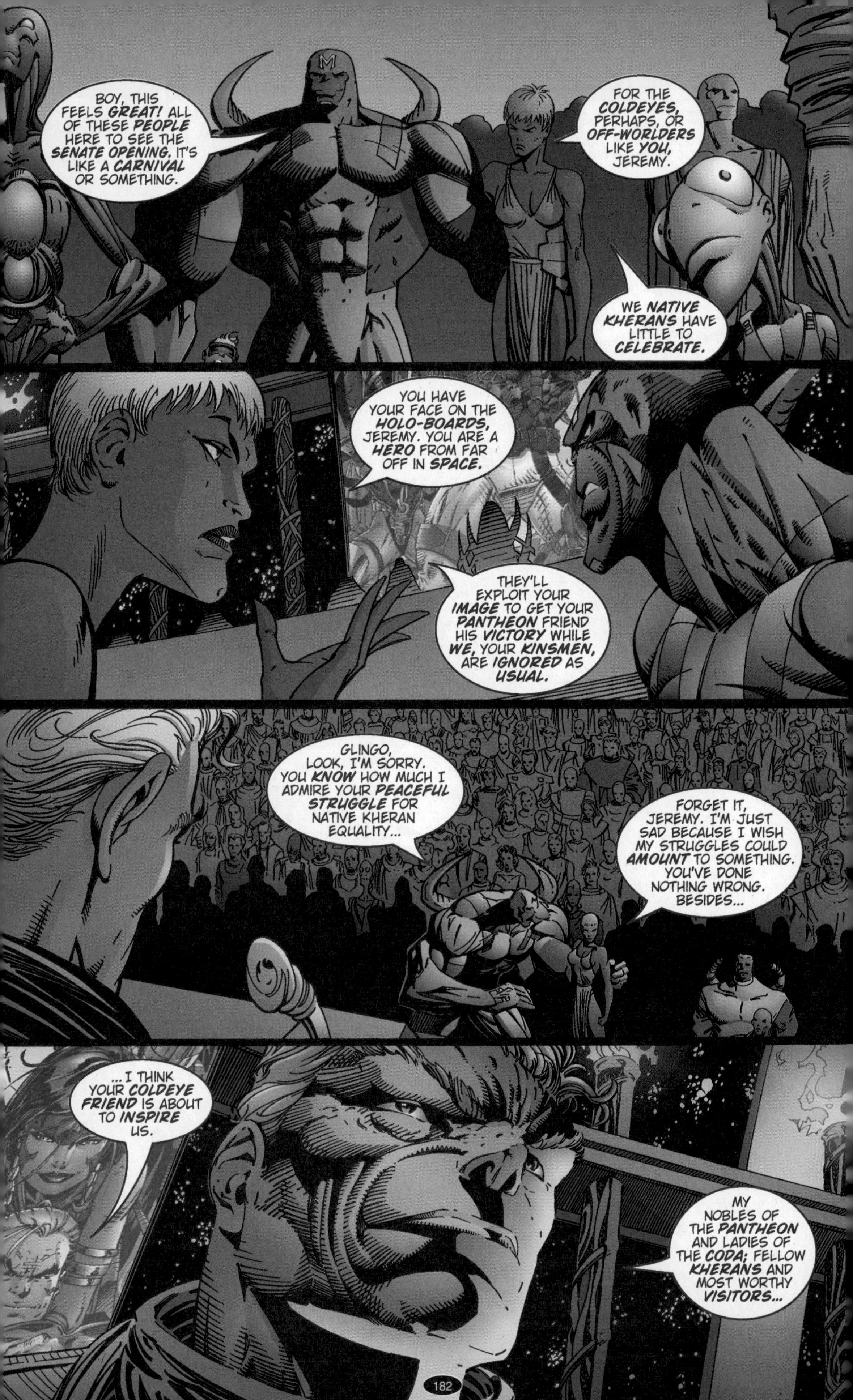
BOY, THIS FEELS GREAT! ALL OF THESE PEOPLE HERE TO SEE THE SENATE OPENING. IT'S LIKE A CARNIVAL OR SOMETHING.
FOR THE COLDEYES, PERHAPS, OR OFF-WORLDERS LIKE YOU, JEREMY.
WE NATIVE KHERANS HAVE LITTLE TO CELEBRATE.
YOU HAVE YOUR FACE ON THE HOLO-BOARDS, JEREMY. YOU ARE A HERO FROM FAR OFF IN SPACE.
THEY'LL EXPLOIT YOUR IMAGE TO GET YOUR PANTHEON FRIEND HIS VICTORY WHILE WE, YOUR KINSMEN, ARE IGNORED AS USUAL.
GLINGO, LOOK, I'M SORRY. YOU KNOW HOW MUCH I ADMIRE YOUR PEACEFUL STRUGGLE FOR NATIVE KHERAN EQUALITY...
FORGET IT, JEREMY. I'M JUST SAD BECAUSE I WISH MY STRUGGLES COULD AMOUNT TO SOMETHING. YOU'VE DONE NOTHING WRONG. BESIDES...
...I THINK YOUR COLDEYE FRIEND IS ABOUT TO INSPIRE US.
MY NOBLES OF THE PANTHEON AND LADIES OF THE CODA; FELLOW KHERANS AND MOST WORTHY VISITORS...

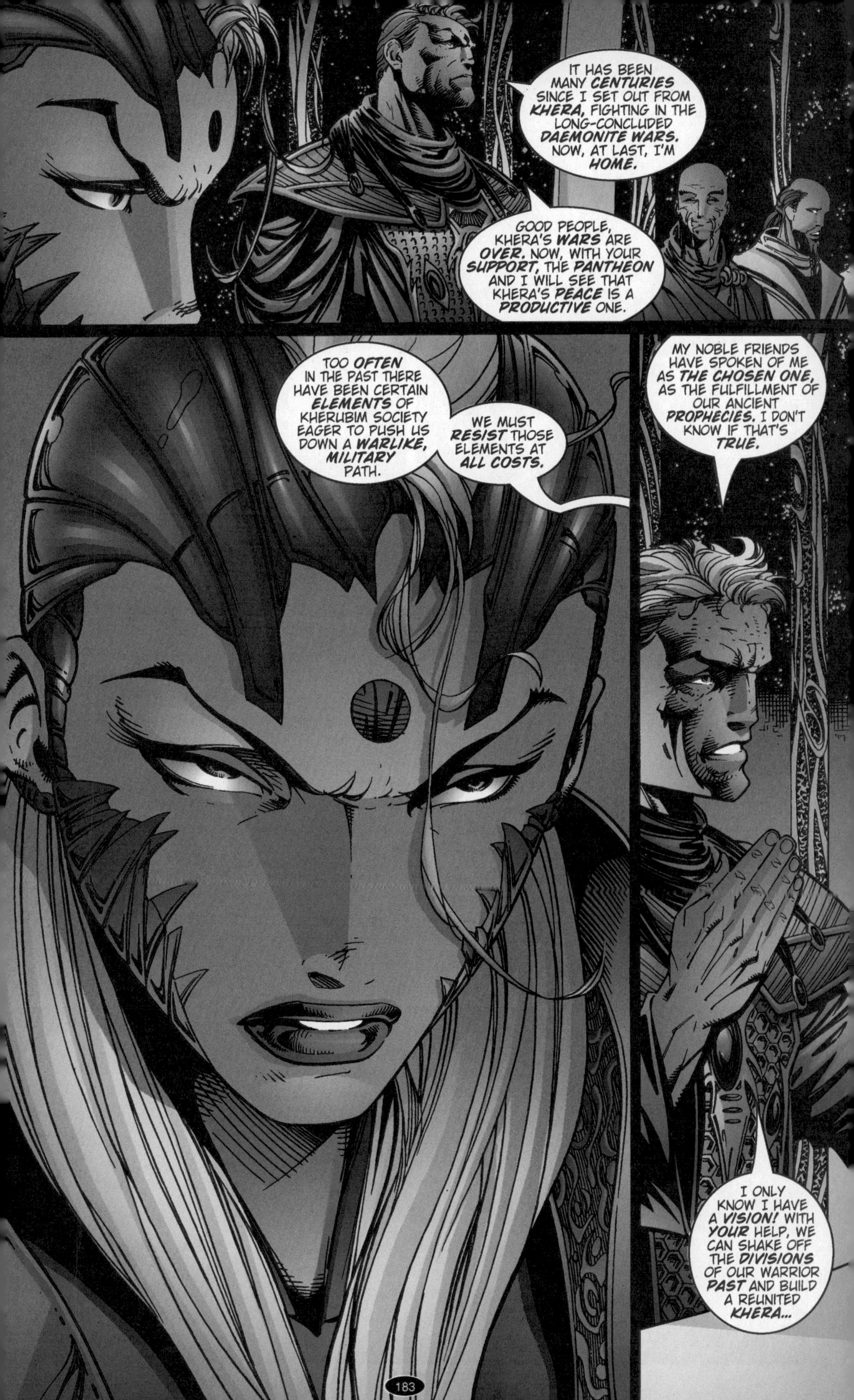

IT HAS BEEN MANY CENTURIES SINCE I SET OUT FROM KHERA, FIGHTING IN THE LONG-CONCLUDED DAEMONITE WARS. NOW, AT LAST, I'M HOME.
GOOD PEOPLE, KHERA'S WARS ARE OVER. NOW, WITH YOUR SUPPORT, THE PANTHEON AND I WILL SEE THAT KHERA'S PEACE IS A PRODUCTIVE ONE.
TOO OFTEN IN THE PAST THERE HAVE BEEN CERTAIN ELEMENTS OF KHERUBIM SOCIETY EAGER TO PUSH US DOWN A WARLIKE, MILITARY PATH.
WE MUST RESIST THOSE ELEMENTS AT ALL COSTS.
MY NOBLE FRIENDS HAVE SPOKEN OF ME AS THE CHOSEN ONE, AS THE FULFILLMENT OF OUR ANCIENT PROPHECIES. I DON'T KNOW IF THAT'S TRUE.
I ONLY KNOW I HAVE A VISION! WITH YOUR HELP, WE CAN SHAKE OFF THE DIVISIONS OF OUR WARRIOR PAST AND BUILD A REUNITED KHERA...

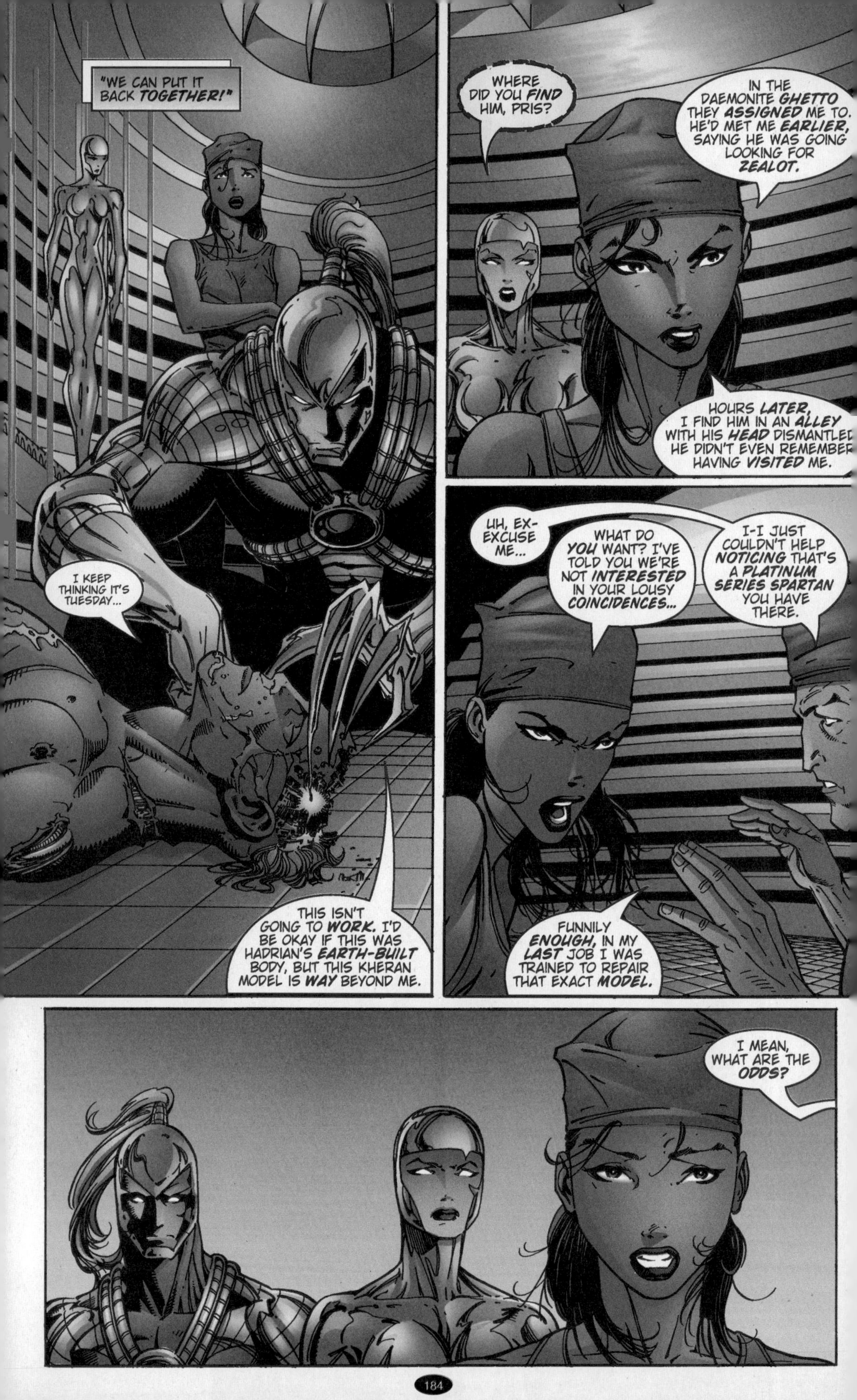
"WE CAN PUT IT BACK TOGETHER!"
I KEEP THINKING IT'S TUESDAY...
THIS ISN'T GOING TO WORK. I'D BE OKAY IF THIS WAS HADRIAN'S EARTH-BUILT BODY, BUT THIS KHERAN MODEL IS WAY BEYOND ME.
WHERE DID YOU FIND HIM, PRIS?
IN THE DAEMONITE GHETTO THEY ASSIGNED ME TO. HE'D MET ME EARLIER, SAYING HE WAS GOING LOOKING FOR ZEALOT.
HOURS LATER, I FIND HIM IN AN ALLEY WITH HIS HEAD DISMANTLED. HE DIDN'T EVEN REMEMBER HAVING VISITED ME.
UH, EX-EXCUSE ME...
WHAT DO YOU WANT? I'VE TOLD YOU WE'RE NOT INTERESTED IN YOUR LOUSY COINCIDENCES...
I-I JUST COULDN'T HELP NOTICING THAT'S A PLATINUM SERIES SPARTAN YOU HAVE THERE.
FUNNILY ENOUGH, IN MY LAST JOB I WAS TRAINED TO REPAIR THAT EXACT MODEL.
I MEAN, WHAT ARE THE ODDS?

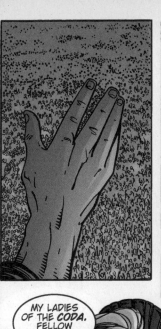

WOW. APART FROM THAT "CHOSEN ONE" BIT, I THOUGHT EMP WENT DOWN REALLY WELL.

IT WAS THE USUAL SMUG PANTHEON FLAG-WAVING, THAT'S ALL. MY BROTHER THINKS ONLY VIOLENCE WILL MAKE THEM TAKE NOTICE.

HUSH, NOW. THE REAL WARMONGERS ARE ABOUT TO SPEAK...

MY LADIES OF THE CODA. FELLOW KHERANS.

I AM ZANNAH, AND I HAVE NOT COME TO FLATTER OR IMPRESS YOU. I TOO HAVE RETURNED AFTER MANY CENTURIES...

...AND I SEE DECADENCE. I SEE THE SICKNESS OF THE WEAK!

RATHER THAN REST UPON THE GLORIES OF OUR PAST, WE MUST MAKE PLANS FOR KHERA'S NEXT TEN THOUSAND YEARS!

SHE'S RATHER GOOD. DID YOU CATCH THAT JAB AT THE PANTHEON?

INDEED. SHE WOULD HAVE MADE A SPLENDID SPEAKER...

...WERE SHE NOT DESTINED FOR MORE GLORIOUS SERVICE AS A MARTYR.

IF THERE ARE TO BE VICTORIES AND GLORIES IN OUR PLANET'S FUTURE, WE MUST STRUGGLE FOR THEM; PAY, IF NEEDS BE, WITH OUR LIVES...

185.

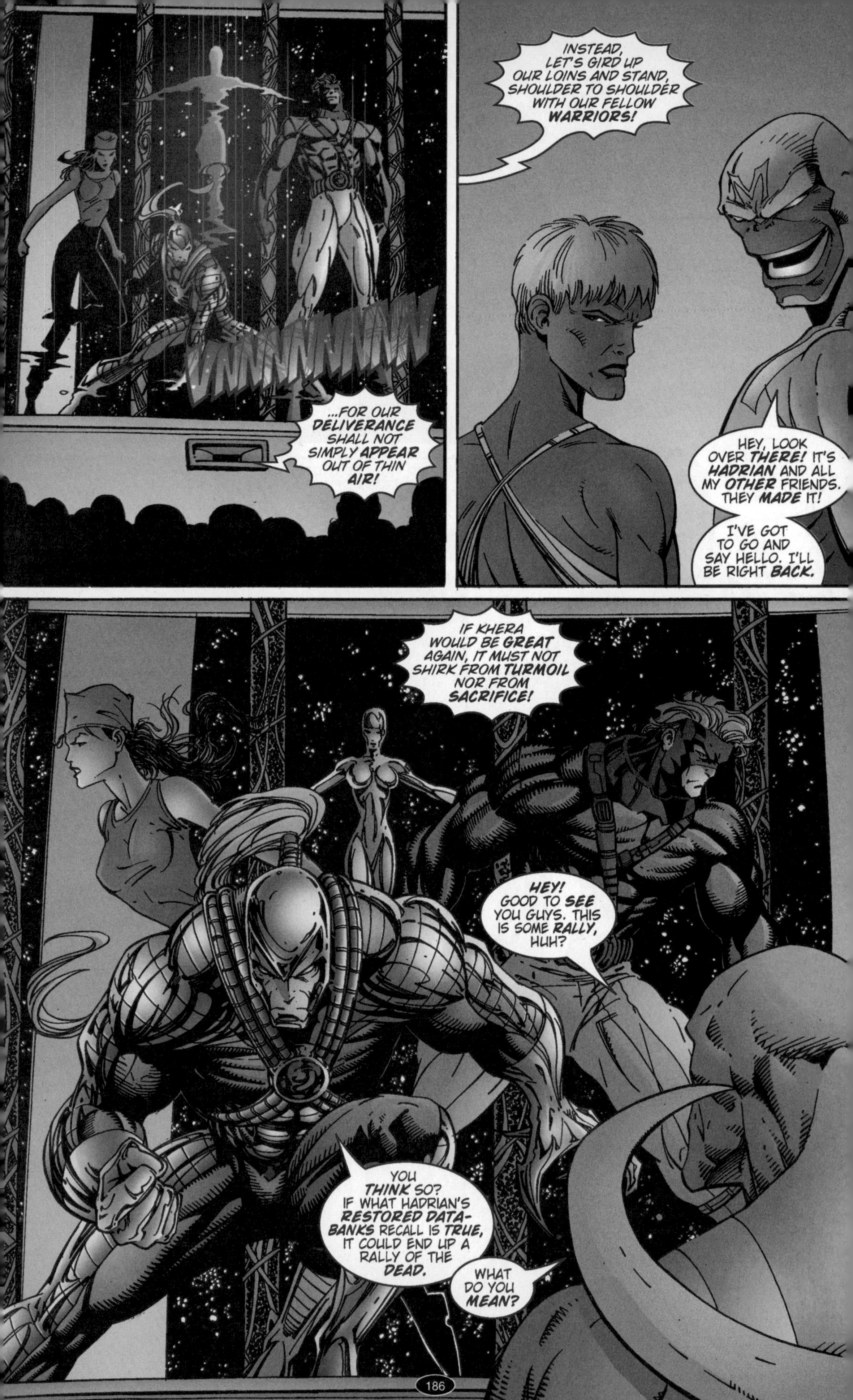
VNNNNNNNNN
...FOR OUR DELIVERANCE SHALL NOT SIMPLY APPEAR OUT OF THIN AIR!
INSTEAD, LET'S GIRD UP OUR LOINS AND STAND, SHOULDER TO SHOULDER WITH OUR FELLOW WARRIORS!
HEY, LOOK OVER THERE! IT'S HADRIAN AND ALL MY OTHER FRIENDS. THEY MADE IT!
I'VE GOT TO GO AND SAY HELLO. I'LL BE RIGHT BACK.
IF KHERA WOULD BE GREAT AGAIN, IT MUST NOT SHIRK FROM TURMOIL NOR FROM SACRIFICE!
HEY! GOOD TO SEE YOU GUYS. THIS IS SOME RALLY, HUH?
YOU THINK SO? IF WHAT HADRIAN'S RESTORED DATA-BANKS RECALL IS TRUE, IT COULD END UP A RALLY OF THE DEAD.
WHAT DO YOU MEAN?

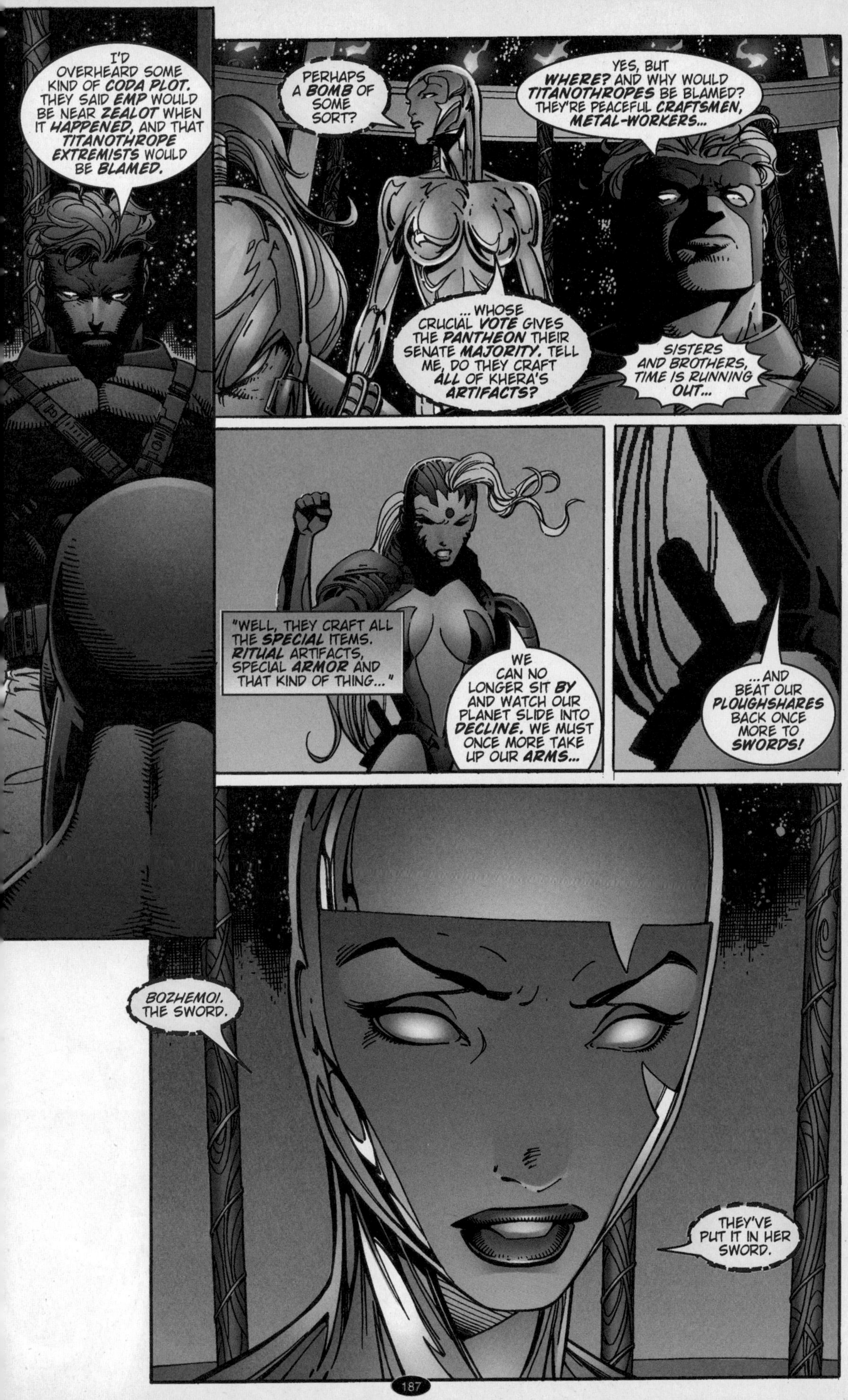
I'D OVERHEARD SOME KIND OF CODA PLOT. THEY SAID EMP WOULD BE NEAR ZEALOT WHEN IT HAPPENED, AND THAT TITANOTHROPE EXTREMISTS WOULD BE BLAMED.
PERHAPS A BOMB OF SOME SORT?
YES, BUT WHERE? AND WHY WOULD TITANOTHROPES BE BLAMED? THEY'RE PEACEFUL CRAFTSMEN, METAL-WORKERS...
...WHOSE CRUCIAL VOTE GIVES THE PANTHEON THEIR SENATE MAJORITY. TELL ME, DO THEY CRAFT ALL OF KHERA'S ARTIFACTS?
SISTERS AND BROTHERS, TIME IS RUNNING OUT...
"WELL, THEY CRAFT ALL THE SPECIAL ITEMS. RITUAL ARTIFACTS, SPECIAL ARMOR AND THAT KIND OF THING..."
WE CAN NO LONGER SIT BY AND WATCH OUR PLANET SLIDE INTO DECLINE. WE MUST ONCE MORE TAKE UP OUR ARMS...
...AND BEAT OUR PLOUGHSHARES BACK ONCE MORE TO SWORDS!
BOZHEMOI. THE SWORD.
THEY'VE PUT IT IN HER SWORD.

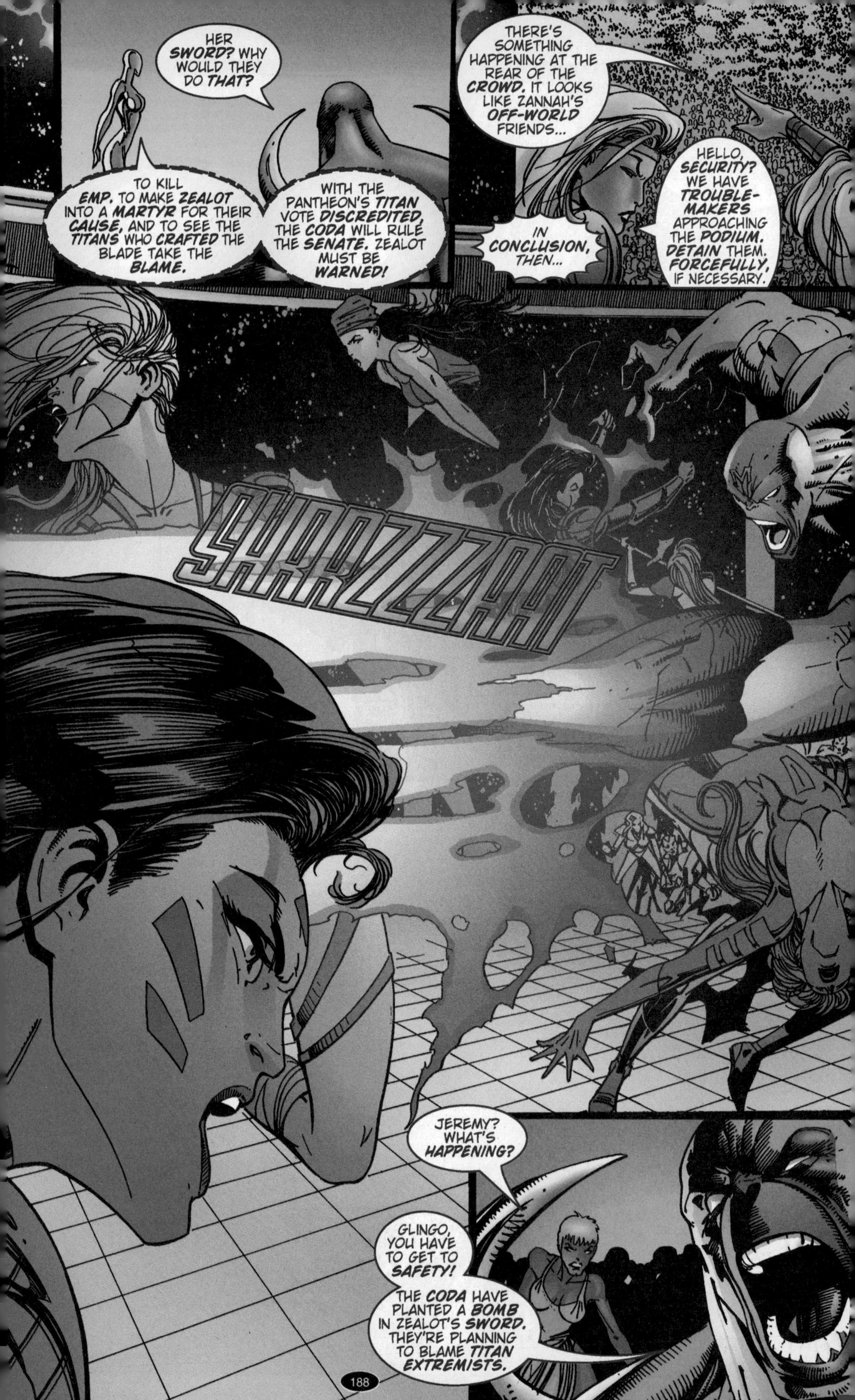

HER SWORD? WHY WOULD THEY DO THAT?
TO KILL EMP. TO MAKE ZEALOT INTO A MARTYR FOR THEIR CAUSE, AND TO SEE THE TITANS WHO CRAFTED THE BLADE TAKE THE BLAME.
WITH THE PANTHEON'S TITAN VOTE DISCREDITED, THE CODA WILL RULE THE SENATE. ZEALOT MUST BE WARNED!
THERE'S SOMETHING HAPPENING AT THE REAR OF THE CROWD. IT LOOKS LIKE ZANNAH'S OFF-WORLD FRIENDS...
IN CONCLUSION, THEN...
HELLO, SECURITY? WE HAVE TROUBLE-MAKERS APPROACHING THE PODIUM. DETAIN THEM. FORCEFULLY, IF NECESSARY.
SKRRZZZAAT
JEREMY? WHAT'S HAPPENING?
GLINGO, YOU HAVE TO GET TO SAFETY!
THE CODA HAVE PLANTED A BOMB IN ZEALOT'S SWORD. THEY'RE PLANNING TO BLAME TITAN EXTREMISTS.

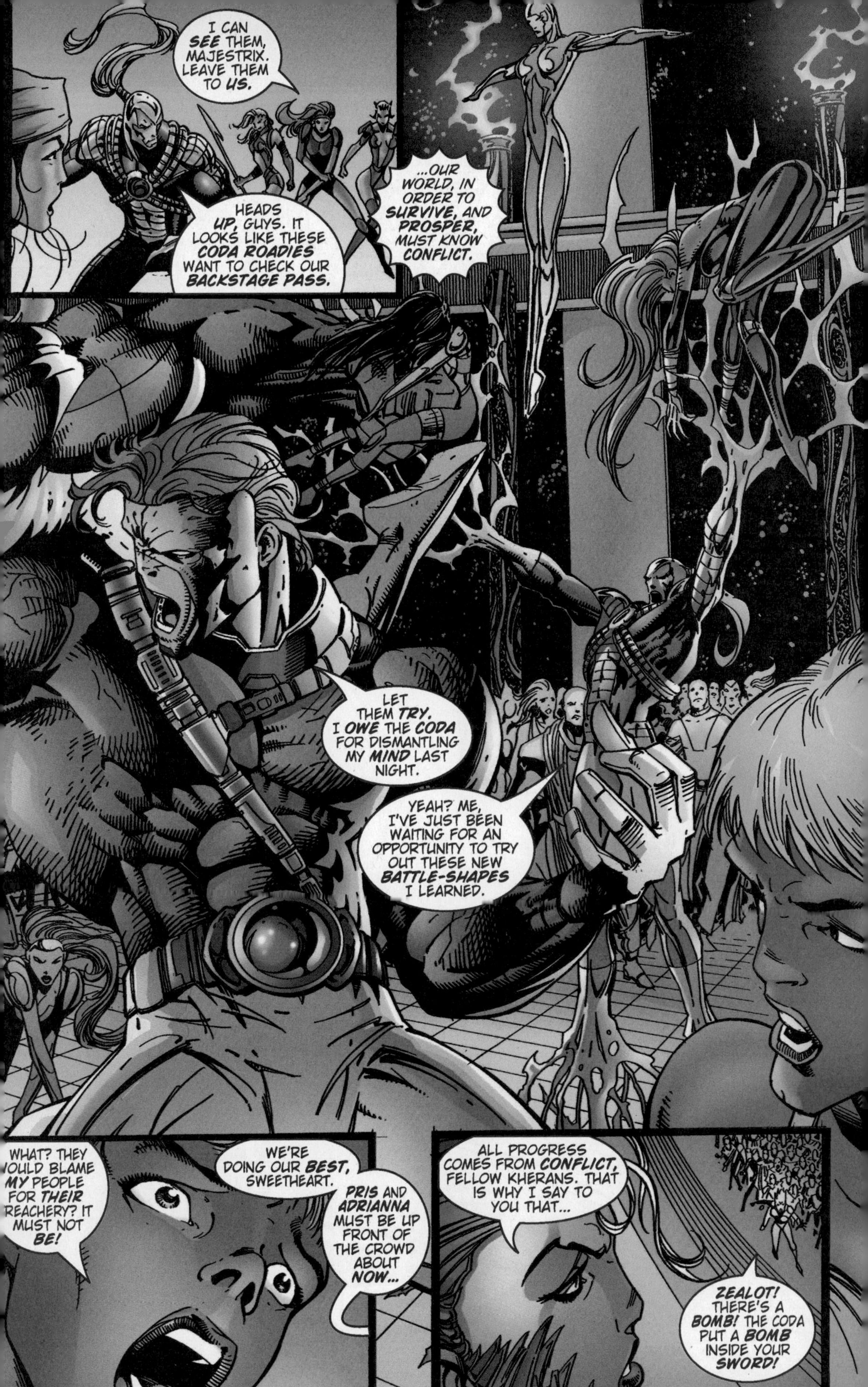
I CAN SEE THEM, MAJESTRIX. LEAVE THEM TO US.
HEADS UP, GUYS. IT LOOKS LIKE THESE CODA ROADIES WANT TO CHECK OUR BACKSTAGE PASS.
...OUR WORLD, IN ORDER TO SURVIVE, AND PROSPER, MUST KNOW CONFLICT.
LET THEM TRY. I OWE THE CODA FOR DISMANTLING MY MIND LAST NIGHT.
YEAH? ME, I'VE JUST BEEN WAITING FOR AN OPPORTUNITY TO TRY OUT THESE NEW BATTLE-SHAPES I LEARNED.
WHAT? THEY OULD BLAME MY PEOPLE FOR THEIR REACHERY? IT MUST NOT BE!
WE'RE DOING OUR BEST, SWEETHEART.
PRIS AND ADRIANNA MUST BE UP FRONT OF THE CROWD ABOUT NOW...
ALL PROGRESS COMES FROM CONFLICT, FELLOW KHERANS. THAT IS WHY I SAY TO YOU THAT...
ZEALOT! THERE'S A BOMB! THE CODA PUT A BOMB INSIDE YOUR SWORD!

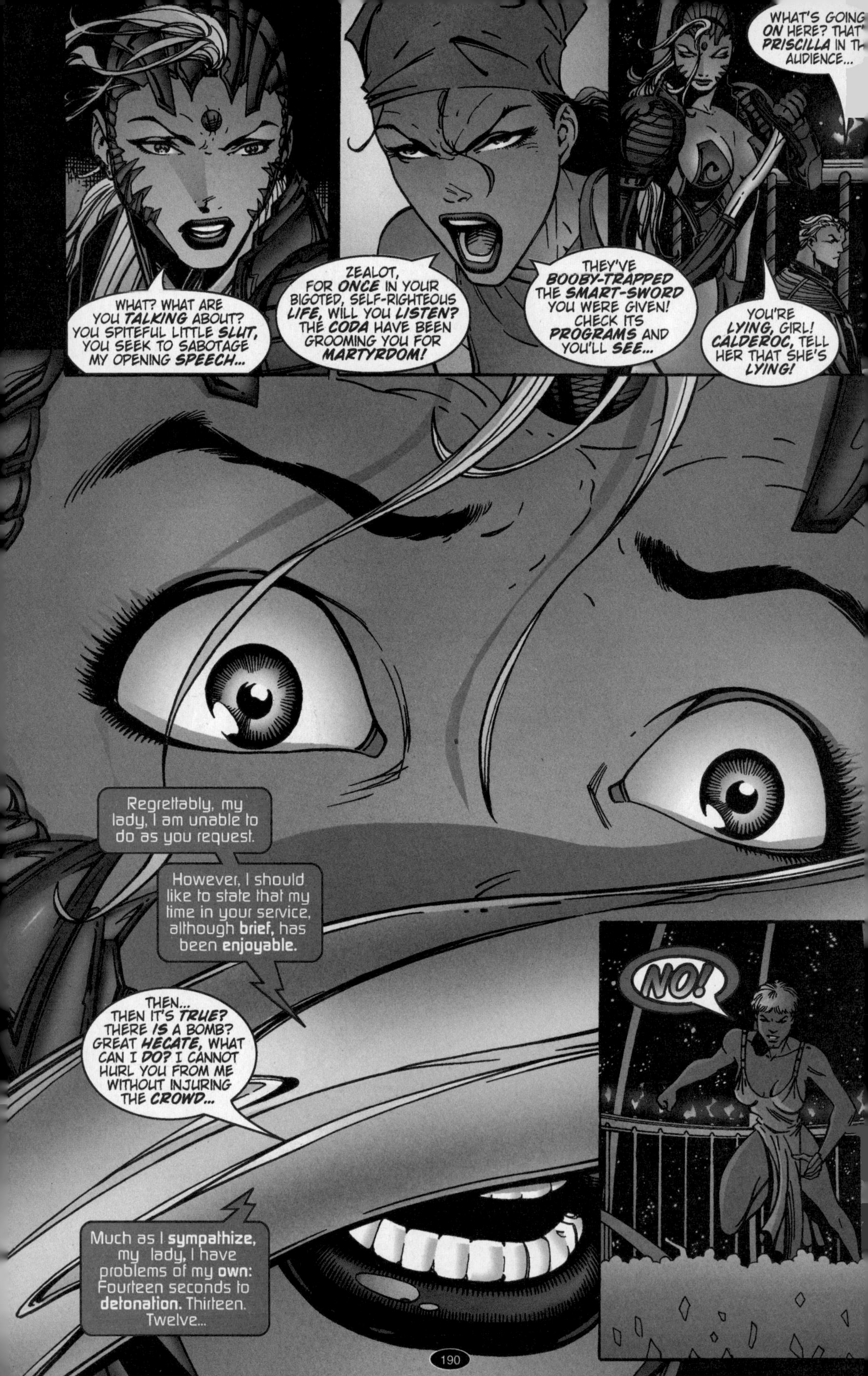
WHAT? WHAT ARE YOU TALKING ABOUT? YOU SPITEFUL LITTLE SLUT, YOU SEEK TO SABOTAGE MY OPENING SPEECH...
ZEALOT, FOR ONCE IN YOUR BIGOTED, SELF-RIGHTEOUS LIFE, WILL YOU LISTEN? THE CODA HAVE BEEN GROOMING YOU FOR MARTYRDOM!
WHAT'S GOING ON HERE? THAT' PRISCILLA IN TH AUDIENCE...
THEY'VE BOOBY-TRAPPED THE SMART-SWORD YOU WERE GIVEN! CHECK ITS PROGRAMS AND YOU'LL SEE...
YOU'RE LYING, GIRL! CALDEROC, TELL HER THAT SHE'S LYING!
Regrettably, my lady, I am unable to do as you request.
However, I should like to state that my time in your service, although brief, has been enjoyable.
THEN... THEN IT'S TRUE? THERE IS A BOMB? GREAT HECATE, WHAT CAN I DO? I CANNOT HURL YOU FROM ME WITHOUT INJURING THE CROWD...
Much as I sympathize, my lady, I have problems of my own: Fourteen seconds to detonation. Thirteen. Twelve...
NO!

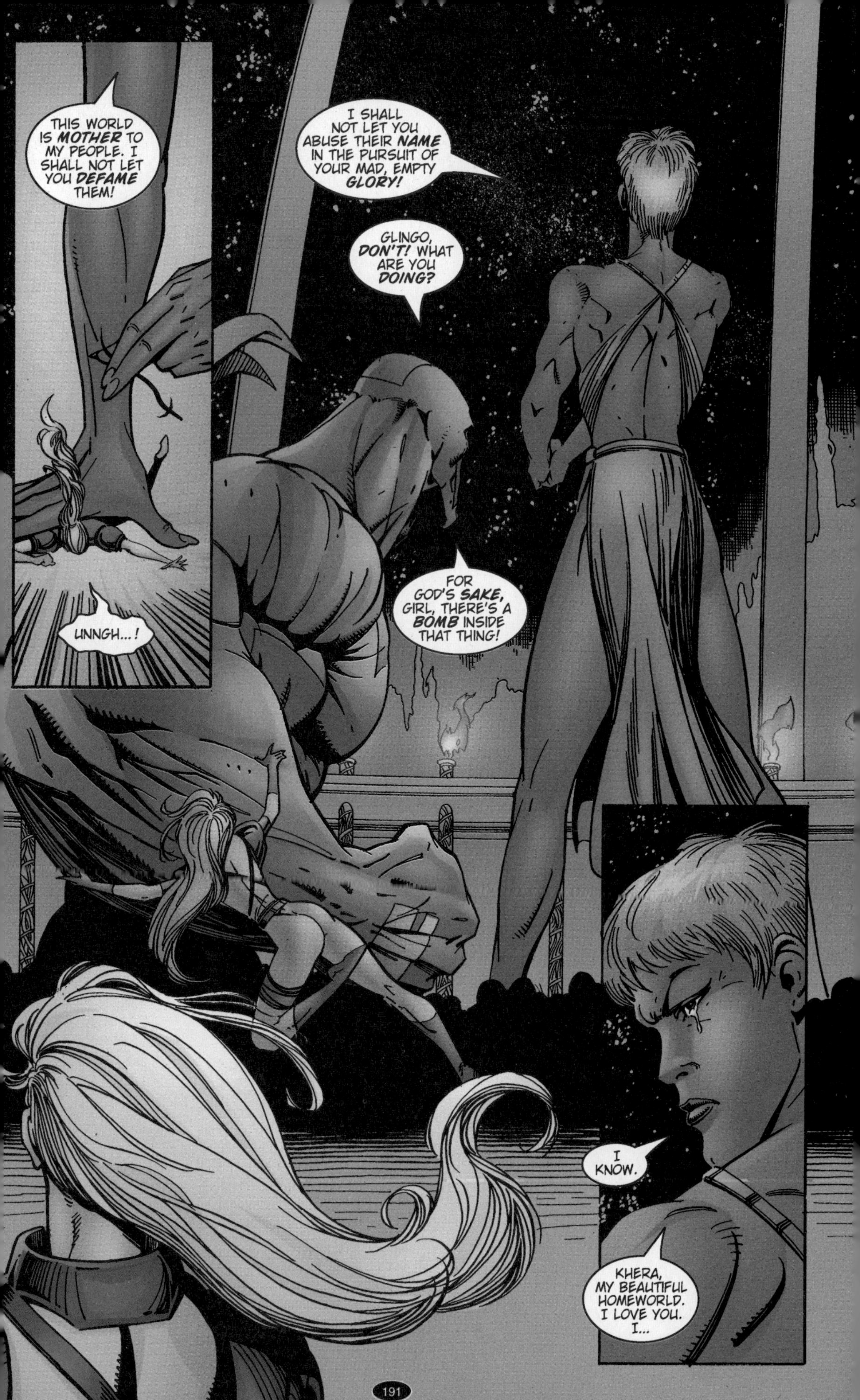
THIS WORLD IS MOTHER TO MY PEOPLE. I SHALL NOT LET YOU DEFAME THEM!
UNNGH...!
I SHALL NOT LET YOU ABUSE THEIR NAME IN THE PURSUIT OF YOUR MAD, EMPTY GLORY!
GLINGO, DON'T! WHAT ARE YOU DOING?
FOR GOD'S SAKE, GIRL, THERE'S A BOMB INSIDE THAT THING!
I KNOW.
KHERA, MY BEAUTIFUL HOMEWORLD. I LOVE YOU. I...

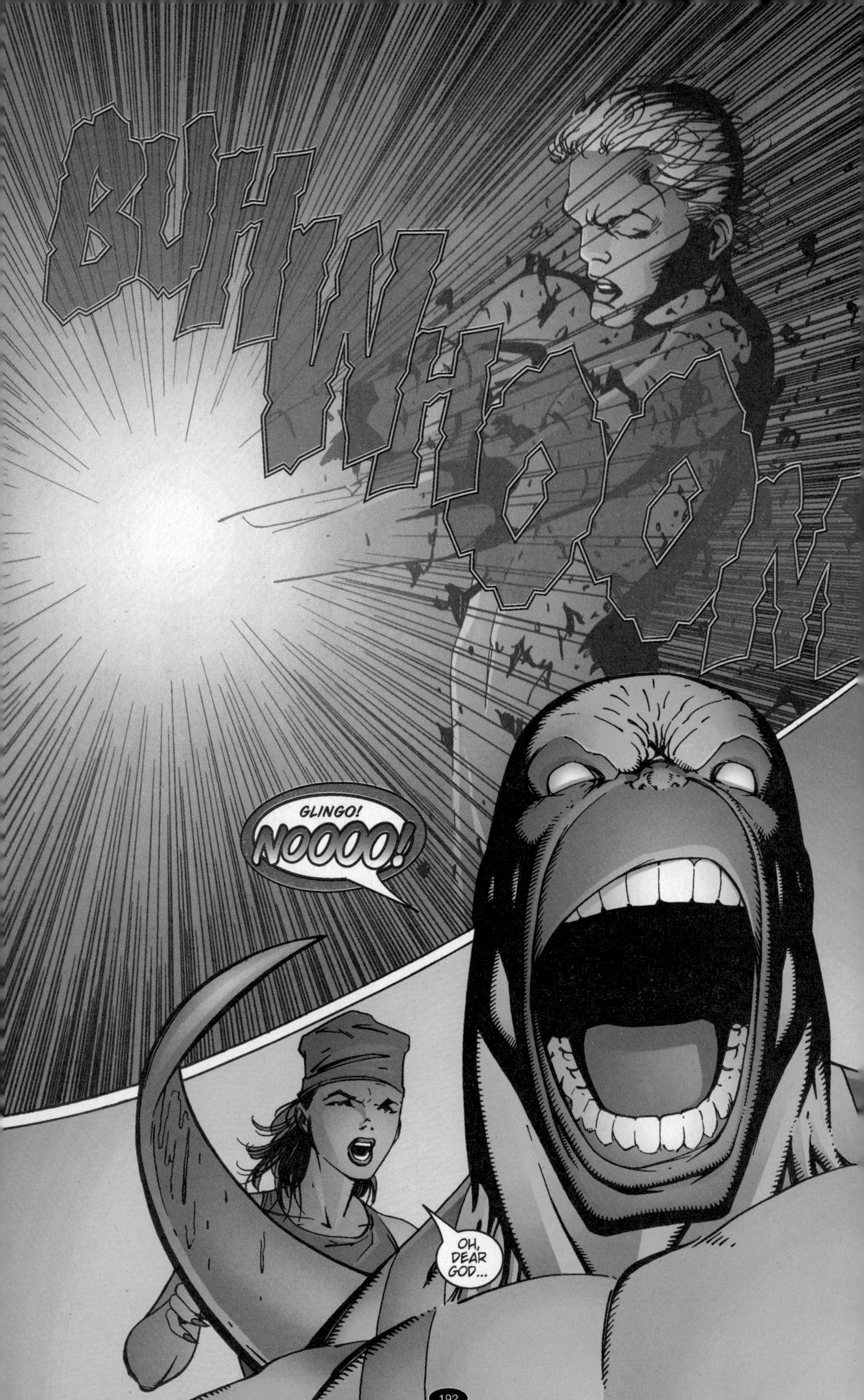
BUHWHOOOM
GLINGO! NOOOO!
OH, DEAR GOD...

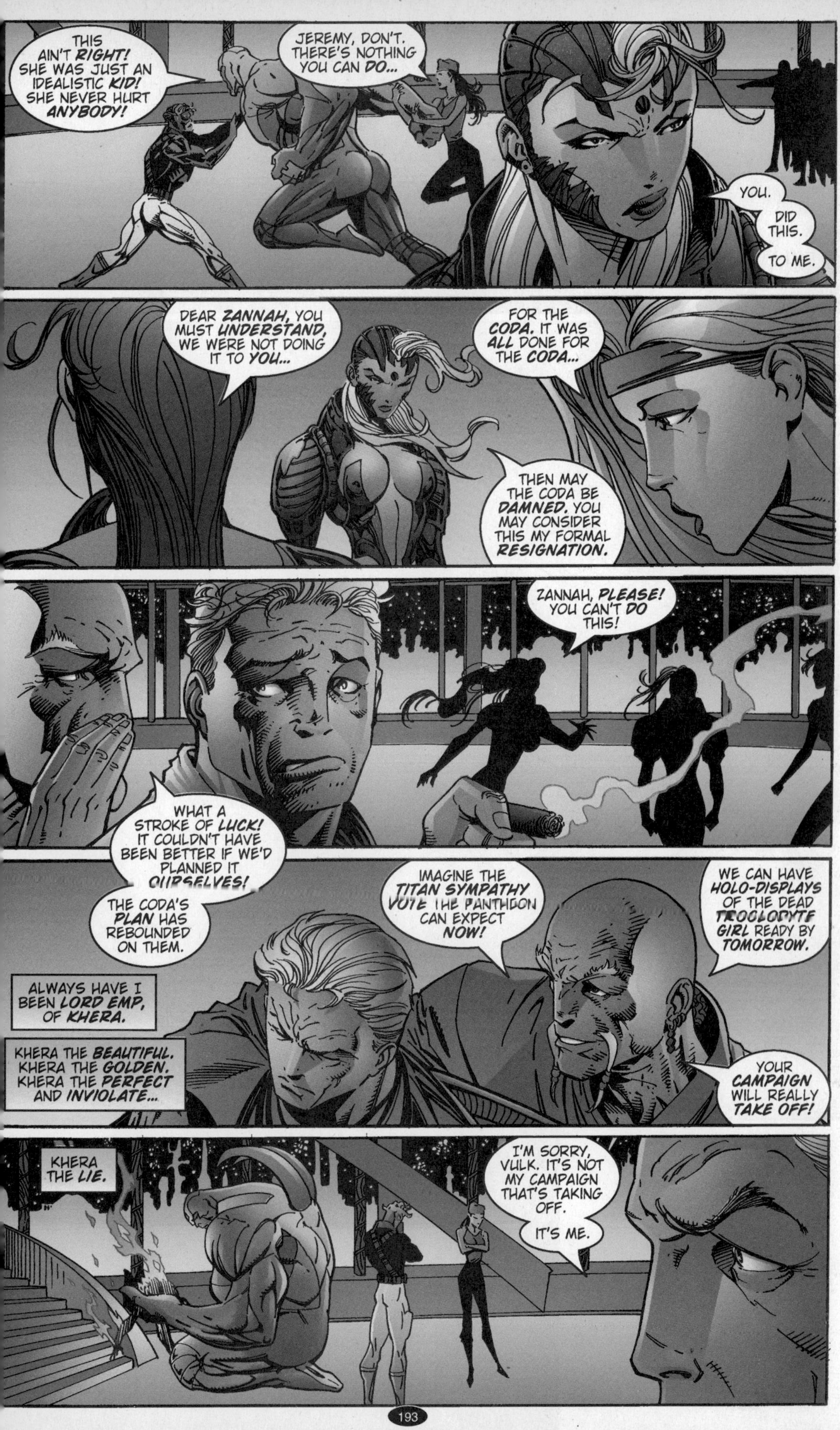
THIS AIN'T RIGHT! SHE WAS JUST AN IDEALISTIC KID! SHE NEVER HURT ANYBODY!
JEREMY, DON'T. THERE'S NOTHING YOU CAN DO...
YOU.
DID THIS.
TO ME.
DEAR ZANNAH, YOU MUST UNDERSTAND, WE WERE NOT DOING IT TO YOU...
FOR THE CODA. IT WAS ALL DONE FOR THE CODA...
THEN MAY THE CODA BE DAMNED. YOU MAY CONSIDER THIS MY FORMAL RESIGNATION.
ZANNAH, PLEASE! YOU CAN'T DO THIS!
WHAT A STROKE OF LUCK! IT COULDN'T HAVE BEEN BETTER IF WE'D PLANNED IT OURSELVES!
THE CODA'S PLAN HAS REBOUNDED ON THEM.
IMAGINE THE TITAN SYMPATHY VOTE THE PANTHEON CAN EXPECT NOW!
WE CAN HAVE HOLO-DISPLAYS OF THE DEAD TROGLODYTE GIRL READY BY TOMORROW.
ALWAYS HAVE I BEEN LORD EMP, OF KHERA.
KHERA THE BEAUTIFUL. KHERA THE GOLDEN. KHERA THE PERFECT AND INVIOLATE...
YOUR CAMPAIGN WILL REALLY TAKE OFF!
KHERA THE LIE.
I'M SORRY, VULK. IT'S NOT MY CAMPAIGN THAT'S TAKING OFF.
IT'S ME.

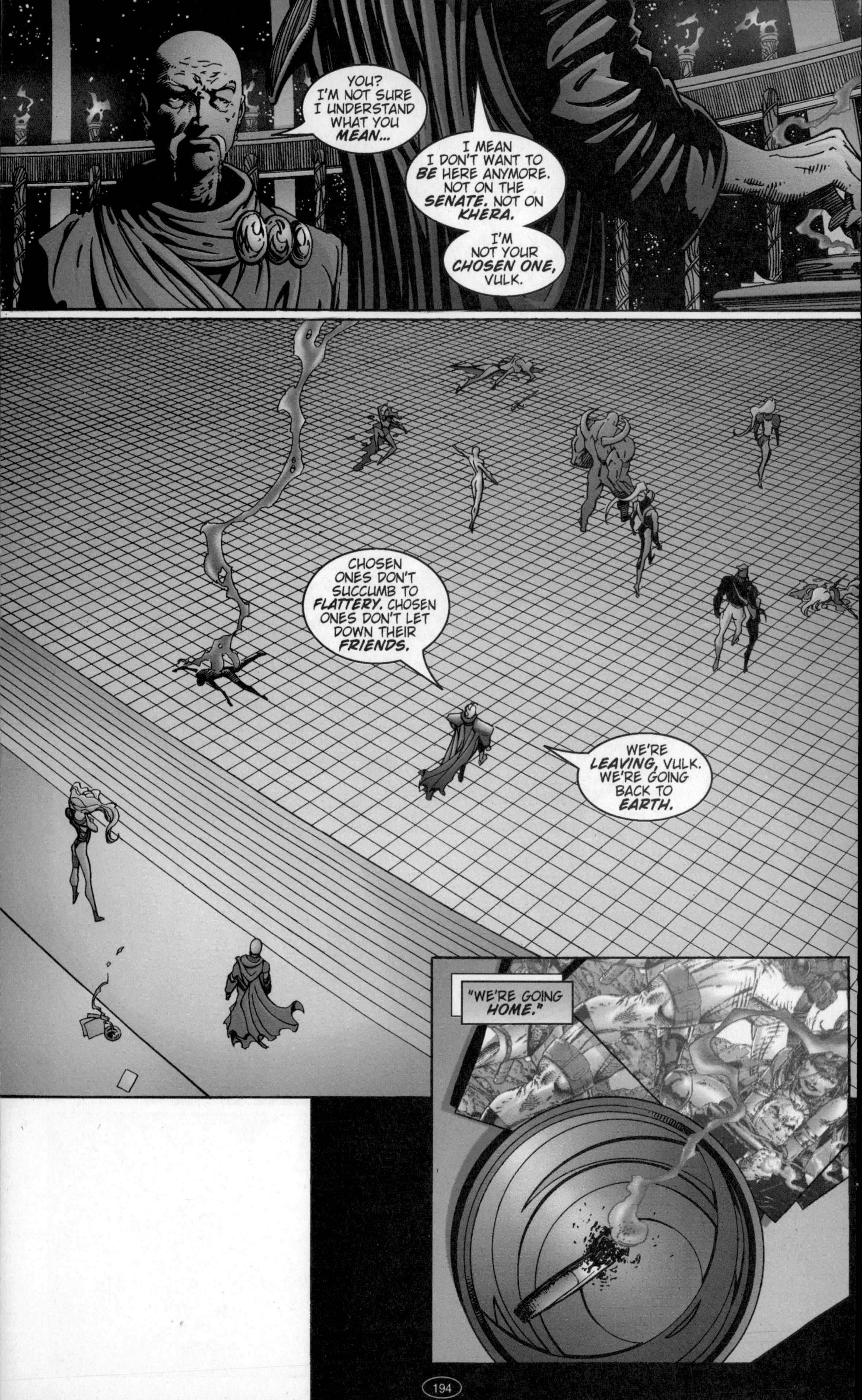
YOU? I'M NOT SURE I UNDERSTAND WHAT YOU MEAN...
I MEAN I DON'T WANT TO BE HERE ANYMORE. NOT ON THE SENATE. NOT ON KHERA.
I'M NOT YOUR CHOSEN ONE, VULK.
CHOSEN ONES DON'T SUCCUMB TO FLATTERY. CHOSEN ONES DON'T LET DOWN THEIR FRIENDS.
WE'RE LEAVING, VULK. WE'RE GOING BACK TO EARTH.
"WE'RE GOING HOME."

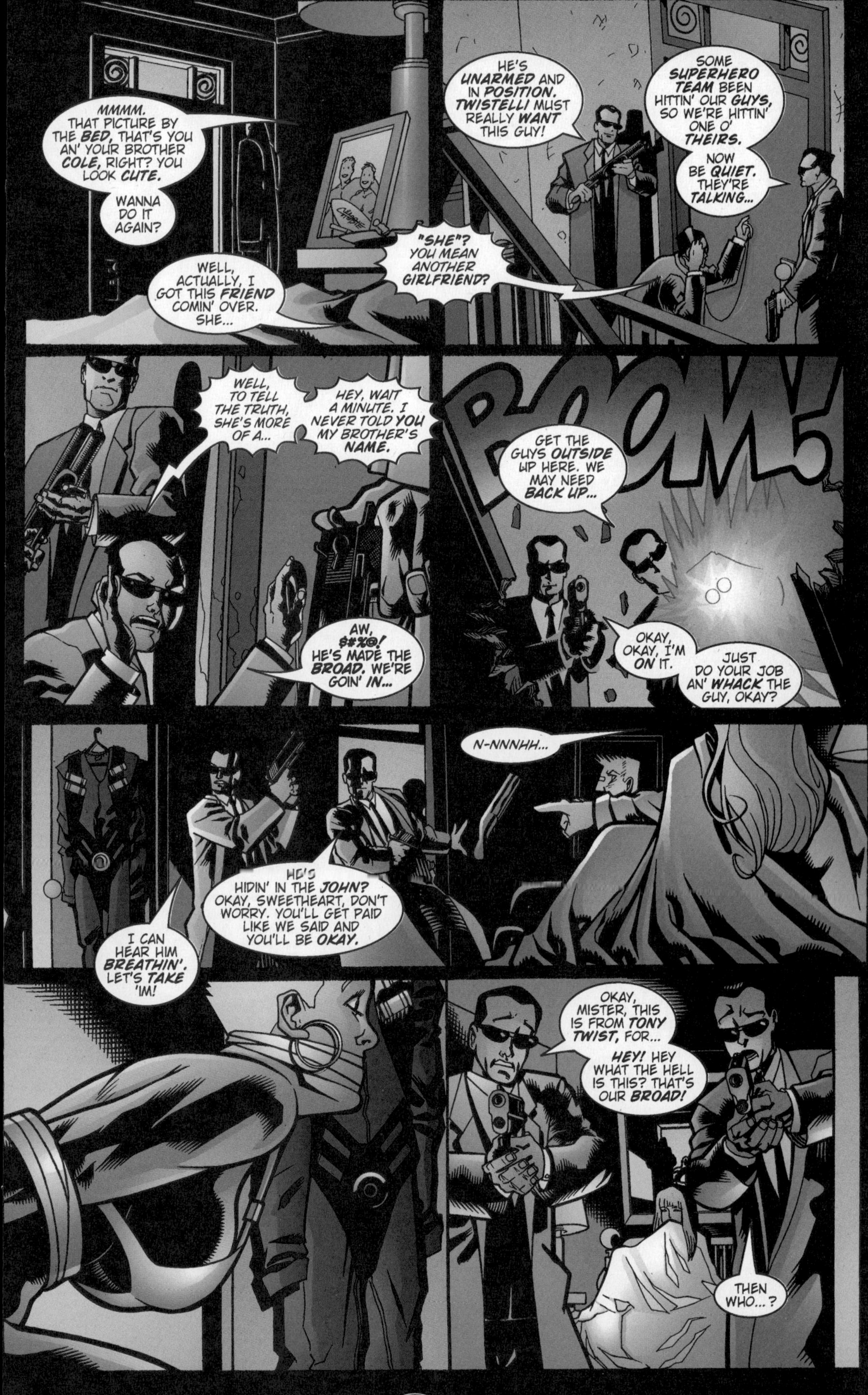
MMMM. THAT PICTURE BY THE BED, THAT'S YOU AN' YOUR BROTHER COLE, RIGHT? YOU LOOK CUTE.
WANNA DO IT AGAIN?
WELL, ACTUALLY, I GOT THIS FRIEND COMIN' OVER. SHE...
"SHE"? YOU MEAN ANOTHER GIRLFRIEND?
HE'S UNARMED AND IN POSITION. TWISTELLI MUST REALLY WANT THIS GUY!
SOME SUPERHERO TEAM BEEN HITTIN' OUR GUYS, SO WE'RE HITTIN' ONE O' THEIRS.
NOW BE QUIET. THEY'RE TALKING...
WELL, TO TELL THE TRUTH, SHE'S MORE OF A...
HEY, WAIT A MINUTE. I NEVER TOLD YOU MY BROTHER'S NAME.
AW, $#%@! HE'S MADE THE BROAD. WE'RE GOIN' IN...
BOOM!
GET THE GUYS OUTSIDE UP HERE. WE MAY NEED BACK UP...
OKAY, OKAY, I'M ON IT.
JUST DO YOUR JOB AN' WHACK THE GUY, OKAY?
I CAN HEAR HIM BREATHIN'. LET'S TAKE 'IM!
HE'S HIDIN' IN THE JOHN? OKAY, SWEETHEART, DON'T WORRY. YOU'LL GET PAID LIKE WE SAID AND YOU'LL BE OKAY.
N-NNNHH...
OKAY, MISTER, THIS IS FROM TONY TWIST, FOR...
HEY! HEY WHAT THE HELL IS THIS? THAT'S OUR BROAD!
THEN WHO...?

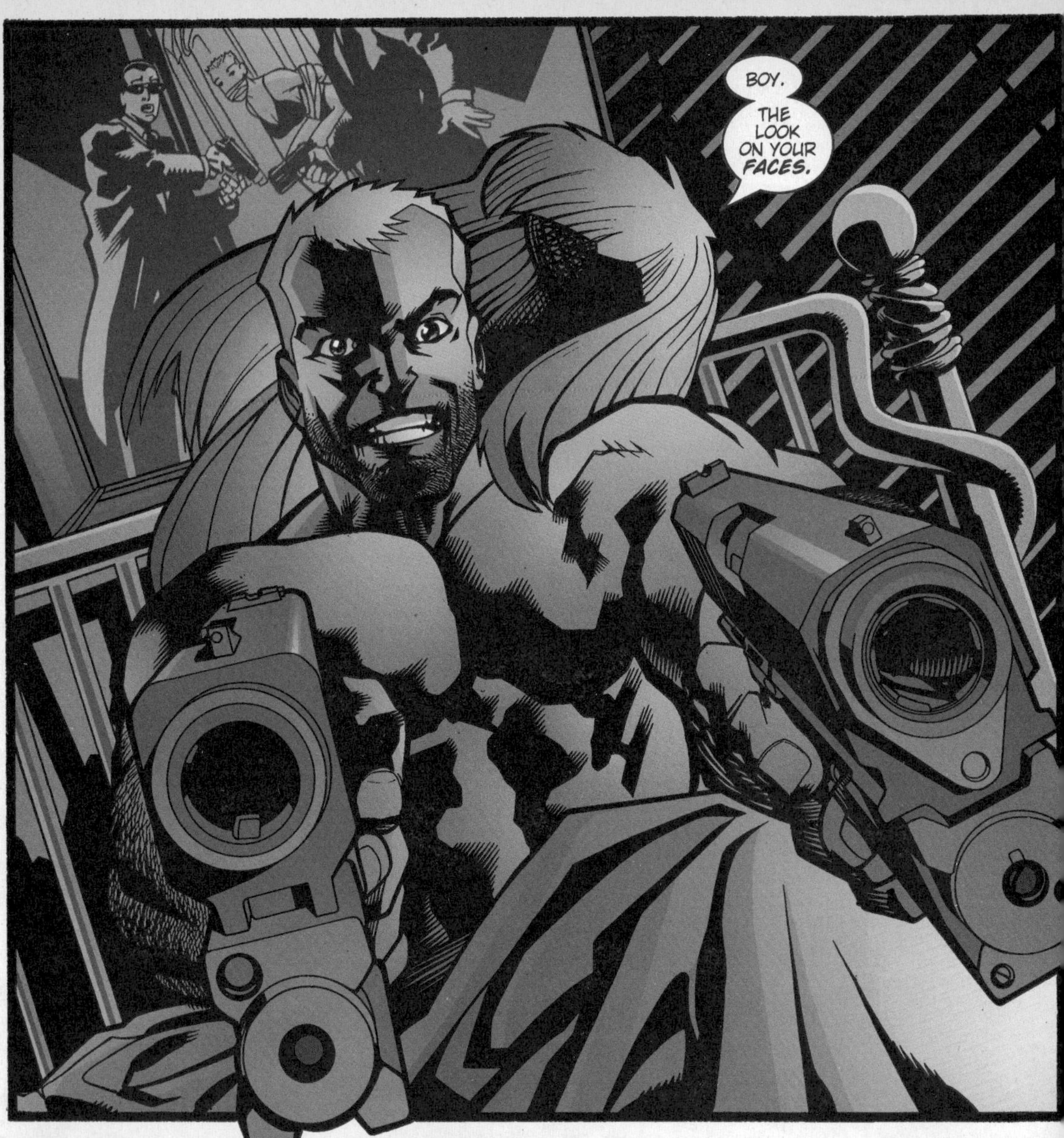
BOY.
THE LOOK ON YOUR *FACES.*

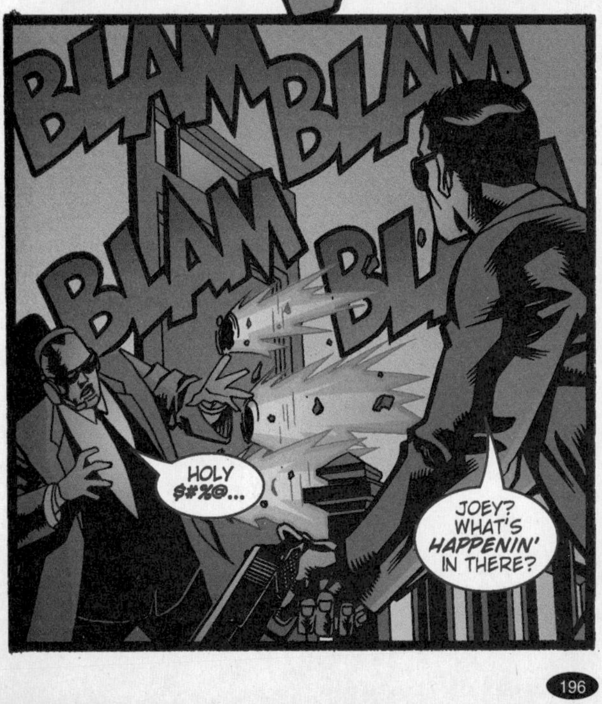
BLAM BLAM
BLAM BL
HOLY $#%@...
JOEY? WHAT'S *HAPPENIN'* IN THERE?

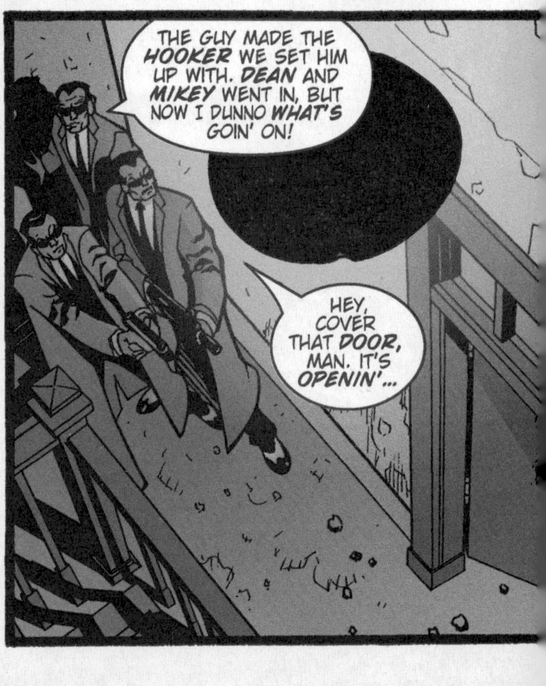
THE GUY MADE THE *HOOKER* WE SET HIM UP WITH. *DEAN* AND *MIKEY* WENT IN, BUT NOW I DUNNO *WHAT'S* GOIN' ON!
HEY, COVER THAT *DOOR,* MAN. IT'S *OPENIN'*...

BRAKKABRAK

HE'S BUSTIN' *OUT!* HOLE THE *CREEP!*

GET THE REST O' THE MEN IN HERE! THIS GUY'S *DANGEROUS!*

BLAM BLAM BLAM BLAM

NAH! NAH, IT'S *OKAY!* WE GOT 'IM! *THAT'LL* TEACH HIS PEOPLE TO START *VENDETTAS* THAT THEY CAN'T *FINISH!*

TURN 'IM *OVER.* LET'S GET A *LOOK* AT...

...*HIM.*

AW, GOD. AW, NO...

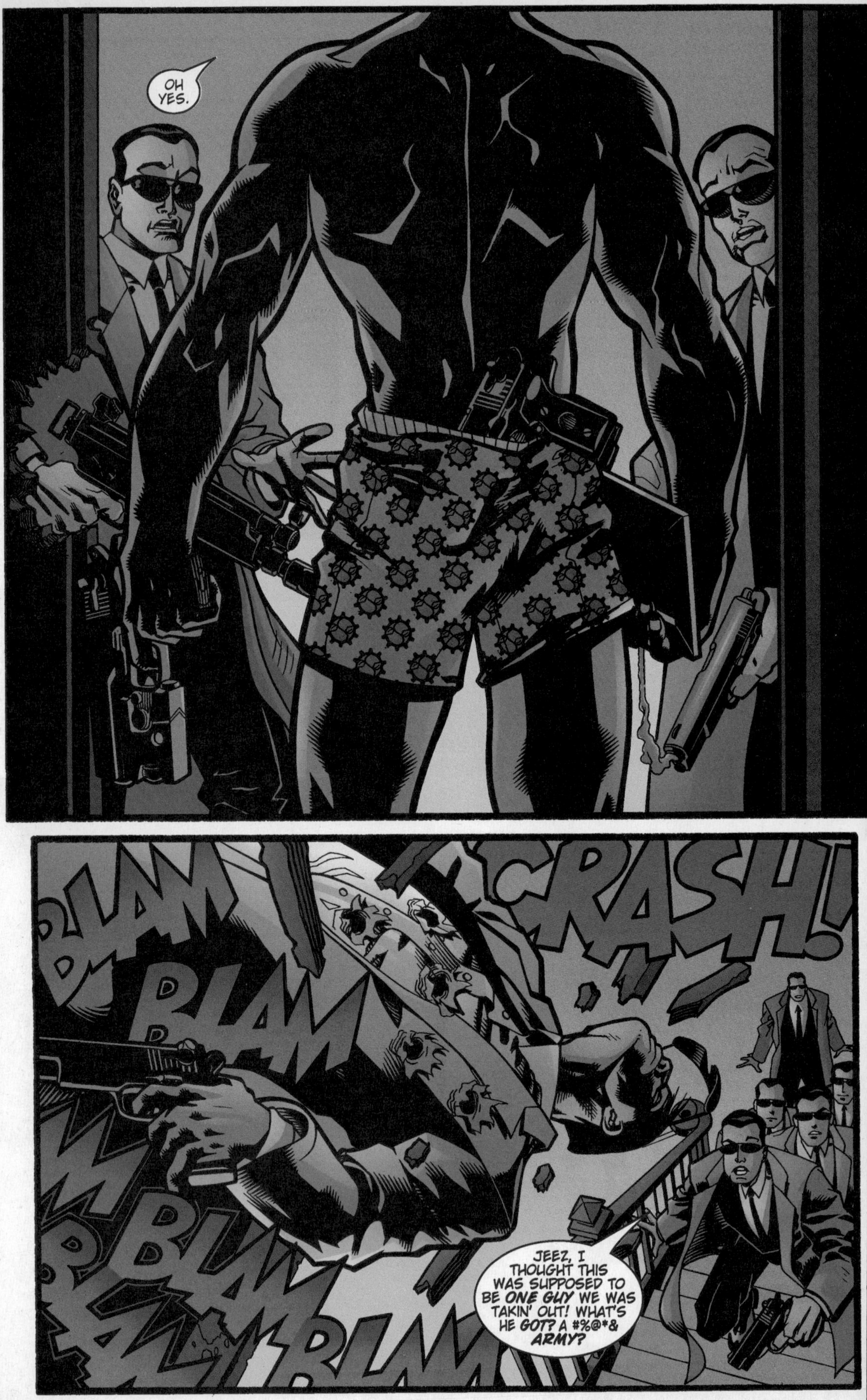
OH YES.
BLAM
CRASH!
BLAM
BLAM
BLAM
JEEZ, I THOUGHT THIS WAS SUPPOSED TO BE *ONE GUY* WE WAS TAKIN' OUT! WHAT'S HE *GOT?* A #%@*& *ARMY?*

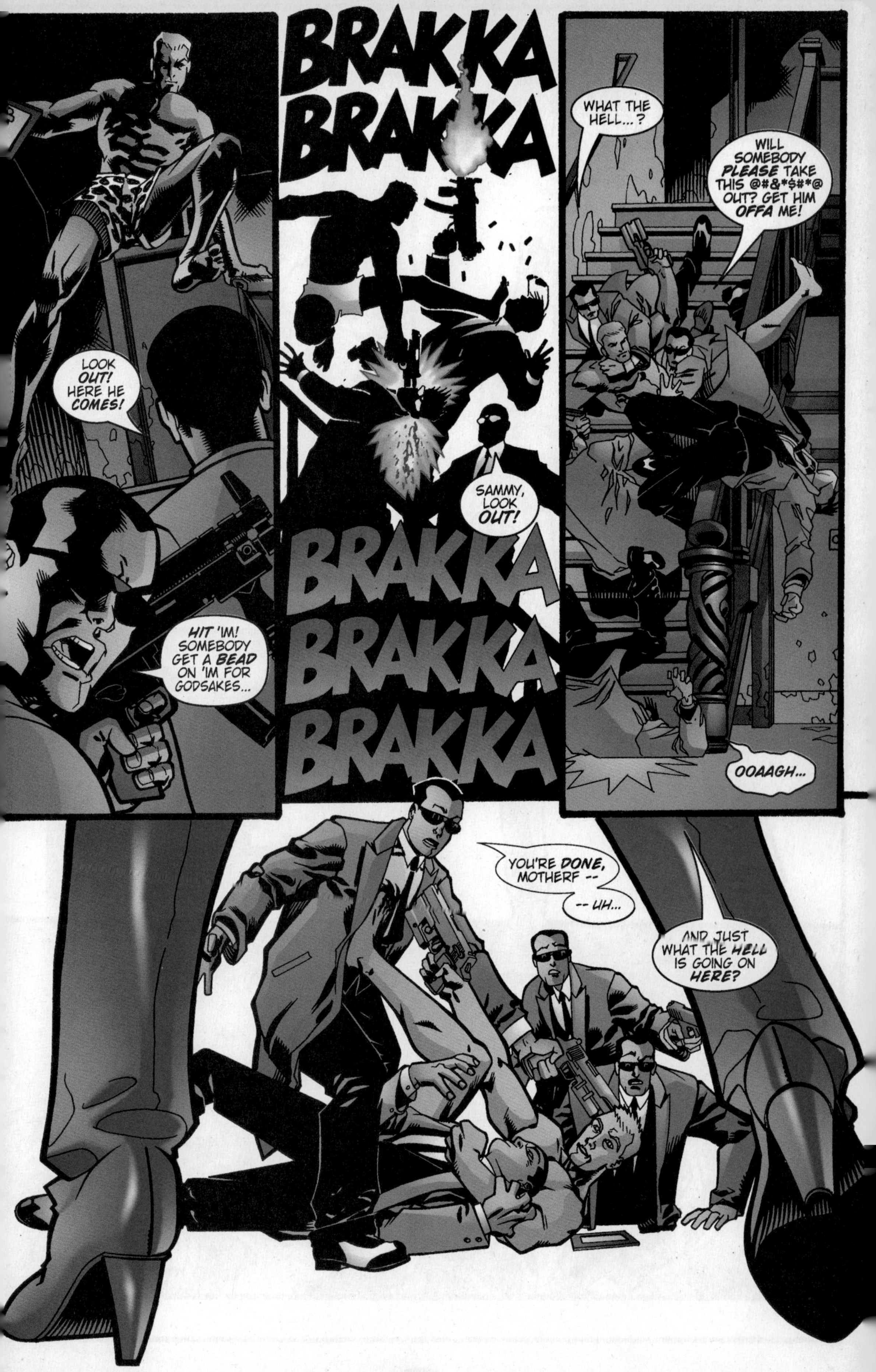
LOOK OUT! HERE HE COMES!
HIT 'IM! SOMEBODY GET A BEAD ON 'IM FOR GODSAKES...
BRAKKA BRAKKA
SAMMY, LOOK OUT!
BRAKKA BRAKKA BRAKKA
WHAT THE HELL...?
WILL SOMEBODY PLEASE TAKE THIS @#&*$#*@ OUT? GET HIM OFFA ME!
OOAAGH...
YOU'RE DONE, MOTHERF --
-- UH...
AND JUST WHAT THE HELL IS GOING ON HERE?

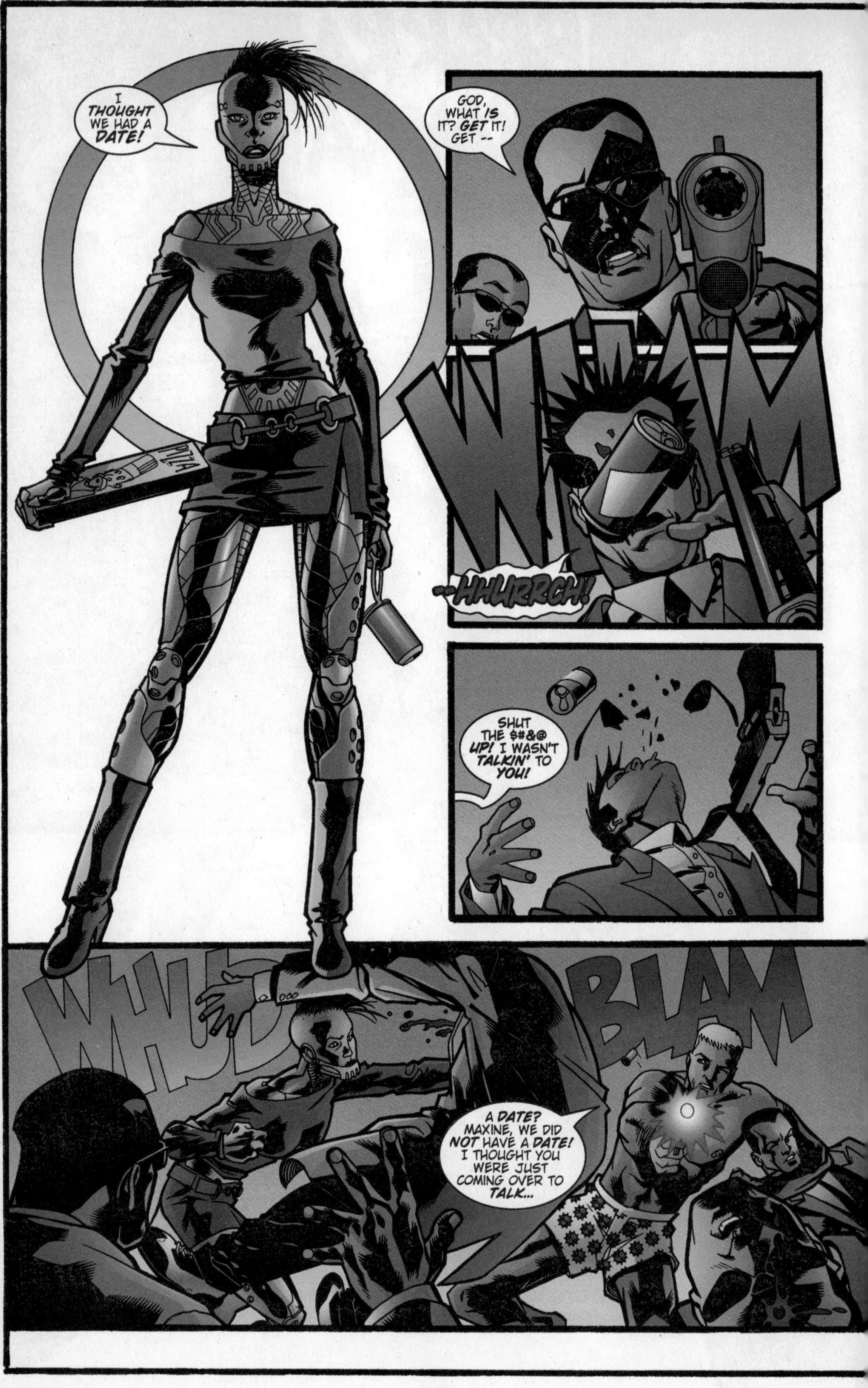
I THOUGHT WE HAD A DATE!
PIZZA
GOD, WHAT IS IT? GET IT! GET --
--HHURRCH!
SHUT THE $#&@ UP! I WASN'T TALKIN' TO YOU!
BLAM
A DATE? MAXINE, WE DID NOT HAVE A DATE! I THOUGHT YOU WERE JUST COMING OVER TO TALK...

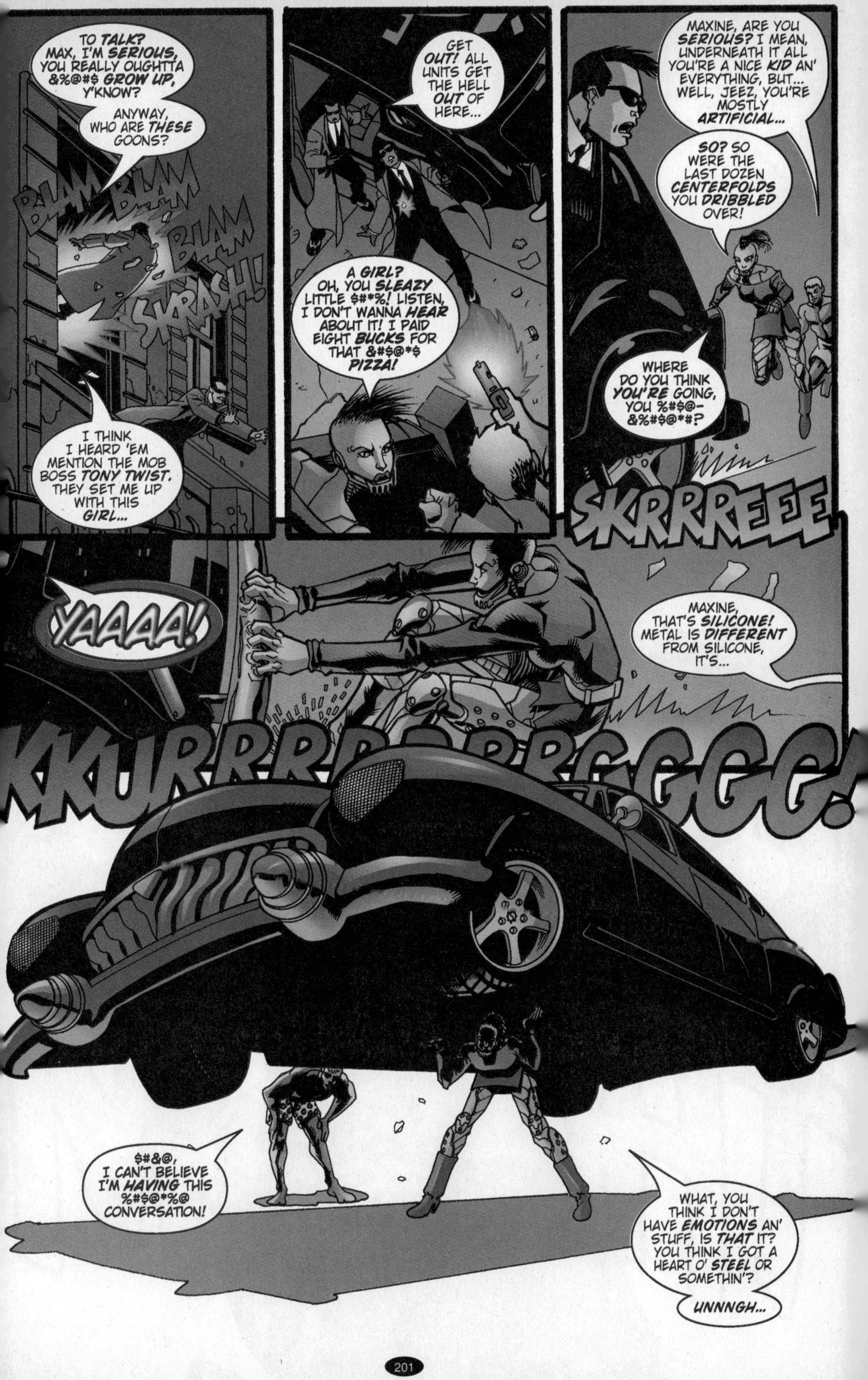

TO TALK? MAX, I'M SERIOUS, YOU REALLY OUGHTTA &%@#$ GROW UP, Y'KNOW?
ANYWAY, WHO ARE THESE GOONS?
BLAM BLAM
BLAM
SMASH!
I THINK I HEARD 'EM MENTION THE MOB BOSS TONY TWIST. THEY SET ME UP WITH THIS GIRL...
GET OUT! ALL UNITS GET THE HELL OUT OF HERE...
A GIRL? OH, YOU SLEAZY LITTLE $#*%! LISTEN, I DON'T WANNA HEAR ABOUT IT! I PAID EIGHT BUCKS FOR THAT &#$@*$ PIZZA!
MAXINE, ARE YOU SERIOUS? I MEAN, UNDERNEATH IT ALL YOU'RE A NICE KID AN' EVERYTHING, BUT... WELL, JEEZ, YOU'RE MOSTLY ARTIFICIAL...
SO? SO WERE THE LAST DOZEN CENTERFOLDS YOU DRIBBLED OVER!
WHERE DO YOU THINK YOU'RE GOING, YOU %#$@-&%#$@*#?
SKRRREEE
YAAAA!
MAXINE, THAT'S SILICONE! METAL IS DIFFERENT FROM SILICONE, IT'S...
KKURRRRRRRRGGGG!
$#&@, I CAN'T BELIEVE I'M HAVING THIS %#$@*%@ CONVERSATION!
WHAT, YOU THINK I DON'T HAVE EMOTIONS AN' STUFF, IS THAT IT? YOU THINK I GOT A HEART O' STEEL OR SOMETHIN'?
UNNNGH...

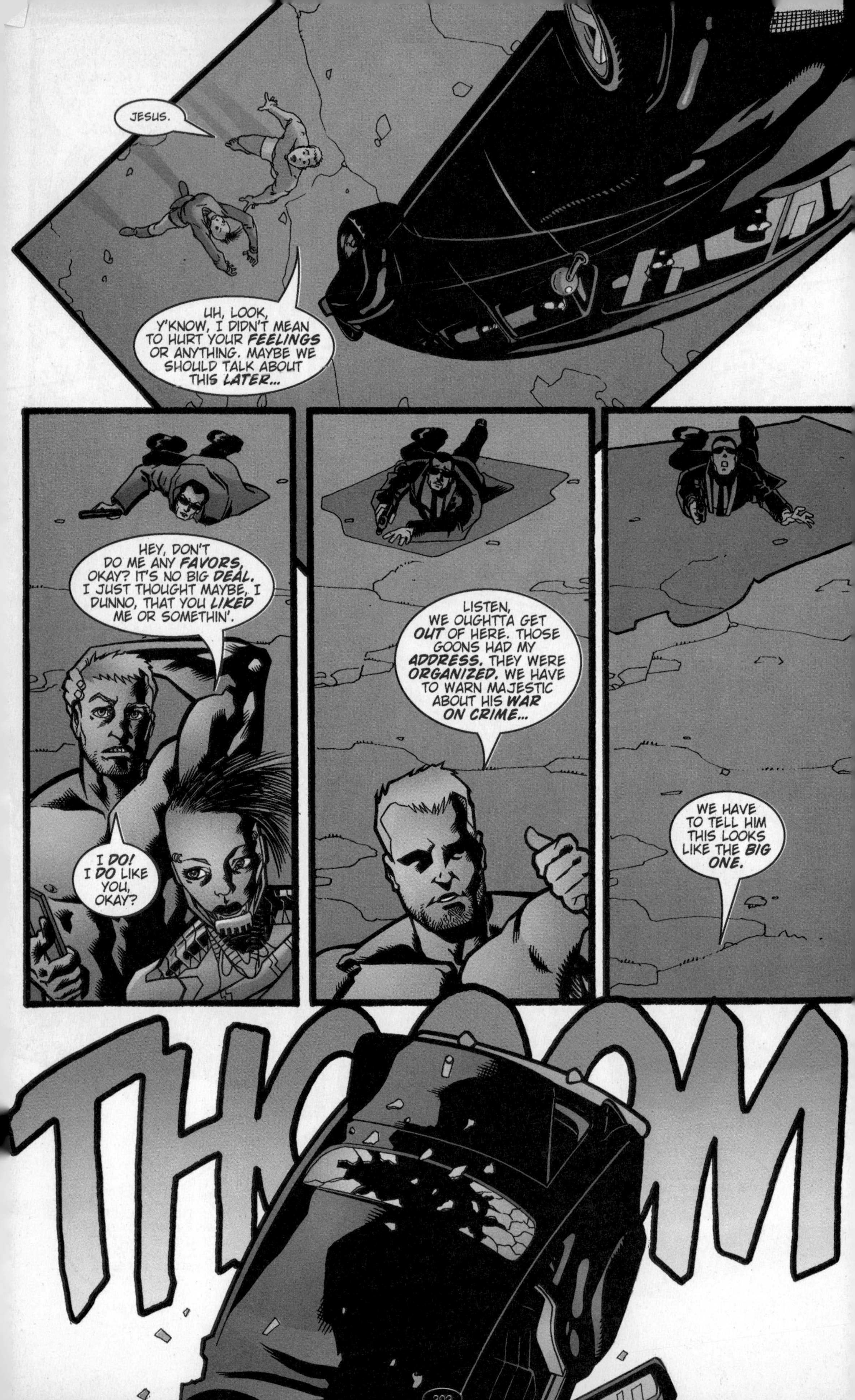
JESUS.
UH, LOOK, Y'KNOW, I DIDN'T MEAN TO HURT YOUR FEELINGS OR ANYTHING. MAYBE WE SHOULD TALK ABOUT THIS LATER...
HEY, DON'T DO ME ANY FAVORS, OKAY? IT'S NO BIG DEAL. I JUST THOUGHT MAYBE, I DUNNO, THAT YOU LIKED ME OR SOMETHIN'.
I DO! I DO LIKE YOU, OKAY?
LISTEN, WE OUGHTTA GET OUT OF HERE. THOSE GOONS HAD MY ADDRESS. THEY WERE ORGANIZED. WE HAVE TO WARN MAJESTIC ABOUT HIS WAR ON CRIME...
WE HAVE TO TELL HIM THIS LOOKS LIKE THE BIG ONE.
THOOM